Designing and Conducting Research in Education

Designing and Conducting Research in Education

Clifford J. Drew
University of Utah

Michael L. Hardman
University of Utah

John L. Hosp
Florida State University, Florida Center for Reading Research

SAGE Publications
Los Angeles • London • New Delhi • Singapore

For information:

Sage Publications, Inc.
2455 Teller Road
Thousand Oaks, California 91320
E-mail: order@sagepub.com

Sage Publications India Pvt. Ltd.
B 1/I 1 Mohan Cooperative Industrial Area
Mathura Road, New Delhi 110 044
India

Sage Publications Ltd.
1 Oliver's Yard
55 City Road
London EC1Y 1SP
United Kingdom

Sage Publications Asia-Pacific Pte. Ltd.
33 Pekin Street #02–01
Far East Square
Singapore 048763

Printed in the United States of America

Library of Congress Cataloging-in-Publication Data

Drew, Clifford J., 1943-
Designing and conducting research in education/Clifford J. Drew, Michael L. Hardman, John L. Hosp.
    p. cm.
Includes bibliographical references and index.
ISBN 978-1-4129-6074-8 (pbk.)

  1. Education—Research—Methodology. I. Hardman, Michael L. II. Hosp, John L. III. Title.

LB1028.D7 2008
370.7′2—dc22   2007016668

This book is printed on acid-free paper.

07 08 09 10 11 10 9 8 7 6 5 4 3 2 1

Acquisitions Editor:	Diane McDaniel
Associate Editor:	Elise Smith
Editorial Assistant:	Ashley Plummer
Production Editor:	Libby Larson
Copy Editor:	Teresa Herlinger
Typesetter:	C&M Digitals (P) Ltd.
Proofreader:	Joyce Li
Indexer:	Jeanne Busemeyer
Cover Designer:	Janet Foulger
Marketing Manager:	Nichole Angress

Brief Table of Contents

Contents

Chapter 2: The Research Process   29

Chapter 3: Ethical Issues in Conducting Research   55

PART III. DATA ANALYSIS AND RESULTS INTERPRETATION   241

Chapter 10: Statistics Choices   243

Chapter 15: Interpreting Results

Appendix: Random Numbers Table

Glossary

References

Index

About the Authors

Preface

This book is designed for use in the very first course in educational research, which may involve students at any level and is frequently offered at both the undergraduate or beginning graduate levels depending on the student's program. The purpose of this book is to provide a first step into the world of research, for consumers of research and also for students who will be actively involved in conducting research. The material presented here can serve as an initial conceptual framework for students without a background in research. From this beginning, students may then either proceed to more advanced work or end their study of research methods with a general working knowledge of what research involves.

This book reflects some very strong beliefs held by the authors. One basic belief is that the study of research methods and their use is surrounded by a number of academic myths. Further, we believe that if you strip away these myths, research methods are not difficult. Some of the academic myths related to research methods include the notions that research is synonymous with statistics, that studying research methods is too difficult for some students, and that research is reserved for a chosen few. We do not subscribe to these beliefs, and over 75 years of combined experience teaching research methods supports our position. Even when we do discuss statistics, our emphasis is on selecting the correct analysis rather than computation. Another academic myth is that research has little to do with our daily lives. We do not subscribe to this belief either, and we find many applications in our daily lives. One final belief has been particularly important to us in teaching this material over the years. We believe this is fun content, and that viewpoint has seemingly been appreciated by our students.

TOOLBOX OF EDUCATIONAL RESEARCH

The world of educational research has experienced a number of important developments over the past few decades, and this book emphasizes those changes. In particular, you will find examinations of quantitative, qualitative, and mixed-method research approaches, which have emerged as vital components in the toolbox of educational research. As methodologists, we believe strongly in multiple research methods and approaches. The basic design of an investigation represents the foundation on which successful research is built, irrespective of methodology or approach employed. We have used this same philosophy in presenting action research through all the steps, from a research question to interpreting results. We describe action research studies in each chapter, taking the student through various challenges presented by environmental circumstances often encountered in field settings.

For additional
simulations visit
www.sagepub
.com/drewstudy

PEDAGOGICAL FEATURES

Research Design Simulations

As instructors, we believe in practice, which is why you will find problem simulations in each chapter that are helpful as students move through the material. These simulations address each step in the research process, from the idea stage through implementation and results interpretation. In the very early parts of the book, students are asked to develop research ideas into researchable questions. They are then given research questions for which they develop designs, and the process moves forward through selecting appropriate statistics and interpreting results. These simulations have been field tested on students over many years.

The simulations may be used in a variety of fashions, depending on the instructor's preference. They may be effectively used in class sessions for both individual and small-group participation. It seems to be more effective to complete the relevant simulations immediately after reading a given section than to wait until the entire chapter is read. Each simulation is accompanied by simulation feedback at the end of the chapter. Usually it is helpful for a student to read this feedback immediately after completing a given problem. The feedback provides a check on the student's performance for that problem and is useful before proceeding to the next simulation or further reading. In addition, throughout the book, readers will find terms that are printed in boldface, which means their definitions can be found in the glossary at the back of the book.

For more research
in action tips visit
www.sagepub
.com/drewstudy

Research in Action

Research in Action boxes are included in each chapter to highlight ways that research is integrated into every educator's life. Each box starts off with a list of "key points in the chapter reflected in this box" that ties the chapter to the boxed material. Next, each box includes "objectives to learn from this box" to help students understand the purpose of the boxed material. Each box also includes scenarios that describe student experiences with research. The boxes end with a "Think about this" section that reflects on what has been learned from the research scenarios. Overall, these boxes are a great resource to help students understand how they might encounter and use research in their everyday life.

ORGANIZATION OF THE TEXT

The way this book is organized reflects our belief in terms of how educational research should be taught; we begin with a background on research and then walk students through the research process from beginning to end.

Part I provides basic background information about research—what it is, why it is important, and an overview of the fundamental steps in the process. Chapter 1 does this by defining research, dispelling misconceptions, discussing why research is important, and providing an overview on the foundations of research. Chapter 2 describes the research process from beginning to end. Chapters 3 and 4 lay the groundwork for ethical issues, participant selection, and participant involvement. In Chapter 5, background is provided on the steps to follow in helping select and develop ways of collecting measures. The research overview in the first five chapters reflects the view of an outsider looking into the research process and experiencing this new world for the first time.

Part II examines a variety of research designs as well as major issues often encountered in planning and implementing studies. Chapter 6 begins with quantitative methodologies, moves on to discuss experimental variables, criterion measures, single subject and group designs, and then concludes with the importance of planning ahead for data analysis. Chapter 7 focuses on non-experimental studies, beginning with survey research and moves to observation as a data collection approach. Chapter 8 discusses qualitative and mixed-method approaches. Chapter 9 explores the pitfalls encountered in research designs. This part of the book continues emphasizing pre-implementation planning in order to maximize the strength of research designs and minimize contaminating influences.

Part III completes the research process by exploring statistics, data tabulation, and analysis and interpretation of results. Chapter 10 begins with a discussion of what statistics are and why we use them. Chapter 11 discusses the various components of data aggregation and tabulation as well as how and when to use tables and graphs. Chapter 12 discusses descriptive statistics including central tendency and dispersion. Chapter 13 moves ahead to inferential statistics and Chapter 14 examines the analysis of qualitative data. Chapter 15 completes the last leg of the research loop with a focus on interpreting results.

The remainder of the book includes an appendix with a random numbers table and a glossary. Together these chapters provide all of the necessary information needed to complete a course in educational research.

SUPPLEMENTAL MATERIALS

Designing and Conducting Research in Education comes with a variety of supplements designed with both faculty and students in mind.

Instructor's Resource CD-ROM

This CD offers the instructor a variety of resources that supplement the book material, including sample syllabi, teaching tips, PowerPoint® lecture slides, lecture outlines, classroom activities, additional simulations, media resources, and more. Also included is an electronic Test Bank, which consists of 20–30 multiple choice questions with answers and page references, 10–15 true/false questions, as well as 10–15 short answer and 5–10 essay questions for each chapter. Instructors can create, deliver, and customize tests and study guides using Brownstone's Diploma test bank software.

Web-Based Student Study Site

www.sagepub.com/drewstudy

This Web-based student study site provides a variety of additional resources to enhance students' understanding of the book content and take their learning one step further. The site includes comprehensive study materials, such as chapter objectives, e-flash cards, practice tests, and more. Also included are special features, such as How to Read a Research Article, Learning from Journal Articles, Expanding on "Research in Action," and a variety of educational research Web resources.

Acknowledgments

We are indebted to many whose wisdom and frustrations have contributed to the conceptualization of this volume. It is always risky to name specific individuals because some will undoubtedly be overlooked. Such practices are, however, customary and appropriate despite the risk. First and foremost are our students, who have helped us learn to teach about research, served as primary impetus for the book, and also served as the research participants as we tried out new material or new simulations. Sincere appreciation is also extended to our colleagues who read portions of the manuscript and made suggestions. We are particularly grateful to our reviewers,

James E. Barr, *Nicholls State University*
Sheryl Boris-Schacter, *Lesley University*
Nancy Brown, *Oakland University*
Yvonne N. Bui, *University of San Francisco*
MaryAnn Byrnes, *University of Massachusetts Boston*
A. Keith Dils, *King's College*
Debbie L. Hahs-Vaughn, *University of Central Florida*
Dwight Hare, *Mississippi State University*
Steven A. Harris, *Tarleton State University*
Douglas Hermond, *Prairie View A&M University*
Shouping Hu, *Florida State University*
John A. Huss, *Northern Kentucky University*
Jenifer Moore, *National Center for Rural Early Childhood Learning Initiatives*
Alfred P. Rovai, *Regent University*
Joan P. Sebastian, *National University*
Wayne H. Slater, *University of Maryland*
Patience Sowa, *Rockhurst College*
Hersh C. Waxman, *University of Houston*
Cherng-Jyh Yen, *The George Washington University*

They provided invaluable feedback and suggestions that helped guide our work.

Clifford J. Drew
Michael L. Hardman
John L. Hosp

Part I OVERVIEW OF RESEARCH

Part I provides basic background information about research—what it is, why it is important, and what the fundamental steps are in the process. Chapter 1 begins with a definition of research, dispelling a number of misconceptions about the process and those who conduct it. These points are combined with discussions of why research is important in the lives of both consumers as well as professionals in education. The rationale for conducting a study is also examined. The overview on foundations of research concludes with an examination of how research and science fit with other "methods of knowing," general descriptions of the different types of research, and how to proceed in selecting a research topic and molding it into a research question.

Chapter 2 describes the research process from beginning to end. The discussion explores where to find research ideas and how to identify them from readings, previous studies, and daily life. The scientific method is discussed, from the perspective of how research ideas become focused and molded into specific research questions, the types of questions studied, and how these steps proceed into planning the research design. The chapter continues with steps on how to implement a study, including collecting data, ensuring reliability, analyzing the results, and drawing implications for practice- and data-based decision making.

Chapters 3 and 4 lay the groundwork for locating and protecting research study participants. Ethical considerations, informed consent, and protecting participants from harm are extremely important in conducting educational research. Investigations involving children present a number of particularly challenging issues in conducting research to improve education. Ethical issues must be balanced with the significance and need for the study in moving forward with participant selection. In Chapter 5, these steps are followed by the basic process of selecting and developing ways of collecting data. The process of defining and selecting criterion measures is discussed with careful attention to data reliability and validity. Selecting a measure is examined in terms of how sensitive it is and how well it communicates the purpose of the research. Challenges presented by various measures and instruments are discussed as well as how to avoid specific problems. The discussion concludes with the development of instruments to collect data, including questionnaires as well as observation protocols.

The research overview in each of the five chapters in this section emphasizes the view of an outsider looking into the research process and experiencing this new world for the first time. The discussion on developing research topics, questions, and plans for implementing studies de-emphasizes the use of jargon and focuses on why research is important and how the beginning researcher can get started. This is the point of departure for education students who may either choose to actively engage in the process or become consumers of research themselves.

1

THE FOUNDATIONS OF RESEARCH

CHAPTER OBJECTIVES

After reading Chapter 1, you should be able to do the following:

+ Present a simple working definition of research.

+ Describe and correct misconceptions about research.

+ Describe why research is important to consumers.

+ Describe why research is important to professionals.

+ Discuss different reasons why studies are conducted, from basic to action research.

+ Describe different ways of knowing information, from tenacity to the methods of science.

+ Distinguish inductive from deductive reasoning.

+ Discuss differences between science and common sense.

+ Describe general differences between quantitative, qualitative, and mixed methods of research.

+ Discuss selecting a research topic and molding that topic into a research question.

+ Examine using research results in data-based decision making.

Research means different things to different people. A layperson's view of research may be limited to descriptions seen in advertisements and on television (which are really marketing and may not involve research at all). Likewise, if you ask six different scientists what research is, you may receive six different answers. Some may respond with very lofty and complex-sounding definitions. Others might be somewhat more casual in their responses, using more commonplace terms.

Students often find it difficult to determine a clear and useful definition of research. Many research courses begin with a discussion of some particular focused content. Unfortunately, that content often focuses on a limited part of the research process, such as statistics, and does not place it in the context of the world around us. Some might think that the definition of research is supposed to become self-evident as the discussion progresses. Perhaps an instructor assumes that you already know what research *is* and that your purpose in taking the course, or reading a research text, is to become thoroughly familiar with details of the process. Before going any further, let us examine this basic question: what is research?

Research is a systematic way of asking questions, a systematic method of inquiry. The purpose of research is to obtain knowledge or information that pertains to some question. The question may be simple (e.g., "Which of these teaching methods is most effective?") or it may be more complicated. The emphasis of this definition is the term *systematic*. There are many ways of asking questions and obtaining information. Research is a method that attempts to undertake this task in a systematic fashion to obtain objective and unbiased information. The definition of research presented above is simple. There are many descriptive characteristics involved in different types of research that we will see throughout this book. At the outset, however, a general definition will serve quite well.

The term *research* has traditionally generated a variety of misconceptions on the part of those not involved. To students, it sometimes seems like a shroud of secrecy has been placed over the act of research, either purposefully or by accident. The net outcome of this situation is a general lack of information concerning what goes on in a research laboratory, the nature of the research process, and what research results mean. All of this tends to generate a mystique and suspicion of the whole process on

---

BOX 1.1   Conventional Wisdom Versus Science

An experienced scholar recently presented the results of a survey he conducted at a national meeting. This survey investigated student perceptions of research that *they* (the students) had conducted for their own graduate programs. After completing their studies, the vast majority of students reported that they *did not change their minds* when their findings contradicted conventional wisdom. These students *did not believe* the results from their own research. They were more inclined to continue believing conventional wisdom (or mythology) than their own data. These students tended to view their research results as being separate from their own daily lives.

What are your thoughts about this viewpoint? What would you think if you learned that something you long believed was not supported by evidence?

---

the part of lay and student populations. The process of conducting research is anything but mystical, and it certainly is not mechanistic. This will become increasingly clear as you progress further into the content of this book.

Research has typically been an anxiety-producing topic for students. In fact, the most consistent description of what research is may be found among students. From a student perspective—particularly the beginning student—research generates a certain amount of mental anguish, perhaps even outright fear. To many students, research is basically an academic hurdle to be conquered but has little relevance to the "real world" we live in (see Box 1.1 for an illustration of this). In addition, for many students, research is synonymous with statistics, and that implies mathematics. These perceptions are unfortunate misconceptions that must be corrected to better understand the research process. For example, it is critical to understand from the outset that research is much more than statistics. Statistical analysis represents only one step in the overall research process. The statistics used in research would be better viewed as tools, like the way an automobile mechanic uses screwdrivers and wrenches. The mechanic's tools are of little value if there is no clear understanding of how a car works. Likewise, the researcher who does not know how to initiate the logical process of asking questions will have little meaningful use for statistical or other scholarly tools. Some research tools involve no statistics whatsoever.

PERSPECTIVES OF EDUCATIONAL RESEARCH

This discussion of research began with some brief attention to what research is and is *not*. We also began with a general definition of research as a systematic method of inquiry. It is important at this point to examine why the study of research design is useful. The purpose of this section is to address that question from two perspectives: that of the consumer and the professional.

Research and the Consumer

In discussing issues related to the importance of studying research, we initially focus on the consumer perspective. This view provides one of the most compelling rationales available for becoming familiar with the research process. We are consumers of research in nearly every facet of our daily lives—clearly, research *does* relate to the real world.

Almost daily, the news media report the results of drug research and product recalls on medicine and many other consumer products because of faulty research. In some cases, research results suggest a risk to consumers; in others, the results simply indicate that there is no positive effect. We also hear many reports about government requirements related to education, such as the No Child Left Behind (NCLB) Act and fluid requirements for educational curriculum related to science such as teaching evolution. Both of these latter topics are high profile and attract national attention. Many research outcomes have educational impacts in some very practical ways. For example, we know a lot more about the effectiveness of various instructional techniques in reading, math, and other academic content areas than we did 30 years ago. We know that the direct and explicit teaching of letters and words, as well as syntactic, phonetic, and semantic analysis improves literacy program effectiveness for children with intellectual disabilities. This approach is known as *direct instruction* and emerged prominently in research literature within the last 30 years (Hardman, Drew, & Egan, 2006; Katims, 2000).

Science and research produce new knowledge on a daily basis (e.g., effects of implementing educational programs for young children), and that new knowledge provides society with more choices. Providing more choices is a strong, consumer-oriented rationale for research, *but* the consumer must be equipped to take advantage of new options (Jones & Kottler, 2006). In most cases, the individual consumer will need to interpret the research results and be able to determine what those results mean for his or her life.

Distinguishable Differences in Research for the Consumer

It is important for us to be able to distinguish between a sales pitch and research evidence. Product advertising in the media often resorts to assertions about research, with subtle and not-so-subtle claims that scientific studies have *proved* the superior effectiveness of whatever product is being sold. While some might be truthful, there are many such statements that are simply advertising claims cloaked in a research covering to enhance appeal. Lay research consumers can see through such statements with some basic knowledge about the research process and make personal decisions about claims of scientific support. One indicator of a marketing exaggeration is when the narrative says that something was *proved*; scientists will almost never use the term proved.

Students of research quickly become quite cynical concerning the manner in which research is used and misused to manipulate consumers. A few examples make this point clear. Some of the worst offenders in terms of misusing research are the people who develop and present advertising on television. It seems that one technique of selling a product on television is rather simple: Employ an unknown actor, put that individual in a white coat behind a desk (with rows of books on the wall), and the product to be sold suddenly appears scientifically credible. If the advertisement is a bit more aggressive, the actor may also tell some sort of research story to drive the point home. The story may begin like this: "At a famous research center in the East . . ." One example of this type of selling is a commercial in which a well-known toothpaste was claimed to be "unsurpassed in the prevention of cavities when compared to the other leading brands of toothpaste." The wording of this line is carefully drafted and important. The implication is that this brand (Brand X) is more effective in preventing cavities. However, that is not what was said. The term *unsurpassed* specifically means that the other leading brands were not any *better* than Brand X. Most likely there was no difference between them. Certainly, if Brand X was really *more* effective, the advertisers would emphatically say so.

Parents are immediately thrust into the role of educational consumers as their children approach school age. They may be faced with decisions about whether early school experiences are productive for their children. Digging through the research literature is a cumbersome process to determine preschool effectiveness, and even reports about the topic that appear in the media can be challenging to understand. It is worthwhile to know some general research methods information to help figure out what is being said. What *does* a positive correlation between participation and later academic performance mean? What does a comparison between two approaches to early childhood education tell us? These are the types of consumer questions that are floating around out there. They are also circumstances where knowing about how research is conducted is very helpful to understand what is being reported.

Research as Information and Its Implications

Lay consumers are inundated on a daily basis with what appears to be research information and its implications. Without some knowledge of the research process, they are at the mercy of those who present the information. Laws requiring truthful advertising will not help people make intelligent decisions. On a personal level, it is your child who is about to go off to preschool. You are the one who has to make a consumer decision about the nature of preschool experience that you think is best for your child. It is important for you, as lay consumers, to have enough background about research methods to make intelligent judgments regarding claims that are supposedly based on research. It is important to have enough information to know what research generally says about preschool experiences. It also may be worth knowing why some people are raising such a fuss about NCLB; after all, doesn't that law relate to all children receiving what they deserve? Read over the "About Simulations" piece and complete Simulation 1.1 to see if the implied cause of the results makes sense.

ABOUT SIMULATIONS

Topic: What simulations are and how to approach them

Background statement: This class may be an unusual one for many of you. For one thing, some of you may be frightened about this content and anything that has to do with the word "research." Many students don't know what research is but are pretty certain that they aren't smart enough to understand it, let alone conduct research. You will survive it, and later you will wonder what all the mystery was about. Although there are terms in research that are not common in the lay world, for the most part, research can be explained in common English.

As you proceed through this content, there will be points when you are instructed to complete what we call "simulations." At that point you should take a few minutes to work on the simulation. The notion is that the material presented *simulates,* or mimics, problems that have just been covered, either in the text or as an in-class topic. These are *not* math problems because this material does not involve math. Basically you are asked to write out responses. You can work individually or in small groups, whichever suits your own temperament and how your instructor wants it done. In many cases, we encourage students to work together on these because the group work seems to have great instructional value and it certainly is more fun. When you are finished (or totally frustrated and cannot go further), turn to the written feedback for that simulation. Each simulation has written feedback, with the same number, in the feedback section of each chapter. Your instructor may circulate among you as you are working on your simulations. This is done to be helpful, not snoopy.

The simulations are all important to complete, so don't just blow them off as something that is not helpful. In our 40 years of experience, the simulations are the element of this course that has been consistently rated as excellent and useful by the students in our classes. Have fun with this material. If this is your first step into research methods, that may sound like a strange statement, but just relax a bit and enjoy this experience.

For additional
simulations visit
www.sagepub
.com/drewstudy

Simulation

Simulation 1.1

Topic: Research and the consumer

Background statement: Janet and her husband have always had a great interest in education. The significance of that interest intensified when their young son Ben began preschool and the curriculum included an exposure to symbolic arithmetic. Janet had concerns that this part of the preschool curriculum was inappropriate and far above what young children could handle. Her husband, Andrew, believed exposure at this age was not a bad thing and that Ben could handle it.

Not knowing where to turn for additional information, Janet went to the Internet and did a search on preschool children and math. She found a number of reports that dealt with preschool and to her surprise, she found some research by faculty at Harvard that focused on the topic of symbolic arithmetic. What further surprised her was that the report, published in late 2005, suggested that preschool children were able to perform some symbolic math tasks fairly well. In addition, the study indicated that the children studied seem to have an understanding of abstract number concepts and can use them before they start elementary school.

Does this research mean that Janet is wrong and Andrew is correct? As a consumer of research, what do the results mean and what conclusions can be drawn?

Write your response, then turn to page 27 for Simulation Feedback 1.1.

SOURCE: Preschool Children Display Innate Skill With Numbers, Addition. (September 9, 2005). *Science Daily.* Available online at www.Sciencedaily.com

Research and the Professional

The perspective of a research consumer is also relevant to most professionals. Professionals often encounter situations similar to those confronting lay consumers. The content may be different since, as a professional, you are consuming work-related items or services, rather than weight-loss pills or another lay-oriented product. However, because professional consumers have to select from an array of competing products, they still need to be familiar with the research process. Once again, a few examples illuminate this point, some also involving the news media. One serious illustration of the misuse of research information occurs regularly in schools across the United States. Headlines scream that a state's third graders performed 2 points below (or 10 points above) the national average on this year's standardized reading test. The story often attributes the blame or credit for these scores, whether explicitly or implicitly, to the teaching staff. In fact, there may be a variety of influences that are likely to be contributing to these scores. For example, it may be that a local high-tech scientific firm moved its design plant, thereby relocating most of its scientists to another community. If the children of these scientists (who would tend to perform better academically) represent a significant group in the school's enrollment, schoolwide average performance could easily decline by two points because these children are no longer there.

Another practical example of research in education relates to the question of how important the principal is in a school. This is an interesting question because some cynics inside and outside the profession occasionally claim that educational administrators, such as principals, are on the frivolous side of the budget and we should divert all of the administrative budget directly into the classroom. Teaching effectiveness is the number one influential factor in student learning. However, research indicates that the second most important influence is school leadership—that is, principal effectiveness (Leithwood, Louis, Anderson, & Wahlstrom, 2004; Mazzeo, 2003). So it might not make a lot of sense to take educational administrators out of the school environment. Furthermore, other research also suggests that we do know something about preparing both effective teachers and principals (Davis, Darling-Hammond, LaPointe, & Meyerson, 2005; Natalicio & Pacheco, 2005). These are examples of how research can address practical questions for professionals in education and are examples of **applied research**—that is, research that addresses questions with some clear application rather than testing a theory.

Most professional practitioners deliver service in one form or another on a daily basis. Counselors interact with clients, educators teach students, psychologists use tests to evaluate individuals, and so on. Knowing this raises product selection questions: Why does a professional select a particular technique, strategy, or measurement instrument? Which counseling method, teaching procedure, or test should be used and why? Test selection questions are not easily or simply answered. This is particularly true since professional consumers receive a variety of sales pitches, often resembling the television advertisements we all see. Everyone wants you to use their test, or their instructional package or process. There are limited consumer safeguards, and the professional consumer still has the basic responsibility of evaluating the manner in which a procedure, technique, or test instrument was developed and the degree to which it fits a particular need (e.g., American Psychological Association, 2005; Jones & Kottler, 2006). Clearly some methods have been developed on a very sound basis with a solid research foundation, whereas others have not.

The selection of instructional materials presents an interesting consumer dilemma. In some cases, committees appointed as "State Textbook Commissions" or some such body make statewide decisions. These committees may develop a list of approved textbooks or instructional materials. While the criteria for selection may be well articulated, there are some circumstances where the selection of instructional materials is based more on marketing effectiveness than on research evidence. Some book or material selections may be made on the basis of secondhand information from others. Perhaps a teacher casually indicates that a particular material is "good." The basis for the "good" rating may remain unspecified, or there may be a careful assessment regarding developmental level, for example. It may be that the individual making the recommendation mentions that "the material is based on research that indicates this type of instructional materials engages students more actively than some others, which leads to better academic achievement." However, this is not a typical basis for such a suggestion. Further investigation concerning the research results and the technical soundness of such research (if it actually exists) is even less typical. The immediate pressure of teaching or other duties often precludes such investigation.

This all begins to sound very much like the sales proposition involving that infamous "research center in the East." In fact, there are more similarities than many professionals would like to admit (teachers are certainly not the only professional consumers involved). Professional practitioners (administrators, psychologists, supervisors, technology managers) often find themselves inundated with salespeople and advertisements expounding the virtues of a wide variety of products. The marketing process for professional products has the same goal as in any other arena—selling. The same tactics are often used, and a substantial number of professional consumers are ill-equipped to evaluate or question the "research" claims used to sell these products.

Professional research consumers need to examine workplace products carefully as they make selections. If the circumstance involves teaching young children, do the materials appear appropriate for the developmental age of the children being taught? What does the early childhood research suggest about teaching techniques that are effective with this age of children? What does the research suggest about using objects that they can manipulate as they are learning basic arithmetic skills? Are the instructional products sequenced in a manner that is appropriate for their developmental level? There are many variations on questions that should be asked about the research literature as professional consumers. In many cases, it is important to know some basic information about how research is conducted in order to evaluate products.

Keeping Current With Research

There is no intent here to suggest that everyone has to become a practicing researcher, gathering data through surveys or experiments. We *do* contend, however, that some understanding of the research process is important to be an intelligent consumer in your role as a professional just as it is for laypeople. Certainly many decisions do not require an awareness of the scientific method. There are many times, however, when it would be most helpful to be able to question some of the claims made by people who are selling a message that is presumably based on research. It is difficult to imagine how one can intelligently keep current in the professional literature without an understanding of the research process. It is clear in most fields that a person *cannot* succeed as a professional without reading the relevant literature and making some thoughtful judgments. Most professionals have long since learned that they should not accept everything they read without question.

There are a variety of means used by most professionals to keep current on developments in their fields. Almost without fail they subscribe to or review authoritative publications (e.g., journals, monographs, annually published compendiums, Web sites of professional organizations). These sources either present or summarize research results and trends in their fields. Increasingly, electronic bulletin boards and other online publications provide summaries of the latest information and debates in the field. Part of the challenge with these sources is filtering through opinions and unfounded assertions versus other information that is based on solid investigation that has passed the test of review. Some information available on the Web is no more substantiated than casual hallway conversation. Other information has undergone the evaluations and quality tests of what we call "blind reviews" (prepublication evaluation of the study and its methodology by qualified scientists who are "blind" regarding who wrote the manuscript). It is important to have this latter filter to provide some confidence regarding the source of information—well-planned investigation versus an assertion without supporting evidence.

DEFINING WAYS OF CONDUCTING RESEARCH

It is worthwhile to briefly discuss why research is conducted and examine the perspective of some who become researchers. The reasons for conducting research are as varied as the people who are involved. Some will suggest very grand and glorious motivations such as solving the ills of society. Others might be much more personal and indicate that research is just plain fun. Neither of these extremes should be ignored; they are both genuine and powerful reasons for conducting research. Research is conducted to describe what is, why it is, and to determine how a particular event happens (Black, 2001; Joseph, 2004; Sapsford & Jupp, 2004). Research is also undertaken to test the usefulness of a treatment for some social or educational problem. Research may be undertaken to gather data on the effectiveness of a reading program, perhaps comparing it to another program offered by another vendor. Other examples of research might study how well a treatment works to help students who have difficulty attending to a task (Carradice, Beail, & Shankland, 2003; Gelfand & Drew, 2003; O'Donnell, 2004).

The "Ivory Tower" Research

The previous points indicate that research is conducted to solve problems, to expand knowledge, and to increase understanding. These examples also include topics that have very practical utility. Both lay and professional groups commonly accept these reasons. However, the comment concerning "research is fun" raises a completely different justification that is not generally discussed. Some would claim that the amusement of an investigator is not an adequate rationale for conducting research. Such justification sounds too frivolous and all too much like the "ivory tower." This type of argument represents a way of thinking that demands that all research must directly relate to the immediate solution of a practical problem. However, it ignores the fact that many problems cannot be immediately and effectively solved until a foundation of basic knowledge exists. Often the development of such a body of knowledge is only possible through the accumulative investigations of many researchers who may well be studying questions that seem removed from the practical, "real world."

The demand that every piece of research be immediately and obviously relevant also ignores the history of solutions to immediate problems that have resulted because some researcher was indulging a curiosity many years before. It is not uncommon to find answers that may be theoretically interesting but will not find their way into application until problems arise at a later time. From our point of view, indulging an investigator's curiosity is a very good reason for conducting research. The benefits from a practical perspective may not be immediate, but such immediacy is less important than a more reasoned outcome later that ultimately leads to more effective decisions. Box 1.2 sketches one researcher's work that *would not* have been undertaken, and almost wasn't, if the test was immediate practicality.

Basic Versus Applied Research

The previous discussion also relates to a debate regarding basic versus applied and theoretical versus **action research.** Some would contend that the application(s) of basic research are too remote to be engaged in by investigators in service-delivery professions like education. Those on the other end of the continuum assert that

---

BOX 1.2   Basic Research and Application

Genetic targeting was developed in the early 1980s and allows manipulation of an individual gene. Mario Capecchi, the scientist involved, had to "bootleg" the investigations, performing the experiments on the side as he was doing his other research. Funding agencies were not convinced that targeting a specific gene was possible and were unclear what you would do with the process (this latter being the practical importance question). However, genetic targeting is now used commonly in battles against certain diseases. It permits removal of a particular gene, which can then be replaced by another that has very secific characteristics. One use of this process is the ability to "turn on" certain types of biological conditions. Some examples are more well known because they receive attention in the popular press, such as various forms of cancer. Thus, a line of investigation that was once considered of questionable practicality and even questionable possibility is now employed in thousands of laboratories around the world as scientists study diseases of many types.

SOURCE: Quinn, S. (2005). *The life and career of Mario Capecchi.* Five-part series on genetic science. Salt Lake City, UT: KUER FM90. Available online at http://www.publicbroadcasting.net/kuer/news.newsmain?action=article&ARTICLE_ID=726571

applied research is of lesser worth because it is hampered by the many challenges and "messiness" of life (and therefore is not *really* research). This is a popular argument in some circles, although not one in which we wish to engage. Basic research involves investigation of questions that are interesting but may have no application at the present time, like Capecchi's initial experiments in Box 1.2. This is sometimes called *pure* research, but that term connotes a value judgment that is not particularly helpful (as compared with *impure* research?). Research that is considered applied research moves along the continuum with the intent of the results being put into use rather immediately. For example, determining the amount of instructional time allocated for reading in a classroom provides an example of applied research. Some evidence suggests that the amount of time allotted to reading during a day is surprisingly small (Edmonds & Briggs, 2003; Foorman & Schatschneider, 2003). This could suggest that simply providing more time for reading might improve that skill.

Action Versus Theoretical Research

Action research is closely allied to the applied end of the continuum and is undertaken to determine results related to a specific action or decision (Hendricks, 2006; Schmuck, 2005). Action research is often undertaken by teachers to determine the effectiveness of a specific teaching intervention in a particular setting. The example presented above involving reading time allocation might lead to an action research study. Identifying a meager amount of time being allocated to reading could be considered identifying a problem. An action research intervention study might investigate whether or not providing *more* time actually enhances reading skills. A further intervention might study how much student engagement in reading (as manipulated by the teacher) would change reading skills. Both of these examples might be categorized as action research and together would reflect a systematic inquiry into classroom practices (Mertler, 2006). Both studies emerge from theories about the amount of practice and the level of engagement that is important for skill acquisition or improvement. Both address practical questions that may have rather immediate implications for the way a teacher operates his or her classroom. Such research provides considerable practical benefit for teachers. The Research in Action box presents two action research studies for you to examine.

Discussions concerning applied versus basic or theoretical versus action research are confusing because the issues have been argued as both method issues and value judgments. This is unfortunate because a great deal of time and energy has been spent on the debate itself. Essentially, the argument can be reduced to the value judgment issue regarding whether or not a requirement of immediate applicability should be a determiner of the value of research. If conducted carefully, the methodology is the same; only the content and setting differ. The task here, however, is to explore technically sound research designs, not debate value judgment issues. There is good reason to conduct both basic and applied research. There is *no reason* for conducting research that is unsound, regardless of the topic.

Personalized Approach

We are strong advocates of a wide array of reasons for conducting research. Most active researchers seem to be motivated by a variety of reasons for undertaking investigations. This places the question of "Why conduct research?" on a very personal level, which seems quite appropriate. We have already noted that research is fun (not discounting the fact that it is also work). It is most certainly a pleasure to obtain an answer to a question that one has, regardless of whether curiosity, theory, or immediate social problems that motivate the research. There is tremendous personal satisfaction in gathering your own data. Not only is it satisfying to determine whether a teacher-initiated intervention results in student learning, it is also gratifying when you can share those findings with other teachers such as the many teacher-oriented action research Web sites (Mertler, 2006). In addition to feeling good about your own teaching, you can potentially help others with similar questions.

As the years have passed, we have begun to appreciate other personal benefits of conducting research. One important part of the process is writing. The expression of thoughts, ideas, and findings, *in writing,* is one of the most demanding tasks a person can undertake. It requires a completeness and clarity of communication that is not involved in routine conversation. Spoken communication, even in formal circumstances, often includes nonverbal gesturing to accentuate, provide emphasis, and complete thoughts that are only partially expressed by the actual words. Most people do not even notice these behaviors because they are so accustomed to both using and experiencing them. Although nonverbal aids may be acceptable in verbal communication, writing does not permit such luxuries. Consequently, it is challenging for most people to write clearly. Despite the struggle, a great deal of satisfaction accompanies completion of the writing.

RESEARCH IN ACTION

KEY POINTS IN THE CHAPTER REFLECTED IN THIS BOX:

- The research ideas will be generally identified.
- The method of science is examined as one way of knowing information among others.

For more research in action tips visit www.sagepub .com/drewstudy

OBJECTIVES TO LEARN FROM THIS BOX:

- Understand how action research ideas begin in a field setting and emerge from the problems or questions in that setting.
- Reflect on how action researchers choose among different ways of thinking about their beliefs.

SCENARIO 1: STUDENT ENGAGEMENT IN READING

Emily is a teacher and researcher who has always been interested in how to engage students in the material they encounter in school. She thinks that students who are engaged in a topic will learn more easily and master the content better than students who are not engaged. She views this as a very practical problem, one of how to actively involve her students in the topics she is teaching. She believes this involvement or engagement has a very beneficial effect on her students' learning. For her, it is an action research possibility because it can directly translate into something she can implement in a classroom.

Emily's idea for research is to demonstrate how student engagement enhances students' motivation for school topics. Her area of particular interest involves how students learn to read and how to improve their reading performance. Combining these two interests, Emily has found some literature that seems related to her ideas (Guthrie & Cox, 1998). She begins to investigate the articles of John Guthrie and his associates and starts thinking about how to study student engagement and reading.

Although Emily firmly believes in engagement, she has some options in how she develops her ideas. She could continue to assert her belief strongly without any further investigation on her part, or she could reference the writings of Dr. Guthrie and be satisfied with that approach. Another approach would be to systematically investigate the topic of engagement and its effect on reading instruction. These options involve three different ways of knowing something or establishing a belief (tenacity, authority, and the method of science). She decides to follow the method of science, which will lead her down a path of actually conducting some research. As she proceeds, she will think through the differences between a commonsense view of the topic and one that involves scientific methods (including the concept of control). She will also make some choices regarding which types of research methods might be used effectively.

Think about this: How does the action research topic of reading engagement emerge from the classroom setting? How is the method of science different from other ways of knowing about the influence of student engagement in reading?

SOURCES: This action research scenario is roughly based on the work of John Guthrie at the University of Maryland and Emily Anderson Swan at the University of Utah (Guthrie & Anderson, 1999; Swan, 2003).

SCENARIO 2: STUDENT SELF-ESTEEM

Daniel is interested in self-esteem, learning disabilities, and diverse students. This is a broad range of topics and he has ideas about all of them. He believes that having learning disabilities influences self-esteem. He also thinks that there are cultural matters that influence students' self-esteem. Daniel has some options regarding his beliefs about these topics. As a teacher, he sees his students with learning disabilities on a daily basis. He observes their self-esteem as being pretty low. These students often express themselves in ways that lead Daniel to think they don't have very high self-concepts, and they often behave in ways that reflect this same low personal evaluation of themselves. Often this seems related to their learning disability.

Daniel also has some Latino students with learning disabilities. They seem to also have low self-esteem, but there appear to be differences between his Latino students and those that are Caucasian. Daniel thinks that it is wrong to just say that all students with learning disabilities have similarly low self-esteem. It appears to him that both Latino and Caucasian students with learning disabilities have low self-esteem but that there are important differences between the two groups of students. Daniel has firmly and vocally expressed his view about these differences, but some of his coworkers challenge him. They seem to believe that a low self-esteem is similar for all children. Daniel begins to read the scientific literature in two areas: self-esteem related to students with disabilities and self-esteem related to students with different ethnic backgrounds.

Daniel has found the method of tenacity to be unsatisfactory because simply expressing his belief strongly is not convincing to his coworkers, and their questions trigger his own curiosity. He is a little frustrated by his reading because he finds that there are few studies comparing minority and Caucasian students in terms of self-esteem. He also finds there are some measurement issues regarding self-esteem itself. Everyone globally and grandly asserts that it is important, but they are a bit vague on what self-esteem is and how to measure it. Reference to authority in terms of the published literature doesn't provide clear direction. Daniel believes that he can learn something about self-esteem in his Latino students that is different from his Caucasian students. He also thinks that he can learn something that will help him work with both groups of students differently and more effectively as a teacher. He decides he will conduct a study on the self-esteem of Latino and Caucasian students with learning disabilities to at least see if he can identify differences that might be useful to him in his teaching efforts.

Think about this: How does the action research topic of differences in self-esteem emerge from Daniel's classroom setting? How is the method of science different from other ways of knowing about the influence of ethnicity differences on self-esteem?

SOURCE: This action research scenario is roughly based on Rubin, D. (2000). *Race and self-esteem: A study of Latino and European-American students with learning disabilities.* Unpublished master's thesis, University of Utah, Salt Lake City.

The entire research process, from designing a study to writing the report, can be one of the most growth-producing experiences available. Each step requires the exercise of disciplined thought balanced with an appropriate dose of creativity. Conducting research has many similarities to other creative acts. You can nearly *feel* the mental growth when a study is completed. For us, this is a very compelling, personal reason for conducting research and one that is more powerful than any of the lofty justifications typically offered.

FOUNDATIONS OF RESEARCH

Research is part of our daily life whether we are conscious of its presence or not. Each of us as individuals may not be actively engaged in what most would consider research, but most of us are consumers of scientific investigations in our daily lives. This is easy to see if we use technology in our work, such as using hydraulic pressure principles if we are operating earth-moving equipment. It is less obvious in the context of how we think. However, research is based on some ways of thinking and certain methods of establishing beliefs. This section will briefly examine certain approaches to formulating beliefs and show how they relate to science.

The purpose of research is to obtain knowledge or information. Research is a systematic method of asking questions, involving the scientific method, and inquiring about phenomena (Hart, 2003; Middleton & Brown, 2006). Both the scientific method and other systematic research traditions are somewhat different from the way people generally conduct their daily lives. This section discusses the placement of research, and therefore science, in relation to various methods of knowing about the world.

Four Ways of Knowing or Fixing Belief

There are a variety of ways of knowing something or fixing belief that are relevant to much of the research conducted today (Goodwin, 2005; Wacome, 2003). Four of these methods of knowing include tenacity, authority, a priori, and science. Each approach involves a different set of characteristics and sources of information. In addition, each of these methods is used to a greater or lesser degree by different groups of people as they pursue knowledge (Jupp, 2006). The different ways of establishing belief are useful in placing research in perspective with regard to other approaches to inquiry.

Tenacity

If a person uses **tenacity** as a method of knowing a fact, then that fact is thought to be true because "it has always been true." This approach comes from the idea that an individual holds tenaciously to existing beliefs. If something is known by the method of tenacity, essentially a closed system exists—meaning no new information is put into the system. In fact, the very nature of tenacity may prompt the individual to hold to a belief even in the face of nonsupportive evidence (Evans, 2002). People often become so accustomed to ordinary life events that they selectively ignore information that contradicts previously held beliefs (perhaps the students in Box 1.1 are an example). Certainly there are circumstances in education where tenacity is used, even though most of us would like to think that what we do is based on scientific evidence. For example, the academic or school year has been established to be about the same time of the year in most geographic locations for a very long time. Originally, it may have followed that schedule in order to allow older schoolchildren to help with harvesting crops. When educators began to suggest operating schools on a year-round basis to better use facilities, they encountered significant resistance. Although many students were no longer involved in agriculture, tenacity was a strong support base for not changing the academic schedule.

Authority

Another approach to knowing or fixing belief—**authority**—cites an eminent person or entity as the source of knowledge. If a well-known individual or an "expert" (an authority) states that something is the case, then it is so (at least according to some people). The authority's declaration relieves the believer from going elsewhere to obtain informaton. The method of authority is not definitively a "bad" method of knowing. Much depends on the authoritative source and on the way in which the believer uses the method. If it is used totally in a nonthinking, closed-system fashion, there are obvious weaknesses. Used in this manner, no consideration is given to nonsupportive or conflicting evidence. When this is the case, the progress of knowledge and ideas is painfully slow and depends totally on the progress of the authority.

A Priori

A third way of knowing or fixing belief is called the **a priori method.** A priori, by definition, refers to "before the fact" and is primarily based on intuitive knowledge. In subscribing to the a priori method, something is known before information is gathered or even in the absence of experiential data. Usually the a priori approach is logical or in harmony with reason. The reasoning can be a weakness, however. Unless the information system is open to data gleaned from experience (experimentation or observation), an error of logic may begin a line of reasoning that is characterized by progressive errors.

Method of Science

The fourth method of knowing is called the **method of science.** The method of science is different from the other three ways of fixing belief. External experience through observation is the foundation of this method. The method of science has a *built-in self-correction factor,* which distinguishes it rather dramatically from the other ways of knowing. This self-corrective factor is operative because the system is open and public. A scientist's work is public not only in terms of end products (published results), but also in the means by which those ends were obtained. In their publications, researchers must describe the procedures, materials, and participants. Investigators must explain and demonstrate the logic used to reach the conclusion in their publications. This ensures that future investigators have the opportunity to learn from those before them. Independent replication operates the self-correction factor of science, and all knowledge must remain open to eventual change or correction if new data come to light. This discussion also highlights the importance of publishing by researchers. Without rigorously reviewed publications, researchers wouldn't be able to demonstrate their investigations to others.

Research has its foundation in the method of science. However, one has only to read a research article to observe great variation within the method of science and the use of at least segments of two other methods of knowing. Certainly reference to authority is operative in research—investigators are continually citing the work of others. This use of the method of authority, however, is different from using authorities solely as a closed system in which conflicting evidence is not acknowledged. Furthermore, research openly challenges authority when evidence is not in agreement. Research also uses basic components of the a priori method of knowing—logic and reason. Again, the way in which logic and reason are used in research is considerably different from the use of the a priori method as the sole source of knowledge. Researchers are required to clearly demonstrate the path of reasoning by which conclusions are reached in their writing. If the logic is faulty or conflicts with observed evidence, it is challenged by the method of science. By virtue of its public nature, science can effectively use portions of the other methods of knowing and avoid pitfalls inherent in them. Refereed review of scientific research by peers capitalizes on the virtues of these qualities.

Inductive and Deductive Reasoning

Reasoning and logic represent vital components of the research process, as noted above. If these elements are absent, the research process is weakened and jeopardized so severely as to render it useless. Without the input of reasoning, knowledge would not progress at all since the relationship of one idea to another, or of data to an idea, is based on this essential element.

Two distinctive types of reasoning are involved in the broad spectrum of research efforts—deductive and inductive reasoning. *Deductive reasoning* uses logic that moves from the general to the specific. Statements initiated from a general idea, model, or theory characterize deductive reasoning, and from these statements something is inferred about a specific case ("If the [general] theory is correct, then I should be able to observe this [specific] behavior in children."). *Inductive reasoning*, on the other hand, reflects the reverse type of logic. Inductive reasoning uses logic that is launched from a specific case or occurrence and moves to inferences about the general ("If a [specific] behavior occurs, then this [general] theory is supported.").

Both types of reasoning are used in behavioral research. Examples of deductive reasoning may be found in introductory statements of research articles. Deductive reasoning is being used when researchers examine a general theory, model, or body of knowledge about teaching and hypothesize a specific behavior they expect to observe when they apply this in a classroom. Inductive reasoning often drives exploratory, qualitative inquiry; where theory is lacking or just developing; when the area of study is new; or when controlled, experimental research has suggested behavioral patterns exist that the researcher would like to examine in natural settings. Inductive reasoning is also the primary means by which data generalization is accomplished. When a researcher is writing the discussion section of a research article, the discussion is mostly based on data collected. From the data (specific observations), inferences are drawn about the general theory or model reviewed in the introduction. Generalizations may be made about a population (general) from the participants' performance (specific).

Differences Between Experimental Science and Common Sense

There are several distinctions between science and common sense that are useful in placing the scientific method in the context of daily life. There is a general theme that threads its way through the differences. Science is characterized by a more systematic approach to problems than common sense, and it always leaves the door open for new approaches or knowledge that may change beliefs about truth or reality (Goodwin, 2005; Wacome, 2003).

Theoretical Structures and Concepts

There is a distinct difference between science and common sense in the use of theoretical structures and concepts. Science *systematically constructs theories and conceptual schemes, uses them, and submits them to repeated tests*—the scientist is never *certain*. A person who operates primarily on a commonsense basis often does not use theory and concepts in the same fashion. Often theories and concepts are applied loosely and not systematically. Explanations of events may not be supported by logic relating that explanation to a conceptual scheme. They may not even relate to accurate data about the events.

Theory Development and Testing

A second difference, closely related to the first, speaks to the issue of theory development and testing. The method of science *systematically generates and tests theories, hypotheses, and ideas.* The term *systematic* here again becomes the key. If a given theory is presumed to work under conditions X, Y, and Z, science demands the systematic examination of events under conditions X, Y, and Z. A commonsense approach to testing, on the other hand, tends to be much less concerned with systematically testing an idea under all relevant conditions. *Selection bias* frequently enters into the choice of situations in which the theory is tested and the viewing of test results. Often an idea such as "all republicans are conservative" is tested unintentionally under conditions that ensure support for a preconceived notion. Information that does not support the hypothesis may be discounted or ignored and not included as a part of the test. Proverbial "in-law" stories exemplify this type of information bias.

Concept of Control

A third difference between science and common sense involves the **concept of control.** This concept will become a central focus in later chapters on experimental designs. Here again, a systematic approach is preeminent. All science arose from the *observation* of naturally occurring events. Education and the social and behavioral sciences cannot always control natural processes in existing groups, cultures, or settings. Experimental science relies on the concept of control, which essentially involves *eliminating possible influential variables except the one being tested.* Common sense, in contrast, may operate in such a loose fashion that several factors are allowed to vary at once. This may mean that any one of two or three influences *might* have generated the results observed, in addition to the one being studied. Under such circumstances, scientists would probably throw up their hands and view the data as uninterpretable, certainly not attributing the results to any one influence. From the less systematic framework of common sense, interpretation may suggest a result caused by one influence, which, since two or three are operating, may be in error.

Relationships Among Phenomena

A fourth distinction between science and common sense involves the interest level concerning relationships among phenomena. The layperson is frequently interested in relationships among phenomena in a somewhat loose and unsystematic fashion. Interest is primarily generated when there is great personal relevance involved. In contrast, *the scientist becomes almost obsessed with the relationships among phenomena, whether personally relevant or not.* There seems to be a continual question-asking process in operation (e.g., "I wonder if this material would be more effective if . . ." or "I wonder if that behavior is influenced by . . .").

Explanations of Phenomena

The fifth difference between science and common sense relates to explanations of phenomena. *Explanations of events that flow from the method of science tend to be stated in terms of the observable, the logical, and the empirically testable* (Berthold, Hakala, & Goff, 2003; Thomas & Rosqvist, 2003). A commonsense explanation, on the other hand, frequently involves reference to metaphysical influences. Metaphysical explanations cannot be tested. Such statements as "Working hard is good for one's moral character" and "Suffering builds character" are metaphysical statements.

There is certainly a conceivable continuum between the science method and common sense. The primary factors that seem to be involved are concepts of systematic inquiry, logic, objectivity, and observable phenomena. Read over Simulation 1.2 at the end of this chapter to see how you would outline the differences between science and common sense.

Simulation

Simulation 1.2

Topic: Science and common sense

Background statement: You are a graduate student at Southeastern Unified College (SUC). One of the faculty has become ill, and you are substituting as the instructor in the introductory research class. In your first lecture, you are going to be discussing the differences between science and common sense. What five points will you emphasize? Give examples of each.

Write your response, then turn to page 28 for Simulation Feedback 1.2

For additional simulations visit www.sagepub .com/drewstudy

RESEARCH TYPES AND METHODS IN BRIEF

Research projects begin with a question, as seen in Figure 1.1. The **research question** then leads to a planning process where the scientist maps out a plan (often called a design) for the study that will gather information and answer the research question. The steps between a research question and interpreting the information are characterized by various activities and procedures aimed at the process of gathering data systematically and objectively. These place certain requirements on the information-gathering process to eliminate or minimize bias and errors in answering the research question.

As a researcher plans the study, he or she may use a number of different approaches to design. Different approaches or methods have various features as part of their procedural protocol and are often labeled by elements of those features (e.g., quantitative studies gather information in numbers or quantities; qualitative studies use a narrative to describe situations). We will briefly outline different research methods below. Each method may be used with different research questions, and in some cases the choice of design is made based on the comfort level and background of the investigator.

Quantitative Research

Studies using quantitative methods collect data in the form of numbers. In this approach to research, the occurrences of behaviors are counted, correct answers or errors are counted, and other types of measures are recorded in terms of quantity. **Quantitative research** tends to be planned and details specified rather extensively before a study begins. The research question or questions are specified in detail. Operational steps of how the study is to be carried out are typically specified and gathered into an itemized operational guide or protocol for actually conducting the study. Often the plan or design of the study is arranged to control outside influences. The plan for the study will also include a description of the participants and how they are to be sampled, what testing or data collection instruments are used, and what specific procedures are employed to gather the data.

Data analysis for quantitative research also has a long history of using statistical tools, and those components are also planned and specified before the study begins. This type of analysis leads to explanations that are divided into parts—for example, the interpretation of a participant's behavior in class may focus on a very limited set of stimuli rather than a global explanation of the broad context of the whole classroom. This interpretation might suggest that a particular child's attention to spelling materials is controlled by the visual stimuli on the paper, as opposed to a broader description of classroom stimuli like his or her classmate's behavior, noise level, lighting, and so on.

From this thumbnail sketch, it is clear that researchers using quantitative methods make detailed plans before the study begins. This is worth noting because when we examine qualitative research, we will find that some elements are intentionally left undefined. There are also some subtypes that need to be mentioned because they have descriptive labels you will often encounter: experimental and nonexperimental research.

Experimental Research

Imposing or manipulating certain conditions in order to see how participants respond characterizes **experimental research.** For example, suppose we were interested in the effectiveness of a particular method of teaching arithmetic. An investigator using experimental research methods would be inclined to impose the intervention (teaching method) on a group of children and measure how well they learn math. The experimenter will prefer to define all the procedures, data collection processes, and study protocols in advance, adopting many of the broader elements outlined for quantitative methods. The researcher will also tend to sample a group of children and is likely to count the number of correct responses on an arithmetic test. This counting of the children's correct responses is the investigator's approach to determining how much they learned. The experimenter will typically use the elements of research methods described for quantitative methods above, as well as manipulate or impose the intervention or treatment.

Nonexperimental Research

Nonexperimental research methods are distinguished from experiments in that they do not impose a treatment or intervention to see how participants respond. Nonexperimental studies are more characterized by gathering data as it occurs or exists in a natural environment. For example, surveys or questionnaires are typically viewed as being used in nonexperimental studies. This type of research typically asks the participant (the person completing the questionnaire) to respond to survey questions when and where they encounter the questionnaire. This may be in the person's office, on the Web, in his or her kitchen, or some other setting, but is characterized by data collection in that situation rather than manipulating a set of conditions to see how participants respond.

The data collected may be in the form of numbers or a narrative, depending on the nature of the question and the preference of the researcher. For example, the survey may ask respondents how old they are, which would likely result in numbers. They may be asked to express how well they approve of their schools and the education their children are receiving, which could result in responses on a 1 to 5 scale—also numerical information. However, respondents may also be asked to write a short narrative reflecting their feelings about a political question, which would result in data in the form of words and would be treated differently than the numbers in the analysis.

Nonexperimental quantitative studies tend to also be planned in detail ahead of time. For example, the survey researcher will always draft and revise a questionnaire multiple times in order to get the wording just right. Because nonexperimental research may collect data in narrative form and also study participants in their natural environments, these studies have elements of qualitative as well as quantitative methods. This is a characteristic we see emphasized in mixed methods.

Qualitative Research

Qualitative research methods may outline the broad scope of a study but may not specify as much operational detail. Qualitative researchers tend not to tamper with natural settings where the data are to be collected. Some qualitative researchers may decide to let hypotheses and definitions emerge as the study proceeds. The data collected might lead a researcher down a path of investigation that was not anticipated before the study began. Researchers seek validity or accuracy by obtaining information from multiple sources—a process known as *triangulation*. Triangulation means that the investigator may, for example, ask for descriptions of an event from two different people and also see how the event is described in official records by the government. This process is the researcher's attempt to ask what the story is from multiple sources, not just one source, thereby trying to find out what *really* happened. Data are recorded in terms of narrative descriptions, not numbers. Researchers using qualitative methods will describe what else is going on rather than controlling it, trying not to tamper with the natural setting they are studying. When presenting the results, researchers using qualitative methods will tell the story in narrative form, describing the whole setting and broad scope of the study.

Mixed Methods

Mixed method studies employ elements from more than one approach, often capitalizing on the strengths of each process. Investigations using **mixed-method research** may count participants' correct responses (quantitative) and also collect narrative descriptions of some behaviors or information (qualitative) in order to construct a data set that more completely answers the research question. For example, using mixed methods the researcher may count the children's correct responses to arithmetic problems (numbers—quantitative) and then also ask them how they felt about having to do the arithmetic (words—qualitative). This allows the researcher to learn information and draw inferences that could not be achieved by using a single type of protocol. Mixed-method research approaches provide the potential for substantial strengths that the component approaches cannot achieve when used singly.

THE RESEARCH PROCESS

Reference has been made to the research process, although thus far only certain portions of it have been described. As a whole, the research process can be conceptualized in a circular or closed-loop fashion in the manner illustrated in Figure 1.1. The

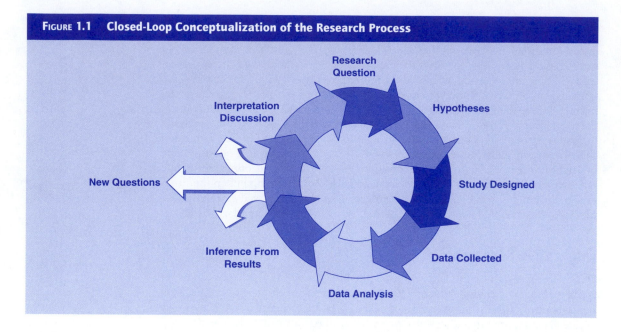

FIGURE 1.1   Closed-Loop Conceptualization of the Research Process

process begins with the research question or problem. The research problem is then developed into more focused questions, which lead to hypotheses in the form of very specific statements that characterize each and every comparison or relationship being studied. From the hypotheses, the study is designed or planned in detail with very specific written statements of what the questions are and what procedures will be used to collect data to answer those questions.

At this point, the investigation is ready to be implemented, which begins with data collection. This is the component where the researcher gathers information through a questionnaire, testing children or observing in a classroom. Once the data are collected, they need to be analyzed to determine what the results indicate. This is then followed by an interpretation of the results regarding the research question(s) (inference about what the results mean). The inference or interpretation may lead to new questions, discussion about any theory that might have prompted the study, and some interpretation about what the results mean for practical applications. This simple description of the research process includes many different components, and it mirrors the general structure of this book.

Selecting a Research Topic

A research topic or idea may emerge from theoretical dilemmas presented by other studies, a practical problem needing solution, or the curiosity of the individual undertaking the study. For example, a teacher might identify a research topic about how much instructional time should be allocated for reading each day. Such a topic might address the teacher's problem of how to manage time, combined with a need or desire to raise student reading skills and test scores. In this case, the general topic is an applied research question and one that could easily lead to action research. That is, a study of the topic could result in an action by the teacher such as rearranging his or her instructional time to focus additional time on reading. Given the nature of this topic, the next step is to develop specific research questions from the topic, and those questions will then lead to the hypothesis or hypotheses.

Distilling the Topic Into Research Question Format

Distilling the topic or idea into research question format means moving from the general topic to a specific question or questions. In our example, the curiosity about instructional time for reading may lead to several possible research questions. In one case, the teacher-researcher may first want to know how much time is currently allotted for reading instruction.

This would logically lead to a descriptive research question—that is, simply asking for a description of what is currently allotted. Such a question would then suggest that the teacher-researcher record the number of minutes each day allotted to reading instruction. Referring to Figure 1.1, the research process might move past hypotheses directly to study design. This is acceptable since in this situation we don't have particular hypotheses in mind, merely a description of what currently is the case. The design or plan for the study would likely involve a research assistant recording the numbers of minutes each day that are allotted to reading instruction, while the teacher continues his or her daily routine in a normal fashion (without making any changes). Recording time might continue over a week or over any specified period of time that the researcher believes represents what is normally done.

Another approach might lead to a difference question, which might ask, "Is there a difference in the amount of instructional time allocated to reading as compared to math, science, or any other specified topics of interest?" In this situation, the teacher-researcher is still obtaining a general description of his or her instructional day, but the amount of time is recorded for each subject area. This type of research question is a difference question that involves comparisons. The minutes are recorded for each content area over a week's period (or whatever period has been specified). In this study, there may be some hypotheses and they may indicate that, "There is no expected difference in the number of instructional minutes allotted to math as compared to reading" (or math vs. reading vs. science). This is called a *null hypothesis* because it predicts no difference.

Notice how the research question format is much more specific and detailed than the research idea or topic. Distilling research topics into research questions involves becoming much more detailed. A proper research question should be sufficiently specific that it leads the researcher to the hypotheses and logically to how the study is implemented. In both examples, the distillation is a logical progression.

In the case of quantitative research and all experimental designs, the research topic must be distilled into a very specific question, which will then lead to a hypothesis or several hypotheses. Research addressing immediate practical problems is often called action research, because it is prompted by an immediate action or decision that needs to be made. This is the type of study example suggested above. In addition to the previous examples, such studies might investigate questions like which of two or three teaching techniques shows greater improvements in achievement scores (e.g., as on a criterion-referenced test). These circumstances will involve a very specific question or questions and lead to hypotheses and then to detailed operational steps for data collection in the design phase.

Qualitative research often explores naturally occurring events or processes, which is different from the experiment mentioned above where the researcher tries out two or three different teaching protocols. Because qualitative studies may emphasize studying events as they naturally occur, some of the detail about what goes on is less prescribed. However, although the specific activities may be less prescribed or prearranged, the research must be consistent with general questions about how and why things occur. Qualitative studies must also be designed (planned) in a manner that will avoid potential difficulties and permit the researcher to answer the question. The research design is critically important and involves rigorous and meticulous planning.

Moving From the Question and Hypothesis to the Design

The next stage continues to represent a logical flow, and it leads to the design or plan for the study. In both the descriptive and the difference questions above, the next step is simply to specify how the study is to be implemented. This design process will again become quite specific and detailed. It is the road map or study protocol and involves specifying how the data are to be collected and under what conditions. This is the next step in Figure 1.1. Let's take our difference question example and develop a design statement.

In this study, our hypothesis stated that there was no difference in the amount of instructional time allocated to math, reading, and science. In order to obtain an accurate set of data, several items are important. One involves the teacher not changing what he or she is normally doing. The research question and hypothesis must be fairly tested by gathering data under routine and normal circumstances. It is recommended that there be an observer or research partner who records the data. This allows the teacher to continue teaching normally. It is also important for the observer to be able to distinguish between the content areas so he or she will be able to record the minutes allocated to each content area accurately. This often means that very precise statements need to be developed ahead of time that describe markers or characteristics of instructional time for each topic. The more detailed these statements are, the easier it will be to achieve accurate and reliable data collection. These statements become the design or plan for study implementation.

Planning will include the operational steps of actually conducting the study and recording data. This is followed by the many steps involved in executing the investigation with data being collected and then analyzed. Once this is done, the results must be interpreted in terms of the research question that completes the loop. If executed properly, the question should be answered or at least a first step should be taken toward achieving this end.

Using the Research in Data-Based Decision Making

The final steps in closing the loop of Figure 1.1 show several points that involve inference from results, the emergence of new questions, and interpretation of the data. Interpreting the data will result in a discussion about whether the study supported earlier findings in literature that was reviewed as the study was begun. The new questions may lead to further studies to achieve greater clarification or following some new line of investigation that might have surfaced. Interpretation of the meaning of results may also lead to using the research outcomes for data-based decisions, which is often the purpose of action research. In our earlier example on instructional time, the teacher-researcher may find that the amount of instructional time allotted for reading does differ from that of math and science and that reading has been receiving less time. This might lead our teacher-researcher to recheck the literature, which suggests that academic achievement measures do seem to be enhanced if they are given more instructional time. The next step may be to revise his or her time allocation between content areas in order to find additional time for reading instruction. This provides an example of an instructional decision that might be made based on data from a piece of action research. Making decisions about instruction is a very important benefit for educational practitioners and one of the appealing features of action research.

The discussion above presents a simple view of the overall research process. As is always the case, the devil is found in the details. A variety of challenges may surface at each step and many specific points have been omitted here. These will be discussed in greater depth throughout this book. What has been examined, however, is the research process as a whole. Many characterizations of research have been guilty of focusing on one portion or emphasizing one step to the exclusion of others. Such a limited perspective frequently gives laypeople and beginning students an inaccurate view of what is really involved in research. Creating such perspectives (knowingly or unknowingly) has generated many misconceptions and often contributed to unfavorable opinions about research. We hope that this book will serve to inform as well as correct misconceptions in cases when that is appropriate.

Chapter Summary

+ A simple working definition of research is a systematic way of asking questions.

+ Some of the misconceptions about research include terms like mechanistic, mystical, and others. In reality, research is often not conducted in a laboratory and is not mechanistic, nor is it mystical.

+ Research is important to consumers because we receive information daily about products we use and much of that information is derived from research. It is important to distinguish between research and marketing.

+ Research is important to professionals because they are consumers of research and are often involved in making decisions based on information from research.

+ Research is conducted for many different reasons ranging from solving basic theoretical problems to making decisions about which reading program to use for specific children in the classroom.

+ The different ways of knowing about something range from tenacity—something is true because it has always been true—to the method of science, which involves collecting data on questions in a systematic and open manner.

+ Deductive reasoning involves logic that progresses from general ideas to specific cases, whereas inductive reasoning starts with a specific case or observation and progresses to more general ideas.

+ Science systematically uses, tests, and constructs theories and concepts, whereas common sense may use them selectively and not systematically under all conditions. Science tries to control all influences except the one under study, while common sense may allow multiple influences to operate in addition to the one under study.

+ Quantitative research involves collecting data in the form of numbers and planning studies in specific operational details, often manipulating the environment to determine what happens. Qualitative research means collecting data in narrative formats, tends to leave the environment in a natural format, and may leave many details of the study undefined at the beginning. Mixed-method research employs elements from both quantitative and qualitative procedures.

+ A research topic may surface from reading or a daily dilemma. The topic may be general and will be molded into a specific research question.

+ Results from research can often be used to make decisions about matters in daily life, such as how much time should be allotted to teaching math or science or what happens to academic achievement when more time is given to a content area which may then lead to the decision to allot more instructional time to the topic.

Key Terms

Action research. Research undertaken to determine results related to a specific action or decision. Action research is often conducted by teachers to determine the effectiveness of a specific teaching intervention in a particular setting.

Applied research. Research involving studies that address questions with some clear application rather than testing a theory.

A priori method of knowing. Refers to things that are known "before the fact" and is primarily based on intuitive knowledge. In subscribing to the a priori method, something is known before information is gathered or even in the absence of experiential data.

Authority method of knowing. This method of knowing or fixing belief cites an eminent person or entity as the source of knowledge. It is based on the idea that if a well-known authority states that something is the case, then it must be so.

Basic research. Basic research involves investigation of questions that are interesting but may have no application at the present time.

Concept of control. The process of holding all possible influences constant except the experimental variable, which is what is being studied. For example, if the researcher is comparing the effectiveness of Reading Programs A and B, the reading programs should be the only factor that is different between the groups. All other influences (e.g., intelligence or age) should be equivalent.

Experimental research. Imposing or manipulating certain conditions in order to see how participants respond characterizes experimental research. An investigator using experimental research methods would be inclined to impose an intervention, such as a teaching method, on a group of children and measure how well they learn math.

Mixed-method research. Mixed-method studies employ elements from more than one approach to research, often capitalizing on the strengths of each procedure. Investigations using mixed method research may use both quantitative and qualitative methods.

Nonexperimental research. Nonexperimental research methods are distinguished from experiments in that they do not impose a treatment or intervention to see how participants respond. Nonexperimental studies are more characterized by gathering data as it occurs or exists in a natural environment.

Qualitative research. Research that involves collecting data in the form of words or a narrative that describes the topic under study and emphasizes collecting data in natural settings.

Quantitative research. Studies using quantitative methods collect data in the form of numbers. In this approach to research, the occurrences of behaviors are counted, correct answers or errors are counted, and other types of measures are recorded in terms of quantity.

Research question. A focused and often detailed statement of the research topic to be studied. The three types of research questions often studied in education are descriptive, difference, and relationship.

Science method of knowing. The method of science as a way of knowing is based on external experience through observation. Data are collected about a topic to determine the existence of a phenomenon.

Tenacity method of knowing. This method involves thinking that something is true because "it has always been true." This perspective comes from the idea that an individual holds tenaciously to existing beliefs.

Student Study Site

The companion Web site for *Designing and Conducting Research in Education*
www.sagepub.com/drewstudy

Supplement your review of this chapter by going to the companion Web site to take one of the practice quizzes, use the flashcards to study key terms, and check out the many other study aids you'll find there. You'll even find some research articles from the Sage Full-Text Collection and a step-by-step guide that will show you how to read an educational research article.

Simulation Feedback

Simulation Feedback 1.1

Neither Janet nor Andrew should jump to the conclusion that he or she is correct and the other position is incorrect based on this research evidence. Research results accumulate over a period of time. This particular study indicated that preschool children have some capacity to deal with symbolic math concepts, perhaps more than was thought before. However, this is just one piece of evidence. Many studies have been performed, each with a slightly different *specific* research question, and the accumulated evidence will perhaps answer the questions of these well-meaning parents. Research evidence accumulates somewhat like the way a complex jigsaw puzzle is assembled—after many pieces are fit into place, the picture begins to emerge.

For additional simulations visit www.sagepub .com/drewstudy

This research reported that preschool children are able to perform some mathematics at an age that surprises many of us. The study Janet found indicated that the children probably can handle the curriculum (assuming it is presented in an appropriate manner). Like many areas of study, there are some related questions that haven't been posed yet, such as, "Will this type of curriculum presented this early help Ben, or might it be detrimental?" Addressing these questions would involve additional studies with research questions like the following (insert your own child's name in place of Ben's): "What are the effects of introducing math concepts to preschool children?" "Are these effects beneficial or detrimental to Ben's development?" "Is such exposure likely to enhance Ben's ability to do math later?" "Will this early exposure make him more afraid of math when he gets older (or less afraid)?" Each of these could be the research question for one or more studies, and each might help fill in the puzzle with an additional piece of information. All assembled, they may tell parents a lot about preschool curriculum that involves math.

As a research consumer, you will be best served by examining an accumulation of research results on any topic. Each study will likely have results that are fairly focused on a narrow topic. The narrow focus is necessary for a quality investigation, as we will see. As we proceed, you will become more familiar with this focused approach and you will begin to feel more comfortable as a consumer of research.

Simulation Feedback

For additional simulations visit www.sagepub .com/drewstudy

Simulation Feedback 1.2

Probably the quickest way of providing feedback in this simulation is to refer to sections of this chapter regarding the differences between science and common sense. Certainly you will want to discuss how theories and the development and testing of them relate to both common sense and science. It will be extremely important to examine the concept of control and how it is central to science but less so in commonsense discussions. Finally, you will probably discuss differences between science and commonsense approaches to examining different phenomena and their relationships, and explanations about them.

2

THE RESEARCH PROCESS

FINDING A TOPIC TO INVESTIGATE

Research can be conducted for a wide variety of reasons. Studies can be undertaken to (1) try out new methods or techniques, (2) to indulge the investigator's curiosity, (3) to establish the existence of behavioral phenomena, and (4) to explore the conditions under which certain events occur. These reasons cover a lot of territory. However, the point to be emphasized for beginning students is that **research ideas** come from many sources.

The Process of Discovering an Idea

Ideas for research come from everywhere. There is an abundance of them. The challenge for a beginning researcher is knowing where to find them and narrowing the focus, which lead to pinpointing a research topic. Someone who is working on an idea assumes ownership of that idea or problem, although ownership is not exclusive—history is replete with examples of multiple researchers working on the same or similar topics. You can build on someone else's research as long as you give that particular person appropriate credit in your publication. As a matter of fact, this reference citing not only does not devalue your current work, it also makes good sense from a research perspective. Moreover, it is a very public means of tracing your logic as you think through different ideas and the nuances of your reasoning as you link one idea to the next and then to the research question.

Reading Published Articles

The world of practicing investigators and their research ideas should also be examined briefly. Many research ideas studied by professors do not come solely from topics existing in their minds. In many cases, the experienced researcher obtains ideas for investigation by reading articles written by other people. As these articles are read, a new research idea may emerge by identifying a gap in the information presented. Such an information gap might involve a variety of topics. For example, it may be that the study being reported in the article did not focus on children of a particular age group (say, 10 to 12 years of age). If a teacher has a class of children that are 10 to 12 years old, he or she may be very interested in data on that group. Since children of that age were not included in the article, this represents an information gap. If a researcher reading this article thinks the study could be improved (or made more applicable to his or her classroom) by studying such children, this may be the target for his or her next study. Actually, such information gaps are sometimes mentioned in the discussion sections of research articles in statements about implications for future research. Implications for future research are an integral part of many published articles and are nearly standard in theses and dissertations.

In most cases, implications for future research are easily identified in an article, since the author typically uses such phrases as "future research should . . ." or "additional study is needed to . . ." or "further investigation might . . ." In the case of the example above, you might find a phrase in the article such as this: "Future researchers might find it useful to include participants from 10 to 12 years of age because [of the social skills they are developing at this age, or because of their emerging academic skills, or whatever other reason that makes this an important group to study]." If these gaps and speculations are of interest to you, they will most probably become *your idea* on which to work. What about the source? Are such ideas "original"? According to the literal interpretation often used by students, they may not appear to be *original,* but, in fact, a spin-off (or tangent) from someone else's idea is considered in the field to be a *valid contribution* to the field of study, as long as specific content or ideas are not copied verbatim or used without citing sources.

Reading Literature Reviews

Students should identify broad areas of interest and then read articles in those areas as a means of identifying and narrowing their research ideas. One of the most efficient approaches is to read the literature reviews on general areas like reading comprehension, character education, or school organization. **Literature reviews** are very helpful because the author has done a lot of work searching, reading, and assembling articles on a topic area. Some journals primarily or even exclusively publish literature reviews, which are very rich and scientific sources of information on a topic (see, for example, the following journals: *Psychological Bulletin, Review of Educational Research*). Other journals occasionally publish reviews but also publish a mixture of articles that report single investigations as well as literature reviews. In all cases, such articles can generate many research ideas to be used for theses or dissertations in the same way that was described earlier. No matter what the topic, there are always specific ideas that emerge in literature reviews suggesting future research.

Literature reviews are important for students to learn about for other reasons besides identifying research ideas. As you prepare to begin your project, you will also have to review literature in order to justify and build your case for conducting your study. Beyond the research ideas that can be drawn from literature reviews, it is also instructive to examine how authors assemble such written documents. You will likely have to write a literature review as one of the early chapters in your thesis or dissertation—don't panic, the idea of a *chapter* sounds quite daunting, but you will be able to work through it one topic at a time.

As you read published literature reviews, you will see that the authors use a structure for the article that is important as you begin your first chapter. The very beginning of the article introduces a reader to the topic in a general way. In the first paragraph or first few paragraphs, an author will indicate what the topic is (e.g., the effect of instructional time on academic achievement), indicate in a general way why it is important, and likely state explicitly that "the purpose of the present article is to review the literature on academic achievement and to draw implications for classroom management." Often the author will present this first introductory statement very briefly—within one to three paragraphs. Completing an introductory, general orientation for the reader is important because readers are best served when they know in general terms what topics are going to be examined, why the author thinks a topic is important, and what implications or interpretations the author is going to present at the end. This allows a reader to make some determinations about whether he or she is interested in continuing to read and invest time on the topic as presented by the author.

The purpose of the literature review is to examine research and findings from research over a broader scope of topics than is possible in any single empirical study. A literature review on instructional time allocation may cover studies that have investigated the *amount* of instructional time devoted to particular curricular areas such as math, reading, and social studies. The review may also cover investigations of how teachers *manage* classroom time allocation in any single day, a week, or even a longer period of time. Depending on an author's conceptualization and the availability of published investigations, the writer will use headings to separate subtopics within the broader overall topic. Those headings represent subtopics, or miniature reviews on various pieces of the literature (e.g., what are the variations in instructional time allocations in most classrooms today, or what are the apparent effects of time spent on academic achievement). There will also be a heading near the end of the literature review that may be called "Implications for Classroom Management" or something similar, which is where the author draws his or her conclusions from the research reviewed. As was mentioned earlier, authors of literature reviews will also make statements like "future research may find it fruitful to . . ." and these are nice places to find research ideas.

As noted before, when you approach your thesis or dissertation, you will begin by writing a chapter that reviews the literature on your topic. In this chapter, you will outline for your readers (your supervisory committee) what your topic is and why it is important, and you will finish your chapter by very specifically stating your research question. Your literature review will inform your audience and lead logically to a justification for conducting your study.

Justifications for conducting your study often fall into one or more of several categories. Your study may be justified because "this particular research question has not been investigated before," and it is important for the educational well-being of students. Another justification might be "although it has been investigated, previous studies had flaws in their research methods" and it is important for the educational well-being of students. A third type of justification might be "although the topic has been investigated, it has not been studied with these particular children" and it is important for the educational well-being of those students. Notice the recurring tag line about being *important for the education of students*. This reasoning is important in educational research and is one you should use in some form.

Like the literature review structure described above, your general topic will have subtopics. For example, suppose you are interested in academic assessment of children learning English as a second language. Some of your logical subtopics might include headings such as the following: (1) assessment instrument development, (2) academic assessment in various content areas, (3) assessment or testing of second-language learners, (4) test bias (both instrument bias and procedural bias), and perhaps others depending on the nature of your study. It is likely that you will conduct electronic searches on these topics in the library and develop headings within your literature review that are based on them. Your headings are likely to evolve and shift over time as you become better acquainted with the published articles on various topic areas.

Replicating Previous Studies

Many faculty view student theses as learning experiences and therefore are delighted to have students replicate or duplicate previous studies. Replications provide added evidence to the growing data accumulation on any topic, which students should understand is also important. Thus, faculty advisors will often suggest research ideas to students that are replications of earlier studies. Even if students are handed a research topic in this way, it is still important for them to conceptualize the scientific and practical logic leading to the topic and not just conduct a study in a mindless manner because their adviser told them to do so. All researchers create a logic trail that builds a case for undertaking their study, as we noted before. Part of that logic trail will include reviewing existing literature on *your* topic.

Finally, student research ideas can also emerge in effective and creative ways as students work with their faculty mentors on research underway. This type of collaborative effort can be enormously productive for both the student and faculty member.

Student Research Ideas and Educational Objectives

Good guidance for beginning student researchers is often difficult to find. In some cases, students are given a document that outlines format, reference forms, and other information, often covering the technical aspects of manuscript production for their thesis or dissertation. Manuscript production is a type of information that is easy to describe in a student handbook. It is not uncommon for these documents to provide guidance concerning font size and what type of paper is to be used in the thesis or dissertation. However, this is not the most important information that most students need as they begin their research careers. It is more important to examine the educational objectives involved in a thesis and to help students develop their research ideas and research plan. There is some difference of opinion among faculty whether student thesis research is viewed as a learning experience or as an examination of competency. The current authors strongly believe that it is a learning experience.

Objectives for a Thesis

Students may also encounter a belief by some faculty that a student's thesis or dissertation should be related to a theory. Practically speaking, and also considering reasonable educational objectives, sometimes it makes sense to relate a student's research to a theory and sometimes it does not. In many cases, students are studying topics that are related to practice rather than theory. For example, they may simply be interested in which of two teaching methods works more effectively. On the surface, students may conduct such a study as a pilot investigation, just to whet their skills with the research process. After the pilot study, they may get a little more involved with the theory underlying each teaching method. Although the second study might also compare different teaching methods, the research may be following two theories of instruction. It makes some sense to relate a study to theory if the student is interested in becoming a teacher or researcher who will be expected to publish theoretically related scholarship. However, many students are not planning for an academic or scientific career at that point in their lives. At best, they are going to be consumers of research. For them, a requirement that they develop a theory-driven research project contributing to scientific literature probably makes little sense and is a meaningless academic hurdle. They can learn about investigations just fine by studying an applied question like which of two instructional methods is most effective for teaching spelling (Johnson, 2005). This is more consistent with a reasonable educational objective of learning basic elements of research.

STEPS IN THE SCIENTIFIC METHOD

We will examine variations in the research process as appropriate. However, it is important to begin our examination of the research process with the closed-loop notion shown in Figure 2.1 since it demonstrates the steps involved, from investigating an idea to developing the research question. The research question may then

---

FIGURE 2.1   **Closed-Loop Conceptualization of the Research Process**

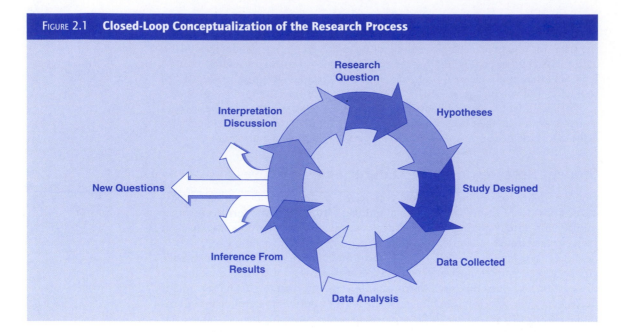

lead to some hypotheses or "guesses" about the topic under study, which in turn may lead to a design or plan for the investigation. Data are then collected and analyzed to answer the question, which hopefully closes the loop. Along the way, additional questions often emerge as topics for future research.

Distilling the Idea or Problem

Ideas for research always go through some evolution. In most cases, they will become more specific and more focused the longer they are discussed. You will likely define more terms and describe your **participants** in more detail. These changes will occur as you read more about the topic and as you discuss it with colleagues. This change process will continue until you have enough of the operational details specified to guide the actual process of conducting a study. Usually, this set of operational definitions can be turned into a research proposal for your thesis supervisory committee.

Once the research idea or topic area is identified, the next process involves distilling the problem. *Problem distillation* refers to the process of refining the problem or idea and making it sufficiently specific so that it can be investigated. Transforming a broad idea into a more specific, researchable question is critical before beginning a study and usually involves seemingly endless definition and description.

Problem identification and problem distillation are a continuous process of defining the details and procedures for a study. For an experienced researcher, these steps are often indistinguishable. They are differentiated here somewhat artificially for instructional convenience to guide beginning investigators through a process with which they are not very familiar. Figure 2.2 outlines the processes of distilling a general idea into a researchable question. As suggested by the funnel-shaped outline, distillation processes involve becoming increasingly specific in the definition of terms and activities, such as how you "test" participants, and when and where you test them, as well as describing the participants, their backgrounds, important characteristics, and abilities.

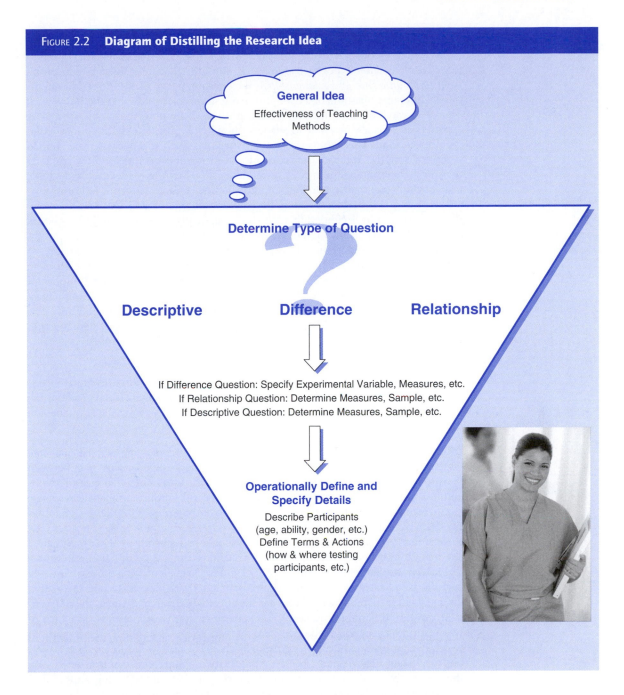

FIGURE 2.2   **Diagram of Distilling the Research Idea**

General Idea
Effectiveness of Teaching Methods

Determine Type of Question

Descriptive   **Difference**   **Relationship**

If Difference Question: Specify Experimental Variable, Measures, etc.
If Relationship Question: Determine Measures, Sample, etc.
If Descriptive Question: Determine Measures, Sample, etc.

Operationally Define and Specify Details
Describe Participants
(age, ability, gender, etc.)
Define Terms & Actions
(how & where testing
participants, etc.)

As a research problem is identified, it is often in the form of a fairly general question. For example, in reading an article you may encounter something that makes you wonder, "What are effective teaching methods?" The investigation that you have been reading studied the effects of students' response time, but something seems troublesome about that. At this point, you may recall from your own experience that response time seems to have different effects depending on how meaningful the material is. This represents a stage of initial problem identification that tends to focus and guide additional reading and search of existing studies. You are beginning to distill the problem into more specific form.

Types of Questions

Early in the process, it is very important to determine the type of research question to be studied. Three types of research question are typically studied in education: *descriptive, difference,* and *relationship.* Is the question being asked a descriptive question, a difference question, or a relationship question? It is critical that you know what type of research question is being studied from the beginning. As you become more experienced, it is also possible to shape a question or push a topic into a particular type of question. This means that a topic area or a particular idea may be studied using a descriptive, difference, or relationship question, depending on how you plan the study. Determining the type of research question being asked seems like a simple task, but it is one that repeatedly baffles beginning research students. However, it is a crucial step. If the researcher does not know what type of question is being asked, there is a very poor likelihood that the study can be planned successfully. We should also note that it is possible for more than one question to be included in a single study, but it is extremely important to be explicit about how many questions and what types that you want answered before moving forward with a plan. Distilling the problem area or idea into research questions is always challenging and particularly important in action research because these studies are typically conducted in field settings where there are lots of distracting influences. Determining the type of question and how many specific research questions, if there is more than one, is a crucial step in action research. The Research in Action box sketches this process for two studies.

Descriptive questions. **Descriptive questions** ask, "What is . . . ?" or "What does . . . ?": What does this culture look like, or what does this group look like? Descriptive studies are basically static and there is no manipulation of a treatment, such as a teaching method. Descriptive studies are frequently undertaken in surveys and qualitative investigations.

Difference questions. **Difference questions** make comparisons and ask the question, "Is there a difference?" Comparisons may be made either between groups (e.g., between two groups of children receiving different math instruction) or between measurements within a single group (i.e., pre- and posttests on the same group). In many cases, these comparisons are made between the average scores of the groups if the data are quantitative. Such a question may be phrased, "Is there a difference in the average scores between these groups (or treatments)?" Difference questions are frequently used in experimental research, although nonexperimental studies may also compare groups or cultures.

Problem distillation for a difference question involves identifying the experimental variable as indicated in Figure 2.2. The experimental variable refers to the factor that an investigator manipulates to see what the effect is. (This is also called the *independent variable* by some researchers.) For example, if you were interested in which of two reading instruction methods was more effective, you might design a study in which two groups were taught, one using Method 1 (CORI in our Research in Action box) and one using Method 2 (DAP). After the two groups had been instructed with their respective methods for a specified time, you would then test both groups to find out which had the better score. All other important characteristics between the groups are supposed to be equal (like age, academic ability, etc.). If all of these other characteristics are equivalent, you are likely to draw a conclusion that the method used to teach the group that performs better is more effective. In this example, the experimental variable is the *teaching method* (which is what you were investigating). Figure 2.3 is a diagram of the study. This study is for a difference question, comparing two teaching methods for reading (i.e., CORI vs. DAP). You would probably be testing the two groups using some reading test as the measure. You would likely conclude that the teaching method for the group that performs better is more effective, assuming other important matters between the two groups are equal. Figure 2.4 illustrates another study from the Research in Action box, this one examining self-esteem differences between Latino and Caucasian students with learning disabilities.

RESEARCH IN ACTION

KEY POINTS IN THE CHAPTER REFLECTED IN THIS BOX:

- The research ideas will be distilled into research questions.
- Determine what types of research questions are being asked.

For more research in action tips visit www.sagepub .com/drewstudy

OBJECTIVES TO LEARN FROM THIS BOX:

- Determine what types of research questions are being asked.
- Visualize the question with a diagram.
- Begin to refine the research questions and think about the design and implementation of the study.

Background: Below you will find two action research scenarios, one related to student engagement in reading and the second involving student self-esteem. For each scenario, the portion presented will relate to selected key points discussed in the chapter. In this case, we are focusing on how the research ideas will be distilled into research questions and determining what types of research questions are being asked. Follow the development of these research questions. You may also wish to develop your own research questions and work through the progression to a study you could undertake.

SCENARIO 1

Emily is interested in the effects of engagement on how young students learn to read. To her, it seems that students who are engaged in academic subjects are more excited about them and learn more quickly. One of the subjects she is teaching her young students is beginning reading.

Initially, Emily views her research question as a difference question that compares students who are engaged with those who are not engaged. From her review of literature, she decides that using conceptual knowledge is a good mechanism to engage the students. This conceptual knowledge includes ideas the students are interested in and concepts or questions they have about the world around them. For Emily, this is what she calls *concept-oriented reading instruction* (CORI). She is initially viewing this as a difference question that compares students taught using a CORI method to students taught using *drill and practice* (DAP). Thus, she has a difference question. A diagram for Emily's action research study is shown in Figure 2.3.

Think about this: How does the action research idea regarding reading engagement become more focused and specific as it evolves into the research question stage? What type of research question or questions is Emily developing? What does the study diagram look like?

SOURCE: This action research scenario is roughly based on Swan, E. A. (2003). *Concept-oriented reading instruction: Engaging classrooms, lifelong learners.* New York: Guilford Press.

SCENARIO 2

Daniel wants to see if his students with learning disabilities have different self-esteem depending on whether they are of Latino or Caucasian descent. He believes that his students have rather low self-esteem, and it seems to him that his Latino students' self-esteem is somehow different from that of his students who are Caucasian.

Daniel has waded through a lot of literature. His reading has indicated that matters are not at all clear regarding what self-esteem *is,* and furthermore, there are different types of self-esteem that have been studied. Daniel sees his study as a general difference question between Latino students and Caucasian students. He initially outlines three difference questions with three types of self-esteem. They are as follows:

1. Do Latino students with disabilities have a different global self-esteem from European American students with disabilities?
2. Do Latino students with disabilities have a different private self-esteem from European American students with disabilities?
3. Do Latino students with disabilities have a different public self-esteem from European American students with disabilities?

A diagram for Daniel's study is found in Figure 2.4. This diagram illustrates a difference question. Daniel has three of these as outlined above.

Think about this: How does the action research idea regarding self-esteem in Latino and Caucasian students become more focused and specific as it evolves into the research question stage? What type of research question or questions is Daniel developing? What does the study diagram look like?

SOURCE: This action research scenario is roughly based on Rubin, D. (2000). *Race and self-esteem: A study of Latino and European-American students with learning disabilities.* Unpublished master's thesis, University of Utah, Salt Lake City.

FIGURE 2.3   Diagram of an Action Research Study Comparing Two Teaching Methods

**Experimental Variable
Teaching Method**

Group 1	**Group 2**
Method 1	Method 2
CORI	DAP

FIGURE 2.4   Diagram of an Action Research Study Comparing Latino and Caucasian Students

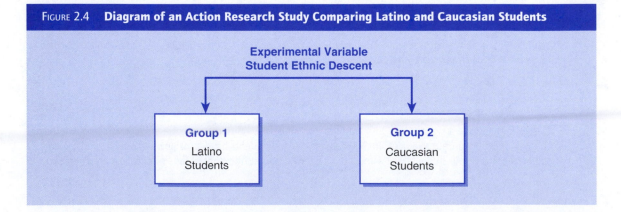

**Experimental Variable
Student Ethnic Descent**

Group 1	**Group 2**
Latino Students	Caucasian Students

Relationship questions. **Relationship questions** explore the degree to which two or more phenomena relate or vary together. For example, a researcher might be curious about the relationship between intelligence and math scores. Structured as a relationship question, the statement would be, "As intelligence varies, what *tends* to happen to math scores?" More specifically, if intelligence increases, do math scores *tend* to increase or decrease, or is there no systematic tendency? The researcher records both intelligence and math scores on a sample of participants to determine the relationship between them. With two scores on each participant (an intelligence score and a math score), the investigator then computes a correlation coefficient, which is a statistical analysis that provides an estimate of the degree to which the variables relate. It is important to emphasize that you are determining to what degree intelligence and math scores relate—what *tends* to happen to math scores when intelligence increases. You are *not* comparing intelligence and math scores.

The Operational Definition

Another important task involved in problem distillation relates to operational definition. In this part of distillation, a researcher needs to carefully consider and identify the following factors important to the study:

- Steps to be taken
- Measurements to be recorded
- All other characteristics, settings, or features

This essential phase of problem distillation must precede implementation of the study. The level of detail needed is often surprising to beginning research students, but the more specific the itemization that can be articulated at this stage, the better the planning will be. This will reduce the likelihood that unanticipated events will surface that can cause data collection errors. The operational definition will always be done in writing so you can refer back to it and so you can share it with your colleagues for their review and suggestions.

Suppose for the moment that a researcher is going to study the effects of material meaningfulness on learning. Distillation of the problem will require operational definition of all terms, procedures, and measures involved in the study. An example of this definition process is found in the term "learning," which is what we are going to measure. While we want to study learning, learning cannot be measured directly since it is something that occurs cognitively and beyond our direct observation. Consequently, the investigator must *infer* that a certain amount of learning has occurred based on how well participants perform. If the students do well on a test, it might be concluded that considerable learning has occurred, whereas if they do poorly, you might infer that they didn't learn much. We are going to infer about how much learning has occurred by *measuring* test scores. This is our criterion measure and is also called a *dependent variable* since the level or score is presumably dependent on our teaching. Several measures may be recorded that reflect different aspects of learning. For example, you might measure the rate of acquisition. If you do, it is crucial to specify *how* this is to be measured. The point to be made here is that learning must be rigorously defined in terms of what is observable so that it can be measured.

Problem distillation for nonexperimental research is also important. Once again, the same principles apply as discussed before. The topic under study must be clearly in mind before the planning can begin. For example, if you were interested in learning about study behaviors of college sophomores, a survey might be an appropriate method for conducting the research. In such a situation, *study behaviors* would be the "problem," and you would then have to specify the precise behaviors to be investigated. If you don't define what study behaviors are (e.g., cramming, reading material over time), it will be difficult to identify them. Without this type of definition, a survey can be like a fishing expedition: you may end up on the lake simply pulling in everything you can get and keeping anything that bites.

Serious definition efforts will be required for the survey on study behaviors, and the definitions must include operational terms that can be translated into a description of procedure. Each aspect of the idea must be operationally defined in the same manner to fully distill the problem. The distillation process (as discussed above) involves several essential activities:

1. Determine what type of question is being studied.

2. If you have a difference question, you need to specify what the experimental variable is, and then determine what you are going to measure, who your participants are, and so on.

3. If you have a relationship question or a descriptive question you will not have an experimental variable so the next step is determining measures, sample, and so on.

4. For all types of questions, you will need a complete operational definition of all necessary terms. All of these processes of defining and describing will literally provide an operational script to follow so you can do the study. This operational script needs to spell out all of the details of what you do, because any steps you leave out become points where you can weaken the study by making an error.

There are some qualitative approaches to research that allow definitions to emerge as the research goes forward. This makes the definition process obviously less structured than the approach we have described above. While such approaches may work well for experienced qualitative investigators, we do not recommend them for beginning researchers. There is simply too much room for error, which could be dangerous, especially if you are conducting a study required for graduation (like a thesis or dissertation). Such an approach will put you at risk for not knowing *when* you're finished, because you cannot check off the steps in the process.

Formulating a Specific Research Question

You are producing a written proposal as you proceed through the narrative outlined above. As you move from a broad idea through the type of question and operational definitions, you have outlined a short thesis proposal. Each department has slightly different formats but generally this process ends with some type of written proposal document that outlines your study for your adviser and supervisory committee. There are two other points that need to be considered in this document: (1) building the case for conducting your study, and (2) including hypotheses and what they look like.

Building Your Case

As indicated earlier, you need to build a case for conducting your study in your thesis proposal. This is also something that practicing researchers do as they outline the logic trail that builds the justification for undertaking a study. This process of building the case for a study occurs as the research idea is described. In a proposal document, the writer states the research idea and begins distillation or narrowing of the topic. As this is done, literature is reviewed that relates to the topic, covering studies that have relevance to the area being investigated. The purpose of this literature review is to outline what research has been published that has a bearing on different aspects of the study being proposed. For example, some studies may have been published that investigated younger children than you plan to in your study,

Simulation

For additional
simulations visit
www.sagepub
.com/drewstudy

Simulation 2.1

Topic: Problem distillation

Background statement: One of the most crucial operations in the early planning stages of research is problem distillation. This is the process of refinement that changes a general, frequently vague idea into a specific, researchable question.

Tasks to be performed:

1. Read the following stimulus material, which represent research ideas stated in somewhat general terms.

2. For each statement, restate the idea in a distilled form that makes it more specific and a researchable question. Your restatement may be rather lengthy. In the statement, specify what is necessary to indicate the experimental variable (keeping in mind the principle of generality). Make the statement as specific as possible in terms of operational definitions.

Stimulus material: The idea to be distilled reads as follows: "Assess the effects of variation in teaching experience on material evaluation."

Write your response, then turn to page 54 for Simulation Feedback 2.1.

---

use different instructional materials, or elicit written as opposed to verbal responses from the participants. These all become relevant to your literature review and are woven into the justification for conducting your study.

There are a number of typical reasons why a study should be done. Although these are stated in general terms, they can be translated into building a case for conducting your own investigation. In the process of reviewing related literature, you will find one or more of the following reasons may support undertaking your study:

After reviewing the literature, it becomes clear that the study has not been done (and it is important to education).

After reviewing the literature, it appears the study has been done, but it was conducted badly and has methodological flaws (and it is important to education).

The study has been done, but not with *these* children, or in *this* setting, with *these* materials . . . (and is important to education).

The current study will resolve or work around the problem and therefore have important value.

In this list of reasons, we included the phrase "and it is important" to state that it is not enough to just point out that the study has not been done. There are a lot of studies that have not been done but they may not be important, either theoretically or for practical purposes. As you build the case for conducting your study, it is necessary to spell out the details of *why* your particular investigation is important. The rationale might be centered on a piece of theory that still needs developing. It may also be that the study has practical value, and the results will help us instruct children more effectively. The practical approach here is what many call *action research,* in that the study is important to conduct because results are likely to change or improve our educational practice. Using reasons such as these, you strengthen the justification for undertaking your study by specifying why it is important.

Hypotheses

Proposals for theses or dissertations often include hypotheses, particularly if the study uses experimental methods. Hypotheses are useful in this context as they help the beginning researcher to be very clear about his or her research questions. When they are written down in your proposal, your hypotheses will make it clear where your thinking is still a bit fuzzy and needs clarification. You will probably need to read completed dissertations to see examples since hypotheses are seldom published in professional journals.

An experimental **hypothesis** represents the ultimate specific, descriptive statement in problem distillation. Such hypotheses are statements made in *very* specific terms, and each one is typically a statistically testable prediction. Hypotheses like these might appear in your proposal:

1. Participants will not differ in mean correct responses as a function of high versus low meaningful material.

2. Participants will not differ in correct responses as a function of 5-second versus 20-second response time.

These hypotheses were adapted from a study that compared student academic performance on two types of material (high meaningfulness vs. low meaningfulness) and under two response-time conditions (5 seconds to respond vs. 20 seconds to respond). As suggested by these examples, a hypothesis is written for each comparison or experimental variable (in this case, there are two experimental variables: material meaningfulness and response time). With the research problem distilled to this level of specific detail, planning the study is simple because the larger composite idea has been broken into its most fundamental components: two experimental comparisons. These hypotheses were used in an experiment that collected *quantitative* data.

Null and directional hypotheses. One factor that may cause confusion involves the use of null and **directional hypotheses.** *The null hypothesis predicts no difference between comparison groups.* The hypotheses above on material meaningfulness and response time are both null hypotheses. **Directional hypotheses,** on the other hand, *do predict a difference and indicate the expected direction of that difference* (i.e., which group will perform at the higher level). If we were to change the first hypothesis above to a directional form, it might say, "Students receiving the high meaningful material will have significantly more correct responses than those receiving the low meaningful material."

This example of a directional hypothesis makes sense because we would expect participants receiving highly meaningful material would do better than those taught with material of low meaningfulness. However, beginning researchers are probably better served if they use **null hypotheses** for several reasons. One reason is that seasoned researchers have usually tried directional hypotheses during their careers and may have obtained results that didn't always support the direction. This makes it more difficult to explain why the results turned out as they did and not as you expected. It is more challenging to change your thinking if your directional guess is wrong than it is to use a null hypothesis to begin with. For a beginning researcher, the null hypothesis is valuable for clarifying the question, even if it serves little other purpose. Under most conditions, a researcher is well-served with a null hypothesis, and nothing is gained by predicting the direction of differences. For statistical testing and problem distillation purposes, the null hypothesis works very well and is probably used more frequently by practicing researchers than the directional hypothesis.

Design and Implementation of the Study Plan

The most important decisions affecting the soundness of an experiment are made *before initial data collection.* The pre-study planning that determined how the data was to be gathered directly influences the strength of any piece of data. The more clearly the problem is articulated (distilled or defined), the easier the data-related planning will be accomplished. A basic concept that influences data quality is that of *control.* Control has an enormous impact on what can be said about the meaning of data. In an experiment, for example, it is desirable to be able to say that the data reflect the experimental variable. The researcher will be able to do this *only if there is confidence that the data do reflect the experimental variable, which is the topic of interest,* and *not some other influence that should have been eliminated.* This is generally known as controlled observation in experimental design. You can only infer that a change in your experimental variable influenced change in the criterion measure if all other possibilities can be discounted as causes of the change. This principle is a central aspect of experimental research design and an important consideration in the quality or accuracy of the data.

A second consideration involved in data planning relates to the *generalizability* of results. To what degree do the results generalize or have meaning beyond the specific participants and exact setting used in the research? Essentially, the topic being addressed here involves the reliability of data obtained. How reliably can one obtain the same or similar results in circumstances beyond those where the data are collected?

Reliability of Data

Data reliability is an important factor in research and basically relates to how dependable the information is that the investigator collects. Data reliability surfaces in all research methods even though different terminology is used to refer to it. Quantitative researchers may talk about the "consistency" of a participant's scores from one test to another (Fraenkel & Wallen, 2006). Qualitative researchers use terms such as "trustworthy" or "authoritative" to describe data reliability (Creswell, 2005; Denzin & Lincoln, 2005). In all methodologies, however, the reliability of data is important. Several factors influence the reliability of data.

Participants in the study. Perhaps the most obvious influence involves the participants in the study. If it is desirable that results be applicable to a given group of individuals, the participants in the investigation should look like that group in terms of age, schooling, and other characteristics. Usually this larger group is defined as the population to which generalization is desired. The researcher wants to achieve generalizability, that is, to be able to observe the same or similar performance in the general population that was evident in the sample of participants. To obtain this data reliability between participants and population, the experimenter must be able to assume that the participants are representative of the larger population.

Stability of measures. A second factor to be considered in data reliability involves the *stability of measures* being used in the research. Stability is also related to generalizability, although most discussions of generalizability focus on participant sample considerations. In the context of data reliability, a primary concern is that the measure is sufficiently stable so that a *participant having the same status* (e.g., physical, motivational, or anxiety level) and *performing at the same level as an individual* *in the broader population, will obtain the same or a similar score on the measure* (e.g., providing the same or similar answers on a survey questionnaire). Thus, for the results of an investigation to be generalizable, the measures recorded must be stable enough that a given score or answer is likely to recur under the same conditions. If a measure is unstable, the data may indicate two different scores for the same participant status. Although behavioral science is plagued by measurement problems, it is usually possible to select or contrive measures that are adequately stable. Of course, this does not mean that there is no variation in the behavior. Instead the concern is that the measure is sensitive to variations in performance and not capriciously variable when performance is not changing (i.e., the variability in the measure is coincidental to performance variation).

Forms of instrumentation. The instrument used for collecting data has a lot to do with the reliability of the data. Instrumentation takes many different forms ranging from a paper-and-pencil questionnaire to a test presented on the computer that each participant completes at the keyboard. Instrumentation also includes human observation in situations where that is involved in the data collection protocol. In each case, steps can and should be taken to make the collection of data as reliable as possible. We will now discuss selected approaches.

If a survey is being used for data collection, then the questionnaire is the instrument being used for data collection. Questionnaires have a long history of use as data collection instruments, and considerable information is available regarding how to enhance data reliability (Hutchinson, 2004; Nardi, 2006). For example, it is important for survey questions to be uncomplicated, to ask for only one piece of information from the respondent, and to avoid wording that will bias respondents' answers. It is also vital that the questionnaire be as brief as possible and have a response format that is easy and convenient for the respondent to complete. In some cases, the survey will be administered in paper-and-pencil form, whereas in others the respondents will complete the questionnaire on a computer, on the Web, or some other medium (Leece et al., 2004; Mertens, 2005). Data reliability using these varied formats and presentations for questionnaires involves examining the interaction between the respondent and each question. Attempts are then made to improve the likelihood that a respondent will give the same answer to the same question when it is presented repeatedly.

Instruments may also be in the form of a test, which in many ways is like a questionnaire. A test might be in paper-and-pencil format, or it might collect data from the respondents through their interaction with a computer. Tests might ask the respondents for information they have learned such as academic content or information about traffic laws for a driver's test. In all cases, reliability of the data will be improved if the question is unambiguous, simple, and has a distinctly correct or incorrect answer. Each of these features will contribute to a respondent giving the same answer to the same question on multiple occasions, which enhances data reliability.

Another instrument example involves the use of human observers where the observers become the instrument for data collection. Reliability of data collection in circumstances where observers are collecting data can be enhanced in a number of ways. For example, the behaviors that an observer is watching for (and then recording on a laptop or data sheet) need to be clearly defined so they are easily seen, easily distinguished from other behaviors, and conveniently recorded. Reliability is improved by making it easy for the observer. If it is easy for the observer to see the target behavior and to record that as a piece of data, reliability is going to be improved and the observer is more likely to record the occurrence of a behavioral event in the same way, repeatedly, when he or she sees it. In addition to making behavior definitions very clear, researchers often provide considerable observer training to improve data collection.

In some cases, mechanical instrumentation may be used to achieve improved measurement precision and data reliability. For example, a stopwatch may be useful if one is measuring time, and not highly vulnerable to error, especially when the observer has easily identifiable cues for operation of the stopwatch. However, reduced measurement reliability may result if it is not obvious when to begin and terminate instrument operation, or if operation of the stopwatch is cumbersome.

Some electronic devices are available that may be used to permanently record actual participant responses if the research procedures permit (e.g., audio or video recordings). Such approaches then allow the recorded responses to be removed to another site and analyzed later in a careful manner, without the pressure of ongoing procedures. Types of recording instruments vary and techniques are continually being improved. Audio devices may serve well to record verbal responses, and video equipment may similarly be appropriate for image records of ongoing behavior sequences. In addition, a variety of physiological instruments, such as the electroencephalogram, polygraph, and others, may be used if that type of data is desired. The advantages of such devices are clear. Data may be permanently recorded, and analysis or categorization may be accomplished later in a relaxed and thorough fashion. Such recording of responses permits the review of performance if any uncertainty exists concerning the nature of the response. This allows multiple checks to be made on the categorization of responses, which in turn improves potential data stability.

The use of permanent recording devices seems to be desirable insurance for research in situations where such procedures are possible. We have used permanent mechanical and electronic recorders as well as human observers many times, and we offer a note of caution: Recording devices are not a panacea. Their utility is only as good as the soundness of the equipment. More than one experimenter has been dismayed when the recordings were prepared for viewing or listening and there was no record because of undetected technical failure. This unfortunate situation, of course, means lost participants, lost data, lost time, and occasionally a completely aborted study. It is always prudent to double-check equipment before it is used in a study. It is also important to be aware of the possible impact on participants' behavior when a recording device is brought into the environment. Participants may respond differently when such equipment is used since it is not part of their routine. They may become nervous, or act in a manner they believe is socially appropriate or expected. The researcher must consider these issues since the recorder itself may alter the data.

Data instability. Several examples have been given of measures or procedures that may be used to improve data stability. A variety of measurement situations also may contribute to a higher risk of instability. The probability of greater measure instability is always increased when heavy reliance is placed on observer judgment regarding a participant's response. This may occur under several conditions. The greatest variation is generated when an observer is requested to record behaviors that are not well defined or easily observable. Recording data reliably becomes more difficult when fewer distinct cues are available. Likewise, when rating scales are used to assess concepts that are poorly defined or defined in vague terms (e.g., attitudes, self-concept, anxiety), an observer is presented with a more difficult task, and often greater data instability results. Such situations may be encountered in interviews or mail-out or electronic questionnaires where it is unclear what the participant's response should be or how it should be recorded.

Four basic approaches can help minimize such difficulties. First, the behavior or performance to be measured must be as clearly defined as possible. Second, the more distinct the cues are for an observer, the greater the chance that accurate response records will result. Third, multiple observers can be trained to a point where reliability will be high among a group of judges as a whole. Using this latter technique, the multiple observers serve as checks on each other, which places less reliance on a single individual's judgment. Finally, when rating scales are used (e.g., the Likert 1 to 5 scale), each point on the scale can be as tightly anchored as possible.

A tightly anchored scale might involve very specific descriptors (e.g., 1 = 0 days per week, 5 = 7 days per week). Such arrangements can greatly increase data stability simply because a respondent's interpretation of vague descriptors (like "seldom," "often") is less involved.

Planning aspects of data collection are an extremely important operational element of the research process. It is easy to see how investigations may be seriously jeopardized by errors in data collection. The data are the central representation of participants' behavior under the research conditions. Consequently, the soundness of the data must be insured to every extent possible.

Data Collection

The **data collection** phase refers to the actual execution of the investigation. This may include the process of administering a questionnaire, conducting an interview, or presenting a math test to a participant and recording responses. *This is the point at which the study is implemented.* Activities involved in implementation are most frequently described in the "procedures" section of a research article.

The most critical elements of data collection are performed before the actual beginning of participant testing—the detailed planning of each step. Planning has been stressed throughout this discussion and is being raised again to emphasize its importance. At least two types of factors warrant attention before data collection begins. First, there are many operational details that should be planned ahead of time and that are so central to research, they are almost routine. These are present in nearly all data collection procedures. The second type of factor is much less predictable—anticipating the unexpected. Planning for an unexpected event is precautionary in its attempt to avoid incidents that are sporadic but may jeopardize the soundness of data collection procedures. In planning for both types of factors, the best preparation is research experience. The most effective method of learning about such factors is to work with a seasoned researcher over a period of time on different investigations and to note carefully the details that receive attention. (This is the most effective manner in which to learn research.) In lieu of such an internship, some areas will be suggested here that may warrant preliminary planning.

Important Considerations When Collecting Data

Regarding the nearly standard concerns, probably the most effective planning device is to *mentally or even actively rehearse* the entire procedure in detail. A series of questions is usually helpful:

1. *Where are you going to observe or administer the task to participants?* This is a question that has more tentacles than are apparent at first. Attention to location is certainly important and a great deal depends on the requirements of the method being used. If a study is being conducted in a school, do you need a separate room or will you be observing more natural settings such as classrooms? If you need a separate room, will there be one available in that school, or will you have to make other arrangements? Suppose you have a room. How close is it to the source of participants? This has certain ramifications for other questions involving transporting participants to the test area.

   There are also considerations regarding the physical details of the site. What are the characteristics of the research site that would be desirable for your purposes? If you are conducting naturalistic observation, are you going to be in the room with the participants or will you be hidden—perhaps observing through a one-way mirror? If you need a separate research space, should it be a relatively distraction-free room so the participants can focus on their task? What about air circulation? Might that be important? Final decisions on many of these details will depend on visiting the site. However, they should also receive advance attention so you can keep in mind what will or will not be appropriate. Frequently advance planning involves the assessment of general tolerance levels that are acceptable regarding the characteristics of the site (e.g., just how stimulus-free *must* it be?). Air circulation may not generally be a problem, but when the principal shows you the room (which turns out to be an unused walk-in food locker), it may suddenly present a difficulty.

2. *Where are the participants, and how do you gain access to them?* If you are observing in a classroom, how do you gain entrance—and when? If the study requires working with children in a separate space, do you contact the teacher(s) with a prearranged list, or do they merely send children as they are free? This latter situation is desired by some teachers but could present certain sampling problems unless precautions are taken (see Chapter 4). The distance from the source of the participants to the test site is usually not a big problem. One must be concerned, however, about the mental set that participants receive during the walk to the research room. If an investigator is walking down the hallway with a child, what is said in conversation on the way can influence the child's view of the study, which may impact their responses and alter your data.

3. *If you're in a separate room, what furniture is necessary in that space, and how should it be arranged?* For example, do you want a table between you and the participant for research materials?

4. *Are your data collection sheets in proper order for the participant's appearance?* This applies in both separate research spaces as well as observations in natural settings. It is not very natural or professional for you to be fussing around with your data sheets when participants enter the classroom, nor do you want your personal organization to be part of the experience when a participant comes into the research space. Both of these activities may influence the participants' behavior. For example, do the data sheets contain space for complete and convenient recording of descriptive information concerning the participant (e.g., name or code, age, gender, and data)? Are the data sheets designed for complete and convenient recording of data? Often data recording has to be performed with one hand while the other hand manipulates research materials such as cards with words or pictures on them. Can you do this efficiently and smoothly? While fumbling around with data sheets might be embarrassing, more importantly it may contribute to data errors or influence the participant's behavior.

5. *Are your other research materials in order?* In a way, this is part of item 4 above, but worth additional emphasis. Is instrumentation, such as a stopwatch or video recorder, in place and in good working order? How should this be accomplished to save time and not make the participants nervous?

6. *What are your interactions going to be with participants?* If you're conducting an experiment, what instructions are you going to give them? Give detailed consideration to the nature of interactions between you and your participants. What you say and do will influence the environment. If you're conducting an experiment or administering a test, it is a sound procedure to have instructions typed out and either memorized or read verbatim. In a slightly different context, never send a questionnaire out without a carefully constructed cover letter. The wording is crucial to the response.

7. *What is the time interval for participants to respond?* Is it 5 seconds in an experiment or 3 weeks for a mailed questionnaire? (Do not forget to allow time for the mail delivery if you are using the mail.) What do you say or do if this interval is exceeded?

8. *Say you're working one-on-one with participants. What is your response to the participant if an error is committed?* Likewise, what is to be said if a correct response

is made? Not only will your response influence any future behaviors of the participant, but you would also be surprised at how some of your verbal interchanges might become public.

9. *How do you exit or dismiss the participant when the research is completed?* This is obviously crucial when a researcher is in direct contact with the participant(s). What should you say?

These questions are merely examples. They are relevant in a high proportion of research procedures but may not include everything that should be considered in a given investigation.

An Essential Rule for Data Collection

Beyond the mental rehearsal, there is an additional step that will provide further safeguards against errors. In fact, this step is so essential that it should be a standard rule. In preparation for data collection and where possible, *the researcher should actually practice the entire procedure from start to finish.* Pretest the questionnaire on a few individuals who are similar to the participants to be used. Practice the experimental procedures or interview in a similar fashion. Practice the observation process in realistic settings, including coding the data.

This rehearsal will serve two important purposes. First, it will usually highlight procedural elements that did not receive attention previously. Such decisions and preparations can then be accomplished before the study is to begin, which minimizes the risk of losing participants because of procedural error. Second, it will give the researcher practice and self-confidence and polish the performance of data collection procedures. This is essential, and it is surprising how much researcher improvement will be evident in the first few practice trials.

Anticipating Contingencies in the Study

It is not possible to anticipate every contingency by following a checklist of standard procedures. Unexpected situations usually arise when the procedural rules are stretched by deviant participant performance or behavior. Tales of antics by participants are exchanged in research labs much in the same way that fish stories are circulated among anglers. In many cases, a researcher's judgment is tested to a considerable extent to preserve order in the investigation setting. It is also not uncommon to lose participants because of deviant behavior, responses, or performance. This possibility can be avoided to a degree by pre-investigation planning. Such planning usually involves attempts to anticipate possible behavioral extremes before the fact. In most cases, this part of the planning involves a series of "what if" questions. Some possible decision questions are suggested here.

1. What if a participant indicates openly (or subtly) that participation in the study is no longer a desirable activity? This is a possibility and presents a definite decision point for the researcher.

2. What if a participant asks to have the instructions repeated? What if a youngster being observed decides to engage the observer in a conversation? Are these permissible or will they contaminate the data?

3. What if a participant in an experiment makes an error and then *immediately* corrects it ("Oh no, the answer is . . .") in a fashion that gives the impression that the correct answer *may* have been known in the beginning? Will you count it?

4. How many consecutive incorrect responses are permissible before a participant is deleted from the study, and is deletion the appropriate action? It is important to determine this ahead of time because some participants with

learning problems may persevere far beyond what is imaginable before they are deleted from the study. Make your rule ahead of time.

5. You're working alone with a child in a separate research space. What should you do if someone knocks on the door or enters the room without knocking while the study is in session?

6. Should records be kept out of the participants' view? How should this be accomplished? In fact, should the timing (if this is a part of the procedures) and data recording be performed surreptitiously?

7. What is to be the response if a participant gets up and walks around the table to see the materials?

8. What should you do if a fire drill is staged?

It is impossible to anticipate all the contingencies that will occur during data collection. These represent only a few drawn from the authors' experiences. It is helpful to consider these as well as others you might think of. Data collection is both exhilarating and nerve-racking. It may also be repetitive and boring in certain cases. There must, however, be something addictive about data collection since researchers keep returning to it again and again. Table 2.1 presents a data collection

TABLE 2.1   **Data Collection Checklist**

Pre-Implementation Planning

Clear statement of research question
Clear definition of experimental variable if difference question
Clear definition of criterion measure
Clear definition of study participants

Preparation of Measures for Data Collection

Determination of measure stability and reliability
Development of instruments to collect data
Plan and practice implementing data collection (including unexpected events)

On-Site Data Collection Preparation

Determination of exactly where data are to be collected
Determination of physical characteristics of data collection site
Determination of furniture or other space considerations in data collection site
Determination of how participants will be located and how you gain access
Preparation and pretesting of data collection sheets or other data collection mechanism
Preparation and pretesting of other research materials

Practice Procedures and Instructions to Participants

Practice verbal and physical interaction steps.
Determine and practice participant response-time intervals.
Determine and practice your responses to participant errors and correct responses.
Determine responses to potential unusual responses or behavior by participants.
Determine interaction protocols for moving participants to and from site.
Rehearse potential "what if" situations (e.g., refusal to participate, fire drills, others).

Practice Complete Protocol From Start to Finish, Multiple Times

summary, although you will need to add items to this checklist that are unique to your data collection circumstances.

Data Analysis

Once the data are collected, the next step is analysis. This step will be treated in considerable detail later in the text and will only be discussed briefly here in the context of the scientific method. **Data analysis** probably carries more negative connotations than any other single part of the research process. Actually, most quantitative analyses are merely combinations of elementary arithmetic operations. In most cases, if one is reasonably prepared with the skills of addition, subtraction, multiplication, and division, the essential components are present. Actual performance of these operations may be guided by any one of several step-by-step quantitative analysis handbooks on the market. Such handbooks are based on a viewpoint that there is little value in memorizing formulas—either by a student or a practicing researcher. Consequently, the discussion of analysis procedures in later chapters will include several references to computational handbooks. Selection of the *appropriate* analysis is often more challenging than performing the computation, and vastly more important.

Qualitative data are usually recorded in the form of words rather than numbers. Often the data reflect an attempt to capture the perceptions of the participants from the inside. Most analysis of qualitative data is also undertaken with words as the researcher attempts to isolate themes, identify trends, interpret, explain, and even undertake conceptual comparisons. Some consider qualitative data to be less about behavior and more about actions—and these actions carry implications about intentions, meanings, and consequences (Dalute & Lightfoot, 2004; Denzin & Lincoln, 2005; Neuman, 2006). While some beginning students may find comfort in the absence of mathematics, they should understand from the outset that qualitative analysis is not any easier and it is a very time-consuming and intense process.

Interpretation From Results

The data or results are not an end but merely a means by which educational, behavioral, and social descriptions may be made. Such a statement may appear somewhat obvious, but beginning researchers often have the mistaken impression that once the data are analyzed, the study is completed. Quite the contrary. One of the most exciting processes has just begun—that of data interpretation and inference. *Inference* is the interpretive process a researcher uses to construct a descriptive statement from the data; it is the explanation and interpretation of the results. Principally based on logical conclusions from the data (related back to the research question that prompted the study), the outcome of the inference may be found primarily in discussion sections of research articles.

Why It Happened and What It Means

When making an inference, it is not appropriate to use a "shotgun" search for explanations. During this part of the research process, data are examined in a way that attempts to close the information loop. At the beginning of the study, there was a research question. This question was distilled, details were defined, some hypotheses were generated, and an investigation was designed and executed to gather data relevant to that question. The process of interpretation and inference translates the results back into behavioral descriptions of what happened in order to propose an answer to the original research question. Figure 2.1 illustrated the closed-loop conceptualization of the research process and the role of inference in that model. The researcher builds a logic trail from the results to *infer* (1) why the results occurred as they did, (2) what the results might mean for any theory or literature that was involved in conceptualizing the study, (3) what the results might mean for practice or practical applications, and (4) what the next study or studies might be that are based on these findings.

One important point needs to be considered regarding the inferences drawn from data. For some beginners, there is a tendency to consider the results as "proving" that a particular interpretation is the case. For example, a beginning researcher might infer that his or her "results prove that long practice sessions are more effective for learning vocabulary than shorter, spaced practice sessions" (in fact evidence, suggests that this is not the case). There is probably no single term that makes an experienced researcher shudder as much as "prove." Quantitative science has its foundation based on chance or probability theory, and qualitative research emphasizes the uniqueness of interactions and events. A consequence of this is that results *tend* to confirm or support a descriptive statement, or, alternatively, the results *tend* to be in disagreement with or negate a statement.

In quantitative research, results of statistical analyses are stated in terms of probability. The statistical statement of $P < .05$, often seen in published research articles, means that "the results obtained may be expected to occur due to chance alone only 5 times out of 100." The reverse or flip side of this same statement addresses the presumed effects of the treatment. The results obtained may be expected because of influences other than chance (inferring the potency of your treatment) 95 times out of 100. Inferences in discussion sections of research articles are usually written in such terms as, "These results would seem to suggest . . ." rather than saying that the results "prove" certain statements. Quantitative researchers write this way because they are working from probability bases, not because they are that unsure of their work. Qualitative researchers are very clear about the fact that they are working with interpretations, explanations, and inferences from the observations they make. They, too, are working with some level of probability of correctness or some level of confidence. However, since qualitative investigators are not working with numbers, they do not assume to know what that probability is. They rely on the concept of trustworthiness to protect the research's rigor (see, for example, Cassell & Symon, 2004; Neuman, 2006).

Meaningful Interpretation

In the process of designing an investigation and interpreting the results, researchers (particularly experimental researchers) attempt to eliminate alternative explanations. If this is not accomplished and there are multiple possible explanations for a given result, the investigation has not been efficiently designed and a meaningful interpretation cannot be expected. Such an essential relationship between study design and study outcome also points up something that will be reflected throughout this text. Although the total research process is composed of several component functions, a crucial relationship ties each component together into an integrated operation. A serious weakness in any part of the research method threatens the worth of the total effort. Consequently, each segment must be addressed with equal seriousness and with consideration for its bearing on every other segment.

Chapter Summary

✦ Research ideas emerge from many different sources including journal articles, literature reviews, previous studies, and combinations of these plus personal experiences.

✦ Justifications for conducting studies may include the fact that a topic has not been investigated before, previous studies contained flaws in their methods, and studies have not been conducted with a particular group of participants, and they always include the reasons why the topic is important for the educational well-being of students.

✦ Distilling a research idea involves refining the topic into an increasingly specific and focused statement until it can be summarized into an explicit research question or set of research questions.

✦ Descriptive research questions ask "what is" and describe a group of participants, a setting, or a procedure. Difference questions make comparisons between groups, between times (e.g., before and after a treatment), or between groups that have received different treatments. Relationship questions explore the degree to which two or more phenomena relate or vary together in a group, such as measured intelligence and reading scores.

✦ Operational definitions during idea distillation include specifically defining the steps to be taken in implementing the study; describing what measurements are to be taken; and writing down the details of participant characteristics, the settings where data are to be collected, and all other factors important to actually conducting the study.

✦ Null hypotheses predict no differences (for difference questions) or no relationship (for relationship questions), while directional hypotheses predict which group will perform better or that there will be a relationship between measures.

✦ The design or plan for a study will include very specific details about what type of question is being asked, what the experimental variable is for a difference question, and what the criterion measure will be in specific terms. The design will also outline steps to be taken to maximize data reliability, exactly who the participants are, and details of an operational script for the researcher to follow in conducting the study.

✦ Data collection will involve administering the questionnaire if one is being used, administering a test, and observing or conducting an interview with the participants. Specific pre-implementation planning should be written down completely and pilot or practice sessions should be conducted with individuals that are similar to the intended participants.

✦ The data analysis to be used will depend on the type of question being studied, the type of data collected, and the number of participants in the study. Selecting a data analysis at this point in the study will be aimed at noting that there are different analyses for each type of question and that selection is based on these factors. Interpreting results will involve constructing a descriptive statement of what happened and what it may mean in light of the literature reviewed and its implications for teaching or other educational practice.

Key Terms

Data analysis. Refers to a step in the research process where the investigator summarizes data collected and prepares it in a format to determine what occurred. For quantitative studies, data analysis will mean summarizing the numbers, whereas for qualitative studies, it will involve reviewing the narrative data to determine trends.

Data collection. The data collection phase of research refers to the actual execution of the investigation and involves recording data in some form. This may include the process of administering a questionnaire, conducting an interview, or presenting a math test or other type of test to a participant and recording responses.

Data reliability. Refers to how dependable the information is that the investigator collects. When a researcher repeatedly observes a behavior, how consistent is his or her recording of what occurred? The level of consistency will impact the reliability of the data.

Descriptive question. Descriptive questions ask "What is . . . ?" or "What does . . . ?": For example, what does this culture look like, what does this group look like, or at what level does a particular group of participants perform?

Difference question. Difference questions make comparisons and ask the question, "Is there a difference?" Comparisons may be made either between groups (e.g., between two groups of children receiving different math instruction) or between measurements within a single group (i.e., pre- and posttest performance by the same group).

Directional hypothesis. The directional hypothesis predicts a difference and the direction of that difference; for example, "Participants receiving treatment Method A will make significantly more correct responses than those receiving treatment Method B."

Hypothesis. A statement used in research to help clarify the research question. It is presented as a declarative statement of prediction. Two basic formats are used, the *null hypothesis* and the *directional hypothesis.*

Literature reviews. Literature reviews are articles or chapters in which an author has read and interpreted the published research studies on a given topic such as reading comprehension.

Null hypothesis. The null hypothesis predicts no difference; for example, "Participants will not differ in mean correct responses as a function of treatment method."

Participants. A term that refers to the individuals on whom the data are collected in a study.

Relationship question. Relationship questions explore the degree to which two or more phenomena relate or vary together such as intelligence level and reading skills.

Research idea. Topics identified by researchers that represent interesting areas for investigation. Research ideas often involve rather general topics, which are then refined into a more detailed, focused, and specific research question.

Student Study Site

The companion Web site for *Designing and Conducting Research in Education* www.sagepub.com/drewstudy

Supplement your review of this chapter by going to the companion Web site to take one of the practice quizzes, use the flashcards to study key terms, and check out the many other study aids you'll find there. You'll even find some research articles from the Sage Full-Text Collection and a step-by-step guide that will show you how to read an educational research article.

Simulation Feedback

For additional
simulations visit
www.sagepub
.com/drewstudy

Simulation Feedback 2.1

Although a variety of approaches may be taken with any given problem distillation, the most obvious in relation to the instructions would appear to be as follows:

1. The beginning point is the idea statement, "Assess the effects of variation in teaching experience on material evaluation."

2. The experimental variable is *teaching experience.* This means that differing amounts of teaching experience will be involved in the subject characteristics. Probably one would want two or three levels of teaching experience represented, such as beginning teachers in their first year of teaching, teachers in their third year of experience, and teachers in their fifth year. Pressing this explanation a bit further, one may wish to constitute three groups of teachers, each with a different amount of experience. The diagram below presents a pictorial illustration of this experimental variable.

3. From the diagram below, it is evident that the three groups will be compared with regard to some variable. This leads to the principle of operational definition. Several parts of the idea require definition; one part is material evaluation, which is what will be measured. The subjects will be evaluating some material, and the researcher will be determining if the different amounts of experience (the experimental variable) influence the way in which the material is evaluated. In other words, do teachers who are in their first year of teaching, as a group, evaluate material differently from those in their third year of teaching or those in their fifth year? It will be necessary to define in operational terms what the material and the evaluation are to be. Exactly how will the researcher record or assess the teachers' evaluation of the material? You can see that this moves into the realm of what is to be measured. Are you going to have the teachers rate the material on some scale such as the following?

Excellent		Average		Poor
1	2	3	4	5

Begin thinking in operational terms as you distill the problem.

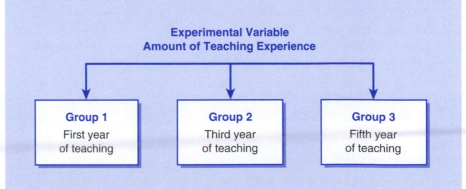

Experimental Variable
Amount of Teaching Experience

Group 1	**Group 2**	**Group 3**
First year of teaching	Third year of teaching	Fifth year of teaching

3

ETHICAL ISSUES IN CONDUCTING RESEARCH

CHAPTER OBJECTIVES

After reading Chapter 3, you should be able to do the following:

+ Describe the three elements of informed consent for ensuring the protection of human subjects.

+ Discuss who must consent to participation in a research study and how it should be given.

+ Describe "harm" as a potential hazard to participants, and identify strategies for determining its level of acceptability within a research study.

+ Identify the issues in research that directly affect the "privacy" of an individual.

+ Define "deception" and the rationale for why it may be used in a research study.

+ Distinguish between ethical considerations in quantitative and qualitative research.

+ Understand the role of institutional review boards in monitoring ethics in research.

+ Understand the importance of maintaining integrity in the execution of a research study and the dissemination of results.

Ethics has become a cornerstone for conducting effective and meaningful research. As such, the ethical behavior of individual researchers is under unprecedented scrutiny (Best & Kahn, 2006; Field & Behrman, 2004; Trimble & Fisher, 2006). In today's society, any concerns regarding ethical practices will negatively influence attitudes about science, and the abuses committed by a few are often the ones that receive widespread publicity (Mauthner, Birch, Jessop, & Miller, 2003).

This chapter focuses primarily on issues, activities, and situations that are far from black and white in terms of ethics. A balanced presentation remains our goal. There are no simple answers or solutions. Although guidelines are suggested, each researcher must be responsible for ethical issues within an investigation. This chapter will not provide a "complete ethical checklist" that covers all questions, settings, or concerns. Such a task would be impossible and not terribly helpful in considering the variety of research situations that may be encountered. Although some guidelines are relatively firm, the best insurance against unethical research practices is the knowledgeable individual scientist who can intelligently consider the circumstances being faced.

Researchers with their inquiring minds are compelled to press on in the development and dissemination of new knowledge. The question becomes not only a matter of whether it is ethical to conduct research, but also whether it is *unethical not to* engage in inquiry. Are researchers guilty of unethical conduct if they do not engage in systematic inquiry conducted with the safety of participants in mind, and with fully informed consent? While ethical considerations may initially be viewed as roadblocks to beginning a study, they are clearly integral to the process. Attention to the ethics of an investigation requires extra thought and effort, but the payoff for a study that is both methodologically intact and ethically sound is extremely exhilarating.

ENSURING THE PROTECTION OF HUMAN PARTICIPANTS

Every researcher has a responsibility to protect the participants in an investigation. The *Ethical Principles of Psychologists and Code of Conduct* of the American

Psychological Association (APA) notes that psychologists must be concerned with "the welfare and protection of the individuals and groups with whom psychologists work and the education of members, students, and the public regarding ethical standards of the discipline" (American Psychological Association, 2002, p. 3). Similarly, the *Ethical Standards of the American Educational Research Association* (AERA) states, "It is of paramount importance that educational researchers respect the rights, privacy, dignity, and sensitivities of their research populations and also the integrity of the institutions within which the research occurs. Educational researchers should be especially careful in working with children and other vulnerable populations" (American Educational Research Association, 2002, p. 3). Although the purview of APA and AERA is psychology and education, respectively, social science and educational research involve many other fields of study where professionals serve in multiple roles (e.g., researchers as well as laboratory supervisors, administrators, teachers, or mentors) (Behnke, 2004; Diekema, 2005; Haverkamp, 2005).

Whether a researcher is a psychologist, educator, or anthropologist, the primary responsibilities to participants are clear: obtain consent, protect from harm, and ensure privacy. However, there is one area of responsibility that is often less clear for both the researcher and the participants: intentional deception. These areas are covered in more detail below.

Consent

Consent involves the procedure by which an individual may choose whether or not to participate in a study. The researcher's task is to ensure that participants have a complete understanding of the purpose and methods to be used in the study, the risks involved, and the demands placed upon them as a participant (Best & Kahn, 2006; Jones & Kottler, 2006). The participant must also understand that he or she has the right to withdraw from the study at any time.

The two forms of consent are direct and substitute. *Direct consent* is the most preferred because agreement is obtained directly from the person to be involved in the study. *Substitute consent*, or third-party consent, is given by someone other than the person to be involved in the study. Substitute consent may be obtained when it is determined that the person does not have the capacity to make the decision or is dependent on others for his or her welfare, such as children under the age of 18 or people with cognitive or emotional disabilities (Nagy, 2005a; Roberts, Geppert, Coverdale, Louie, & Edenharder, 2005). Both direct and substitute consent must meet the requirements for **informed consent.**

From a legal standpoint, *informed consent* involves three elements: **capacity, information,** and **voluntariness.** All three elements must be present for consent to be effective (Drew & Hardman, 2007). It is also important to understand that consent is seldom (if ever) permanent and may be withdrawn at any time. (The act of withdrawing consent must also include the elements of capacity, information, and voluntariness.)

Capacity

Capacity is a person's ability to acquire and retain knowledge. The ability to evaluate the information received and make a choice based on this evaluation is fundamental to the element of capacity. Based on the person's ability to acquire, retain, and evaluate information, he or she is deemed *competent* or *incompetent*. Competence is partially determined by legal qualification and ability. Legal qualification is most often viewed in terms of age; individuals under the age of majority (generally 18 years) are considered to be legally unable to make certain decisions. Children's rights are then legally protected by obtaining permission from parents or legal guardians. Children's rights are ethically protected when the person giving the consent has a primary interest in the child's welfare (Field & Behrman, 2004).

The second factor in determining competence is the individual's ability to give consent. (Does the individual understand the nature and consequences of giving consent?) This factor is again relevant to the involvement of children in research studies but is also applicable to others as well (e.g., persons with cognitive or emotional disabilities, or those who are incarcerated) (Hardman et al., 2006). First, from a legal standpoint, a person is considered competent unless they have been adjudicated through the court system as being incompetent. It cannot be assumed that because individuals of adult age may have a cognitive or emotional disability they are not competent to make decisions regarding their individual welfare. Second, even if the individual is deemed legally competent, it does not relieve the researcher of the responsibility to ensure that the participant understands the information provided and can exercise the free power of choice. Clearly the capacity element is not simple. It often becomes even more complex in the context of implementation, which is discussed in later sections of this chapter.

Information

Determination of whether information has been communicated to a participant in an effective manner is based on both *substance* and *manner*. What information was given, and how was it presented? The information must be planned and presented so it can be completely understood, and it must be fully understood by the participant. It is the researcher's responsibility to see that this is accomplished. This perspective places a great responsibility on an investigator and makes assurance that effective consent has been obtained even more complicated.

Voluntariness

Voluntary consent is concerned with each individual's ability to exercise the free power of choice without the intervention of force, fraud, deceit, duress, or other forms of constraint or coercion. This right to exercise choice must be present throughout the entire research process. The intent of this interpretation is that no such "constraint or coercion" must be either explicit or implicit on the part of the investigator.

The collective consideration of all three elements of consent has great impact on the manner in which a study is planned and executed. Each research situation presents a different set of circumstances, and consent procedures must be adapted accordingly. For investigators in certain areas (e.g., child development, cognitive disabilities, mental health), the type of participants frequently studied requires special consideration and protection (see, for example, Hardman et al., 2006; Roberts et al., 2005). Such participants will receive repeated attention in our discussion and examination of consent issues regarding *who* and *when*.

Who may give consent? The first answer to this question is the parent, guardian, or other agent legally responsible for the person and authorized to act on the person's behalf. Although this may seem simple, it is not, and the prerogative of consent is not constant. It varies greatly from situation to situation and among participants. The question of who may give consent is not a difficult one for those who have not been adjudicated as being "incompetent." Adults can give their own consent to participate in research. It is also clear that they must consent on a *voluntary* basis and with complete information concerning the nature and consequences of participation. Many individuals deemed incompetent and in need of special protection are thought to be unable to give consent on their own. They may be lacking in capacity because of cognitive or emotional disabilities, or because they are legally too young.

They may appear very vulnerable to either explicit or implicit coercion (thus violating the truly voluntary element of consent). They may have a combination of these and other characteristics that render them unable to exercise free will and make decisions. For such individuals, the question then becomes one of who can give consent on their behalf (and what should be considered in the process).

The parent, guardian, or other agent (e.g., institutional administrator) may give consent unless it comes to someone's attention that the *interests of the person who is consenting are at odds with what may be the interests of the subject.* For situations in which participants cannot provide their own consent, the researcher should not assume that "parental" consent is sufficient (Drew & Hardman, 2007). There is a need to constantly be vigilant in these situations. The American Psychological Association (2002) suggests that obtaining legal consent from the parent or guardian does not relieve the researcher of respecting the wishes of the child. The APA suggests,

> For persons who are legally incapable of giving informed consent, psychologists nevertheless (1) provide an appropriate explanation, (2) seek the individual's assent, (3) consider such persons' preferences and best interests, and (4) obtain appropriate permission from a legally authorized person, if such substitute consent is permitted or required by law. (p. 7)

Thus, consent from both the guardian *and* the child is needed.

It is important to note that the conventional wisdom associated with consent may not be appropriate for children. Consent, as a legal term, is not considered appropriate to use with minors. As noted in the APA code above, a child's agreement or refusal to participate is more appropriately described as assent or dissent. Researchers have investigated the ability of children to give consent because of ongoing concerns that these young participants are at risk for some level of implicit coercion (see, for example, Roberts et al., 2005). Findings do confirm that children have some capacity to make decisions about their participation, but there appear to be age-related problems regarding the degree to which they can do so freely. Some evidence suggests that children at about the seventh-grade level struggle to understand their prerogatives compared to adults (Diekema, 2005). The notion of not agreeing with their adult consent-giver (parent or guardian) is not only difficult to understand for children, it is inconsistent with much of the other information they receive daily. This is even more challenging for younger children and for those with cognitive disabilities (Field & Behrman, 2004; Gelfand & Drew, 2003). Investigators must use their best professional judgment in determining who should be involved in the consent process (see Box 3.1).

When must consent be given? Some research circumstances clearly require consent, whereas others are more subject to debate. Risk to participants may include a number of different situations, ranging from actual physical harm in the form of pain to potential psychological harm such as emotional stress. Similarly, the forfeiture of personal rights may vary greatly, from a serious invasion of privacy to a situation in which the participants are not threatened in any significant fashion.

The factors involved when consent should be obtained are similar to those regarding who can provide effective consent. Researchers must exercise their best professional judgment. However, the rule of thumb is *when in doubt, ask for permission.* If it is unclear whether or not consent is needed, it is prudent to err on the side of caution. Smith (2003) noted that the APA allows for no consent to be obtained when such avoidance is coded in federal law or regulations, *or* when the research is unlikely to distress or harm participants and involves one of the following:

The study of normal educational practices, curricula, or classroom management methods conducted in educational settings

Anonymous questionnaires, naturalistic observations, or archival research for which disclosure of responses would not place participants at risk of criminal or civil liability or damage their financial standing, employability, or reputation, and for which confidentiality is protected

The study of factors related to job or organization effectiveness conducted in organizational settings for which there are no risks to participants' employability, and confidentiality is protected. (pp. 56–57)

BOX 3.1   AERA Guiding Standards for Educational Researchers Working With Children and Vulnerable Populations

Education, by its very nature, is aimed at the improvement of individual lives and societies. Further, research in education is often directed at children and other vulnerable populations.... We should strive to protect these populations, and to maintain the integrity of our research, of our research community, and of all those with whom we have professional relations. We should pledge ourselves to do this by maintaining our own competence and that of people we induct into the field, by continually evaluating our research for its ethical and scientific adequacy, and by conducting our internal and external relations according to the highest ethical standards.... Educational researchers should be especially careful in working with children and other vulnerable populations.... Standards intended to protect the rights of human subjects should not be interpreted to prohibit teacher research, action research, and/or other forms of practitioner inquiry so long as: the data are those that could be derived from normal teaching/learning processes; confidentiality is maintained; the safety and welfare of participants are protected; informed consent is obtained when appropriate; and the use of the information obtained is primarily intended for the benefit of those receiving instruction in that setting.

AERA Standards

Educational researchers should

- exercise caution to ensure that there is no exploitation for personal gain of research populations or of institutional settings of research.
- not use their influence over subordinates, students, or others to compel them to participate in research.
- be mindful of cultural, religious, gender and other significant differences within the research population in the planning, conduct, and reporting of their research.
- consider and minimize the use of research techniques that might have negative social consequences, for example, experimental interventions that might deprive students of important parts of the standard curriculum.
- be sensitive to the integrity of ongoing institutional activities and alert appropriate institutional representatives of possible disturbances in such activities which may result from the conduct of the research.
- communicate their findings and the practical significance of their research in clear, straightforward, and appropriate language to relevant research populations, institutional representatives, and other stakeholders.

SOURCE: Adapted from American Educational Research Association (2005). Ethical Standards II. Guiding Standards: Research Populations, Educational Institutions, and the Public. [on-line]. Retrieved September 23, 2005 from http://www.aera.net/aboutaera/?id=174.

RESEARCH IN ACTION

Key points in the chapter reflected in this box:

- Anticipating the various ethical issues in conducting action research.
- Determining what approvals will be needed from institutional organizations.
- Checking guidelines regarding participant consent and assent.
- Anticipating questions about potential hazards, confidentiality, and other risk factors presented in action research studies (all of which will be asked by approval groups such as IRBs and school research committees).

For more research in action tips visit www.sagepub .com/drewstudy

Objectives to learn from this box:

- Understand how action research conducted in a field setting present challenging contexts pertaining to anticipating ethical issues.
- Reflect on how action researchers anticipate and resolve potential risk issues.
- Determine how consent and assent are obtained for these action research studies.

Scenario 1: Student Engagement in Reading

Emily is beginning to study the effects of engagement on how young students learn to read. She is using what is labeled as concept-oriented reading instruction (CORI) as a means of engaging the experimental group, and her comparison group is going to receive drill and practice (DAP) on words and sentences. Emily reviews the notes on action research found in the AERA Guiding Standards and is a little confused by the wording. Both reading instruction approaches are found in different teacher's teaching styles and she is not sure whether she can consider both of her instructional methods to be normal teaching processes. Surely Emily intends to maintain confidentiality, protect her students' welfare, and the information will be used to benefit students' instruction in general. But do the guidelines mean that she doesn't need consent because this can be considered a normal part of the teaching process?

Emily will need to have her research approved by the Institutional Review Board (IRB) for her university. The best guideline for her to follow is found in the wording "when in doubt, obtain consent." In fact since she is studying young students, Emily will need to obtain consent from her students' parents and also have her students complete an *assent* form that indicates they agree to participate. Before she can begin the study she will need to outline the details of her protocol and have it approved by the IRB. She will need to also obtain permission to conduct her study in the school district where the students are enrolled and then seek consent from parents and assent from the students themselves.

It is unlikely that there is much if any potential hazard to the students. Emily will need to maintain confidentiality of her students' performance (her data). Although confidentiality is an important matter, the data do not raise huge red flags regarding sensitive information. Emily's study will not likely encounter significant ethical issues.

SOURCE: This action research scenario is roughly based on Swan, E. A. (2003). *Concept-oriented reading instruction: Engaging classrooms, lifelong learners.* New York: Guilford Press.

SCENARIO 2: STUDENT SELF-ESTEEM

Daniel is beginning a study to see if his students with learning disabilities have different self-esteem depending on whether they are of Latino or Caucasian descent. He believes that his students have rather low self-esteem and it seems to him that his Latino students' self-esteem is somehow different than that of his Caucasian students.

Both groups of students are normally in Daniel's classes although they are not typically asked questions about their self-esteem. Daniel will need to obtain approval from the IRB at the university because he will be conducting this study as part of his degree program. He will also need to obtain permission from the school district as well as consent from the parents and have the students complete an assent form. Consent and assent forms will be part of the protocol to be approved by the IRB and the school district as will any questionnaire that Daniel intends to use with his students.

Because of the nature of his study, Daniel will have to pay particularly close attention to two of the standards in the AERA Standards. These include being attentive to cultural, religious or other significant matters in all aspects of his research since he is comparing Latino and Caucasian students. The second will be focusing on and minimizing the any potential negative social consequences of asking his participants about self-esteem matters. Daniel's study does raise some attention level because of his comparison groups but any issues can be minimized by careful protocol review and adequate sensitivity.

Think about this: Are you using children and what is the definition of children? What participant consent actions must you take for using children as participants that differ from using adults? What risk factors might be present if any? Who should approve the plan for the study and how do you contact them?

SOURCE: This Action Research scenario is roughly based on Rubin, D. (2000). *Race and self-esteem: A study of Latino and European-American students with learning disabilities.* Unpublished masters thesis, University of Utah, Salt Lake City.

How should consent be obtained? The method of obtaining consent will vary greatly depending on the situation involved and the degree of potential risk for participants. Consent may be obtained less formally (i.e., verbally) if the study creates little or no risk or potential invasion of privacy. In such circumstances, participants may be verbally informed of the nature of the investigation (assuming that the capacity element is present) and give consent verbally. Consent should be obtained in writing in other situations when participants are placed in a more "risky" position (e.g., potential harm, stress, substantial invasion of privacy). This is typically accomplished by providing both written and verbal explanations of the study, and the subject indicates consent by signing the written form. In certain cases, the provision of both verbal and written explanations is not possible, such as in a survey using mailed questionnaires. Usually the subject's willingness to complete a questionnaire is adequate indication of consent. A written explanation of the survey should be included with the questionnaire (often as a part of the instructions *on* the questionnaire) with a clear indication that responses to the questions are voluntary. In all cases, the researcher must remain cognizant of the three elements of consent and also inform the subject that consent can be withdrawn at any time. It is also routine and *required* that research conducted through colleges or universities involve written consent. Figure 3.1 is a sample assent form for children (parental agreement would also be needed).

FIGURE 3.1   **Sample Assent Form University Of Utah**

ASSENT TO PARTICIPATE IN RESEARCH

(Include title of study and Principal Investigators name headers on each page)

Purpose of Research

We are asking you to take part in a research study because we are trying to learn more about . . . (Outline what the study is about in language that is appropriate to both the child's maturity and age.)

Procedures

If you agree to be in this study you will . . . (Describe the procedures and the duration of participation. Describe what will take place from the child's point of view in a language that is appropriate to both the child's maturity and age.)

Risks

(Describe any risks to the child that may result from participation in the research.)

Benefits

Your involvement in this study will help us to understand . . . (Describe any benefits to the child from participation in the research.)

Alternative Procedures and Voluntary Participation

If you don't want to be in this study, you don't have to participate. Remember, being in this study is up to you and no one will be upset if you don't want to participate or even if you change your mind later and want to stop. Please talk this over with your parents before you decide whether or not to participate. We will also ask your parents to give their permission for you to take part in this study, but even if your parents say "yes," you can still decide not to do this.

Confidentiality

All of your records about this research study will be kept locked up so no one else can see them. (Explain how the records will be kept confidential.)

Person to Contact

You can ask any questions that you have about the study. If you have a question later that you didn't think of now, you can call me (insert your name and telephone number) *or ask me next time.* (If applicable: *You may call me at any time to ask questions about your disease or treatment.*)

Consent

Signing my name at the bottom means that I agree to be in this study. (If the study is related to treatment, insert the following: *My doctors will continue to treat me whether or not I participate in this study.*) *My parents and I will be given a copy of this form after I have signed it.*

_____	_____
Signature of Subject	Date
_____	_____
Signature of Witness	Date

Harm

Psychologists must take reasonable steps to avoid harming their clients/patients, students, supervisees, research participants, organizational clients, and others with whom they work, and to minimize harm where it is foreseeable and unavoidable. (American Psychological Association, 2002, p. 6)

When psychologists become aware that research procedures have harmed a participant, they take reasonable steps to minimize the harm. (American Psychological Association, 2002, p. 12)

Participants, or their guardians, in an [educational] research study have the right to be informed about the likely risks involved in the research and of potential consequences for participants, and to give their informed consent before participating in research. . . . Participants in research should be made aware of the limits on the protections that can be provided, and of the efforts toward protection that will be made even in situations where absolute confidentiality cannot be assured. It should be made clear to informants and participants that despite every effort made to preserve it, confidentiality may be compromised. (American Educational Research Association, 2005)

The most basic concern in all research is that *no individual is harmed by serving as a participant,* as suggested above by the APA and AERA codes of ethics. In the context of research ethics, **harm** may be broadly defined to include extreme physical pain or death, but also involves such factors as psychological stress, personal embarrassment or humiliation, or myriad influences that may adversely affect the participants in a significant way.

Potential Hazards to Participants

Certain types of investigations present potential harm to participants. Research that involves physically dangerous treatment may present real possibilities for harm if the treatment is "inflicted" on the participants. Unfortunately, there are examples of investigations in which ethical principles were violated in an extreme fashion (see Young, 2005). Other areas of research are specifically designed to investigate the effects of psychological or emotional stress. Such research represents extremely difficult circumstances, especially when the procedures involve actual "infliction" of stress. There is always the possibility that a subject may become seriously ill (e.g., have a stroke or heart attack) as a result of the stress. In addition, the possibility exists that the stress itself may be harmful to participants from a psychological standpoint.

Vulnerable populations. Some studies may be characterized as high risk for harm because of the participants involved. By virtue of characteristics associated with age or disability, an individual can be rendered relatively powerless in exercising free will when choosing whether or not to serve as a research participant. These participants may be less capable of understanding potential harm, or they may feel openly or implicitly coerced in some fashion. People who are institutionalized or incarcerated, such as prisoners, persons with severe disabilities, or people with serious mental illness, may agree to participate in a study either because they "should to show evidence of good behavior" or to gain approval from supervisors. Unfortunately, some troubling examples of ethical violations have occurred with studies involving these individuals (Field & Behrman, 2004; Moser et al., 2004).

Highly vulnerable populations should not be taken advantage of in the name of science. Researchers investigating topics involving these individuals must exercise extreme care. Very young children, the elderly, or people with disabilities may be easily convinced that most activities are important, are of little harm, and should be engaged in for the benefit of society (Drew & Hardman, 2007; Quadagno, 2005).

Determining the Degree of Harm

Vulnerable participants pose a dilemma because of the important need to study these individuals in order to improve their lives and to benefit society. Consequently, a researcher will likely encounter such ethical dilemmas sooner or later. Thoughtful and knowledgeable consideration must guide the process. The researcher must determine what constitutes significant risk, and carefully weigh potential benefits versus potential harm to the subjects.

How much is harmful? Researchers continually face questions regarding what is meant by a *high degree* of vulnerability and a *potential, substantial,* or *significant* risk. Although the above terms suggest quantification, they refer to issues that are difficult to quantify. Basically, such terminology focuses on perceptions, values, or judgment. As such, there is little probability of consensus concerning their meaning. Even so, these issues cannot be ignored and every researcher must eventually face the question, "How much [harm] is harmful?"

Researchers must decide how much threat, stress, or pain should be considered harmful. Their determination might fall near one end or the other of the continuum (i.e., nothing should ever be done in research that would pose the slightest imposition or threat of stress on a subject versus the interests of science and society are always paramount—individual distress or harm should be discounted in favor of the potential benefit for the larger number). Neither of these extremes can be accepted as a blanket rule. The continuum must be explored more completely and judicious caution exercised.

Some researchers may attempt to fall back on *consent* as a means of dealing with issues related to harm. They may argue that potentially harmful studies can only be undertaken if the participants have effectively consented (have the capacity to understand the potential risk, full information concerning any harm to them that may occur, and voluntarily agree to subject themselves to such potential harm). However, since consent is an essential prerequisite to these investigations, it adds little to our understanding of how much harm is acceptable. Consent, even under the most careful precautions, does not render an investigator free to ignore further responsibility regarding potential harm.

What is the cost/benefit ratio? Another approach to addressing the issue of harm is the cost/benefit ratio. This approach involves a comparison of the potential benefits of a given study with the potential risks to the participants. Presumably, if the benefit of the study outweighs the potential harm, the study is considered ethical, and the opposite would also be true. For example, suppose an investigation were proposed that had potential for solving the inflation problem in the United States. However, to conduct the study, a sample of 1,000 participants would be required to divulge personal details concerning amount and sources of income, as well as the manner in which every dollar was spent. Certainly this represents a substantial invasion of privacy—but there is also a dire need to solve the inflation problem. Do the benefits outweigh the harm? This becomes a matter of individual judgment.

The idea of assessing costs and benefits has considerable appeal. Yet how is this task accomplished? It may be a rather simple matter in business, but in many cases we are confronted with factors that defy measurement. How does one evaluate and predict the harm that might be inflicted on a participant? An equally difficult question involves how one measures and predicts benefit. Or, how does the process of balancing subject harm with potential benefit proceed? These problems lack precise solutions and require careful evaluation. The evaluation process must involve a review by professionals other than the investigator proposing the study (often an institutional or agency "human subjects review board"). If assessments were the sole prerogative of the researcher, a conflict of interest could influence the decision. (After all, the researcher has a vested interest in the study.)

As much as possible, research should be planned and executed in a manner that minimizes harm to participants. A study is always more ethically justifiable when the probability of risk is minimized. In addition, the researcher must be concerned about how long the harmful effects will last after the study is completed, and if they are reversible. It is most desirable to deal with an effect that can be easily reversed and has a short post-investigation duration. A potential harmful effect should be detected early so that the study can be terminated if necessary.

Privacy

The value attached to individual **privacy** has varied throughout history, and vast differences are still evident from one country to another. Privacy has, however, become a "right" that is highly treasured in contemporary Western society.

Science is based on the collection and analysis of data. Educators as well as behavioral and social scientists collect and analyze data concerning people, both as individuals and groups. This is the point at which the goals of research and the right to privacy may come into conflict. Frequently, research of this nature is aimed at obtaining information concerning attitudes, beliefs, opinions, and behavior. Thus, pursuing the goals of science, while guarding against unnecessary invasion of participants' privacy, presents complex issues.

Issues in Research Affecting Privacy

As with other ethical considerations, privacy has become an increasingly valued right. Seeking privacy is an act of seclusion or confidentiality—removed from public view or knowledge. Total privacy is virtually nonexistent, and people are required on occasion to yield a certain amount of privacy for one reason or another. In some cases, this is done voluntarily to obtain something in return (e.g., a person divulges certain personal information to obtain a credit card). Even in these circumstances, there have been rather dramatic changes recently in the kinds of information that can be requested.

Sensitivity. In considering privacy related to the conduct of research, several factors must be addressed. First, the sensitivity of the data in the view of the individual or group being studied must be considered. For example, certain types of information may be viewed as sensitive under any circumstances. For example, data concerning sexual preference represents information that many people would want to keep private. Other information may be less sensitive, such as one's favorite color. In addition, many types of information would be considered situationally sensitive, information that would be divulged under certain circumstances but not others (e.g., age, weight, or personal income).

The setting. The setting in which research is being conducted may also be an important factor in considering a potential invasion of privacy. On one end of the continuum, there are those settings that are nearly always considered private, such as a person's home. The other end of the continuum might be represented by a setting in which privacy is not generally assumed, such as a public park. Some settings may be only situationally private—a person's home cannot be considered private when a realtor is showing it to a prospective buyer. Clearly, the researcher must consider the setting in which the data are collected if undue invasion of privacy is to be avoided.

Information. A final point regarding privacy involves how public the information is. Subjects may not believe that their privacy has been seriously threatened if only one or two people know (e.g., the researchers collecting the data). It is a totally different story, however, if the investigators publish personal information and opinions in the newspaper. In so doing, they have made the information available to the general public. This makes it possible for the public to identify *individuals*. Such a breach of confidence should never occur, but this example is not without some base in reality. The researcher must remain very alert concerning the degree to which private information remains confidential, particularly when such information is of a sensitive nature.

A researcher cannot ignore privacy in any study. If a potential problem exists, consent should always be obtained. In addition, the participants should be assured that the data will be held in strict confidence to protect anonymity. Few studies *require* that data be maintained in a form in which participants can be personally identified. As a rule of thumb, researchers should invade the privacy of participants as minimally as possible. If a potential of privacy risk exists, the investigator should take every precaution. Any study that substantially invades privacy may obviously place the participants at risk. Such procedures also place the conduct of science at risk by reducing the public trust vital to the successful pursuit of knowledge.

Deception

Research deception involves an intentional misrepresentation of facts related to the purpose, nature, or consequences of an investigation. In this context, **deception** refers to either an *omission* or a *commission* on the part of the researcher in terms of interactions with participants. An omission deception could mean that the investigator does not fully inform participants about important aspects of the study. Part or all of the information is withheld. A commission involves a situation in which the researcher gives false information about the investigation, either partially or totally. In the first case, participants may not even be aware that a study is in progress, or they may only be informed about a portion of the investigation. In the second situation, participants generally are aware that they are involved in some type of study or activity that is out of the ordinary, but may be given misleading information regarding the actual purpose of the study or activity. In either case, the researcher is misrepresenting the study.

Regardless of the precise nature of deception, it has become a very prominent issue for investigators concerned with the ethics of conducting research. As we move through the first decade of the 21st century, deception is receiving widespread attention in educational and social science research with increasing concerns regarding its use on the Internet (Keller & Lee, 2003; Lichtenberg, Heresco-Levy, & Nitzan, 2004; Mishara & Weisstub, 2005; Nagy, 2005c; Pittenger, 2003).

Reasons for Deception

There are a variety of reasons that deception may be used in research. These include deceiving participants who have become "test-wise" and are suspicious that the purpose of the study is hidden, reducing the amount of influence a group can have on an individual respondent, and pragmatics (limited finances, time, and data sources).

Hidden agenda. Some research participants have become "test-wise" and often believe the "real" purpose of a given study is hidden. This is truer for certain populations than others (notably college sophomores, one of the most "studied" groups in the United States). If participants are *that* suspicious, they may be expected to answer, perform, or generally respond in an atypical manner. Such responses may seriously threaten the soundness of an investigation. Participants may attempt to respond in a manner that they think the researcher desires, or they may try to out-guess the researcher and "sabotage" the study. Some populations are studied frequently, and others are even professional research participants. (Some college students earn part of their monthly income by serving as participants in studies about response to advertisements.) There is even evidence that participants are "wising up" to the research process.

The APA Code of Ethics notes that "Psychologists do not conduct a study involving deception unless they have determined that the use of deceptive techniques is justified by the study's significant prospective scientific, educational, or applied value and that effective non-deceptive alternative procedures are not feasible" (American Psychological Association, 2002, p. 11). APA continues by noting that deception is not used if it can be expected to cause physical or emotional suffering, *and*, if used, the deception must be explained to participants as early as feasible.

Individual influences. Suppose a study were being conducted on group control of individual actions. In this type of investigation, the study might focus on the amount of influence a group had on individual opinions about the use of drugs. This might be the type of study that would involve intentional deception to a considerable degree. If the participant being observed was suspicious about the purpose of the investigation, he or she might be more or less resistant to group pressure than normally would occur. The researcher would need to account for such an influence by deceiving the participant. The individual may be directly deceived about the purpose of the study, or information may be withheld. If the participant were openly informed about the nature of the study, the outcome would be jeopardized. In this case, the use of intentional deception could backfire. The researcher cannot reveal the exact nature of the investigation, but the participant may be generally suspicious and alter behavior because of those suspicions in a manner unknown to the investigator. Intentional deception is used to control factors important to the study, but suspicion of deception creates problems for control.

The control exerted may relate to the technical soundness of the study or it may relate to the generalizability of the findings (matters that will be examined in detail in later chapters). If one group of participants receives different treatment (deception) than another, the comparison may not *really* involve the treatment. Likewise, if deception is either real or perceived by participants, results might not be transferable to the outside world. Methodological reasons for using intentional deception represent a double-edged sword: they have both advantages and disadvantages. The judgment of the investigator regarding this issue will likely be tested.

Pragmatics. Some reasons for using deception are purely pragmatic. Limited finances, time, and data sources have often led researchers to use deception. For example, if it is too expensive, time consuming, or not feasible to observe a natural occurrence of a particular phenomenon, it might be best studied by creating a simulated incident. Such a situation may arise when the researcher is studying something that only occurs rarely or creates dangerous circumstances when it does occur (e.g., emergencies). This type of deception could involve a staged purse-snatching or mugging with observations focused on the reactions of witnesses. Such an example would necessarily involve deception (and also no pre-study consent) if the witnesses are to behave naturally.

Is deception ethical? The previous discussions illustrate the reasons why researchers use deception and also some of the problems involved in its use. But is deception ethical? One of the most fundamental arguments against deception is that it is unethical and degrading to the participants involved. Lying is generally viewed unfavorably in our society and even deemed immoral. This value places the conduct of science in a dilemma. Science is presumably undertaken for the benefit of society, so should it be associated with acts that are generally thought to be malicious? This is a question that has no direct answer since it is couched in such polarized terms.

Most people would agree that research cannot be clearly declared either ethical or unethical. There are many shades of gray and myriad matters that must be considered. One of the most serious issues facing researchers and the use of deception is the issue of consent. If participants are involved in activities that present potential risk to them, consent is necessary. However, in studies using deception, informed consent is likely absent. If a study uses deception, participants must at least be given enough information to know the possibility of risk and then voluntarily decide whether or not to participate.

Simulation

Simulation 3.1

Topic: Ethical issues related to participants

Background statement: You are planning a study, which will involve an investigation of a new social studies program with high school students during their sophomore year. You have obtained your subject pool using matched samples from two different social studies classes that form two groups, one that receives the new social studies program (treatment) and one that will receive a placebo activity (control). What ethical issues must you consider in planning your study?

Write your response, then turn to p. 80 for Simulation Feedback 3.1

For additional simulations visit www.sagepub .com/drewstudy

ETHICAL CONSIDERATIONS IN QUANTITATIVE AND QUALITATIVE RESEARCH

In this section, ethical considerations are addressed in the context of quantitative and qualitative research. The purpose is to inform researchers as to the ethical issues that may be specific to a given research approach. Although the discussion here is necessarily brief, the reader is referred to other sources with more in-depth information on the issues.

Ethics and Quantitative Research

Quantitative research involves studies in which the data that are analyzed are in the form of numbers. In this research approach, behaviors are counted, correct answers or errors are counted, and other types of measures are recorded in terms of quantity. Quantitative research involves both experimental and nonexperimental research. Ethical issues in experimental research focus on protecting individuals that *receive* an intervention. For example, an intervention may involve training participants in group communication where a great deal of *self-disclosure* is required. Self-disclosure is a technique whereby people are encouraged to discuss their feelings, attitudes, and experiences (some of which may be quite personal). Does the researcher have the right to use such a treatment? Dealing with this question is a personal decision on the part of the researcher. As discussed earlier, the researcher clearly has the responsibility to fully inform participants about the nature of the activities in the process of obtaining consent, and make it clear to participants that their consent may be withdrawn and they may elect to discontinue the activities at any time. Assuming that the investigator handles consent appropriately, both in planning and executing the experiment, the problem should be lessened, although perhaps not completely eliminated.

In addition to the problems related to participants who *receive* an experimental treatment, there are also difficult ethical issues involving those who are in a "placebo" or control group. Such would be the case where one group of students in a high school receives a newly developed science program (experimental treatment) that appears to be very effective, and a second group receives the science program that was used for many years with limited effectiveness (control group). One ethical perspective is that the researcher has the responsibility to provide the new treatment to all participants. However, some researchers may have a very different view. This opposing perspective is often called the *natural state argument*. This argument contends that the untreated participants are not being denied a benefit they already have; they are merely being left in their natural state. In the example above, the high school students in the control group continued to receive the science program that had been used in the school for many years.

Clearly, neither of the above positions is acceptable for all research (Field & Behrman, 2004; Gross, 2005; Roberts et al., 2005). There remains a critical need to conduct a scientifically sound test. One approach to this dilemma represents a compromise that attempts to meet the goals of research and also the ethical need for providing benefit to all participants. In our example above, it may be possible to first conduct the study as initially planned—with a treatment group and a placebo comparison group. Then, after the investigation is complete and the data collected, researchers could provide the new science program to the participants in the comparison group if in fact it was a more effective program. In this way, treatment is not withheld from anyone in the study, and the data are not contaminated. Although this is a reasonable compromise, ethical issues remain. Some would contend that the delay in treatment is still harmful to the placebo group. This may be true if the duration of the study is extended over time, but if not, such an argument loses its potency. Another issue may be expense: if the treatment is quite expensive, the researcher may have difficulty funding treatment for the second group. Although this may be a problem, it is not a very compelling argument. To remain ethical, the researcher should plan a budget to allow for treatment of the comparison participants. None of this discussion has great significance for interventions or treatments of unknown effectiveness, but becomes more relevant as evidence of promise accumulates for any given treatment.

Ethical issues also exist in conducting nonexperimental research where an investigator does not impose or manipulate conditions. Although ethics in nonexperimental designs (e.g., survey research) are often less complex or harmful than experimental studies, it is important for investigators to be aware of basic principles for protecting the participants, including "full disclosure and consent." For example, in survey research, each respondent should be fully informed as to the purpose of the study, participant demographics (e.g., teachers, college students, the general public), confidentiality of responses, how the results are intended to be used, and who will have access to the data. Bacon and Olsen (2005) also indicate that survey researchers have the ethical responsibility of "not wasting" a respondent's time and to only collect data that has utility (real use). Schenk and Williamson (2005), in discussing the ethical responsibilities involved in conducting nonexperimental research on children, suggest "if the information gathering activity will not directly benefit the children involved or their community, do not proceed" (p. 17).

Ethics and Qualitative Research

Qualitative research involves data that are recorded in narrative descriptions, not numbers. Researchers use qualitative methods to observe and describe conditions rather than control them. A basic ethical principle for qualitative researchers is this: *Do not tamper with the natural setting under study.*

Participant and nonparticipant observations are integral components of qualitative research and are used widely in the fields of education, sociology, and anthropology. Each presents unique ethical issues in regard to consent, privacy, and deception (Brinkmann & Kvale, 2005; Haverkamp, 2005).

Informed consent is necessary but can be problematic when relying on observations in a qualitative research study. Although potential harm from treatment is not generally a threat, there are other ethical concerns. Clearly, there is a substantial threat to privacy. A revelation of observed conversations and behaviors could cause harm to participants in their families, communities, or place of employment. In addition, the actual research participants, who have given consent, may not be the only people observed. In natural settings, people move in and out of interactions and settings for many reasons (Creswell, 2005; Denzin & Lincoln, 2005). For example, a researcher has permission to study formal and informal counselor–student interactions in a middle school setting. Informed consent has been obtained from the counselors, students, and parents of the students who are in formal counseling. However, the researcher plans to follow the counselors while they work during the day and record informal interactions among students throughout the school and between the counselors and the students. How is consent obtained from all the students and their parents? Is consent necessary? The accepted rule of thumb for such nonparticipant observation research is that consent is not necessary when (a) access to the setting is approved by the agency or institution, (b) participants who are actively involved have given informed consent, and (c) other observed behavior is considered public and observable by anyone present in the setting. In other words, if other students or teachers in the school overhear the conversations that the researcher is observing in a public place, they do not require additional consent.

This rule of thumb does not always guarantee, however, that difficulties with consent will not occur. The definition of "public" is open to debate. For example, a doctoral student at a leading university was recently conducting nonparticipant observational research for his dissertation. The student obtained consent to observe a YWCA board meeting from the president and members of the board. However, an influential community member speaking at the meeting refused to participate when told he was under observation as part of a research study. The entire board meeting came to a halt.

Participant Observation

Participant observation also presents unique ethical challenges. The participant observer often lives, eats, and sleeps on a daily basis with those under observation. In such a study, a broad range of details is observed and recorded regarding participants' cultural mores, interaction patterns, social structures, and daily behaviors. The participant observer may directly probe into many facets of the lifestyle of the participants—public, private, and often sensitive. With such a pervasive scope of observation, an invasion of privacy is inevitable. This makes informed consent absolutely necessary.

The nature of participant observation research raises some serious difficulties with regard to consent. Specifically, this research methodology often requires that only the core group of participants know the researcher is not just another member of the group. Is it adequate to obtain consent only from the group leader (e.g., the tribal leader, the school principal, the teacher, the fraternity president)? Another problem in observation studies involves the *effects* of obtaining consent *on the behavior of those being studied*. An important strength of observation research is the study of participant routine behaviors within the natural environment. By obtaining consent, a researcher may alter this natural behavior. Many researchers seek to mitigate these effects by asking an inside informer to watch for changes in the customary behavior and interactions of the group and warn the researcher if routines are altered.

Another potential difficulty with observation methods—particularly participant observation—arises as those under observation become increasingly comfortable with the researcher's presence. By virtue of the observer's role, the participants may forget that they are being studied. Some question exists whether this means they are no longer consenting because their consent is no longer "effective" in the pure sense.

Privacy Issues

Invasion of privacy represents a substantial risk in qualitative research because of the sensitive data often collected and analyzed (Baez, 2002; Nagy, 2005b). One of the traditional methods of circumventing privacy problems—anonymity—is a way to protect individual participants. In reporting the results of observation studies, fictitious names are often used to disguise the identity of individuals, groups, agencies, and locations. Although this technique is adequate in most circumstances, it sometimes fails. Some of the published information may involve behavior that could be considered embarrassing and potentially damaging to the participants, and the people involved may know each other well enough to establish who was being discussed.

Finally, anonymity does not solve privacy questions related to sacred data in cultural studies. Revealing sacred information related to ceremonies, taboos, or stories, while central to a research process, may never be appropriate. Tony Hillerman described this dilemma aptly in his novel *Talking God* when he said, "The museums of the world are filled with the gods of conquered peoples."

Degree of Deception

The aura of deception may also surround ethical questions in qualitative studies. In one sense, the participant observer is by definition a "deceiver." Even with consent, the participant observer affects the behavior of others in the study by his or her behavior. This is a serious problem that cannot be ignored by researchers using this approach. It also raises complex questions about potential harm. In extreme forms of participant observation, the observer might encourage others to engage in behaviors that might be harmful, illegal, or both. Qualitative researchers must continually ask themselves (and the appropriate review committees), "What harm may be incurred by the deception involved in my study?" (See Box 3.2.)

MONITORING ETHICS IN RESEARCH: INSTITUTIONAL REVIEW BOARDS

While the investigator is ultimately responsible to ensure that no ethical violations occur in a given study, the federal government has also established an additional assurance in the conduct of research—the **institutional review board** (IRB). IRBs are composed of five or more members who are representatives of the institution (e.g., faculty members or administrators) as well as laypeople who have no association with the institution. The IRB is charged with reviewing the purpose of the research and the proposed methodology as it relates to potential risk or benefits to the participants involved. This review body is also directly concerned with issues of informed consent and a subject's right to privacy. As described by the American Psychological Association (2002), the researcher must receive institutional approval (through an IRB) where the focus is on protecting human subjects.

BOX 3.2   Ethics of Undercover Research

Ethnographies, or detailed descriptions of a culture, require anthropologists to immerse themselves in the day-to-day lives of their subjects. But what if immersion involves a researcher not revealing his or her identity?

This question was important for Rebekah Nathan, who determined that she could not have made a meaningful study of students unless she blended in with them—and did not fully explain who she was. That, the professor writes in *My Freshman Year,* required "a delicate balancing act between truth and fiction." (Rebekah Nathan is a pseudonym, and her university is not identified in her book.)

Ms. Nathan says she followed the ethical protocol of "informed consent" when conducting formal interviews with students. She identified herself as a researcher (though not as a professor at the university), explained her study, and obtained written permission to publish the subjects' words.

However, in day-to-day interactions, Ms. Nathan let students assume she was one of them.

Lois Weis, a professor of sociology of education at the State University of New York at Buffalo who read the book, does not think Ms. Nathan compromised her ethical obligations as a researcher. "It seems to me that she made wise decisions," says Ms. Weis, who has conducted numerous ethnographical studies and is the coauthor of *Speed Bumps: A Student-Friendly Guide to Qualitative Research* (Teachers College Press, 2000).

"Certainly in this kind of research there can be a lot of misunderstandings, miscommunications, and certainly research subjects could end up feeling hurt or used," Ms. Weis says. "But that could happen whether they knew that she was a researcher or not."

Margaret A. Eisenhart, a professor of educational anthropology and research methodology at the University of Colorado at Boulder, who also read *My Freshman Year,* disagreed with Ms. Nathan's undercover approach.

Protecting the Subject

"My job as an ethnographer is to protect the people I'm working with in the same way I'd want to be protected if I were in the subject's shoes," says Ms. Eisenhart. "It is just simply unethical to do something which is primarily for your own benefit, to advance your own career."

She rejects the idea that Ms. Nathan would have jeopardized her research if she had been up front with her subjects. Ms. Eisenhart says that in one of her own studies she was able to gain the trust of students and accompany them on social excursions, even dates, without concealing her identity. That research was the source for the book *Educated in Romance: Women, Achievement, and College Culture* (University of Chicago Press, 1990), which she wrote with Dorothy C. Holland.

"I don't think it was hard to get people to open up once they relaxed about who we were," Ms. Eisenhart says of their study.

The American Anthropological Association's code of ethics does not explicitly advise against undercover research, though it once did. Some anthropologists believe the practice is unethical in all cases, while others say it depends on the context, says Stacy Lathrop, staff liaison to the association's ethics committee.

"We all play multiple roles in our life, and you have to navigate between those," Ms. Lathrop says. "Participant observation is like life, dynamic and changing. As in human relationships, sometimes you do keep secrets."

SOURCE: From Hoover, E. (2005, July 29). "The ethics of undercover research," *The Chronicle of Higher Education*, A37. Reprinted with permission from *The Chronicle of Higher Education.*

Psychologists [must] inform participants about (1) the purpose of the research, expected duration, and procedures; (2) their right to decline to participate and to withdraw from the research once participation has begun; (3) the foreseeable consequences of declining or withdrawing; (4) reasonably foreseeable factors that may be expected to influence their willingness to participate such as potential risks, discomfort, or adverse effects; (5) any prospective research benefits; (6) limits of confidentiality; (7) incentives for participation; and (8) whom to contact for questions about the research and research participants' rights. They provide opportunity for the prospective participants to ask questions and receive answers. (p. 11)

Many researchers are supportive of IRBs and view them as a protection for not only human participants but researchers as well. The IRB can assist the researcher by identifying potential pitfalls that could be overlooked by an individual investigator, thus protecting reputations and avoiding litigation. Other researchers see the IRB as a governmental intrusion into the research process. They view them as overly cumbersome, unnecessary, and dictatorial. From the latter viewpoint, IRBs were established to deal with the very few who violate ethical standards, while punishing the many ethical researchers with unwieldy governmental requirements (see, for example, Kleiman, 2003; Rae & Sullivan, 2003).

Federal Requirements for IRBs

Regardless of the position taken on the need for IRBs, they are a federal requirement. Institutions receiving federal funding must establish committees to approve *all* human and animal research. This includes student research for theses and dissertations, as well as individual faculty endeavors. Investigators must receive IRB approval on any research involving human or animal participants whether or not the study is receiving federal dollars. An institution that fails to meet IRB requirements may put its federal funding in jeopardy. Collegial review bodies such as IRBs do not negate the individual researcher's responsibility for ethical decision making. The final ethical responsibility rests with the investigator.

ETHICS AND PROFESSIONALISM

Ethics and professionalism could easily consume an entire volume, but will only receive a cursory examination in this chapter. Our focus is on three issues: (1) integrity during the execution of the study, (2) integrity related to publishing, and (3) sanctions for breaches of integrity. Hopefully, these topics will provide a background and sensitivity that will prompt further thought and inquiry by the beginning researcher as questions arise.

Integrity During Execution of the Study

Any breach of integrity during the execution of a research study, whether it be unintentional errors or outright falsification of the data, seriously weakens or even invalidates the investigation. One of the basic purposes of science is the acquisition of objective and accurate data about real phenomena. Reality is fluid, situational, and certainly variable depending on one's perspective. However, somewhere underlying the conduct of science, there is a philosophical assumption that some "truths" can be determined. This places a very important responsibility on scientists to undertake their efforts in a totally honest fashion. This is not a statement that reflects a value judgment or a moral stand. It simply emphasizes a fundamental principle on which scientific investigation is based.

This chapter has addressed the importance of **integrity** in research and focused thus far on the execution of the study. The question raised in this context relates to why breaches of integrity occur. Although a variety of influences result in these problems, none makes such acts justifiable. However, their discussion assists our understanding and promotes preventive action.

Factors influencing breaches of integrity involve some rather powerful social pressures, particularly among beginning researchers. One of the most powerful factors is the pressure to publish, often characterized as a "publish or perish" mentality. Researchers are constantly pressured to "get into print," which is always particularly acute early in a career (Parasuraman, 2003; Weerasekera, 2004). This pressure may place such a stress on investigators that they plagiarize the work of others, and alter or fabricate data. To protect against such acts, investigators must be overly diligent in their efforts to be objective.

Plagiarism involves misrepresenting someone else's work as your own and is clearly unethical. Plagiarism may be defined as the following:

> The intentional unacknowledged use or incorporation of any other person's work in, or as a basis for, one's own work offered for academic consideration or credit or for public presentation. It includes, but is not limited to, representing as one's own, without attribution, any other individual's words, phrasing, ideas, sequence of ideas, information or any other mode or content of expression. (University of Utah, 2005)

Data alteration may be described in terms of *trimming* and *cooking*. Trimming occurs when the researcher smoothes irregularities in the data to achieve a better fit between actual and expected results. Cooking occurs when the researcher retains or reports only those findings that fit the hypothesis. Both variations, while more subtle than complete fabrication, still represent dishonest science.

Ethical problems may also arise when strong pressure (often implicit) leads to inaccurate data collection. For example, such pressure may occur when a research assistant believes that significant results *must* be obtained and either consciously or unconsciously alters the data. Other circumstances may have the same net outcome. The data collection process is often laborious, boring, or even extremely difficult. This has led to incidents in which research assistants actually record fictitious data rather than conscientiously observe participants (sometimes known as *dry labbing*).

Research assistants and beginning researchers are not the only scientists vulnerable to breaches of integrity. In fact, some very prominent individuals, with widely known reputations, have been accused of conducting unethical research. One example concerns the work of Sir Cyril Burt, a noted British psychologist. Burt is a particularly difficult case since the allegations of scientific misconduct against him were made after his death, making it impossible for him to respond. The controversy is further complicated by two factors: (1) there is no question that Burt was a very well-known scientist—he was knighted in 1946 in recognition of the importance of his work; and (2) the topic of his investigations was, and remains, very controversial—the heritability of intelligence. The allegations include (1) estimating certain levels of intelligence (based on estimates by parents of certain twins) but later reporting such estimates as solid data, (2) listing people as coauthors on research reports who may never have existed, and (3) producing data that represented answers supporting his theoretical beliefs that are unusually "precise" fits with predictions (some say impossible). These points have been countered by supporters of his work on the basis that while the inconsistencies may represent a degree of carelessness, basically the errors are trivial, do not seriously undermine the strength of the heritability of intelligence position, and certainly do not warrant the accusations of fraud. The arguments have been intense on both sides, often representing varying perspectives on the intelligence issue as much as the problems involved in the ethics of science. However, one cannot ignore the difficulties and suspicions generated in relation to the conduct of research (Joynson, 2003). In one sense, the scientific endeavor is as much on trial as the work of Burt, which illustrates very well the fundamental problems involved with breaches of integrity (confirmed or alleged). It should be noted that this is not the only example—other fields of science also have their unfortunate incidents.

Every researcher must take precautions against breaches of integrity related to the execution of research. However, it is impossible to have *every* data collection effort fully supervised or observed by more than one researcher. Ethical integrity in science, as in many other fields, is mainly an individual undertaking. Hopefully, one precaution that may have an important influence is a more open discussion of the resulting problems and the potential outcomes.

Integrity Related to Publishing

Publishing is an integral part of the overall research process. Chapter 1 characterized the research process in a closed-loop fashion: An investigation is undertaken to answer a question of presumed importance. The process is not completed until the results are interpreted in relation to the question that closes the loop. The work of a scientist is public, and publishing is the means by which it is made public. For the most part, a published research report describes the closed loop and takes the form of an article in a professional journal. The research question is presented, accompanied by the rationale concerning why the question should be studied, a description of the execution, the results, and an interpretation of those results related to the question. Considerable detail (e.g., participants, procedures, analysis) is included in such a report, which basically makes the researcher's work open for public scrutiny by the scientific community. This public scrutiny helps to make science objective and is why publishing is an important part of the research process.

Because publishing is an important part of research, it is also an important factor in the career of a scientist. Scholars use publications as one means of determining the capability and performance of a researcher. Successful publication of research in a respected journal or book provides at least some evidence that the work has withstood review by the scientific community. Such evidence clearly enhances the researcher's employability, rank, and salary. In fact, some universities will terminate professors if they have not published a reasonable amount during the first few years of their employment (often the first 5 to 7 years). These realities of academic life place pressure on researchers to publish. Although the pressure is not undue (5 to 7 years is plenty of time), some tend to exaggerate the intensity of this pressure and ethical problems may result, as described below.

Plagiarism and Maintaining Integrity

As per our earlier discussion, ethical problems that may arise include plagiarism and maintaining integrity during the execution of a study. In regard to integrity, there may be a temptation to report the results of a study somewhat differently from what the data collected would indicate. This may be a situation in which significant differences are reported where the data did not actually show statistically significant differences. Such incidents have ranged from circumstances in which "it was close" and the data were changed slightly, all the way to "dry labbed" results. In qualitative research, the scholar may fail to convey quotations or observations that contradict or raise questions about his or her conclusions (Creswell, 2005; Denzin & Lincoln, 2005).

Simultaneous Submission

Another ethical concern related to publishing involves multiple publications of the same article. For example, ethical violations occur if you conduct a survey, write an article reporting the study, and then publish the same article in two different professional journals at the same time. In fact, the rule of thumb that is usually employed does not even permit *submitting* the same article to two different journals at once. This view would hold that you submit the article to one journal and, if it is rejected, you are then free to submit it for review by another journal. Many journals include this requirement in their editorial policies.

The multiple publication issue noted above is much different than an article (already published) that is *reprinted* in another journal or a book of readings. In this latter situation, the journal or publisher desiring to reprint your article must request permission from the first journal before the article can be reprinted. (A credit line must also be listed, clearly indicating that the article is reprinted from another publication.) In addition, the author does not claim such a reprinted piece as a separate and new publication—it is merely noted as having been reprinted.

Ethical Issues in Authorship

Authorship also presents several serious ethical considerations. This is an area in which graduate students and beginning researchers may be particularly vulnerable. One of the first questions relates to who should be listed as authors. *Any individual making a major contribution to the project should be listed as an author.* Obviously, the phrase "major contribution" is open to different interpretations. In this context, it is being used to reflect a contribution involving the conceptualization, design, data collection and analysis, and writing of the manuscript. Several combinations of "and/or" can be inserted between the above activities to determine whether or not authorship is warranted. Once again, this is an area in which one's best ethical judgment must prevail. The issue is mentioned because it seems that integrity occasionally wears thin when it comes time to list authors. Unfortunately, some graduate students have been taken advantage of by unscrupulous professors who only give them a footnote credit line, if that. (A credit line may be appropriate for minor contributions; however, it is *not* appropriate for substantial work involving conceptual and writing efforts.)

A publication may have multiple authors. This raises a question regarding the order of authorship. Who is to be senior author (listed first) and who will be junior author(s) (those listed second, third, and so on)? The order of authorship should be determined in relation to the level of contribution. The person making the greatest contribution should be senior author and the others listed in order of their relative efforts. If the contribution is relatively equal, order should be determined by mutual agreement, a flip of the coin, or some other method that is acceptable to those involved. If order of authorship does not denote level of contribution, the authors must acknowledge this and describe how the order was determined in a footnote at the beginning of a publication (e.g., "authors listed alphabetically"). It is important not to regard author order as a trivial matter—after all, with three authors the citation in text is often "Senior et al., 2006." Would a researcher involved really want to be *et* or *al* if he or she did much of the work? Unfortunately, not everyone adheres to fair and ethical principles when determining the order of authors. The main caution is to be aware that such breaches of integrity do occur. Intellectual property should be discussed openly and frankly regarding your rights as an author (and be certain not to take advantage of someone else) (Nagy, 2005c).

Sanctions for Breaches of Integrity

Some sanctions for unethical conduct are self-evident. Certainly, a breach of ethics that is made public is personally embarrassing and causes professional disgrace. It may cause the loss of a job and result in the inability to obtain other employment in the research community.

Most scientists belong to professional organizations, such as the American Psychological Association, the American Educational Research Association, the American Sociological Association, or some other disciplinary organization. Many of these organizations have formal codes of ethics to guide member activities. They may expel a member for unethical conduct, which is essentially an expulsion from the profession. Sanctions can be very harsh for the person who has been unethical. Each time a breach of ethics occurs, the entire field is disgraced to some degree. Although inconvenience may result, it is important to remember that ethical principles are not only in harmony with science but also represent the basic fiber from which science emerges.

Chapter Summary

+ Every researcher has the responsibility to protect participants in a research study including obtaining consent, ensuring protection from harm, and protecting privacy.

+ Informed consent ensures that each participant has a complete understanding of the purpose and methods used in the study, the risks involved, and the demands of the study.

+ Legally, informed consent involves three elements: capacity, information, and voluntariness. Capacity is a person's ability to acquire and retain knowledge. Information must be presented so it can be completely and fully understood by each participant. Voluntariness ensures each participant's ability to exercise the power of free choice without the intervention of force, fraud, deceit, duress, or other forms of coercion.

+ Consent to participate may be given by an adult, a parent, guardian, or other agent legally authorized to act on a person's behalf. There are a number of factors that determine when consent is required. The rule of thumb regarding risk factors is "when in doubt, ask for permission."

+ The most basic concern in all research is that no individual is harmed by serving as a participant in a study. Particular care should be taken with participants who are characterized as vulnerable to harm, such as people with disabilities, children, or older individuals.

+ There are several factors to consider in protecting the privacy of participants, including the sensitivity of the data in view of the individual or group being studied, the setting in which the research takes place, and how public the information is that is collected and disseminated.

+ Research deception involves the intentional misrepresentation of facts related to the purpose, nature, or consequences of a study. The use of deception must be carefully considered and justified based on significant prospective, scientific, educational, or applied value (American Psychological Association, 2002).

+ Ethical issues in quantitative research focus on protecting individuals who receive an intervention. Qualitative researchers focus on the importance of not tampering with the natural setting under study.

+ Institutional review boards (IRBs) provide assurance that no ethical violations occur in any given study. An IRB is charged with reviewing the purpose of the research and the proposed methodology as it relates to potential risk or benefits to the participants involved.

+ Any breach of integrity during the development, execution, or dissemination of results, whether it be intentional or unintentional, will seriously weaken or even invalidate a research study.

Key Terms

Capacity. An element of consent referring to a person's ability to acquire and retain knowledge.

Deception. Research deception involves an intentional misrepresentation of facts related to the purpose, nature, or consequences of an investigation. In this context, deception may refer to either an *omission* or a *commission* on the part of the researcher in terms of interactions with participants.

Ethics. Ethics in research generally means an investigator has a moral obligation to protect the participants from harm, unnecessary invasion of their privacy, and the promotion of their well-being.

Harm. In the context of research ethics, harm may be broadly defined to include extreme physical pain or death, but also involves such factors as psychological stress, personal embarrassment or humiliation, or myriad influences that may adversely affect the participants in a significant way. Protecting participants from harm is a key consideration in any research undertaken.

Information. An element of consent requiring that information pertaining to a study must be presented so it can be completely and fully understood by each participant.

Informed consent. Informed consent ensures that each participant has a complete understanding of the purpose and methods used in the study, the risks involved, and the demands of the study.

Institutional review boards. Institutional review boards (IRBs) are committees of individuals set up within universities and other organizations to provide assurance that no ethical violations occur in any given study. An IRB is charged with reviewing the purpose of the research and the proposed methodology as it relates to potential risks or benefits to the participants involved.

Integrity. Relates to the honesty of an investigator and how honestly he or she undertakes an investigation. Any breach of integrity during the execution of a research study, whether it be unintentional errors or outright falsification of the data, seriously weakens or even invalidates the investigation.

Privacy. The right of an individual to control distribution of personal information. As a rule of thumb, researchers should invade the privacy of participants as minimally as possible.

Voluntariness. Voluntariness in consent ensures each participant's ability to exercise the power of free choice without the intervention of force, fraud, deceit, duress, or other forms of coercion.

Student Study Site

The companion Web site for *Designing and Conducting Research in Education* www.sagepub.com/drewstudy

Supplement your review of this chapter by going to the companion Web site to take one of the practice quizzes, use the flashcards to study key terms, and check out the many other study aids you'll find there. You'll even find some research articles from the Sage Full-Text Collection and a step-by-step guide that will show you how to read an educational research article.

Simulation Feedback

For additional
simulations visit
www.sagepub
.com/drewstudy

Simulation Feedback 3.1

There are concerns in this simulation regarding the comparison group—they are receiving a placebo rather than the actual treatment. Is this deception? It probably is, but the investigation could be seriously jeopardized if they are specifically and fully informed that they are not receiving the treatment. This may present a rather difficult dilemma, and whether or not you are ethical depends on how procedures are handled. Perhaps you can treat the comparison group after the experiment is completed. Another question, however, must be asked regarding potential harm by withholding treatment from this group for the duration of the experiment and then treating them later. Does this create a problem? You can only make this decision after considering all the facts and issues. Review the relevant portions of the text, think carefully, and by all means obtain approval from your human subjects review committee.

4

PARTICIPANT SELECTION AND ASSIGNMENT

After reading Chapter 4, you should be able to do the following:

+ Understand what questions must be addressed in selecting participants for a research study.

+ Select a representative sample of participants who will participate in a research study.

+ Identify various sampling approaches used in designing a research study.

+ Describe the process for determining the size of the population sample needed in a given research study.

+ Determine participant selection for comparative or difference research questions.

+ Determine participant selection for relationship or correlational research questions.

+ Determine participant selection for descriptive and other research questions.

+ Describe various approaches to assigning participants to groups by chance in an experimental research study.

+ Describe various approaches to assigning participants to groups using controlled methods in an experimental research study.

This chapter examines topics that are most often used in experimental and quantitative research. There are also circumstances in qualitative investigations where the sampling of participants occurs prior to beginning data collection, and sampling is a topic of interest in qualitative research (see, for example, Denzin & Lincoln, 2005; Neuman, 2006). Sampling and assignment are part of the many activities that are involved in the implementation of a research study. Researchers must not take the attitude that these activities are merely logistics and of secondary importance. Although we emphasized the critical nature of pre-investigation planning, it is also important to remain alert during study implementation. Errors during this phase plague investigators in many disciplines and can easily destroy the worth of the most carefully laid plans (Creswell, 2005; Flick, Steinke, & Von Kardoff, 2004). In addition, a complete articulation of each step in implementation, prior to actually beginning a study, is important. Pitfalls will be avoided if the researcher attends to details in planning before they threaten the soundness of an investigation.

PARTICIPANT SELECTION

There are several questions that must be addressed in selecting participants for an investigation: Are the participants appropriate for the research question? Are the participants a **representative sample** of the population that is being studied—that is, can the results be generalized to the larger population? What should be the sample size? To assure that a study is conceptually sound, a researcher must select participants who are appropriate to the topic under study. Child development is hardly being investigated if the participants are college sophomores. Likewise, if the intellectual status of schizophrenic adults is the topic, the participants certainly ought to have been diagnosed with schizophrenia. Consideration of participant variables is a part of operationally defining the population and includes many factors to which the researcher must attend.

An important part of participant selection is the representative nature of the sample. Assuming that a researcher wants to know something about how a given population responds, participants in a study should resemble that population. Because it is doubtful that the entire population can be tested, a sample must be used that will provide results similar to those that would be obtained if the entire population had been studied. The degree to which results are generalizable, or are externally valid, is critically influenced by participant selection.

The issue of how many participants should be involved in a study is related to concerns about the generalizability of results. This difficult question is repeatedly asked by beginning research students. Determining sample size is a challenge because no set answer or rule may be given. Several factors influence decisions regarding an adequate sample size.

Defining the Population

Operationally defining the population under investigation is fundamental, both with respect to identifying appropriate participants for the research question and obtaining a representative sample. A *population* refers to all constituents of any clearly described group of people, events, or objects who are the focus of an investigation. Populations may be quite large (theoretically infinite) or they may be fairly small. For example, a population might be defined as "all third-year nursing students in the United States who are enrolled in degree programs." This population would include a rather large number of individuals who are potential participants. However, one additional restriction in the definition would dramatically reduce the size of this population. If the population were to be defined as "all third-year *male* nursing students in the United States who are enrolled in degree programs," the number of potential participants would be much smaller. The essential factor in population definition involves the units or restrictions that are used to describe the set. In the first example, four restrictions were used in the definition: (1) nursing students, (2) third year of study, (3) in the United States, and (4) enrolled in degree programs. Unless the population is clearly defined, the researcher does not know what units or restrictions to use when selecting the sample of participants (Fraenkel & Wallen, 2006). In addition, without a clearly defined set of characteristics, it is unclear to whom the results are generalizable.

Descriptive Characteristics of Population

The descriptive characteristics used in defining a given research population must relate to the topic under study. If one is investigating some aspect of measured intelligence, then it is logical that the population definition includes some unit that reflects intelligence specifications. Restrictions in the definition are intended to exclude participants with unwanted characteristics. This is an important factor in conducting a precise study and should happen before the study begins rather than making hasty decisions in the field. In the example of nursing students, the population was defined as being enrolled in degree programs. By this definition, the researcher is not interested in students who are enrolled in diploma programs (degree versus diploma is a distinction made in the professional training of nurses), and such students are not eligible to be participants in the study. Often, additional restrictions are added to population statements, such as, "Individuals with marked visual, hearing, or emotional problems that could potentially interfere with task performance will be eliminated before sampling." Such restrictions involve participant properties that are not a part of the investigation and therefore are not part of the study. The following Research in Action box illustrates two action research studies where the characteristics for participants are defined and certain restrictions are specified ("without any diagnosed learning problems" and "None of the Latino students can be classified as a student with English as a Second Language").

RESEARCH IN ACTION

KEY POINTS IN THE CHAPTER REFLECTED IN THIS BOX:

- Defining the population and being specific about participant characteristics.
- Determining how many participants will be needed.
- Deciding on details of participant selection.
- Deciding how participants will be assigned to groups.

For more research in action tips visit www.sagepub .com/drewstudy

OBJECTIVES TO LEARN FROM THIS BOX:

- Understand how action researchers proceed to define the population being studied and are specific about participant characteristics.
- Understand what action researchers consider in determining how many participants will be needed.
- Understand what action researchers consider in determining the details of participant selection.
- Understand what action researchers consider in deciding how participants will be assigned to groups.

SCENARIO 1: STUDENT ENGAGEMENT IN READING

Emily is conducting a study comparing two groups of students, one receiving concept-oriented reading instruction (CORI) and a second being taught using drill and practice (DAP) on words and sentences. She needs to define her population carefully and decides that she will need second- and third-grade students without any diagnosed learning problems. She is going to implement her instructional sessions outside of the regular curriculum, conducting instructional sessions as separate augmentations to the regular school day. She decides that her population definition will therefore have restrictions and not include any students with identified academic or behavioral disabilities.

In planning ahead for her study, Emily determines that she is going to need about 25 participants in each group. Ideally she could sample 50 participants and randomly assign half to the CORI group and half to the DAP group. But in many action research settings this is not possible. So she is going to use intact classrooms with careful attention to average student abilities so one group will not be at a disadvantage over the other. She is also going to find teachers that have similar expertise, experience, and performance evaluations to try to create approximate equivalency between teachers. In order to allow for some dropouts and also to get closer to equivalent situations between the two groups, she decides to use five classrooms in each condition, combining the data for all five CORI classes into the CORI grouping and all five DAP classes into the DAP grouping. Since Emily is in a large urban district, this type of sampling is very feasible. The district prides itself as one that is involved in research to improve practice. The Superintendent and the Board of Education are very proud of this philosophy. Emily is going to use the whole district as her population frame and sample 10 classes from that frame. Then she can establish a good working relationship with the teachers for each condition.

SOURCE: This action research scenario is roughly based on Swan, E. A. (2003). *Concept-oriented reading instruction: Engaging classrooms, lifelong learners.* New York: Guilford Press.

SCENARIO 2: STUDENT SELF-ESTEEM

Daniel is conducting a study to see if his students with learning disabilities have different self-esteem depending on whether they are of Latino or Caucasian descent. He is defining his population as middle school students from grades seven through nine, in resource rooms who are identified as having learning disabilities. All students will have a measured IQ between 85 and 115 and will have a severe discrepancy between their ability and academic scores in at least one area (math calculation, reading comprehension, or written expression). Within this population he is also defining one subpopulation as those of Latino descent (at least second-generation Americans) and a second as being Caucasian. None of the Latino students can be classified as a student with English as a Second Language (ESL).

Daniel decided that he wants a minimum of 15 participants in each of his groups. So he will set his goal of sampling at least 15 Latino students and 15 Caucasian students, all with learning disabilities. This number he believes is minimal to use the statistics he wants for comparing the two groups so he is planning ahead. In order to accomplish this Daniel decides he is going to sample 20 participants for each group, knowing that having more will not hurt him and that he is likely to lose some through attrition. Daniel decides to use stratified random sampling with one strata designated for the Latino group and the second for the Caucasian group. All characteristics between the two strata are defined exactly the same so the two groups should come out very close to equivalent in all characteristics except racial background.

Think about this: For both action research studies in this box, what characteristics are key for defining the populations? Write two lists that include the population characteristics for each study. How many participants will be needed for each action research study and why? How will participants be assigned to groups for each study?

SOURCE: This action research scenario is roughly based on Rubin, D. (2000). *Race and self-esteem: A study of Latino and European-American students with learning disabilities.* Unpublished masters thesis, University of Utah, Salt Lake City.

Following the definition of the population, the researcher must obtain or construct a complete list of all individuals in the population. This list is known as a *population frame.* The construction of a frame can be an extremely difficult and laborious task unless such a listing is already available. Occasionally it is impossible to construct a complete frame as defined by the population (e.g., listing all the fish in Lake Erie).

If it becomes impossible to construct a precise population frame, the researcher may find it necessary to work with a more restricted sample. For example, resources may not permit the construction of a population frame for "all fourth-grade students in the state of Oregon." The experimenter may then decide to form what is known as a *participant pool* by selecting a number of districts throughout the state that are representative of the larger population. From this participant pool, a sample can be drawn to actually participate in the study. Figure 4.1 represents an illustration of this procedure.

This is not an uncommon field procedure and, if implemented with care, it can provide very acceptable results. The participant pool in Figure 4.1 has some advantages beyond cost savings. An investigation is seldom conducted without at least some participant mortality (meaning some drop out, not actual deaths). When participants are lost from the sample, the participant pool can be used as a replacement pool for selecting new participants. Since the original sample was drawn from this

FIGURE 4.1   **Participant Selection Using a Participant Pool**

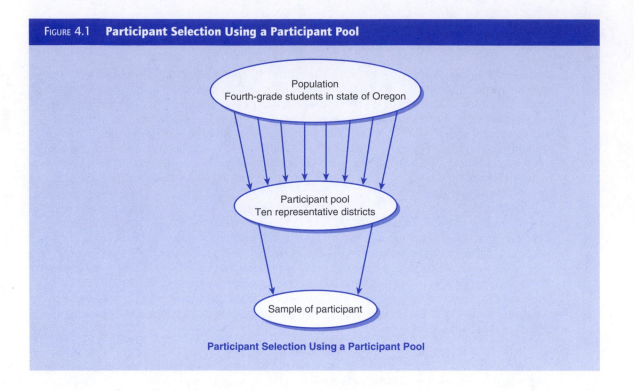

Participant Selection Using a Participant Pool

same source, there is little reason to believe that replacement participants will be different from those selected initially. A researcher will occasionally form a participant pool even when a complete population frame is available. This is done in order to replace participants who are lost or deleted from a study due to procedural errors. This arrangement helps the study implementation because returning to the complete population frame is unnecessary.

Selecting a Representative Sample

Once the researcher has a frame from which to sample, the next task is to select participants who will take part in the study. The sample to be studied must accurately represent the larger population. If the sample is not accurate, interpretations of results may not be accurate for individuals other than those actually used as participants. If a researcher is not aware that a sample is unrepresentative, he or she may draw inaccurate inferences about the population.

A representative sample is crucial at two points during the process of selecting participants. Initially, construction of the participant pool must receive careful attention to ensure a representative group. The earlier example concerning fourth-grade students illustrates this point. If the 10 districts selected for the participant pool are not representative of the state population, any sample drawn from that pool will not produce results that are generalizable to the larger population. The second point at which the researcher must be cautious is when the actual sample is selected from the participant pool. Identical issues are involved here; simply stated, the sample must be representative of the pool if results are to generalize to that pool, and if the participant pool is representative of the population, then results should be generalizable to the population at large.

Simulation

For additional simulations visit www.sagepub .com/drewstudy

Simulation 4.1

For this simulation and in examples throughout this chapter, you will need a random number table such as Table 4.1.

Topic: Population definition

Background statement: This simulation represents one part of a population frame construction for sampling purposes. The population is defined as "all third-year male students enrolled at Whereami State University." Computer printout material was generated for all students and coded with the digit 1 for first-year students, 2 for second-year students, and so on.

Tasks to be performed: Construct a portion of the population frame from the list presented. Do so by placing an X by each name that will become part of that population frame.

Bacco, E. Donald	1		Barnes, Linda E	2	
Bach, Jay T.	3		Barnes, Mike L.	3	
Bachman, Thomas	4		Barnes, Scott	2	
Back, Donald R.	2		Barnhart, Cyrus E	1	
Back, Laura J.	6		Barnumm, Daniel	4	
Backer, Jane Z.	3		Bennett, Ellen	6	
Backman, Fred	1		Berg, William J.	3	
Bacon, Robert F.	3		Bernard, Clifford	4	
Badger, Mike	3		Berrett, Colleen	3	
Bagley, David	6		Best, Sandy	4	
Bagley, Penny	2		Bigelow, Randy L.	3	
Bailey, Bob Jo	3		Bigelow, Robert W.	3	
Baird, James V	6		Bragg, Raymond J.	3	
Baird, Sally Jo	1		Brassiere, Newland	1	
Banks, Vernon L.	4		Burns, Sallie	2	
Bannon, Diane	2		Burton, Archibald	4	
Barber, Anne L.	2		Butkus, Lowell Tom	1	
Barber, Jeanne	1				
Barclay, Larry	3				
Bardin, Robyne Anne	3				
Barger, George	3				
Barker, James R.	3				
Barker, Sara	4				

Write your response, then turn to page 108 for Simulation Feedback 4.1.

TABLE 4.1   Random Number Table

			Column			
Line	1	2	3	4	5	6
1	10480	15011	01536	02011	81647	91646
2	22368	46573	25595	85393	30995	89198
3	24130	48360	22527	97265	76393	64809
4	42167	93093	06243	61680	07856	16376
5	37570	39975	81837	16656	06121	91782
6	77921	06907	11008	42751	27756	53948
7	99562	72905	56420	69994	98872	31016
8	96301	91977	05463	07972	18876	20922
9	88579	14342	63661	10281	17453	18103
10	85475	36857	53342	53988	53060	59533
11	28918	69578	88231	33276	70997	79936
12	63553	40961	48235	03427	49626	69445
13	09429	93969	52636	92737	88974	33488
14	10365	97336	87529	85689	48237	52267
15	07119	61129	71048	08178	77233	13916
16	51085	12765	51821	51259	77452	16308
17	02368	21382	52404	60268	89368	19885
18	01011	54092	33362	94904	31273	04146
19	52162	53916	46369	58586	23216	06691
20	07056	96728	33787	09998	42698	06691
21	48663	91245	85828	14346	09172	30168
22	54164	58492	22421	74103	47070	25306
23	32639	32363	05597	24200	13363	38005
24	29334	27001	87637	87308	58731	00256
25	02488	33062	28834	07351	19731	92420

Sampling Approaches

Several different sampling procedures are used in the behavioral sciences. The conditions of the study determine which procedures are to be used. The crucial nature of participant selection demands that researchers use the most appropriate and rigorous technique possible.

Simple Random Sampling

Random sampling is probably the best-known method of selecting participants to obtain a sample representative of the population. **Simple random sampling** (sometimes called unrestricted random sampling) is a selection process where each individual in the population frame has an equal chance of being chosen. Because each person has an equal chance of being selected, it is presumed that the population characteristics will be represented similarly to the degree that they exist in the population. A random sample does not totally guarantee that all the population characteristics will, in fact, be represented in the sample. However, because chance is used to construct the sample, random sampling greatly reduces the possibility that a biased or unrepresentative group will be selected. More confidence may be placed in the representativeness of the sample when the population is homogeneous with regard to its characteristics. This simply means there is less diversity to be represented. Similarly, when the population is more heterogeneous, there is a greater chance that all features of the diversity will not be represented simply because of the greater variation.

Procedures used to select a random sample are simple and easily implemented. Any technique that ensures that all individuals in the population frame are equally likely to be selected will suffice. For example, drawing names from a fishbowl will approximate a random selection process. It is necessary to have the names on individual slips of paper and to mix them well. Similarly, the names might all be placed on cards that are shuffled, after which the desired number of participant cards is selected from the deck. The shuffling procedure must be conducted carefully, however, if a random sample is to be approximated. Studies have indicated that casual shuffling does not approximate a chance mixing of cards. Probably the most effective procedure for random sampling is also one of the simplest: using a table of random numbers. This technique requires the researcher to assign consecutive numbers to each individual listed in the population frame. This is easy—just make a list of all individuals in the frame and put numbers beside them. Once this is accomplished, a table of random numbers is used to select those who will serve as participants. (Tables of random numbers are found in appendixes of many statistics books, or one might use specially prepared books of tables such as the *CRC Standard Probability and Statistics Tables and Formulae* [Zwillinger, 2000]). To use a random number table, begin with any number in the table and read systematically in any direction (vertically or horizontally). When a number is encountered that matches one of the assigned numbers in the population frame, then that individual becomes a participant. Numbers that are not a part of the frame list are ignored (e.g., if the number 386 appears in the table when the population frame includes only 300 individuals, it is ignored). Numbers already selected are ignored once they become part of the sample (e.g., the second time that 46 appears in the table). This procedure continues until the desired number of participants is obtained. A random number table may be found at the end of this chapter.

Stratified Random Sampling

Stratified random sampling is a useful procedure when the investigation being conducted requires participant selection from more than one population. Such circumstances may exist if the researcher wishes to study two or more groups of individuals who are distinctly different on the basis of some characteristic that is important to the research (the quasi-experimental design discussed earlier in this text). An example of such a situation is a developmental study in which three different age-level groups are being compared on a given learning task. Because developmental level is a part of the investigation, formulation of the three groups at different age levels must occur. One cannot expect to obtain three distinct age-level groupings by random sampling from a single population.

The different developmental levels in this example actually form three different subpopulations known as *strata*. Each subpopulation or stratum constitutes a group to which the researcher may wish to generalize results. For sampling purposes, each stratum must have participants selected from it as if three miniature experiments were being conducted. The participant group for each age level will have to be sampled in a fashion that makes that group representative of the age level of subpopulations being studied. An effective way to accomplish this is to use stratified random sampling from each of the respective subpopulations.

Stratified random sampling is conducted in much the same way as simple random sampling. Once each of the strata is clearly defined, a subpopulation listing or frame is constructed of the individuals who are potential participants. In the example of a developmental study, three frames would be necessary, one for each age range (e.g., group A, 3–5 years; group B, 6–8 years; group C, 9–11 years). The researcher then randomly samples from strata A, B, and C until the desired number of participants is obtained for each.

Stratified random sampling provides a convenient method of obtaining representative samples from the subpopulations. In addition, other variables may be held constant to equalize groups on characteristics other than the one under study. Using our developmental investigation as an example, it is usually desirable to have the different age groups be similar on characteristics like measured intelligence. To accomplish this, measured intelligence is defined in common across groups—that is, all groups are constituted so they have equivalent measured intelligence. You then randomly sample from all the children who were 3–5 years of age who had a measured intelligence between, say, 90 and 110. Next you sample from those 6–8 years of age with measured intelligence between 90 and 110, and so on. There is little reason to expect intelligence differences between groups using this procedure. It is wise, however, to check on this assumption before beginning the experiment. This can be very simply done by computing group IQ means and testing for differences between the groups. If groups are different, samples should be redrawn from each subpopulation until the IQ variable is equivalent between groups. In practice, the control variable means are so similar that equality is obvious even before statistical testing (although you will want to compute the statistics to provide the evidence).

Stratified random sampling is also useful in other situations. Occasionally, the logistics of a large study may make simple random sampling from the total population difficult (e.g., if a national survey is being conducted with field offices located throughout the nation). Administrative convenience may suggest that the regional responsibility of a given field office should be defined as a stratum and that a sample be drawn randomly from that subpopulation. If the sample is drawn with care, there is little reason to expect that it will not represent the stratum. In fact, the combined sample of all strata should represent the larger population.

Proportional Sampling

Some situations may result in unrepresentative samples using either simple or stratified random sampling. For example, such a condition might be found if a particular subgroup of the defined population were a 10% proportion of the total population. In the previous discussion of stratified sampling, we implied that the subpopulation samples would be the same size. This approach would overrepresent the 10% group because without special attention, the subgroups would carry equal weight, which would therefore not accurately reflect the subgroup's actual proportion of the population. To avoid such an error in representation (particularly when the subgroups will be combined to form a single larger sample), it is often useful to sample from subgroups in the same proportion that they exist in the larger total population. This procedure is known as **proportional sampling.**

Proportional sampling can be done in the same fashion as the stratified approach. Subpopulation frames are constituted, after which a sample is drawn from each. The difference in this case is that each subgroup sample is drawn only in the proportion that it exists in the larger population. For example, if two subgroups exist in the population (e.g., nurses), one constituting 90% (female nurses) and the second only 10% (male nurses), then the composite sample from both subpopulations would represent a 90% to 10% split using proportional representation. You can achieve this by randomly selecting participants from one frame (female nurses) until 90% of the total sample has been obtained and then selecting for the second group (male nurses), which constitutes the remaining 10%.

Proportional sampling is used in investigations that have a different purpose from those using equally represented strata. For investigations like the developmental study discussed earlier, with the three different age-level groups, equalized stratified samples are most appropriate. The developmental example is the type of study in which the subsamples are going to be maintained separately and, perhaps, compared. This type of study is different from the national survey example about student nurses where the strata samples will ultimately be combined in a large sample to be totally representative of a national population. In the latter case, the purpose of the study does not include a comparison of the subsamples. Because the inference is aimed more at describing the total national population, representative proportions are more important and proportional sampling would probably be used. This would prevent male nurses from being overrepresented when describing the population.

Systematic Sampling

Systematic sampling is a convenient procedure that has some inherent flaws and should be used very rarely. This type of sampling can produce a representative sample *only* if the population frame is arranged appropriately. Imagine that a sample of 100 participants is to be drawn from a population frame of 1,000. The first task to be performed is to establish what is known as the *sample interval.* Divide the population frame by the size of sample to be drawn. In this example, 100 would be divided into 1,000, resulting in a sample interval of 10. Now the researcher must determine at which point in the population frame to begin drawing participants. This can be accomplished by randomly selecting any number from the first interval. After this has been done, participants are selected by choosing every kth individual from the frame until the desired sample size is obtained. Suppose the randomly identified beginning number in the example was 7. The first participant would be the individual numbered 7 in the frame; then, using the sample interval of 10, numbers 17, 27, 37, 47, and so on, would be drawn until you had selected 100 participants.

Systematic sampling is easily executed in field operations. The precision with which a systematic sample represents the population is equal to that of random sampling *if* the population frame list is arranged in a random order. A variety of precautionary checks are necessary to avoid sample problems. The major point of difficulty involves possible trends in the frame list that would result in systematic bias. For example, if the frame is constructed in a way that individuals are listed in an order of increasing age, bias can easily occur. Because of the systematic age progression from the beginning to the end of the list, two separate samples may be very different depending on the beginning number. The earlier example that began at 7 would have older individuals than a sample that begins at 2 or 3. In either case, the sample mean age may be quite different than the population mean age, making the sample unrepresentative. Similarly, an alphabetically constructed frame may result in a biased sample if influential variables related to surname are operative in the population. Examples of this type of problem may include concentrated pockets of minority groups that have characteristic surnames. Consequently, the usefulness of systematic sampling is determined by the degree to which the arrangement of the population frame is free of influential trends. Identification of a problem area is usually based on logic and experience—that is, you examine the way the population frame list is arranged to avoid sampling errors. There is no checklist of "problems to avoid" that is relevant in all situations. Sampling often requires that a researcher combine component techniques to achieve a desired outcome. This can be done well but requires careful thinking through the process to avoid mistakes that result in unrepresentative samples.

Cluster Sampling

Quite often a researcher will not find it possible or practical to list all individuals who are potential participants when constructing a population frame. It may be that the individuals are already grouped into clusters in some way (e.g., a school or geographical regions would constitute a cluster of students or people). **Cluster sampling** is a procedure whereby the researcher lists all the clusters and takes samples from this list. Thus, instead of sampling individual members of the population, a sample cluster is initially selected from which the participants are then obtained (Best & Kahn, 2006; Knottnerus, 2003; Levy & Lemeshow, 2003). Suppose the researcher was conducting a study involving junior high school students in a large metropolitan area. Rather than constructing the population frame by listing all the junior high students in the area, the investigator lists all the junior high schools (clusters). From this list, a random sample of schools may be drawn, and then actual participants will be selected from those schools. The researcher may elect to use all the students available in the selected clusters or only a sample from those clusters.

Cluster sampling is similar to the participant pool arrangement discussed earlier in this section. Like with participant pools, researchers have to be cautious that the cluster initially selected is representative of the total population. If the clusters are drawn in a manner in which the researcher can have confidence in generalizability, that confidence should be warranted regarding participants sampled from those clusters.

Double Sampling

Double sampling (sometimes called two-phase sampling) is a procedure that is often useful for survey research. The term describes the process pretty well: an investigator accesses the participant twice for data. Two situations warrant the use of double sampling. The first involves situations where the researcher needs an intense or more in-depth follow-up data collection with part of a larger primary sample. Such an investigation may be initiated with a rather large sample, using an inexpensive survey instrument. With the results from the first instrument in hand, a researcher can then sample a smaller group from the first round of participants for purposes of obtaining more detailed data. This smaller group of participants is usually sampled in a way that will ensure a representative sample of the original larger group. It is not unusual for this smaller group sampling to also be accomplished using random procedures.

A second use of double sampling is an attempt to gather missing data. This procedure, which is used most often in survey research, is used to gather the information that is absent because participants failed to return questionnaires during the first phase. The missing data may alter the results of the investigation if those who fail to complete the first questionnaire are, in some fashion, different from participants who do return the instrument. By virtue of their failure to respond, it is probably true that these participants are somehow different (e.g., in their attitude or motivation). To preserve the integrity of the first sample, the researcher may implement the next phase by drawing a second sample from nonrespondents. Usually, the second phase involves procedures that are more persuasive in eliciting responses, such as face-to-face interviews. Caution must be exercised in assuming that the second-phase data are the same as that obtained in the first phase. Certainly, the participants are from the same first sample, but the research conditions have now changed. Even so, double sampling may preserve sample integrity to a greater degree than selecting new participants from the replacement pool.

Sample Size

A question that is frequently asked by beginning researchers is, "How many participants do I need?" This question is often difficult to answer because there is no sample size rule that is correct under all conditions. Given different circumstances, larger or smaller samples may serve adequately. If you are interested in more information regarding appropriate samples, you might review texts that examine this topic in detail (e.g., Knottnerus, 2003; Levy & Lemeshow, 2003).

One rule that does apply regarding **sample size** is that an adequate sample of behavior must be obtained. Certain characteristics of the population will dictate how large the sample must be to accurately predict population factors. If there is little variation in the population (i.e., if the population is homogeneous), a much smaller sample will suffice than if more variation is present. High variability within the population indicates that the sample must be larger to permit more of that variation to be represented in the participants selected. Behavioral science is plagued by considerably more variability than, for example, agriculture or biology. Consequently, samples in behavioral science usually require a larger population proportion for accurate generalization.

How does one determine population variability? The answer to this question is often unsatisfying. Only an estimate of population characteristics can be obtained. If the researcher is conducting an investigation on a given population, there will be some unknowns regarding that population. However, clues about the population's variance may be available in previously published research. Some populations have been shown to be more variable than others over the years. Greater variability is evident, for example, in populations that are quite different on some psychological dimension. People with mental retardation or other disabilities are, for example, more variable in most performance areas than individuals without such conditions (Drew & Hardman, 2007; Hardman, Drew, & Egan, 2006). A researcher can expect more error variance in any group of people with mental retardation, making an adequate sample necessarily larger. Information concerning such variability can often be found in the published literature. In the absence of specific published information (e.g., in the case of a beginning effort in that area), it is usually prudent to proceed cautiously. A pilot study may be useful for obtaining guidance, or the first phase of a double-sampling design may also provide initial information concerning participant characteristics. Often, the early stages of a research program are conducted with a conservative attitude that leads the researcher to obtain larger samples.

Experimental studies asking difference questions are often designed so that the total sample of participants is divided into two or more groups. When treatments are applied to these smaller groups, they essentially become subsamples of the larger group. Therefore, a researcher must consider the number of treatment groups involved rather than the total number of participants in the experiment. For example, an investigator may select 60 participants for an experiment in reading. Suppose the study is designed so that six experimental conditions are required. If these are independent conditions, such an experiment would require that the total sample (N) be assigned in some fashion to six different groups, resulting in a sample size (n) of 10. This sample is placed together in a compartment, referred to as a cell.

A cell n of 10 participants is a rather small sample of behavior that may prove to be inadequate. With only 10 participants per cell, the treatment mean is more vulnerable to change by an atypical performance than if the group were larger.

If researchers do not consider cell size from the outset, they may be dissatisfied with such small subgroups. The most prudent approach to avoiding this difficulty is to determine the desired cell n ahead of time and let the total N be determined by adding together the group n's. Our general rule of thumb is that cell n's should not be smaller than 12–14 (although at times other logistic concerns force deviation from this personal rule). More confidence may be placed in cell sizes of 20–25, which results in rather large sample N's in more complex experiments. Clearly, non-experimental investigations also ask questions regarding subgroups that may be formed for comparisons (Hutchinson, 2004; Nardi, 2006; Neuman, 2006). The subgroups in any study must be of adequate size to provide a credible sample of behavior, opinions, or other data.

It should now be clear that there is no agreement about the "magic" minimal number of participants necessary for a sound study. The number of participants is a serious concern to design strength and research outcomes (see, for example, Lall & Levin, 2004; Lei & Dunbar, 2004). There is even great variability within particular methods. For example, any review of survey studies will show considerable variation between surveys that take regional samples versus those that take national samples. In general, national surveys often use samples of 1,000 or more, whereas regional studies vary considerably but will often use smaller samples. As we noted earlier, experimental studies tend to use much smaller samples than survey research. The best guidance can be found by reviewing recent literature in the area being studied. Current research will provide the clearest indication of "present professional practice" for those substantive areas.

The researcher must also be aware of certain statistical requirements when determining sample size. Frequently, limited participant availability will result in samples that are smaller than desirable. Under such conditions, it may be necessary to alter the statistical analyses that are to be used. A more complete discussion of this topic is found in Part III of this book.

Participant Selection for Different Purposes

Our discussion of participant selection has been quite general up to this point. In this section, we will discuss issues that relate to the type of question being asked.

Comparative or Difference Questions

Two basic concerns of comparison studies are internal and external validity. To recount briefly, internal validity refers to the technical soundness of a study, whereas external validity has to do with generalizability of results. The researcher who is selecting participants for a comparative investigation must attend to both internal and external validity. There may be times during an investigation when concerns about internal validity tend to diminish the generalizability of results. In Chapter 9, this tension is discussed in relation to experimental procedures, but similar conditions exist regarding participant selection. Participants selected for a study must be appropriate for the topic being investigated. If the research question involves studying developmental trends in learning math facts, for example, then several age-level groups might be compared. To accomplish this, stratified age groups are formed with a defined age gap between groups. However, by forcing the composition of such groupings, the generalizability of results may be somewhat restricted.

This statement about restrictions on generalizability does not mean that results do not generalize at all. Indeed, if adequate stratified sampling procedures have been employed, there is reason to believe that the within-group results will generalize. The point being made is that children progress somewhat continuously through a sequence of ages. It is doubtful that the results of such a stratified experiment will generalize completely to children who fall between the experimentally contrived strata. Therefore, results are somewhat restricted regarding external validity by the experimental arrangements necessary for constructing an internally valid study.

A researcher may wish to sacrifice some rigor in either internal or external validity to emphasize the other dimension. Depending on the stage of a program of research, it may be appropriate to concentrate on one type of validity at the expense of the second. Early in a program of research, an investigator may be more concerned with internal validity to ensure a purer examination of basic knowledge. As the research program progresses and data begin to accumulate, more attention may be focused on the generalizability of results. Such changes in emphasis regarding internal and external validity will likely be reflected in participant-selection procedures. As the program of research progresses, it is likely that the researcher will attend more closely to the broadest possible generalizability, and therefore the representativeness of the sample. This is different from a sampling focus that may be used early in a research program. At the initial stages, a researcher is likely to be most concerned that the participants are appropriate to the topic under study. Generalizability is then limited in terms of the broader population of possible individuals to whom results might apply in the future.

Relationship or Correlational Questions

Participant selection for relationship questions is different from selection for comparison questions. The purpose of correlational questions is to demonstrate the degree to which characteristics relate to one another. The reasons for investigating relationships usually involve predicting one variable or set of variables on the basis of measurements taken on the other variable. An example of a correlational study is the use of entrance exam scores to predict college achievement (often in the form of grades). This prediction is based on correlations between entrance exam scores and college grades obtained for previous students. If the relationship determined in a particular study does not generalize to the larger group for which prediction is desirable, the study has lost its value. Therefore, in selecting participants, one must be sure the sample is representative of the population for which prediction is desired.

There are some characteristics of correlational studies that relate results directly to sample selection. One specific factor is the variability in the sample. With a heterogeneous group of individuals, the correlation coefficient will be higher than with a more homogeneous group. If the sample is more heterogeneous (more variable) than the population, the prediction will not be accurate for the larger population. Likewise, if the sample is more homogeneous than the population, the observed relationship (predictive ability) may be lower than is actually possible in the larger population. This highlights the importance of selecting representative samples in all phases of research programs that ask relationship questions.

Descriptive Questions

The researcher investigating a descriptive question intends to describe the characteristics, opinions, or behaviors of a given group, culture, or setting. Participant selection for a descriptive study must emphasize one concern—accuracy of the description (external validity). A descriptive investigation that does not accurately characterize the group being studied is worthless and misleading. Therefore, a representative sample is of crucial importance in the planning of a descriptive study.

Other Questions

Our discussion thus far has focused on sampling procedures within the context of research. A variety of sampling approaches may be effectively used for questions that are not primarily of a research nature. For example, prediction is also undertaken in nonresearch settings such as forecasting election outcomes on Election

Day. Within the last few years, election prediction has become very sophisticated. Many people are amazed when winners are selected accurately with only 1% (often less) of the returns counted. Certainly, such a small sample would make researchers very nervous, particularly if it were not a random sample. However, the procedures used in election prediction are extremely accurate and you cannot argue with success. One reason for such accuracy is that the election sample is not randomly undertaken. A procedure known as *purposive sampling* is used, whereby data are obtained from a particular district that has consistently voted for winners. Because of this consistency over time, that district serves as a better prediction than a random sample of several districts.

Convenience sampling is another example of nonrandom sampling. Participants are selected on the basis of availability, such as students in a college English literature class, or members of a high school hockey team. This procedure is often used when random sampling is not feasible, such as when studying the relationship between participation in varsity sports and academic achievement in an urban high school. In this study, external validity is an obvious problem when using convenience sampling because there is no way to generalize from the convenience sample to a larger population of high school students. However, the primary purpose of this study is to better understand whether or not a relationship may exist. Generalization to a larger population sample is therefore of secondary importance. The findings should not be dismissed out of hand but should be analyzed within the context of the students being studied.

Quota sampling is another nonrandom sampling procedure. This procedure is used when the researcher is unable to use random sampling, but wants a subset of a larger population to which the results can be generalized. As suggested by McMillan (2004), quota sampling involves identifying different composite profiles of major groups in the population, after which subjects are selected nonrandomly to represent each group. An example of quota sampling in educational research may be sampling special education teachers who teach specific areas of disability, such as learning disabilities, emotional disturbance, or autism.

A complete examination of sampling is far beyond the scope of an introductory design text. However, there are complete volumes that focus solely on sampling (e.g., Knottnerus, 2003; Levy & Lemeshow, 2003) for both research and nonresearch questions.

PARTICIPANT ASSIGNMENT

The process of assigning participants to groups is most commonly associated with experimental research, particularly traditional experimental studies. Consequently, this discussion will be primarily couched in terms of experimentation. Researchers involved in nonexperimental comparisons should attend to those issues in this section that may be generalized to nonexperimental approaches. The main focus of participant assignment is the concept of control, which has relevance to all comparisons—experimental or nonexperimental.

Experiments address different questions that involve comparisons between two or more performances. These performances may be the result of a variety of designs such as (a) baseline versus postintervention comparisons in time-series research, (b) pretreatment versus posttreatment comparisons with a single group of participants, or (c) comparisons of two or more groups on a single-performance test. The primary concern of this section is comparing multiple groups that involve sets or collections of participants for the conditions and also require the participants to be assigned to those groups.

Participant assignment in multigroup experiments is an important component of an internally valid study. The problem is how to divide those individuals who are a part of the sample into groups that will receive the different treatments. For example, how does the researcher assign students to reading groups in an experiment that is comparing the effectiveness of three different teaching methods (A, B, or C)? The concept of control refers to the notion that these groups need to be equal in all respects with the exception of the variable under investigation. Therefore, if Teaching Method A is being compared with Method B, the difference in teaching methods should be the only way in which the two groups are not equivalent. The notion of control is *the* central issue in internal validity. Participant assignment to groups is the primary technique for ensuring control.

Assignment by Chance

Assignment of participants to different treatment conditions is often accomplished using a chance procedure. Although this procedure seems to imply that participant assignment is "left to chance," it in no way means that the procedure is unplanned or haphazard. In fact, chance assignment refers to a carefully planned and executed technique in which the researcher uses random selection to form the groups for the study.

Prior to our discussion of assignment approaches, a clear distinction needs to be made between random assignment and random sampling. Random sampling is a separate procedure from random assignment and has a different purpose. The purpose of random sampling is to obtain a representative sample from the population, as we have discussed before. This is important for purposes of generalizing results to the greater population (external validity). Random assignment of participants to different conditions is a technique used by researchers to constitute equivalent groups. The purpose of random assignment is *group* equivalency, since individual variation or individual differences within groups will remain. Another concern is to ensure that participant properties (e.g., motivation or intellect) existing during the pretreatment phase are equivalent. Hopefully, this will permit any posttreatment differences to be attributed to the treatment, which cannot be accomplished without such equivalence (see, for example, Kazdin, 2003). Random assignment involves procedures where participants are assigned to groups in such a way that each participant has an equal chance of being placed in any of the treatment or comparison groups. Within this general procedure, there are several techniques for actual implementation.

Captive Assignment

In some cases, researchers will have the total sample identified and available at the outset of the investigation (as opposed to situations in which all the participants are not present at one time). The participants in this situation are "captive" and we use what is called **captive assignment.** This makes it possible to actually know, from the beginning, which participants, by name, will be in which experimental group. Consequently, somewhat different operational procedures are used to randomly assign participants.

When a researcher has the total sample captive, procedures for random assignment to the experimental conditions are simple. Individuals in the sample are listed by name, forming a sample frame. Once this is completed, the experimenter executes what is essentially a miniature random sample for each of the treatment groups. This might be done using the famous fishbowl technique. Participants are assigned consecutive numbers from 1 to N. These numbers are then written on individual slips of paper, placed in a fishbowl (or hat, or other container), and thoroughly mixed. Placing the participant's name on the slip rather than a corresponding number can also be done. Once either names or numbers are in the receptacle, the participant groups may be randomly drawn. If, for example, the study involved two conditions, the first half of the total sample drawn from the fishbowl forms the first group n and the remaining sample constitutes the second group. Thus, if the sample N equaled 50 individuals, the first 25 slips of paper drawn would constitute the group for treatment A, and the remaining 25 would be assigned to Treatment B. The researcher may choose another procedure to achieve the same end. For example, the decision may be to use the first participant for Group A, the second for B, the third for A, the fourth for B, and so on, in an alternating fashion until both groups are complete. In either case, there is little reason to suspect that bias has been systematically introduced that would make the group different.

Random number tables may also be used efficiently to assign participants to groups. As before, it is necessary to make a list of the participants in some sort of order. This process could be conveniently done with an alphabetical listing. Once this is completed, the random number table is used to assign treatment to the participants in consecutive order beginning with the first name and proceeding through the list. Using the previous example in which there were two experimental conditions, the researcher would be interested only in the digits 1 and 2 as they appeared in the table, with each digit representing one of the groups. The researcher can then begin at any point in the random unit table and proceed systematically in any direction (horizontally or vertically). If the first digit encountered is 2, the participant in the first list position is assigned to Group 2. If the second and third digits are 1, those individuals occupying the second and third list positions are assigned to Group 1. This procedure is continued until all groups are completed. The researcher ignores irrelevant digits (those other than 1 or 2 in this example) and similarly ignores either 1 or 2 after that respective group n is completed. Therefore, after the 25th participant is assigned to Group 2, any further encounters with 2 in the table are ignored. Using the random number table is generally more convenient than drawing from a fishbowl, particularly when large numbers of participants are involved.

Sequential Assignment

Often researchers do not have the entire sample captive (the actual names are not all present before beginning the study) and a different assignment procedure is necessary. A **sequential assignment** method is often used in these circumstances. In a situation in which researchers do not have the exact sample drawn, they may be operating from a participant pool (drawn in a representative fashion). Consequently, the researchers do not know exactly which individuals from that pool will ultimately serve as participants. In addition, the experiment may be conducted over a period of time rather than at a single sitting. Under these conditions, the researchers may gather data on three or four participants one day, another three or four the next, and so on. Individuals from the participant pool show up for the study on a sequential basis. When they do present themselves, the participants must be assigned to one of the treatment conditions in a fashion that will guard against the formulation of biased or unequal groups. Such a setting is not at all uncommon in studies in which participants are individually tested or individually interviewed (Corrigan & Salzer, 2003; Krause & Howard, 2003). If there are many participants in the study, it is usually impossible to test them all in a day.

A slight modification of the fishbowl procedure may be used for this situation. Suppose a study was being conducted with an N of 50 and two experimental conditions (cell n of 25 each). The researcher may simply place 50 slips of paper in the fishbowl, 25 with Condition A written on them and 25 with Condition B. As the first slip is drawn, its specified condition (A or B) is listed, and so on, until all slips have been drawn and their respective conditions listed in order. Once this step is completed, the experimenter is ready for the first participant to appear. That first participant is assigned to the group indicated by the first slip drawn; the second participant is assigned to the second slip drawn, and so on. Using these procedures, it is not likely that the groups will be systematically different.

A similar procedure may be implemented using shuffled cards or data sheets pre-marked by condition. Twenty-five cards would be marked with Condition A and 25 with Condition B. These cards are then shuffled thoroughly (a thorough shuffling is important—casual shuffling is often not random). Once completed, the first partic-ipant to appear is assigned to the condition appearing on the first card. As before, the sequential testing of participants corresponds with the sequence of shuffled conditions.

Alternative procedures for sequential random assignment are also available through the use of random number tables. Assigning digits to represent each of the conditions for which groups are to be formed may be one way to do this. If, for example, six experimental conditions were being studied, then the digits 1 through 6 would be used in the random number table. Suppose it has been determined that cell *ns* for this same experiment will be 20; this would result in a total sample *N* of 120 participants. If the first number encountered is 5, then the first participant to appear will be assigned to condition 5. Likewise, the second may be assigned to 3, and so on, until the total of 120 participants with 20 per group has been obtained. If group 5 is completed with 20 participants, then subsequent encounters with digit 5 in the table are ignored. Usually, a complete list is made of the group sequence (e.g., 5, 3, 1 . . .) before the experiment begins, including the full complement of partic-ipants to be assigned. This way the sequence of assignment is predetermined ran-domly before each participant appears for testing. Computer programs are also available that are specifically designed for sequential assignment situations.

Occasionally, a researcher will wish to exert a bit more control than is possible with the randomized procedures described above. As an illustration, take the six-condition experiment just described. Table 4.2 presents an example of the sequence of participant assignments to conditions. For discussion purposes, however, only a portion of the assignment sequence is provided (recall that the entire participant list will include an *N* of 120). Despite the fact that this is only a partial list, a bias prob-lem is evident in this portion. Note that there is no individual assigned to Condition 4 until the 22nd participant appears. Although the groups will most probably even out by the time the 120th participant is reached, the cell *n* for Condition 4 must be obtained in greater proportion from the later participants than other groups. The problem would be more pronounced if a smaller total *N* were involved in the study. It is not unreasonable to suspect that certain participant variables may be operative in the promptness with which participants appear for experimentation (e.g., moti-vation, interest, or compulsiveness). These variables, which are unknown but highly likely, may be influential in the way in which a participant performs the experimen-tal task. If such influences are operating in, for example, the first 30 or so partici-pants to appear, Condition 4 is likely to be systematically different than the other groups (by the time the 30th participant appears, the group count is as follows: Group 1, five participants; Group 2, five participants; Group 3, seven participants; Group 4, two participants; Group 5, five participants; Group 6, six participants). Condition 4 may have fewer highly motivated, compulsive participants and more of those that are just getting by in life (or perhaps Condition 4 participants are more well-rounded in their personal life and participation in this study competes with many other legitimate life activities). Irrespective of *how* Condition 4 differs, the worry here is that it *does have a likelihood of being different.*

One method of circumventing the above problem is through *block randomiza-tion.* This procedure considers a block to be a sequence in which each condition appears once. The researcher draws participants at random within a block, ignoring all digit repetitions until each condition has appeared once (the completion of a block). As soon as each condition has appeared, a new block is begun, and this procedure is repeated until the sample *N* is totally assigned to conditions. Table 4.3 presents an example of the previously assigned participant pool that has been

TABLE 4.2   Example of a Simple Random Assignment Sequence List for Six-Group Study

Participant Number	Group Assigned	Participant Number	Group Assigned
1	5	36	2
2	1	37	3
3	6	38	1
4	3	39	4
5	2	40	5
6	3	41	6
7	6	42	2
8	2	43	6
9	1	44	4
10	5	45	5
11	5	46	3
12	6	47	1
13	3	48	3
14	1	49	4
15	2	50	5
16	2	51	1
17	1	52	2
18	6	53	6
19	5	54	6
20	3	55	1
21	3	56	4
22	4	57	3
23	6	58	5
24	4	59	2
25	3	60	5
26	1	61	4
27	6	62	2
28	5	63	6
29	2	64	1
30	3	65	3
31	1	66	5
32	2	67	4
33	4	68	1
34	5	69	3
35	6		

TABLE 4.3   Example of a Block Random Assignment Sequence for a Six-Group Study

Participant Number	Group Assigned	Participant Number	Group Assigned
1	5	36	**5**
2	1	37	4
3	6	38	1
4	3	39	2
5	2	40	6
6	**4**	41	3
7	5	42	**5**
8	3	43	3
9	2	44	1
10	4	45	6
11	1	46	5
12	**6**	47	4
13	2	48	**2**
14	6	49	3
15	1	50	5
16	4	51	2
17	5	52	1
18	**3**	53	4
19	5	54	**6**
20	2	55	5
21	1	56	2
22	4	57	3
23	3	58	1
24	**6**	59	4
25	5	60	**6**
26	2	61	6
27	4	62	5
28	1	63	2
29	3	64	1
30	**6**	65	4
31	6	66	**3**
32	1	67	1
33	4	68	5
34	3	69	6
35	2		

sequenced using block randomization. Horizontal lines under the condition digit that completes the respective block set off each block in the table. The participant assignment to conditions is considerably different from what was exemplified in Table 4.2. Because of the control imposed by block randomization, the group proportions existing by the time the 30th participant appears are substantially changed. Beyond this control, however, the assignment within blocks is random, presenting little reason to expect systematic bias between group characteristics.

Comments

It should be evident from the preceding discussion that all random assignment procedures do not *absolutely* ensure the absence of bias between groups. Free random assignment procedures (those without nonchance controls such as are imposed in block randomization) are occasionally vulnerable to the generation of nonequivalent groups. Although such bias occurs infrequently, the statistical theory on which random procedures are based indicates that atypical groups will appear by chance a certain percentage of the time.

There are precautions that may be taken by the researcher to circumvent such occurrences. Captive assignments may permit the researcher certain checkpoints that are not possible with sequential assignment. By virtue of the actual identification of all participants before beginning the study, the researcher may be able to determine equivalency of groups on a pre-experimental basis. To accomplish this, relevant measures must either be available or be administered before the initiation of experimental procedures. Because the exact composition of the groups is known, groups may be compared on these pre-experimental measures before administering the treatments. If the groups are statistically different, they may be thrown back into the sample pool and reassigned until they are equivalent. Such procedures are not possible with sequential assignment because the exact individuals serving as participants in each group are not identified prior to beginning the experiment. Although this is a useful safeguard, its helpfulness depends on the relevance of the pre-experimental measure. If the measure is not related to the experimental task (e.g., if the task involved discrimination learning and the pre-experimental measure is shoe size), it may be of little use in estimating group equivalency with respect to related participant variables. The pre-experimental group comparison also presumes that other unmeasured, experimentally related variables are not different. It is important to remember that precise equivalency may not be determined in a "money-back-guaranteed" fashion. However, the use of certain controls in combination with random procedures greatly enhances confidence that the groups are probably not different in a significant manner.

Sequential assignment does not permit the same pre-experimental checkpoints that captive assignment does. However, certain precautions may be taken. Despite the fact that researchers do not have actual participant names available, they do have the information necessary to scrutinize the sequence of assignment. It is always prudent to carefully examine the assignment sequence list to identify possible idiosyncrasies that may result in biased assignment of participants to conditions. Such an atypical sequence was evident in Table 4.2. If a potential problem is noted, the investigator may then exercise some control options. One possibility may be to specify some a priori rules and reassign in a free random fashion. These rules may be that no more than three (or some specified number) consecutive participants may be assigned to any one treatment condition. Likewise, the block-randomization procedure may be a desirable option to control for extremes in assignment sequence occurring by chance. Sequential assignment (sometimes termed the "trickle process" because the participants trickle in) requires some additional vigilance regarding the formulation of equivalent groups (Corrigan & Salzer, 2003; Krause & Howard, 2003).

There is also a procedure that can be used that does not actually advance group equivalency, but does guard against flagrant misinterpretation of results. Recall the previous discussion of pre-experimental measures on participants that are related to the experimental task. Because complete groups are not identified, such data are not useful before instituting the treatment. These measures may, however, serve for a group comparison on a post hoc basis or after the study has been completed. Such comparisons would provide the researcher with information concerning the pre-treatment status of the groups. If groups are not different, the researcher can inter-pret the data as if group equivalency were in effect before the treatment. If, on the other hand, the groups appear different on a pretreatment basis, considerable care must be exercised in the interpretation of results (if the data are amenable to mean-ingful interpretation at all). An alternative to this last possibility may be found through the use of specific statistical procedures. Analysis of covariance is a method whereby statistical equivalency may be imposed to facilitate interpretation of results if pretreatment differences exist (Rausch, Maxwell, & Kelley, 2003). This procedure, however, in no way offsets the desirability of group equivalency that exists as a part of actual group composition.

The importance of participant assignment procedures cannot be overempha-sized in studies in which group comparisons are being made. In studies comparing groups, participant assignment is a central concern in the technical soundness of an investigation. They demand the researcher's careful attention both in terms of plan-ning and implementation.

Assignment by Controlled Methods

Earlier we discussed participant assignment procedures in which the researcher exerted certain controls rather than using free random assignment. Such procedures primarily rely on chance, with the controls or restrictions being imposed as added modifications. This section explores methods that primarily rely on control and, in some cases, use chance procedures as secondary modifications.

The first method under controlled assignment is *experimental matching*. There are several procedures that generally fall under matching approaches. In general, experi-mental matching differs from random methods in that the researcher attempts to force group equivalency on a given characteristic using data that are available on a pre-experimental basis. For example, suppose it had been determined that measured mental age was an important characteristic related to participant performance on a given task. Under such circumstances, the researcher may wish to have groups that are equivalent on mental age. Using experimental matching, the researcher would see to it that the groups involved were not different on this characteristic.

There are some alternatives in the way an experimental match may be imple-mented. A researcher may decide to perform a group match, in which case the only concern is that group means and variances are equal. Because the primary concern with a group match involves the composite representation of the control character-istic (i.e., means and variance on mental age), this is the focus of monitoring during group formulation. Usually, the entire sample is listed in rank order on the control measure (mental age). With this completed, the highest participant is arbitrarily assigned to one of the conditions (e.g., treatment 1). The second-highest student is then assigned to treatment 2, the third to treatment 3, and so on, until one partici-pant has been assigned to each condition. Once that has been accomplished, the usual procedure is to then reverse the order (begin with treatment 3, then 2, then 1, for purposes of assigning the second participant in each group). This procedure is continued until a complete cell n has been constituted for each treatment and the total N has been assigned. Although this procedure will usually generate little differ-ence in group means, often the researcher will carefully monitor group means to ensure similarity. If statistically different means do occur in following such procedures, group mean adjustments are frequently made. Because the group mean is the concern, adjustments may be made by participant substitution. The use of such procedures to control means may make it difficult to achieve equal variances between groups simultaneously (Corrigan & Salzer, 2003; Krause & Howard, 2003). Although experimental methodologists have noted this difficulty, procedures to avoid it have not received serious attention. It is not uncommon for group matches to primarily focus on means.

A second approach to conducting an experimental match involves the assignment of matched pairs. As the label suggests, this is a procedure whereby a participant-to-participant match is accomplished, again, for purposes of formulating presumed equivalent groups. To perform such a participant assignment, the researcher uses a pre-experimental measure related to performance on the experimental task. The researcher then examines all the scores in the sample, searching for participants with equal or nearly equal scores. If three groups are to be formed, three participants must be drawn with "matched" scores. Such participants are then assigned to the three conditions. This procedure is continued until cell *ns* are completed.

A basic requirement for either group or participant-by-participant matches is the obtaining of a pre-experimental measure on which the control dimension is based. The match measures are usually obtained in one of two fashions: (a) by using a task that is separate but highly related to that involved in the treatment, or (b) by using the initial performance level on the treatment task. The first source of match data seems self-explanatory, but there are specific concerns that must be addressed. Probably the most pressing area involves the strength of the relationship between scores on the control measure and performance on the experimental task. It is prudent for the researcher to have clear evidence of such relationships either from previous research or from pilot correlations computed in preparation for the experiment. If the researcher merely assumes a relationship, the design is seriously weakened in terms of control.

The second source of match data involves initial participant performance on the experimental task. This is frequently a convenient method of obtaining control dimension data. Inherent in this procedure, however, are certain requirements concerning the logistic characteristics of the experimental task. First, it is obvious that the task must be constructed in a manner that includes multiple trials or responses from the participants. Some learning tasks are designed this way and permit a series of trials until the participant's performance reaches a given criterion level. Then, to implement the match, the researcher provides each participant with a few trials on the experimental task. After this has been accomplished, performances on these trials are scrutinized and the match is performed. Finally, the remainder of the experiment is conducted with the difference in treatments being implemented.

Use of an initial performance score for matching data includes one other concern that must not be ignored. This involves the strength of the relationship between performance on the initial trials (match data) and total performance. It seems likely that performance on a beginning task ought to be highly related to subsequent performance on that same task. However, this may not be the case in all circumstances. In fact, on some experimental tasks the initial phases of performance are quite different from the later performance scores. It is unwise, therefore, to assume a relationship in the absence of some evidence, even on the same task. Knowledge about the strength of this relationship will usually come from the literature review.

Experimental matching enjoyed considerable popularity in the early years of behavioral science. However, there were several difficulties encountered with this procedure that have led researchers to favor random assignment to equate groups. The preference for randomized procedures began in the early 1900s and gained momentum until experimental matching of participants began to be viewed as a taboo—a substandard protocol or last resort for establishing group equivalence. The difficulties with experimental matching have been discussed widely, and are sufficiently important that the beginning researcher should at least have cursory knowledge of them (Gelfand & Drew, 2003; Goodwin, 2005). Since there *are* situations where one cannot use random assignment, knowledge of experimental matching pitfalls becomes more important when it must be used.

From the beginning, certain logistical challenges surface with experimental matching. Using *either* group procedures or matched-pairs procedures, it is necessary to have pre-experimental data available on participants before assignment to groups. To have these data available, the sample must be captive—you must actually have the participants identified. If the exact individuals are not identified (e.g., was described under sequential assignment), the researcher cannot obtain match data and perform a pre-experimental match.

One of the most serious problems with experimental matching involves the control variable itself. Because a specific variable or characteristic is chosen as the one on which groups are matched, that characteristic is assumed to be an important factor for control. It has been repeatedly stated that such a variable should not be used based only on assumptive evidence of importance. However, it is not unusual to find this to be the primary basis for choice. In both group and matched-pairs procedures, it is important that sound evidence of the relationship between the match characteristic and performance on the experimental task be available.

Beyond the relationship question, there are some additional implicit assumptions that concern the match variable. Although it is not uncommon to encounter match design studies with more than one control variable, let's just examine the situation where participants are matched on one characteristic (e.g., reading ability, *or* IQ, *or* academic achievement). By selecting that variable for matching or control, the researcher is explicitly indicating its perceived importance. At the same time, one must ask serious questions about the other variables on which participants were *not* matched. (Remember, the focus is momentarily on the case of matching on a single dimension.) Because there is no match on the multitude of other possible dimensions, the assumption may be made that they are not important for control. This is highly shaky reasoning. The important point here is that the logic used in selecting the match variable (that it is important) does not hold true in the reverse (that those not selected are not important). Yet, by ignoring other variables, the design itself may suggest such reasoning.

It is evident that the unattended variables may indeed create problems. In the process of matching participants, the researcher is, in fact, placing participants in groups in a fashion that is systematic. One *serious* unknown factor is the degree to which this process introduces systematic bias between the conditions on the unmatched (perhaps unknown) variables. In fact, there is reason to suspect that this may occur. Random assignment, on the other hand, gives little reason to expect systematic differences between groups. The process involved is aimed at creating groups that are *unbiased on both known and unknown variables*. This is a strength built into random assignment that is absent in matching procedures.

The researcher using matching procedures for participant assignment often uses more than one characteristic for control. It is not uncommon to find matching studies in which several dimensions are controlled ("participants were matched on gender, and IQ, and socioeconomic status . . ."). Two concerns need to be addressed under such circumstances. First, despite the addition of more control variables, the issues previously discussed remain as design concerns. Human participants are extremely complex. It would be nearly impossible for all of the important characteristics that may influence participant performance to be controlled. However, the unknown or unattended characteristics are still highly suspect as potential contaminators. The second concern is one of logistics. As the number of match variables increases, the difficulty of implementing a match is also greatly increased. It is enough of a task to find matched participants on a single dimension. The magnitude of the problem grows substantially by just adding one additional control. Finding an adequate match with more than two controls creates several additional problems. Because of the difficulty in performing such a match, the precision with which it is accomplished is frequently sacrificed. These sacrifices usually begin with rather small deviations (e.g., participants were matched on measured IQ within plus or minus 5 points) but necessarily increase as the participant pool nears exhaustion.

The difficulties discussed above are generally more prevalent in pair-match procedures than in group-match procedures. The fact remains, however, that these pitfalls are found in using any experimental match designs. Random assignment provides a more powerful, less problematic procedure when it can be used.

Chapter Summary

✦ In selecting participants for a research study, it is important to ensure that the participants are appropriate for the research question, a representative sample of the population under study has been selected, the results can be generalized to a larger population, and the sample size is adequate.

✦ A population refers to everyone or everything within a clearly defined group of people, events, or objects constituting the focus of a research study. A participant pool is a subset of participants that are representative of the population sample.

✦ A population sample to be studied must accurately represent the larger population, otherwise the interpretation of results may not be accurate for individuals other than those who participated in the study.

✦ There are various approaches that may be used in sampling populations. The conditions of the study determine which procedures are to be used. Sampling approaches include the following:

★ Simple random sampling: each individual has an equal chance of being chosen.
★ Stratified random sampling: procedure in which representative samples from different subpopulations are obtained.
★ Proportional sampling: drawing samples from a subgroup only in the proportion that it exists in the larger population.
★ Systematic sampling: used in rare circumstances in which a representative sample can be obtained if the population frame is arranged appropriately.
★ Cluster sampling: grouping individuals into clusters (e.g., a third-grade elementary class) whereby the researcher lists all the clusters and then draws samples from the list.
★ Double sampling (two-phase sampling): a participant is accessed twice for data collection (e.g., when a situation warrants an intense or more in-depth follow-up with participants).

✦ It is important for a researcher to have an adequate sample of the population under study. The characteristics of a given population will determine how large the sample must be to accurately predict population factors.

✦ A researcher selecting participants for a comparative or difference investigation must attend equally to internal validity (technical soundness) and external validity (generalizability of results).

✦ A researcher asking a relationship or correlational question attends more to external validity (ensuring the sample is representative of the population for which the prediction is desired).

✦ A researcher asking a descriptive question emphasizes the accuracy of the population description (external validity), including characteristics, opinions, or behaviors of a given group, culture, or setting.

✦ Purposive sampling, convenience sampling, and quota sampling procedures are examples of nonrandom participant selection.

✦ Participant assignment in multigroup experiments is an important component of an internally valid study and must take into account how individuals are divided into sample groups for different treatments.

✦ Assignment by chance refers to a carefully planned and executed technique in which the researcher uses random selection to form groups for a research study.

✦ Captive assignment refers to the identification and availability of a total sample at the outset of the investigation, as opposed to situations in which all participants are not present at one time.

✦ Sequential assignment is a method used in situations where the researcher does not have the exact sample drawn and is operating from a participant pool.

Key Terms

Captive assignment. Refers to the identification and availability of a total sample at the outset of the investigation, as opposed to situations in which all participants are not present at one time.

Cluster sampling. A sampling procedure involving grouping individuals into clusters (e.g., a third-grade elementary class). The researcher then lists all the clusters and draws samples from them.

Double sampling. Also known as two-phase sampling. In this procedure, a participant is accessed twice for data collection (e.g., when a situation warrants an intense or more in-depth follow-up with participants).

Proportional random sampling. A sampling procedure aimed at properly representing characteristics in subgroups, it involves drawing samples from a subgroup only in the proportion that it exists in the larger population.

Representative sample. A representative sample is one where the group selected for inclusion in a study has similar characteristics to the population that is being studied and therefore accurately reflects that population, so the results can be generalized.

Sample size. Refers to the number of participants a researcher selects to be in a study. It is important for a researcher to have an adequate sample of the population under study. The characteristics of a given population will determine how large the sample must be to accurately predict population factors.

Sequential assignment. An assignment method used in situations where the researcher does not have the exact sample drawn and is operating from a participant pool.

Simple random sampling. A sampling procedure where each individual has an equal chance of being chosen.

Stratified random sampling. A sampling procedure used to obtain representative samples from different subpopulations.

Systematic sampling. A sampling procedure used in very rare circumstances in which a representative sample can be obtained only if the population frame is arranged appropriately.

Student Study Site

The companion Web site for *Designing and Conducting Research in Education* www.sagepub.com/drewstudy

Supplement your review of this chapter by going to the companion Web site to take one of the practice quizzes, use the flashcards to study key terms, and check out the many other study aids you'll find there. You'll even find some research articles from the Sage Full-Text Collection and a step-by-step guide that will show you how to read an educational research article.

Simulation Feedback

For additional simulations visit www.sagepub .com/drewstudy

Simulation Feedback 4.1

As indicated in your text, the population frame is constructed by designating all the potential participants, by name, who have the characteristics indicated in the population definition. Recall that the population was defined as "all third-year male students enrolled at Whereami State University." From the partial list that you have, certain students should have an X by their name, thereby becoming part of your population frame. The students listed below should have an X by their name. These are male students with a code of 3 for year of enrollment.

Bach, Jay T.	3
Bacon, Robert F.	3
Badger, Mike	3
Bailey, Bob Jo	3
Barger, George	3
Barclay, Larry	3
Barker, James R.	3
Barnes, Mike L.	3
Berg, William J.	3
Bigelow, Randy L.	3
Bigelow, Robert W.	3
Bragg, Raymond J.	3

Other students in the original list did not combine the characteristics of both male and code 3. Occasionally, you may encounter some difficulty determining characteristics from the information provided. For example, names have definite regional differences in terms of whether they are given to males or females (Billie Jo Bailey). If confusion exists, you must confirm sex by seeking additional information.

5

MEASURES AND INSTRUMENTS

CHAPTER OBJECTIVES

After reading Chapter 5, you should be able to do the following:

+ Describe key features of a criterion measure, including reliability and validity.

+ Develop a written definition of an example criterion measure and describe how you will determine its reliability and validity.

+ Select a criterion measure from a group of alternatives and describe how it has a high level of sensitivity and communication value for your intended audience.

+ Describe an instrument or task that can be used to generate your criterion measure.

+ Discuss how reactive you believe participants will be to your instrument. Also discuss how you will decide which task to administer first in a situation where you need to have participants complete two of them.

+ Describe ceiling and floor effects and how you would alter your measurement or participants in order to avoid both.

+ Discuss particular performance range challenges presented in quasi-experimental studies such as developmental investigations of academic performance.

+ Discuss the challenges involved in constructing a questionnaire, including convincing participants of its legitimacy, and techniques that are useful to facilitate participant completion of the instrument.

+ Discuss pitfalls of questionnaire construction and how to avoid them, including issues related to reading levels, topic sensitivity, length, and question order.

+ Discuss development of observation as a measure, including protocol formats.

SELECTION AND DEFINITION OF A CRITERION MEASURE

In the beginning of the book, we emphasized the importance of careful planning in moving through the research process. At every stage, there are points to consider and decisions to be made while moving from determining the research question to outlining where you are going to find the study's participants. This chapter moves forward in that planning process and addresses some of the points you need to consider in choosing how you are going to measure outcomes. Determining what you are going to measure represents one of the many details that must receive attention in a research investigation beyond sketching the basic design. As we proceed, you will find *what* you are going to measure as well as *how* you are going to obtain those measurements. Consequently, this chapter examines those parts of an investigation that are commonly labeled as measures and instruments or tasks. As researchers, we have to find ways to measure the effects of what we have done.

Features of Criterion Measures

It is important for a researcher to select an appropriate criterion measure during the planning of an investigation and to define that measure in a manner that allows for reliable and valid recording of what happened. **Measurement reliability** refers to the consistency of performance. How consistently does the same performance receive the same score, whether that score is the number of correct answers on a math test or observations of classroom disruptions? **Measurement validity** refers to the degree that a test assesses what it is intended to measure. If you are intending to evaluate the reading level of a child, is the test you're using appropriate for assessing reading performance?

Criterion measure refers to what is measured or counted and is synonymous with *dependent variable,* which refers to the characteristic or performance being measured in the study. It is important to re-emphasize the distinction between dependent variables and the independent variable (sometimes referred to as the experimental variable) used in experimental studies. The *independent variable* is the factor being studied or, in the case of experiments, the **experimental variable.** In some cases, the experimental variable (independent variable) represents a treatment such as comparing one type of teaching method with another. In other cases, the experimental variable represents a group characteristic that is being studied such as comparing learning rates of students with intellectual disabilities with those of students with learning disabilities (Drew & Hardman, 2007). In this example, the experimental variable is the group characteristic of "intellectual" disabilities versus "learning" disabilities.

If a researcher is comparing the effectiveness of two instructional techniques (e.g., Method A versus Method B), the independent or experimental variable is the method of instruction. In this example, the researcher is not measuring the method of instruction; the method of instruction is being studied as an independent variable. The criterion measure is what we use to measure the effectiveness. If the instruction methods were designed for teaching reading, we would need to determine how effectiveness can be assessed. One approach is to measure reading comprehension by the number of correct responses made by participants on a test. In such an example, the number of correct responses would be the criterion measure. In this example of reading comprehension, the criterion or acceptable method for assessing this construct is the number of correct responses.

Criterion is not used here in the same sense as a performance goal to be achieved (e.g., the idea that students must reach a certain performance level or criterion before they are certified as having passed a course). Instead, it is a means of measuring the actual level of performance that a participant accomplished.

Reliability

It is important to be very specific in defining a measure. Selecting a more detailed and specific criterion measure has several advantages. Such definitions leave less room for error and misjudgment, and they improve measurement reliability. A clear definition of what the measure is will make it easier to determine when we have seen a particular performance. For example, if a math problem results in either a correct or incorrect answer, it should be easy to see when a student calculates the correct answer. Such a measure would be very likely to show consistency across different times and observers. It would therefore be a very reliable measure with the same performance resulting in the same score on repeated occasions.

Reliability is often reduced when a criterion measure is described in a rather vague fashion. If a criterion measure definition is not stated in specific terms, the data collector has to exercise more judgment about what is a correct or incorrect answer. This results in data that are less reliable because the same performance may be judged to be correct in one case and incorrect in another. Such a circumstance reduces the accuracy of the data collected because at the end of the study, we don't know whether a student actually completed 30 or 25 answers correctly. This type of situation is far less likely if the criterion measure is defined in a very detailed manner.

A final point on defining the criterion measure also affects reliability. We just noted that the definition needs to be detailed and specific rather than vague or abstract. This is critical, but it is also important that the definition of a criterion measure remain relatively simple even though it is specific. If a criterion measure is defined with a very lengthy description, it becomes too difficult for the data collector to use easily. If a data collector cannot easily apply the definition and very quickly determine whether the answer is correct, reliability will be reduced. Consequently, the ideal definition of a criterion measure is one that is clear and specific but also sufficiently short that it can be readily used in a field setting. The Research in Action box illustrates some of the processes involved in selecting criterion measures in action research examples.

Validity

It is important to select a criterion measure that has measurement validity. In this case, validity means that the measure you are recording actually assesses what it is supposed to measure. When you observe a student responding incorrectly to a math test item, is it appropriate to infer that the student did not learn that math fact? If the answer to that question is yes, then the measure is likely a valid measure. If, instead, there may be other interpretations of the meaning of the incorrect response (e.g., that the student is so anxious that he or she can't respond at all), then we may have a measurement validity problem. It is our job to develop or find criterion measures that allow us to make the necessary interpretations from observed performance (e.g., a correct response means the students have learned the material; an incorrect response means they have not). Of course, there will be a certain amount of variability in each student's performance, but if we can make that interpretation for the most part, then we have a valid criterion measure.

Direct Measurement

It is also important to distinguish between those factors that can and cannot be measured directly. There are some rather common constructs that cannot be measured directly. Their existence must be inferred from the measurement of certain attributes, and these attributes are believed to indicate something more about the abstract construct. Learning is an example of such a construct. You can infer that learning has occurred through observation of a certain performance. In this example, learning is considered the broader construct, whereas the performance (e.g., number of correct responses) is an attribute of learning. When conducting a study that involves such topics, the measure should be selected and defined in a way that it represents a valid assessment of learning.

Because abstract constructs are not directly measurable, they cannot be considered for use as criterion measures. The *attributes* of a construct can achieve the level of specificity necessary in a criterion measure because they are observable, countable, or can in some fashion be directly measured. The construct usually represents a more global or abstract construct (e.g., self-concept, intelligence, or anxiety), whereas the attribute is a more specific, definable, observable type of factor that reflects something about the nature of the construct.

Obviously, the relationship between a criterion measure and the construct under investigation is critical for a measure to be a valid representation of the construct. One must be sure that the criterion measure is indeed an attribute of the construct being studied. This is frequently a challenging area for beginning researchers.

No set of prescribed rules exists for determining that the presumed relationship between criterion measures and constructs being studied is sound (Johnson

R E S E A R C H   I N   A C T I O N

KEY POINTS IN THE CHAPTER REFLECTED IN THIS BOX:

- Selecting criterion measures for both studies involves determining behaviors or responses that can be observed or counted:
  - What are the questions to be asked directly of the participants?
  - What are the behaviors to be counted by observers?
  - What are the instruments that might be used to record data?

For more research in action tips visit www.sagepub .com/drewstudy

OBJECTIVES TO LEARN FROM THIS BOX:

- Selecting criterion measures for both studies involves determining how the behaviors and responses are going to be counted in very specific terms.
- Determining criterion measures in action research requires focusing specifically on participant behaviors and responses that can be counted in an environment that has many potential distractions.

SCENARIO 1: STUDENT ENGAGEMENT IN READING

Emily is trying to determine what measures to assess in a study of reading instruction. She is comparing two approaches to instruction, one involving student engagement through emphasizing concepts of interest to the students (CORI) and the other method using drill and practice on words and sentences (DAP). There are two measures she is interested in. One involves assessing the engagement itself, and the second focuses on how the students perform on reading.

Students who are engaged in the concepts surrounding an academic subject are often very excited about it. They are active and animated. They talk eagerly about the concepts with their classmates. Although such class sessions are noisy and active, the conversations relate to the subject matter and are not disruptive in the same way that negative outbursts are disruptive. Emily wants to measure this activity level and begins by writing a detailed description of what it looks like to an observer: How frequently did the students talk about the subjects involved in the lessons? How often did they come up with questions about the subjects and related questions? She is beginning to define her measure in terms of observable actions by the students during a given period of time.

Emily's second criterion measure is more traditional as one thinks about reading instruction. She wants to compare the groups' performance on the reading content and how well they comprehend passages when asked to read them. These measures will use tests on the content of passages in an attempt to determine how well the students learned to read the material.

Emily's criterion measures are beginning to emerge as she writes the definitions. In each case, she is counting something—whether it is the number of test questions students answered correctly or the number of concept-oriented questions and student-to-student or student-to-teacher interactions that occurred. Her measures will be recorded in classroom settings by observers and by the teacher as tests are reviewed.

Scenario 2: Student Self-Esteem

Daniel is developing the criterion measures for his study comparing the self-esteem of his Latino and Caucasian students. All of his participants will be students with learning disabilities. His criterion measure is going to be self-esteem, and he has already decided there will be three parts of self-esteem he wants to assess: global self-esteem, private self-esteem, and public self-esteem. These are components he has found in the literature and they all pique his interest.

Daniel wants to measure global self-esteem by using the Rosenberg self-esteem scale. This scale has been widely used with adolescents and seems to have validity and reliability that are satisfactory. Daniel has found literature suggesting that global self-esteem can be separated into two parts—public and private. The literature indicates that public self-esteem is based on students' opinion of themselves in the company of others, focusing mostly on perceived intelligence. Private self-esteem reflects how the students view themselves in a more personal context, such as within their peer group or family. Daniel has found literature that includes instruments for both components. He sees that the public and private self-esteem measurements are not as strong in terms of reliability and validity, but he also knows these subcomponents have been studied less by researchers in the field. Daniel's measurement instruments will be read to the students to minimize the effect of various reading disabilities that occur frequently in students with learning disabilities. Students will complete one instrument containing all three self-esteem components as the questions are read.

Daniel's criterion measures will come from students' responses on the questionnaire-type instruments they complete. He knows self-esteem has always been a topic with measurement difficulties, but he also believes in it, believes it is important, and wants to conduct research on it.

Think about this: For both action research studies in this box, what are the specific participant behaviors and responses to be counted? Write two lists that include the details of what is to be counted and therefore the criterion measures for each study. What are the differences in the criterion measures for the reading study and the self-esteem study?

SOURCE: This action research scenario is roughly based on Rubin, D. (2000). *Race and self-esteem: A study of Latino and European-American students with learning disabilities.* Unpublished master's thesis, University of Utah, Salt Lake City.

& Christensen, 2004). Frequently, previous research has resulted in the establishment of accepted criterion measures. A researcher can then rely on this research as a guidepost that will facilitate selecting a measure. When such guidance is absent, however, the researcher must rely on experience, judgment, and intuition to assess the logical relationship between a given criterion measure and the factor being studied.

For example, in a descriptive study of a selected group's reading level, the suggested criterion measure may be an average of the group members' correct test scores. This is a logical criterion measure to the degree that the number correct on that test is an accepted measure for determining reading level. It would be foolish, however, to attempt to describe a particular group's reading level using a criterion measure of the amount of time they spent on homework. Even beyond the matter of accepted measurement units, a criterion measure of time on homework does not hold an intuitive or logical relationship to the purpose of a study that that assesses reading level.

In another example, one would not typically use mathematical computation performance as a measure of self-concept. The behavior observed or counted as a criterion measure must have a stronger intuitive relationship to the construct being studied than is likely between math computation and the elusive construct of self-concept (Fraenkel & Wallen, 2006).

Characteristics of Alternative Measures

Many other concerns must also be addressed in selecting criterion measures. Assuming that a researcher has achieved a measurable level of specificity and that the relationship of the measure to the topic is acceptable, there may still be other decisions to be made. It is not unusual to be faced with two or three possible criterion measures that might be acceptable in terms of specificity and the relationship to the construct under investigation. Under such circumstances, the choice may be based on several considerations.

Measure Communication Value

One characteristic that may favor a given measure over other alternatives is the communication value of the measure (see **measure communication value** in the glossary). Which measure is the most efficient means for investigation and communication about a given problem? For example, in a descriptive study of reading skill level, the criterion measure of correct responses on a word knowledge test might be appropriate. Of course, this is not the only measure for reading skill, but it is one that is fairly easily understood and has reasonably good communication value, depending on the audience. Another measure for reading skill might be visual and auditory discrimination. Such measures may be used for diagnostic reading tests but would probably need translation for most audiences if you are describing overall reading ability. Such a translation is cumbersome and unnecessary because of the availability of word knowledge as an alternative, so there is good reason to prefer a word knowledge test.

Measure Sensitivity

As mentioned, there must be a logical relationship between the measure and the topic under study (an attribute of the construct). The measure must be specific and observable (one must be able to determine its presence either by counting or in some way certifying its existence). Finally, it should be efficient and sensitive to performance differences. Another consideration in the selection of a criterion measure is its sensitivity (Johnson & Christensen, 2004; see **measure sensitivity** in the glossary). One measure might be more sensitive to participant performance differences than other alternatives. It is always preferable to use the most sensitive measure available, assuming that other characteristics do not make its use undesirable (e.g., participant reaction or other logistic difficulties). For example, in cognitive psychology, a lot of research has been conducted on the learning of verbal material. Because of this extensive work, a sophisticated technological base has been developed in certain sub-areas of study.

Substantial research has been conducted on the rate at which study participants acquire knowledge. Two criterion measures for rate of acquisition exemplify the sensitivity issue. For the purpose of illustration, let's say the participants are required to memorize a list of eight pairs of words (e.g., dog–fist, lion–water, baby–sky). They are then shown one half of the pair and asked what word is "paired" with it. One attempt at each of the eight pairs is defined as one trial. As a criterion measure, a researcher records the number of trials it takes a participant to make three correct responses on each pair. An alternative criterion measure might involve counting the number of errors a participant makes in reaching the three-correct-response level of proficiency. In this example, the number of errors is the more sensitive measure, whereas the number of trials represents a less sensitive measure. This is the case because a participant may make various numbers of errors (reflecting variation in acquired knowledge) within a list trial. Consequently, the number of trials may be the same for two participants, but sizeable differences may exist in the number of errors committed. Because errors seem more reflective of the knowledge being acquired, it is the more sensitive measure and is preferred as a criterion measure. Although this example comes from experimental research, the same issue is equally important in other types of investigations.

Comments on Criterion Measures

Selection and definition of a criterion measure in research involves attention to a number of matters. The measure has to be one that can be used with high reliability. This means that the same level of performance by participants must result in the same or a similar score for a high percentage of the time. Reliability is important in order to enhance data accuracy.

A companion of reliability relates to the validity of the measure. As described earlier, validity means that the criterion measure assesses what it is supposed to be measuring and that you can therefore make interpretations about the scores. If you think you are measuring arithmetic skills, the highly valid criterion measure would reflect a student's knowledge in that area rather than something else. An example of a measure with validity problems might be one where performance was largely influenced by the student's reading ability. This might occur in situations where lengthy story problems were presented. It would be an error to interpret performance narrowly as involving arithmetic skill in such a test.

We also examined direct measurement as one feature that is important to be aware of when a criterion measure is selected. Some constructs cannot be directly measured and instead the criterion measure will involve recording data on the occurrence of certain attributes that are elements or components of the construct.

In some cases, there are multiple criterion measures that might be used and the researcher needs to select from the alternatives. Selection of a criterion measure should include attention to reliability, validity, and direct or indirect measurement as we noted. The researcher should also pay close attention to the communication value of any measure that is selected. If one selects a criterion measure that is difficult to communicate about, then interpreting results may be quite difficult. This is particularly vital because interpreting the outcomes of any study is one of the important reasons for conducting research in the first place.

A criterion measure must also be adequately sensitive in order to reflect performance differences by participants when they occur. If a measure is not very sensitive, participants might be performing quite differently but the scores do not reflect that difference. A criterion measure must accurately reflect the participant performance variation.

Finally, selecting and defining a criterion measure also needs to include attention to *objectivity* and *usability*. Most people assume that research is objective—an understanding that is an overriding component of science. However, keeping a watchful eye on the objectivity of a criterion is important so that the data do not accidentally include a bias that significantly influences interpretation possibilities. Usability does not receive a great deal of attention but it is a vital element. It is possible to contrive a criterion measure that is reliable, valid, sensitive, and all those other descriptors, but is *so* challenging to use that data collection is difficult. This type of criterion measure is not desirable. In fact, if the criterion measure is very difficult to implement, the reliability will likely be reduced because the researcher will have problems recording the data. Thus, usability is an important component of selecting and defining a criterion measure.

Simulation

For additional simulations visit www.sagepub .com/drewstudy

Simulation 5.1

Topic: Criterion measures

Background statement: The data collected in a study represent the researcher's evidence of how the participant interacted with the task. Specification of the measure to be recorded is, therefore, a crucial part of planning any investigation. It is also a frequent area of difficulty for the beginning researcher.

Tasks to be performed:

1. Read the following stimulus material, which is a summary statement about a hypothetical study.

2. Suggest a criterion measure that might be appropriate for the investigation.

Stimulus material:

A teacher in your school wishes to compare the effectiveness of two reading programs. The study has been designed in a traditional experimental framework with two groups of participants, one receiving one program and the second receiving the other program. Suggest the criterion measure(s) that may be appropriate.

Write your response, then turn to page 134 for Simulation Feedback 5.1.

INSTRUMENTS OR TASKS

Instruments or tasks are presented to participants in order to generate measurable behavior (i.e., behavior that can be counted, observed, or somehow recorded as the criterion measure). Consequently, there must be a logical relationship between the instrument or task a researcher selects and the construct being studied. The instrument must be designed to generate behavior that is presumed to be an attribute of the topic under investigation. For example, suppose a researcher was conducting a survey about teacher preferences regarding approaches to teaching reading. To determine teachers' attitudes on this topic, the researcher must generate some response from the participant that will identify the individual's preferences. One way of obtaining these data might involve a mailed questionnaire or a personal interview with the participants. In the first case, the questionnaire is the instrument that generates the participant's response, and in the latter example the participant's response is given directly to the interviewer. Either of these approaches could serve the purpose of providing an acceptable criterion measure for the study. The selection of which approach to use depends on many considerations.

Instruments vary greatly from one investigation to the next. Some experimentation may actually include a task that the participants perform and their performance results in the criterion measure. Others may involve the administration of a test instrument of some type. Nonexperimental research may be undertaken by means of surveys (questionnaires and interviews) and observation studies. In both surveys and observation studies, there is often some instrument used to generate data. The researcher must pay attention to the instrument's characteristics, advantages, and potential problem areas.

Participant Reactivity to Tasks

The process of generating the actual data in an investigation can be thought of as an interaction between participant characteristics and the properties of the task or instrument. Once a participant sees (or hears) the task stimulus, his or her responsiveness is changed—that is, the **participant reactivity** has changed. For example, it is likely that a participant's responsiveness will be altered if a part of the treatment involves giving him or her information about the effectiveness of a particular discipline method. It is reasonable to expect that such an experience may result in anxiety, a heightened sensitivity, or any number of changes in participant properties.

Multiple Task Effects

A researcher must be concerned about altered participant properties in situations where the same participants are administered more than one treatment or measure. In the strictest sense, participants are not the same after the first measure has been taken. There are times, however, when it is not feasible to do anything but administer multiple measures. When multiple measures are administered, the researcher has two basic options: (a) systematically administer one measure before the other, or (b) rotate the order of administration in some fashion.

If one measure is obviously *less* vulnerable or sensitive to participant changes, then that measure should be administered second. An example of this is a situation in which teachers were supposed to evaluate certain instructional materials and the researcher also wanted to know how much information the participants had about the material. The measure evaluating instructional materials should be administered first because it is probably more vulnerable to participants' emotions or attitudes than an information test. If the participants did not do well on the information test, the evaluation might be systematically lowered—that is, the participants might rate the materials lower if they think they did badly on the knowledge part, either consciously or unconsciously. It is doubtful, however, that participants will do less than their optimum on an information test as a result of the evaluation rating. Therefore, it seems reasonable that the evaluation measure should precede the information test.

If there is little apparent difference in measure sensitivity, sequence of administration is not an issue. Under these circumstances, the researcher will simply want some assurance that neither measure systematically comes before the other, thereby creating an influence that cannot be accounted for. To accomplish this, measures are generally counterbalanced (i.e., measure A then B; B then A) or randomly ordered. These procedures mask or mix the influence of each respective measure so that there is no systematic impact of one on the other.

Types of Instruments Used in Research

The types of instruments used in research are nearly endless, limited only by the researcher's imagination and the specific nature of the study. Differences are clearly evident between tasks even when several investigations are part of a program of research on the same topic. Researchers are constantly refining their instruments or studying a slightly different component of the same construct. Examples of such evolution of instruments can be found in a number of circumstances in education and psychology. If one reviews the historic changes in intelligence tests, for example, it is easy to see how the instrument format has changed over time. In many cases, such incremental changes occurred because of accumulated research evidence. However, in a few instances the instrument changes have been rather abrupt and not so incremental. These types of format modifications will often occur when a new piece of information is imported from a different field or when the researcher is trying to avoid a particular anomaly in the data. An example of this is using a Likert-type scale that has an even number of response options rather than an odd number (i.e., a 1 to 6 scale rather than a 1 to 5 scale). The even-numbered scale does not permit a middle response and therefore tends to spread the scores out slightly (McMillan & Schumacher, 2006).

Task Performance Range

One of the most frequent problems encountered in task selection involves the range of performance that the task will permit. Task **performance range** refers to the variation in responses possible within the limits imposed by highest and lowest possible performance scores on the task. Take the example of an achievement test being used as a task. Suppose the number of correct responses is the criterion measure. If the total number of questions on the test is 25, the performance range would have a ceiling of 25 and a floor of zero (no correct responses). The desirable situation, of course, is to design the task so that participants can perform without being limited by the task itself. Unless this is the case, the level of performance likely reflects task limits rather than the experimental treatment (e.g., the method of instruction) (Goodwin, 2005; Kazdin, 2003). In many cases, it is difficult to select or design a task that allows participants to perform to their full ability without being hampered by task performance range.

Ceiling effect. If participants in an investigation perform the task so well that they "top out," this is called a ceiling effect. A **ceiling effect** occurs when the performance range is so restricted or limited on the upper end that many participants cannot perform to their greatest ability. Such results are called an *artifact* because they represent an artificially determined performance level generated by constraints of the experiment rather than constraints of ability. Ceiling effect accurately describes what happens to the participants.

Figure 5.1a provides a visual example of results where a ceiling effect has occurred. In this hypothetical experiment, participants with intellectual disabilities were compared with participants of average intelligence to assess the effectiveness of two teaching methods. The number of correct responses on a test was the criterion

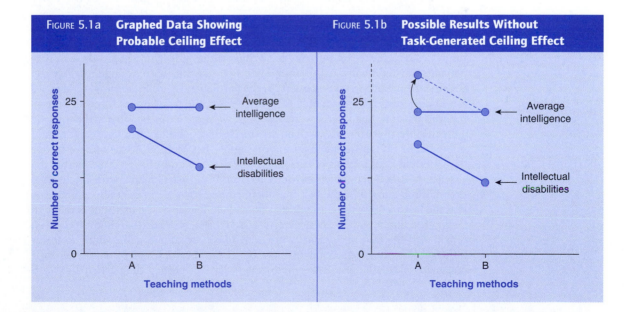

FIGURE 5.1a **Graphed Data Showing Probable Ceiling Effect**

FIGURE 5.1b **Possible Results Without Task-Generated Ceiling Effect** measure with a task performance range of 0–25. If the researcher is not alert to the apparent ceiling effect, an incorrect interpretation of these results may be made. One interpretation might suggest that there is a differential effectiveness between teaching methods for some participants, but not all. Method A seems superior to Method B for participants with intellectual disabilities, but that difference is not evident with average participants. This would be a logical interpretation if the average participants had not performed at or near the upper limit of the performance range. Because their group means are so close to the task ceiling, one might suspect that their performance represents task limitations rather than the effectiveness of teaching methods. This possibility is even more likely when one considers the fact that the results are group *means*. Because the means for the average group are so near 25, it is possible that many of those participants gave correct responses on all test items. There is no way to know how many correct responses they might have made if the ceiling had been raised.

Figure 5.1b shows hypothetical results that might have been obtained if the task performance range had been expanded in terms of upper limits. Interpretation of these data is much different from what was previously suggested under the conditions of the ceiling effect. The data presented in Figure 5.1b suggest that teaching Method A is more effective than Method B for both average participants and those with intellectual disabilities. This represents important information that was not evident in Figure 5.1a. It is also information that is not obtainable because the imaginary study in Figure 5.1a would not permit its observation. With a ceiling effect occurring, one does not know whether any difference existed between Method A and Method B with average participants because the methods were not differentially effective, or the range of task performance was so restricted that these participants could not perform to the best of their ability. The situation represented in Figure 5.1a is referred to as a result where possible differences are "masked."

Floor effect. Task restrictions may occur at the lower end of the performance range as well as the upper end. In situations where variation in participant performance is restricted by the lower limit of the task, results are influenced by what is called a **floor effect.** In the previous example, zero correct responses was the lower limit of possible participant performance. Because zero response is the floor with any task, the difficulty of the material itself becomes a primary determiner of the lower limit.

Figure 5.2a presents results of a hypothetical investigation in which a floor effect appears. Using the same research variables as before, the number of correct responses is the criterion measure for a comparison of teaching methods with participants having intellectual disabilities and participants with average intelligence. Because the mean correct responses for the participants with intellectual disabilities are so near zero, it is reasonable to conclude that the task floor is limiting performance variation. Again, unless the researcher is alert to this possible artifact in the data, the interpretation may well be in error. If the floor effect was ignored, the data in Figure 5.2a might result in an interpretation that Method A was more effective than Method B for average participants. One does not know for certain whether the absence of differences between Methods A and B in participants with intellectual disabilities is caused by the fact that the methods are not differentially effective or that the task itself was so difficult that possible influence of the methods is masked.

Figure 5.2b shows hypothetical results from this same study that might have been obtained if the task performance range had been expanded with regard to lower limits. In this case, such a change might have been accomplished by using less difficult material for the test. Easier items might have permitted the participants with

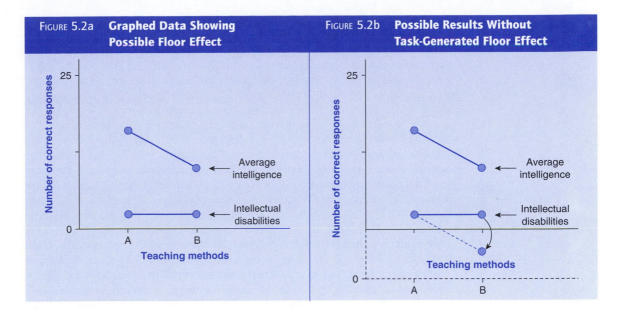

FIGURE 5.2a   Graphed Data Showing Possible Floor Effect

FIGURE 5.2b   Possible Results Without Task-Generated Floor Effect

intellectual disabilities to exhibit some performance variation. Although the floor is still zero correct, it is reasonable that variation of the participants with intellectual disabilities when using less difficult material is more representative of their ability to perform than was the case when the lower limit was masking performance. Interpretation of these data, as before, would probably be different from the interpretation of data in Figure 5.2a. It now seems that Method A was more effective than Method B for both groups of participants.

Ways of avoiding performance range problems. It is desirable to find a task performance range that does not limit the response variation of participants. Because the objective is to study participants (their behavior, ability, etc.), logically, the participant must be permitted to perform. As a researcher progresses in a program of research, it is not uncommon to find that alteration of the task range is necessary. Usually, determining the need to expand the performance range is based on results showing a possible floor or ceiling effect. To avoid a performance range problem, it is possible to either change the task (make it easier or more difficult) or change the participants (younger, brighter, etc.).

Depending on the circumstances, a researcher may elect to use different participants (e.g., younger or brighter). Younger participants, for example, may circumvent a ceiling effect if performance level is related to age. However, researchers should be somewhat cautious in using a participant change to avoid performance range problems. If there is a substantial change in the participant description, it is likely that a different human is actually being studied (i.e., substantial developmental differences). This is a particularly delicate matter if the primary focus of the research is the participant (e.g., response abilities of the participant). It is not always the case, however, that the participant is the central focus. There may be investigations in which the primary interest is the task (e.g., the properties of an instructional package). Under such circumstances, the researcher may be more willing to change participant characteristics than task properties.

Alternatively, the researcher may choose to change the task. Participant characteristics are more commonly the focus of investigation than task properties because we are more often interested in studying the students. Therefore, alteration of task properties represents the most common approach to avoiding a floor or ceiling effect. The fashion in which this can be accomplished is shown in a series of example studies investigating the effects of organizing material on students' learning. Study 1 compares the test performance of participants with and without intellectual disabilities on two lists of words. The first list is organized into sublists by conceptual category (e.g., fruits and trees) and the second is randomly organized (conceptually unorganized). The Study 1 table summarizes the results in terms of mean correct responses by participant group and experimental condition. The total number of words (and possible correct responses) is 25. Inspection of the group means in the Study 1 table suggests that the performance of participants with average intelligence was likely limited by the task ceiling. These results represent, essentially, the same type of data contamination evident in Figure 5.1a. Consequently, the researchers are not able to determine from this study whether or not organization of material has an influence on the recall of individuals of normal intelligence. This topic then becomes the central question for Study 2.

For Study 2, a change in task is necessary to circumvent the ceiling effect. Only participants of average intelligence are used in this study. The age is lowered slightly but not enough to be concerned about the problem of studying a different developmental level. To expand the performance range, two levels of material difficulty are used—easy and more difficult. The easier list had a difficulty level that approximated that used in Study 1. The second set of words was then constituted with a difficulty level substantially above the first. In addition, the list of words that each participant received was lengthened to 30 words. The Study 2 table and figure summarize the results in terms of mean correct responses by list difficulty and

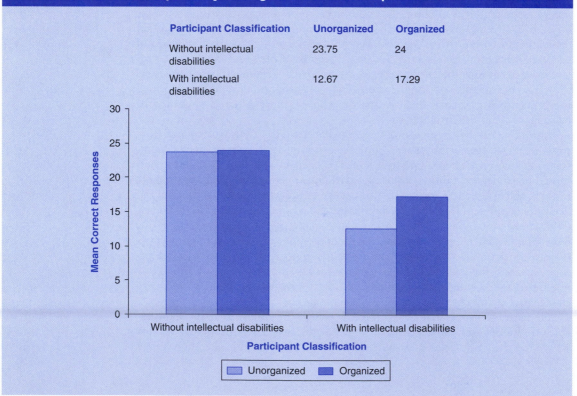

STUDY 1   Mean Correct Responses by List Organization and Participant Classification

Participant Classification	Unorganized	Organized
Without intellectual disabilities	23.75	24
With intellectual disabilities	12.67	17.29

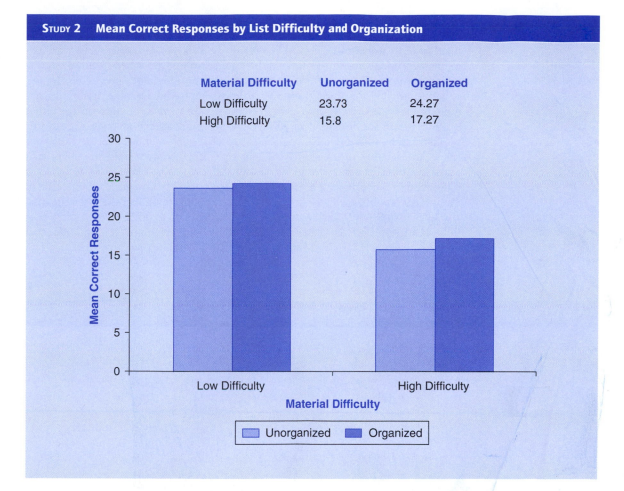

STUDY 2   Mean Correct Responses by List Difficulty and Organization

Material Difficulty	Unorganized	Organized
Low Difficulty	23.73	24.27
High Difficulty	15.8	17.27

organization. Analysis of the data indicates that a significant difference did occur between performance on organized and unorganized material. From this data set, it is evident that a ceiling effect like that found in Study 1 had been sufficiently avoided to permit differences to appear. Inspection of the means, however, suggests that performance on easy material list was approaching the ceiling although not as closely as in Study 1. This was expected since the low difficulty was the same difficulty level used in Study 1, except with a slightly longer list.

Study 2 exemplifies the variety of minor adjustments that may be made to influence the interaction between participants and the task. The age level of participants is slightly different from that in Study 1 (range of 19–24 years, whereas Study 1 had a range of 21–27 years). This probably gives us little to worry about developmentally. Changing the participant age is a technique that can be used, although a dramatic change in age may result in a developmentally different participant, particularly with children (Berk, 2006; Nadelman, 2004). If the participants were young children, they would be developing more rapidly and changing age ranges may result in a different developmental level. A second minor adjustment was made by increasing the list length from 25 to 30 words. Lengthening the task must also be done somewhat cautiously because dramatic changes may also alter the nature of the study. Care must be taken to avoid letting the lengthened task become a test of endurance instead of accomplishing the actual purpose of the investigation. Usually, this problem is avoided by running a quick pilot test of the task.

As suggested, adjusting the performance range can be accomplished in a number of fashions. Decisions are usually made on the basis of clinical experience and inspection of previous task–participant interactions. For example, further adjustments were made in a third study following the two just described (Study 3). A different population was under investigation that had some unique properties causing concern. Notably, this third group was diagnosed as having learning disabilities and therefore was expected to have greater performance *variation* than found in either of the previous studies. Great variability in performance seems characteristic of this population. In addition, this variation is expected at both ends of the performance range. Consequently, three levels of material difficulty were used to ensure that participant performance would fall within the task limits. These were designed as follows: (a) a low-difficulty list that is even easier than the low-difficulty material in Study 2, (b) an intermediate-difficulty list that falls approximately between the high and low list in Study 2, and (c) a high-difficulty list with a difficulty level above that in both Studies 1 and 2. As the results for Study 3 are examined, it is apparent that

STUDY 3   Mean Correct Responses by List Difficulty and Organization

List Organization List Difficulty	Unorganized	Organized
Easy	15.25	16.23
Intermediate	11.59	13.21
High	7.25	7.54

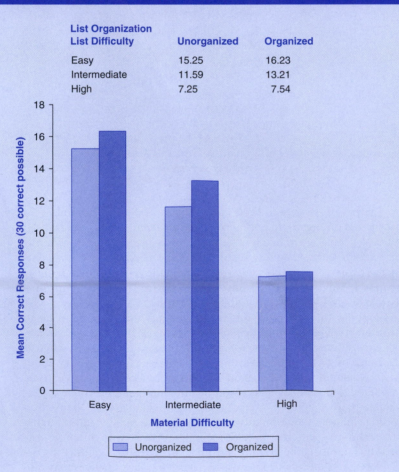

the initial judgment had been correct. All means were nicely plotted and well within the performance limits imposed by the task.

Task performance range difficulties present a particularly challenging problem in certain *quasi-experimental designs*. A quasi-experimental design is one in which an experimenter is comparing groups that are different on the basis of some preexisting condition. Examples of quasi-experimental studies are found throughout the research literature in human development studies (i.e., preexisting age differences), and a variety of educational circumstances where the comparison being made is between groups that are known to be different before the study (e.g., groups of children with differing disability characteristics). The previously cited studies where participants with intellectual disabilities were compared with participants of normal intelligence represent classic quasi-experimental designs. Likewise, studies comparing different cultural or physiologically different groups are examples that are quasi-experimental (Berk, 2006; Gersten et al., 2005).

The problem arises in attempting to design a task with performance possibilities that are broad enough to cover the range of responses in all groups. For example, studies in child development may necessitate a minimum of three levels of chronological age to obtain even a rough picture of developmental trends in performance. It is difficult to gain much developmental information from only two levels. Three or more levels permit a more complete developmental picture. Even with three age levels, the performance range may be extremely problematic. Imagine the difficulty in designing a task that will permit performance of groups with mean ages of 4, 6, and 8 years. Likewise, the problem is equally challenging for groups that are pre-experimentally different on other dimensions. Such pre-identified participant classifications as "high, average, and low achievement" bring with them vast differences in background information and, likely, wide performance ranges. It is possible, for example, that the low-achievement participants may also be poor, which may be accompanied by a multitude of health and cultural influences. When planning an investigation, a researcher must be cautious in selecting the task if a quasi-experimental design is involved. A pilot test of the task with each type of participant group will definitely be necessary to determine the degree to which the task will appropriately allow participants in all groups to perform at their best. The pilot study is always more advisable than investing resources in a full-blown investigation that obtains results contaminated by performance-range restrictions.

The Questionnaire's Purpose and Design

To a beginning researcher, questionnaire studies may seem to be the easiest type of study to conduct. On the surface, it may seem that all you have to do is put the questions to be asked on paper, mail them or electronically distribute them, then sit back and wait for the data to roll in. Electronic distribution may involve putting the questions on the Web and just waiting for electronic responses. This apparent simplicity is deceptive, however. There are many important elements in questionnaire studies that are not apparent on the surface, and several relate directly to the instrument. This section will briefly examine some of the issues related to the construction of a questionnaire instrument. These are areas for focused attention regardless of whether you distribute your questionnaire using snail mail or electronically.

Constructing the Questionnaire

The questionnaire represents the link between a researcher and the data. It must stand on its own because a researcher is not usually present to prompt a response or clarify areas where the participant may be confused. This leads to an important point for designing the instrument. Because a researcher cannot personally work with each respondent (e.g., to clarify a question or prompt a response), it is important to solve as many instrument problems as possible while the questionnaire is being constructed. One critical factor is to anticipate the difficulties that may arise as participants complete your questionnaire. This can be partially accomplished by asking a series of questions but also should involve running a pilot test of your instrument. Pilot tests are enormously helpful in revising your instrument as well as other elements of respondent participation.

Legitimacy of questionnaire. A researcher always wants to know what factors might make a participant fail to respond or what might lead a participant to give inaccurate responses. First and foremost, the respondent must be convinced that the study is legitimate and worth the effort of response—that is, there must be a high level of **questionnaire legitimacy.** Part of this task may be managed through appropriate sponsorship and a well-written cover letter (Hagan, 2006; Wiersma & Jurs, 2005). Respondents are more likely to complete a questionnaire that is sponsored by an agency they view as being legitimate and having a logical stake in conducting the research. Often this is accomplished by a cover letter that appears on letterhead from your college or university. The cover letter should *not* be overly long but should explain the specific purpose of the study and why the research is being conducted. A number of references provide more detailed information on these elements of survey research (e.g., Hutchinson, 2004; Nardi, 2006).

Participant's completion of instrument. The questionnaire itself must also contribute to encouraging participant response in an accurate manner. The amount of effort required on the part of the respondent is also important—the less effort required, the more likely a respondent is to complete and return the questionnaire. The questionnaire should not be so long that it requires a great deal of time and effort to complete. Here again, the effort required by the respondent is of paramount concern—the shorter a questionnaire is, the more likely a respondent is to complete and return it. If there are too many open-ended questions, the respondent may not be willing to take the time to write out the answers (whereas the same information might be obtained by questions for which the participant can merely check off their responses).

Designing the questionnaire. The questions being asked in a questionnaire are central to the data collection process. They must be clearly worded so that there is minimal chance for the respondent to be confused. The best protection against problems such as this is a pilot test of the instrument prior to beginning the study. Pilot tests have been mentioned before. They represent a crucial step and should always be conducted to avoid serious inaccuracies and inconsistencies in the data. However, in addition to the pilot test, there are several points that need attention as the questions are being written. The next section addresses these.

Pitfalls to Avoid in Question Writing

Avoid writing items that actually have two questions included in one, sometimes called *double-barreled questions.* An example of this might be a question like, "Does your company have an explicit recruitment policy for ethnic minorities and women?" This type of question is very typical of verbal conversation but causes serious difficulties on a questionnaire. The problem is the use of the word "and," which may cause confusion for the respondent. What response should be given if the department has a policy for minorities but not for women? If the question is read literally, a "yes" answer can only be given if policies exist for both. A negative response might result if there is no policy for women, minorities, or both. The question might be worded more clearly by substituting "or" for "and," or it might be separated into two questions. Items should always be reviewed carefully to ensure that only one question is involved in each (Bradburn, Sudman, & Wansink, 2004; Hagan, 2006; Wiersma & Jurs, 2005).

All possible precautions should be taken to avoid ambiguous questions. Certainly, the example presented above was vague in terms of what response was desired. There are, however, other types of ambiguity that a researcher should avoid, such as vague terminology. Certain difficult or technical words may not be familiar to the respondents and may, therefore, be ambiguous. (Researchers should not expect respondents to use a dictionary unless they are willing to settle for a very low response rate.) On the other end of the continuum, there may be some terms everyone thinks they know but that have been used too much and so loosely that the meaning has become very fluid (as in the case of slang terms or phrases). Such terms or phrases may generate inconsistent responses because they have different meaning to different people (Nadler & Chandon, 2004). A researcher must be cautious regarding the use of uncommon terms as well as those that are commonly used. The best safeguard against ambiguity in a questionnaire is a pilot test and also a critical review by an independent group of colleagues.

Questionnaire's reading level. Give the questionnaire's reading level extra emphasis. A delicate balance must be maintained between precise and colloquial language. After a researcher avoids the obvious problems of words and slang, attention should be turned to the general wording of the questions. The primary concern here must be the sample of participants being studied in the survey. If the respondents are considered "well educated," the language difficulty level may be somewhat higher than if they are less educated. At times, there may be an inclination to use slang phrases to establish rapport with the respondents (e.g., when studying adolescents' opinions of music). Here again, caution must be exercised because of the problems with slang terminology. The same slang phrases may have widely varying definitions for adolescents in California and in South Dakota and may change weekly.

Sensitive topics. Particular care must be taken when a survey involves sensitive topics (e.g., sex, drinking habits, use of drugs), and questionnaire construction must therefore monitor **questionnaire sensitivity** (its potential to offend) in this sense. Such topics raise the probability that respondents may not return the questionnaire or may respond inaccurately. Although response issues are continuing problems, there are certain precautions that can be taken in questionnaire construction that may help. One of the difficulties noted earlier was the possibility of inaccurate responses. Participants may be inclined to answer in a manner that they think is socially appropriate rather than being completely honest. Questions may be worded in a fashion to partially offset such tendencies. For example, the same item could be phrased two different ways:

1. Do you smoke marijuana?

   Yes

   No

   If yes, how often?

   Once a week

   Once a month

   Every day

2. How often do you smoke marijuana?

Once a week

Once a month

Every day

Never

Participants may give socially appropriate (or legally appropriate) answers in either case, but there is less chance of this happening in Question 2. The wording in Question 1 makes it very easy to say "no," whereas the second wording makes it somewhat more difficult. Other approaches to sensitive topics include wording the question in a manner suggesting that the practice is widespread or that there is no consensus regarding what is socially appropriate. Some might suggest that sensitive topics like those above should be avoided because of the response problems involved. Certainly, less sensitive topics do not present as many difficulties, but researchers cannot avoid an area of study just because it may be troublesome.

Order of questions. The order in which questions appear may also have an influence on participants' responses. For example, it is usually best to place the easily answered questions first. In this way, respondents may become more committed to completing the questionnaire as they proceed because they will have already spent time on the task. Similarly, if there are sensitive questions or open-ended items requiring more effort, these are best placed at the end of the questionnaire. Even if the participant declines to answer these more specific items, the responses to other questions will have already been provided and there is greater likelihood that the survey will be returned.

There are many considerations involved in the construction of a questionnaire. Only a few have been examined here. Beginning researchers who anticipate undertaking such an investigation should consult reference volumes specifically focusing on these types of studies and instruments (e.g., Hagan, 2006; Nadler & Chandon, 2004; Nardi, 2006). Many of the issues discussed in this section are also relevant to constructing structured interview protocols. Such interview studies are similar to questionnaire surveys except that an interviewer personally reads the questions to the participants and records the responses.

Using Observation as an Instrument

Observers must have some means of recording the data. This section will briefly examine data-recording instruments that can be used for observation studies. There are certain types of observation that impose little structure on the data recorded, whereas others involve a great deal of structure. Observations in qualitative studies often favor the former, and researchers may describe a setting and interactions among participants in words and without preplanned organization of the data. Quantitative observation, with more structure, is the primary focus of this discussion because the data-recording instrument is a major source of structure.

Observation Protocols

Observation-recording instruments may be very simple or quite complex, depending on the nature of the study. The data sheet or **observation protocol** (directions or description of how observations are to be done) will probably be simple if an investigation is aimed at recording information on only a few behaviors. More complex instruments are obviously necessary for studies involving many behaviors or many participants who are being observed simultaneously. One important point in developing an observation instrument relates to this complexity factor.

The instrument should never be more complex than necessary to serve the study purposes. Complex instruments require more effort from the observer than those with simple formats. Since more effort is required, there is a greater likelihood that errors will be committed during data collection. This generates more inaccurate data and may reduce interobserver reliability. A delicate balance must be struck between a format that is sufficiently precise to meet the needs of the study and one that is as simple and convenient to use as possible.

Protocol Formats

Formats for observation instruments will vary, depending on the data-recording method being used. For example, the format might be very simple if the researcher is merely counting occurrences—the tally method. Figure 5.3 illustrates a data-recording format using the tally method for counting aggressive behaviors. Note that the categories of behavior are provided on the form for the observer.

The data instrument might look different if the observer were using a duration recording method. Duration data involve the amount of time a participant is engaged in the target behavior. In this case, an observer will note the time that the

---

FIGURE 5.3   Observation Data Sheet Using the Tally Recording Method

		Subject: David	
Aggressive behavior		Session 1	Session 2
Physical			
	Peer	卌	//
	Adult	/	
Verbal			
	Peer	卌 //	卌 ///
	Adult	//	/
Nonagressive behavior			
Physical			
	Peer	/	
	Adult	/	///
Verbal			
	Peer	//	/
	Adult	/	卌

behavior begins (i.e., by starting a stopwatch) and when it terminates (by stopping the stopwatch). This process of starting and stopping the stopwatch may continue (without resetting the watch to zero) for a specified period such as a one-hour reading lesson. The data, then, would be the total amount of time that the participant was engaged in the target behavior (e.g., self-stimulation) during that one-hour observation session. Figure 5.4 illustrates a data form using duration recording.

Observation studies may also use the interval method of recording data. Such procedures focus on whether or not a particular behavior occurred during a given interval. Basically, the observer would place a check mark or a code symbol on the recording form if the behavior occurred during the specified interval. Figure 5.5 illustrates an interval recording form. The codes in this example are simple: *P* represents physical aggressive behavior, *V* represents verbal aggressive behavior, and a blank interval box means that neither of those target behaviors occurred during that interval.

FIGURE 5.4   **Data Form for Duration Recording Method**

Subject:_____   Target behavior:_____

Observer:_____   Date:_____

Location:_____   Activity:_____

Session number:_____   Total behavior
(duration read
from watch)

Time ended:_____

Total session length:_____   _____ hr. _____ min. _____

FIGURE 5.5   **Data Form for Interval Recording Method**

Subject: _____ David _____   Observer: _____ Mary _____

Date: _____ 5/16 _____   Activity: _____ Playground recess _____

Session number: _____ 12 _____   Time started: _____ 9:15 a.m. _____

Target behaviors and codes: _____ Physical agression = P _____

verbal agression = V

Interval length: _____ 15 seconds _____

1	VP	2	P	3	V	4	PV	5	V	6	
7		8	V	9	P	10	P	11	P	12	VP
13	V	14		15		16	V	17	V	18	P
19	VP	20	V	21		22		23		24	
25		26		27	P	28	P	29	V	30	VP

Observation instruments can take many forms as indicated by the examples presented above. As with most research, the specific format must be tailored to fit the investigation being planned. A beginning researcher may find it helpful to review current literature in the area being studied or consult volumes that focus in greater depth on observational recording systems.

COMMENTS

As we have seen, there are a number of matters that we need to pay attention to in selecting a measure for our study. Likewise, we have to determine what type of instrument or task we are going to use to collect our measures. This level of specificity and detail is pretty important as you prepare to undertake your research and it will affect the integrity of your study.

We have examined a variety of types of instruments that can be employed in educational and behavioral research. Each type has certain advantages and some limitations. The researcher may exploit some of the features, but he or she must always be alert so the limitations do not create inaccuracies in the data collected. Table 5.1 summarizes some examples of the research instruments discussed and outlines both advantages and limitations.

TABLE 5.1   Advantages and Limitations of Example Research Instruments

Instrument	Example	Advantages	Limitations
Written or hard-copy instrument on which a participant responds directly	Knowledge test	Format somewhat flexible, questions can be written in different ways & participants can respond in different formats	Written format not flexible enough to follow up on incomplete responses
Paper or hard-copy survey	Mailed questionnaire	Can be widely distributed, does not require face-to-face interaction	Format set once it is developed, must depend on thorough predistribution planning and pilot-testing, respondent response rate is touchy
Electronic survey	Web or e-mail questionnaire	Very inexpensive distribution, very broad distribution possible, very rapid distribution possible	Technical malfunctions, respondents limited to those with electronic access, response rate still touchy with this format—respondents may not respond because they think survey is spam
Face-to-face interaction between researcher and participants	Interviews	Very flexible, allowing follow-up on incomplete responses, clarifications	Expensive, time-consuming, and requires extensive interviewer training; potential data bias or inaccuracy due to face-to-face interactions
Human observation	Human data collection using data sheets	Data collection fairly flexible. Recorders can be trained to a high level of interobserver reliability	Data may be affected by participant reactivity to observer presence. Requires observer training to achieve high level of observer reliability
Electronic observation	Video	Records all behavior that can be reviewed later to enhance interpretation or allow for reexamination at a later time	Technical malfunctions can result in significant data loss. May be obtrusive for participants

Chapter Summary

✦ Reliability of a criterion measure refers to consistency or how often the same performance results in the same score. Validity refers to how well the criterion measure reflects the intended performance.

✦ Your definition of a criterion measure should include how reliability will be determined as well as how you will assess validity. These elements will include multiple administrations of the measure to see if similar scores result from similar performance and how accurately the measure reflected what you intended to assess.

✦ The criterion measure you select should be easily understood by your intended audience and be sensitive enough to reflect differences in participant performance even if those differences are subtle.

✦ The instrument or task you select to generate your criterion measure should result in varying data outcomes when you administer it to participants who are performing the task in a varying manner.

✦ After discussing participant reactivity to your instrument and the effects of administering multiple tasks, try it out on a classmate or acquaintance. When the person has completed the task, ask how he or she reacted and what effects he or she believes occurred.

✦ Ceiling effects occur when there is an inadequate performance range possibility on the upper end of the task, whereas a floor effect is found in a situation where the lower end of performance is restricted. Altering an instrument or task to avoid a ceiling effect could be accomplished by making items more difficult or increasing test length slightly. Avoiding a floor effect can be achieved by making items easier so participants can get more correct answers. Both of these alternatives should be used in moderation.

✦ Developmental studies often investigate performance across multiple age ranges. It is challenging to devise instruments to generate measures across different age ranges, particularly with young children where different skills are reflected at various ages.

✦ The appearance of legitimacy for a questionnaire means that the participant believes the questions being asked are justifiable and worth answering. This belief on the part of participants increases the likelihood they will answer the questions and do so truthfully.

✦ Reading levels should not exceed those of the intended participants and this must always be tested before the study actually begins. Different participant groups come from various backgrounds and question content will have varying degrees of personal or cultural sensitivity (potential to offend). Questions that may have higher sensitivity or potential for offending participants should be placed at the end of the questionnaire. This placement is also true for open-ended questions where participants have to work harder to provide an answer. Questionnaires should always be as short as possible.

✦ Observation protocols should be as simple as possible for the observer to complete and also involve the least amount of judgment for the observer. These characteristics will enhance data reliability.

Key Terms

Ceiling effect. An effect that occurs when the performance range of a task is so restricted or limited on the upper end that the subjects cannot perform to their maximum ability.

Criterion measure. That which is being measured in a study. If, for example, a study were focusing on the height of a particular group, the criterion measure might be inches. *Criterion measure* is synonymous with the term *dependent variable*.

Dependent variable. *See* criterion measure.

Experimental variable. That phenomenon that is under study; the factor that the researcher manipulates to see what the effect is. For example, if the researcher were interested in determining which of two teaching methods was more effective, the experimental variable would be the method of teaching. *Experimental variable* is synonymous with the term *independent variable*.

Floor effect. An effect that occurs when the performance range of the task is so restricted or limited on the lower end that the subjects' performance is determined by the task rather than by their ability to perform. Under such conditions, the task is so difficult that the researcher is unable to obtain any evidence about how the subjects can perform.

Independent variable. *See* experimental variable.

Measure communication value. This term refers to how easily understood a term is by a particular audience. A measure that has good communication value is one that is intuitively understood and not obscure.

Measure sensitivity. Refers to how sensitive a particular measure is to performance differences—that is, when performance changes, how well does the measure reflect those changes?

Observation protocol. A description of what behavior is to be observed and how it is to be recorded as data.

Participant reactivity. The degree to which a participant's behavior or performance is altered by the effects of taking the test, completing the instrument, or otherwise participating in the study.

Performance range. Task performance range refers to the variation in responses possible within the limits imposed by highest and lowest possible performance scores on the task.

Questionnaire legitimacy. Establishment of a study's (and thereby the questionnaire's) degree of respectability, justifiability, or genuine quality through appropriate sponsorship or affiliation with a respected organization or agency.

Questionnaire sensitivity. The degree to which a questionnaire or other instrument has the potential to be personally or culturally offensive due to "sensitive" or controversial topics.

Reliability, of measurement. Reliability refers to the consistency with which a measure reflects a given performance level. A reliable measure should consistently reflect performance change when change occurs.

Validity, of measurement. Validity means that the criterion measure assesses what it is supposed to be measuring, such as addition skills.

Student Study Site

The companion Web site for *Designing and Conducting Research in Education*
www.sagepub.com/drewstudy

Supplement your review of this chapter by going to the companion Web site to take one of the practice quizzes, use the flashcards to study key terms, and check out the many other study aids you'll find there. You'll even find some research articles from the Sage Full-Text Collection and a step-by-step guide that will show you how to read an educational research article.

Simulation Feedback

For additional
simulations visit
www.sagepub
.com/drewstudy

Simulation Feedback 5.1

As with any problem in which one is given a general task to perform, a variety of specific responses may be expected. The crucial issue here is whether you were sufficiently specific and that what you specified can be measured and is a logical criterion measure for the topic. Hopefully, the following will serve to exemplify such specificity for at least one possible measure.

First of all, the criterion measure must be a way of determining the effectiveness of the reading programs. One way of assessing the effectiveness of reading instruction is to measure a student's reading comprehension. However, as noted previously, the term "reading comprehension" is not specific enough to tell you what you are going to count. Frequently, reading comprehension is determined by counting the number of correct responses on a test dealing with a passage the students have read. Correct responses will serve adequately if reading comprehension is what you wish to assess. Do you have something else you want to measure? Is it specified in a measurable form?

Part II RESEARCH METHODS AND DESIGNS

Part II examines a variety of research designs as well as major issues often encountered in planning and implementing studies. Chapter 6 begins with quantitative methodologies and starts this discussion with the crucial matters of the concept of control and how to control factors that contaminate a study. Also essential to this discussion are the concepts of experimental variables and criterion measures. The chapter continues with an examination of single-subject design configurations, moves on to traditional group designs, and finishes with a discussion of the importance of planning ahead for data analysis.

Chapter 7 focuses on nonexperimental studies, beginning with survey research, and moves to observation as a data collection approach. The survey discussion begins with mailed questionnaires as well as those that are electronically distributed, and examines response rate issues and other potential challenges to this methodology. In addition, face-to-face and telephone interviews are discussed as well as focus groups. Observation studies are examined as a nonexperimental method covering matters ranging from identifying the participants through behavior definition and observation reliability.

Chapter 8 discusses qualitative and mixed-method approaches, including issues regarding when qualitative methods are best used and why they present advantages. The strengths of studying events as they unfold in natural environments are examined and data collection for qualitative methodology is explored, including a wide array of data sources. Ethical issues that particularly emerge in qualitative methods are also discussed. Mixed-method designs are explored and an examination of method selection discusses how to take advantage of the particular strengths of each approach.

Chapter 9 explores the pitfalls encountered in research designs beginning with discussions of types of design validity. Threats to internal and external validity are examined as well as general standards of rigor, threats to rigor, and how to defend against them. This part of the book continues emphasizing pre-implementation planning in order to maximize the strength of research designs and minimize contaminating influences.

6

QUANTITATIVE RESEARCH METHODOLOGIES

After reading Chapter 6, you should be able to do the following:

+ Describe how you could control age between two groups receiving different reading instruction methods.

+ Describe how you could control age between two groups where the experimental variable is based on preexisting differences in math skill levels.

+ Describe how you would determine the length of a baseline where there is 30% of variability between data points.

+ Describe how an A-B-A-B design provides more evidence regarding treatment effect than a simple A-B design.

+ Discuss what type of study is particularly appropriate for a multiple-baseline design.

+ Describe how independent group experiments are different from repeated-measures group designs.

+ Describe how mixed-group designs are different from totally independent group designs.

+ Describe some steps that are important in planning ahead for data analysis.

DEFINING QUANTITATIVE RESEARCH

Gathering and analyzing information in the form of numbers distinguishes *quantitative research* methods from other types. Investigators using this approach tend to count some aspect of performance or behavior exhibited by those participating in their study. For example, they may count the number of students' correct reading or math responses to reflect amount learned. Alternatively, they may count the number of classroom disruptions to determine how well teachers are organizing and managing their classes.

Quantitative investigators tend to prefer explicit and detailed definitions as they plan their studies. They are very clear about what type of research question or questions are being asked, exactly how the data are being collected, and the reliability of those collection procedures. To analyze the data, these studies often use statistical tools to examine performances. Different analyses will be used depending on the type of research question being asked and other factors, such as the type of data collected.

As indicated in Table 6.1, quantitative researchers may conduct experiments where they impose a treatment to see how well it works, such as a particular teaching method. Quantitative researchers may also use nonexperimental methods, such as questionnaires to see how teachers perceive the children they are teaching. In the latter case, the teachers may be asked to recall things like how often they see classroom disruptions during reading lessons.

This chapter will examine a variety of research components that are used in quantitative methods. We will discuss some of the basic concepts underlying quantitative methods as well as describe basic design configurations. You will find that the number of design configurations is nearly endless. Practicing researchers assemble the design they are going to use based on the research question being asked and the circumstances presented by the study situation. The basic concepts become the foundation or support, and the final design will be somewhat like an assembled jigsaw puzzle.

TABLE 6.1	**Major Elements of Different Research Methods**
Methods	*Elements*
Quantitative	Prefers explicit definitions and hypotheses
	Prefers explicit procedure description
	Data in numerical scores
	Attention to assessing data and score reliability
	Attention to design validity
	Prefers design or statistical variable control
	Prefers design control of procedural bias
	Prefers random sampling to obtain representative information
	Prefers statistical summary of results
	Prefers dividing phenomena into parts for analysis
Experimental	Manipulates study conditions to observe participant responses
	Imposes treatment or intervention
	Explicitly defines procedures, samples, and conditions for data collection
Nonexperimental	Often studies conditions as they exist in natural environment
	No imposition of treatment or intervention to determine participant reaction
	May use numerical or narrative data
Qualitative	May prefer hypotheses and definitions to emerge in context as study develops
	Data in narrative description form
	Achieves validity by cross-checking data sources (triangulation)
	Prefers narrative & literary procedure description
	Prefers logical analysis for control or accounting for variables (describing what else is going on)
	Relies on researcher to detect & minimize procedure bias
	Prefers expert information samples
	Prefers narrative results summary
	Prefers holistic description (describing the whole picture)
	Prefers not to tamper with natural setting
Mixed Methods	Employs elements from multiple other methods such as collecting both quantitative and narrative information
	Quantitative data may serve as a source of triangulation for the qualitative data, and vice versa
	Qualitative data may be able to investigate why a particular quantitative result was evident
	Quantitative data may be able to provide support for a particular qualitative result

Characteristics of Experimental Studies

Quantitative experimental approaches to conducting research have a long and rich history, including early work ranging from agriculture to psychology and education. Sir Ronald Fisher (1926, 1935) is often cited as the father of quantitative experimental methodology in the social sciences for his work during the early part of the 20th century. His work, plus that of W. A. McCall (1923), set the stage for behavioral science experimental methodology and had a significant impact on current thinking regarding this approach to research. Experimentation is a powerful tool when the topic and setting are appropriate for its use. There are many variations of procedures within experimental and quantitative methods, and they are important and useful as components of a broad, mixed-methods tool kit (Rasinski, Viechnicki, & O'Muircheartaigh, 2005).

Controlling or Manipulating Contaminating Factors

A researcher manipulates the treatment under study, such as the length of time devoted to teaching certain academic content. The factor under study is known as the **experimental variable.** It is also called the **independent variable,** but in this book the term *experimental variable* will be used to avoid confusion with other uses of the term *independent* in certain research contexts.

The factors we are holding constant, that is, *controlling,* are sometimes called *confounding* or *extraneous variables* because they can exert influence in addition to the experimental variable and have potential to confuse our results unless we control them. Control is the essential element in sound experimental design. The fashion in which the **concept of control** is implemented varies a great deal depending on the circumstances involved in the research setting (see, for example, Gay, Mills, & Airasian, 2006; Goodwin, 2005).

Control is often achieved by using certain sampling procedures while in other circumstances it is achieved by particular procedures for assigning participants to groups. For example, either random sampling or random assignment may be used so that the characteristics are *very* similar between the groups to which participants are assigned. It may be important to control age or reading level between two groups, meaning we don't want significant differences between the groups in terms of average age or average scores on a reading test. In order to accomplish this control, we may randomly assign participants to Groups 1 and 2. This would result in both groups having similar group averages in age and reading levels. Sampling and assignment procedures are extremely useful for controlling participant variables, as was discussed in Chapter 4.

Quantitative research is often associated with laboratory investigations in which the researcher tightly controls outside influences that might contaminate the results (e.g., noise, other distractions). If control is successfully accomplished, any change observed in the participant behavior or performance is thought to be caused by the treatment that was manipulated and is being studied. Controlling all influences except the one under study is perhaps the central focus for experimental researchers and is of utmost importance. The goal of control is to be able to attribute a performance level, difference, or change to the experimental variable (the treatment).

The reason that attributing performance to the effect of the experimental variable is so important is that this is the core foundation of a design's validity. As we conduct research on a topic, such as the effects of a reading intervention, we need to be able to attribute any change in performance to that intervention. That requires controlling any other influences such as age. If we don't control those factors, they may make our interpretation difficult or inaccurate. We cannot attribute increases in scores to a reading intervention if there are also age differences that might have contributed to scores that indicate a reading improvement. This is the core of design validity and the strength of a design (its level of validity) is based on the concept of control. Any possible influences except our experimental variable are threats to this design validity. We discuss various threats to validity in Chapter 9.

In many cases, experiments occur in classrooms or other instructional settings and the stereotype of precise laboratory control does not hold true. For example, a researcher may control or manipulate the time allotted to teaching arithmetic, such as 20 minutes, 30 minutes, or similar durations. In this example, the manipulation or treatment would be the amount of time for arithmetic instruction but the rest of the setting and environment might look a lot like a regular classroom. Suppose we found that children receiving 20 minutes of arithmetic instruction did better on tests than those who were taught for 30 minutes. We would like to say that the better performance can be attributed to the amount of time they were taught. However, to be able to draw that conclusion, all other possible influences must be controlled—that is, held constant. We can't have the children in the 20-minute group being brighter, having a better teacher, being better rested, or any of those matters that might make them perform better than the other group. In fact, we want all of these influences held constant between the groups so that neither is advantaged or disadvantaged. When we accomplish this, then we can attribute any performance differences between the groups to the only factor that was different between them—the experimental variable (time of instruction). What is being manipulated (the experimental variable) and the amount of control imposed on other potential influences depend on the research question being asked.

Experimenters take great pains to plan their studies so they will be able to attribute changes or levels of performance to the experimental variable. They do this in a number of ways. Sampling of students as participants is conducted carefully so that, in the example above, the participants in the 20-minute group and the 30-minute group are the same age, intelligence, experience, and so on. The researcher will also try diligently to have teachers between the groups be similar in experience, skill, enthusiasm, and any other matters that might affect instructional effectiveness. Investigators will also do their best to treat the students the same, and teach them in the same way and in the same environment, with the only difference hopefully being the time of instruction, which is our experimental variable in this example. It is easy to see why experimental researchers do so much planning regarding the details of procedures. This is their main avenue for being able to draw inferences about the results they obtain in an unambiguous fashion. Consequently, this is their best mechanism for achieving a high degree of design validity.

Critierion Measures

As we saw in Chapter 5, the selection, adaptation, or development of a workable criterion measure is very important to all research studies. If a researcher is going to observe change in the participants, there must be some way of measuring that change (e.g., improved reading performance, faster time in completing the physical education exercises, reduced number of classroom disruptions). Without a good criterion measure, the researcher won't be able to determine the effects of any treatment. A **criterion measure** is the metric a researcher uses to determine what the level of performance is or if change has occurred.

A wide variety of criterion measures are used in educational and behavioral research. For example, the number of correct responses on a test is recorded. In other cases, the measures might involve the time elapsed to finish a test or lesson, the number of positive interactions among classmates, or any number of other measures depending on the study. The criterion measure is often called the dependent variable, since the change (if it occurs) is presumably dependent on the researcher's manipulation of the experimental variable. For the purposes of this book, the designation of criterion measure will be used. This avoids confusion that beginning researchers often have in trying to remember differences between independent and dependent variables. Remember, *experimental variable* is synonymous with the term *independent variable,* and *criterion measure* is the same as the *dependent variable.*

Quasi and True Experiments: Approaches to Group Experimentation

Sometimes a researcher is interested in a variable that cannot be easily manipulated or has already been "manipulated" by nature. In this type of situation, the experimental variable is formulated on the basis of preexisting differences between comparison groups as distinguished from circumstances in which the researcher creates differences by actually manipulating the treatment. Such a format is known as a **quasi-experimental design**, whereas the term *true experiment* (or just experiment) is reserved for cases involving actual manipulation of the variable by the researcher.

Quasi-experimental comparisons are often used when a researcher is examining developmental differences between age groups. For example, suppose you want to investigate the development of emotional maturity. In this hypothetical study, perhaps you want to see how emotional maturity has progressed at the second, sixth, and tenth grades. This type of design involves selecting students from groups of second, sixth, and tenth graders. These differences in grade level are preexisting because we cannot assign students to such groups randomly. This would be considered a quasi-experimental design because we are making comparisons across groups that have preexisting differences.

Quasi-experimental studies are very useful and rather common in some fields, such as the developmental example above from the field of education. Certain specialties within education have also used quasi-experimental designs rather often, such as special education. Over the years, it has been important to compare instructional strategies used with children who have different cognitive or behavioral characteristics, such as those with intellectual disabilities and those with specific learning disabilities or autism. Quasi-experimental designs become necessities in these types of comparisons because the differing disabilities characteristics are preexisting and are the focus of the investigation.

BASIC EXPERIMENTAL DESIGN FORMATS

We noted before that there are many different design formats. Researchers assemble different configurations to meet the needs of the specific research question, the type of participants being studied, the situation where the study is conducted, and multiple other matters that exist in the investigation. In this section, we will discuss some very basic formats and selected examples of how they might be applied. In all cases, the most fundamental aim will be to arrange the different components so the concept of control is working and the researcher can attribute any outcomes observed to the experimental variable. There will always be other example formats that might be used in particular situations. Those included here are examples of some that are most basic and may be encountered by beginning researchers.

Experimental research in recent years has been characterized by two divergent approaches to designing studies: time series experiments and traditional experimental designs. *Time series experiments* have come into more frequent usage in the past 40 years, often in operant conditioning or behavior modification research (e.g., Horner et al., 2005; Kennedy, 2005). On the other hand, *traditional group experimental designs* have long been used in a variety of settings and disciplines ranging from psychology and education to medicine and pharmacology (e.g., McGrath, 2005; Williams, 2005). Early group experimental design was developed primarily in the context of agricultural research, whereas time series experimentation has come into popular usage predominantly in the realm of behavioral science.

Time Series or Single-Subject Experimental Designs

Time series designs have often been labeled as single-subject or single-case designs because of their frequent use with individual participants (Kennedy, 2005; Sealander, 2004). The single-subject label is commonly used and for that reason we will use that term in this book. It is important to mention that these designs can and are used in situations in which more than one participant is studied. However, it is beyond the scope of this book to explore in depth all the dimensions and details involved in designing investigations. Readers interested in further study should consult sources more focused on time series experimentation (e.g., Horner et al., 2005; Kazdin, 2003; Kennedy, 2005).

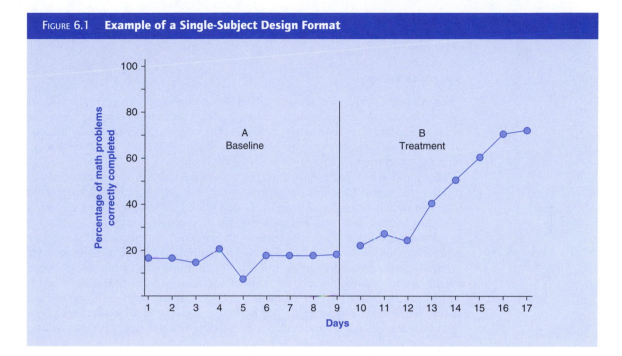

FIGURE 6.1   **Example of a Single-Subject Design Format**

Single-subject design involves investigation that compares different phases of treatment with a single or very few participants. These phases typically compare a participant's performance without treatment (termed a baseline phase) and with treatment (called the treatment phase). The purpose is to determine whether the initiation of treatment will generate a change in the participant's performance or behavior. Figure 6.1 illustrates a single-subject design format.

Important Elements in Single-Subject Research

Several initial factors must be considered essential elements in single-subject research. Single-subject research often involves continuous or nearly continuous measurement. Actually, it involves a series of observations taken on the participant over a specified period. This is a distinctive feature in relation to other research approaches in which far fewer measurements represent the data. The number of measurements or data points recorded varies considerably depending on the situation, which leads to a second basic consideration. Usually, there are a number of phases in any single-subject experiment, each representing a different experimental condition, such as the following:

Baseline (performance before intervention)

Treatment (performance observations during intervention)

Return to baseline (performance observations after reversing to nontreatment conditions)

Before demonstrating the effect of any treatment, it is necessary to determine what the performance level is *without* the treatment influence. This is usually accomplished by recording the performance level of the subject in a natural or non-treated state. Such a condition and the data generated are called a *baseline*. When sufficient data have been recorded to establish the usual or stable baseline performance level, the researcher then begins experimental treatment. For purposes of this discussion, the initiation of treatment will be called the intervention. (In actual experiments, it is usually labeled by the specific treatment term such as "extinction" or "reinforcement.")

Data Stability

The number of measurements or data points within any phase must be sufficient to determine a stable performance estimate. The purpose of changing from one phase to another is to demonstrate behavior change presumably caused by the new condition. This cannot be established with any degree of certainty unless the behavior rate or performance level is stable before the change.

The question of when behavior may be considered stable is one that continually plagues students of time series experimentation (see, for example, Goldberg et al., 2003; Sofuoglu, Gonzalez, Poling, & Kosten, 2003). Obviously, there are some behaviors that are never stable in the sense that no variation occurs, but usually it is possible to establish a reliable estimate of the behavior pattern, which serves as a comparison for the data in the next phase. For example, it may be that considerable variation occurs in the frequency of a behavior, but it is cyclical and varies rather reliably around a particular level at certain times. Figure 6.2 illustrates this behavior and would be considered an adequately stable basis for implementing a phase change. However, the data would not have been considered adequate for a phase change by Session 4 since the regularity of variation was not evident at that point.

Determining Baseline

There are some basic rules of thumb regarding baseline length. Single-subject myths have often indicated a minimum of three sessions of data collection, but more thoughtful explanations indicate that enough observations must be collected to determine

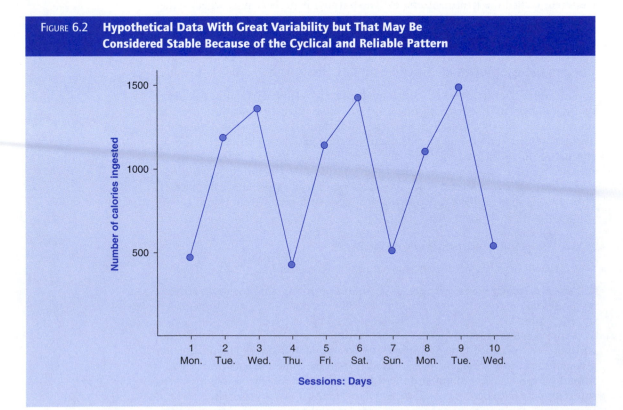

FIGURE 6.2   Hypothetical Data With Great Variability but That May Be Considered Stable Because of the Cyclical and Reliable Pattern

a stable performance estimate (Kennedy, 2005). More sessions of data collection are suggested when more variability is observed in the baseline (e.g., for each 10% of variability, at least one other data collection session is warranted). Variability is easily determined by taking the highest rate minus the lowest rate, and then dividing that by the highest rate. Scheduling difficulties or ethical concerns (e.g., self-abusive behavior) may make this rule impractical, requiring attention or intervention regarding some of the problems causing the data variability (Best & Kahn, 2006).

Types of Single-Subject Designs

The A-B Design

Figure 6.3 shows a data display resulting from a single-subject study measuring math problems completed. This format is known as an **A-B design.** In this type of experiment, the researcher records data on the participant for a time without treatment involved (Phase A, known as baseline). After the researcher has enough data to reliably indicate the participant's untreated performance level, Phase B (treatment) is initiated. The experimental variable in this case is the treatment with two specific conditions in that variable: treatment absent and treatment present. Single-subject experiments represent situations in which the researcher actually manipulates the experimental variable. The investigator will try to control all factors so that the only difference between Phase A and Phase B is the implementation of treatment. This will allow any performance differences between the phases to be attributed to the treatment. The example in Figure 6.3 involves a study that measured math performance, although such research could measure any number of educational content areas or classroom behaviors that were the target for change. In all cases, the key is being able to attribute any performance change to the intervention and to avoid other influences that might contribute to such results in addition to the intervention. A variety of single-subject design formats may be used in different situations and will be explored in greater depth in later sections of this chapter.

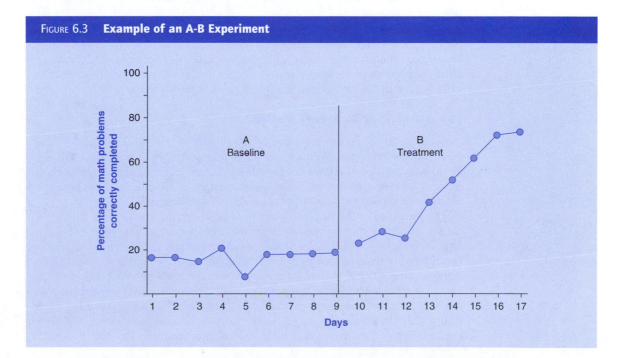

FIGURE 6.3   **Example of an A-B Experiment**

The A-B design is essentially a two-phase experiment. Although it was applied in early research, the A-B design involves some very serious weaknesses and is not used much today. Expanded formats were developed to circumvent the weaknesses and these have mostly replaced its use. It is discussed here only because of its conceptual simplicity, which facilitates basic understanding of time series formats in general.

As mentioned above, the two phases constituting the A-B design are baseline (A) and intervention (B). The baseline condition is implemented first and continued until a satisfactory estimate of pretreatment performance level is obtained. *After a stable rate of baseline behavior has been established, the intervention or treatment condition is begun.* Figure 6.3 illustrates a data display that might result from an A-B design experiment.

The vertical centerline in Figure 6.3 represents the time intervention is begun, or the phase change. One basic assumption of the A-B design is that any observed performance change after intervention is due to the treatment. We noted that above and indicated that it is an important assumption because of our desire to attribute any observed performance change to the intervention. The major difficulty with the A-B design lies in the absence of strong evidence supporting this assumption. Suppose that baseline data are stable and then a rather dramatic performance change is evident, which occurs at the same time as the intervention. In viewing such data, one might be inclined to attribute the performance change to the treatment. This may be the case, but there are some alternative explanations as well. It could be that other influences occurred simultaneously with the initiation of treatment.

In the example in Figure 6.3, the intervention involves Johnny being fitted for glasses. The experimenter would like to say that the dramatic improvement in math performance in Phase B occurred because Johnny is now wearing corrective lenses. However, suppose that about the time Johnny was fitted for glasses, the teacher, distressed by Johnny's poor performance, also began to provide him with one-on-one tutorial assistance. Is the performance change due to the glasses, the tutoring, or both? The experimenter cannot say with certainty. Here is a situation in which the change in performance might be caused either in part or wholly by influences other than the experimental treatment. Without additional convincing evidence, the researcher will find it difficult to be assured that the treatment alone resulted in the behavior change.

One additional note must be made. It has repeatedly been mentioned that the baseline data *must be stable before intervention.* This is an *essential* element in any time series experiment and worthy of repeated emphasis (Kennedy, 2005; Sealander, 2004). Otherwise, performance change evident in the data may merely represent an extension of an already existing trend and may not be due to the intervention at all.

The A-B-A-B or Reversal Design

In an effort to circumvent some of the pitfalls of the A-B design, researchers extended that basic model into a four-phase format known as the **A-B-A-B design.** Frequently called the **reversal design,** it basically involves a sequential replication of baseline-intervention-second baseline-second treatment intervention. Figure 6.4 illustrates a hypothetical data display for an A-B-A-B design.

The purposes of the first two phases in the design are the same as for the A-B design. The B_1 condition is terminated at the time that the performance or behavior level is stable. At that time, the condition is reversed and the pretreatment baseline conditions are reestablished (A_2). The assumption underlying this procedure is that if the treatment being studied is the influential or controlling variable (i.e., the factor influencing the behavior change in B_1), then removal of this treatment condition ought to reestablish the behavior rate at the baseline level. The A_2 condition is continued until the performance level returns to or nears the A_1 baseline or stabilizes. If the behavior rate returns to near baseline level, it is presumed that the treatment is

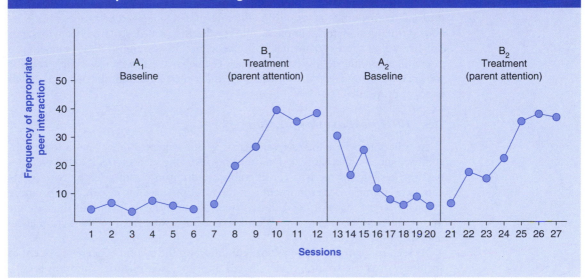

FIGURE 6.4   **Example of an A-B-A-B Design**

the factor influencing the behavior. At this point, the experimental treatment conditions are reinstituted (B_2). If behavior returns to the first intervention level, this is taken as further confirmation that the treatment is controlling the behavior.

The A-B-A-B design is not without weakness, however. First of all, the assumptions concerning the controlling treatment are supported only if the data reverse nicely to or near the initial baseline level when A_2 is instituted. Likewise, as noted previously, if condition B_2 reestablishes the performance at or near that evident in B_1, further strength is provided for an assertion that the treatment is controlling the behavior. However, such support is not available if the data do not fall nicely into this pattern. Suppose the behavior does not reverse in A_2. There may be several reasons for this. The first involves the possibility that the experimental treatment is not controlling the behavior. Other influences occurring at about the same time as the intervention at point B_1 may have changed the performance level (as in the A-B example). Alternatively, the treatment may be so powerful that the effects are not reversible even with treatment withdrawn. A third possible contaminant might be operative. Some unknown influence may have intervened to maintain the B_1 performance level at the same time that the experimental treatment was withdrawn. Another possibility is that the behavior itself is not reversible. Certainly the reinforcement and learning history of the participant has changed, and it is doubtful that the participant during A_2 is the same individual that existed before treatment was ever instituted. This is most relevant in target behaviors in which obvious learning is involved as a function of B_1. Acquisition of learned skill is rather difficult to reverse, and the A-B-A-B design should not be used in such circumstances.

The reversal design must be used with considerable caution. As noted above, it is of doubtful utility if the target behavior involves obvious learning or skill acquisition (e.g., in academic areas). However, it may be used effectively if behavior is being maintained by conditions in the environment such as social praise. If the target is an undesirable behavior, those conditions may be altered to decelerate the emission rate. The primary strength of the design is visible when the data evidence reversal under A_2 and reestablish a changed level under B_2. Without this evidence, the researcher is left primarily to speculation concerning the treatment effectiveness.

Beyond the interpretation difficulties presented by nonreversal, other considerations must receive attention when using the A-B-A-B design. It was mentioned earlier that time series experiments are often conducted for practical purposes rather than primarily for knowledge progress. Under these conditions, it is not unusual to encounter situations in which reversal of changed behavior is undesirable or unethical. If, for example, a child is exhibiting self-destructive behaviors, it is not likely that the experimenter will be inclined to reestablish such behaviors to strengthen confidence in what controlled the behavior. The danger simply may be too great to permit reversal. Consequently, under such conditions the A-B-A-B design is not appropriate.

The Multiple-Baseline Design

In situations where the reversal format is either undesirable or has a low probability of success, alternative designs must be used. One such alternative, the multiple-baseline design, has received considerable attention in recent years by researchers conducting time series experiments. In the **multiple-baseline design,** data on more than one target behavior are recorded simultaneously. Termination of the baseline on the different behaviors is staggered in a fashion illustrated by the hypothetical data display in Figure 6.5.

As seen in Figure 6.5, the baseline condition on the second behavior (percent of spelling words correct) is not terminated until the experimental condition for the first behavior (percent of math problems correct) has been stabilized. Likewise, the phase change for the third behavior (percentage of time on task in physical education) is conducted in a similar fashion as for the data for the second behavior. The assumption underlying multiple-baseline designs is that the second behavior serves as a control for the first, and the third behavior serves as a control for the second.

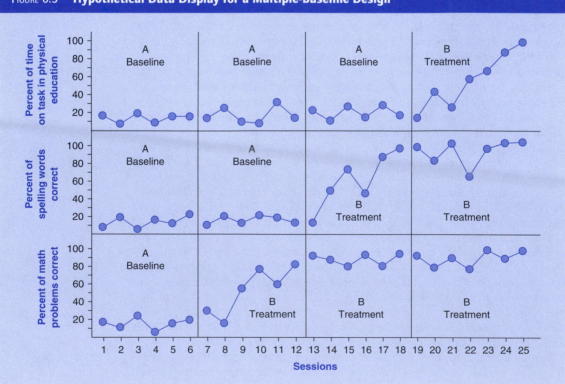

FIGURE 6.5   **Hypothetical Data Display for a Multiple-Baseline Design**

Presumably, the continued baseline level on the second behavior(after B has been instituted on the first) represents what would have occurred with the treated behavior had the experimenter not intervened. Thus, if the intervention on the second behavior also results in a rate change (as exemplified in Figure 6.5), this is viewed as confirmation that the treatment was the influence that generated change in the first behavior. Similarly, the third behavior is viewed as a checkpoint for the second. If the base rate remains stable and then intervention results in a rate change (again as in Figure 6.5), this is viewed as further confirmation that the treatment is the controlling agent. The absence of rate changes in the second and third behaviors under continued baseline conditions (the staggered portion) is of vital importance to this design. Continuation of stable base rates is presumed to indicate the absence of coincidental influences other than the treatment that might have generated changes in the respective treatment conditions.

As with most designs, both in time series and group experimental research, the multiple-baseline design is not without vulnerability to certain pitfalls. Similar to reversal designs, the multiple-baseline approach shows strongest support for basic assumptions when the data fit nicely into the pattern exemplified in Figure 6.5. The two foundation assumptions involved in the design are that (1) the continued or staggered base rates on the second and third behaviors will remain stable while other respective behaviors are under treatment, and (2) the control behaviors will change rates when treatment is specifically applied to them. (The present discussion is worded in terms applicable for three or more behaviors; there are also applications in which two behaviors are used.)

Several difficulties may be encountered with these assumptions. First, suppose continued base rates on the control behaviors do not remain stable (i.e., they also change when treatment is applied at intervention points on other behaviors). One explanation might involve influences other than the treatment that occur coincidentally with intervention. If this were the case, such other influences (e.g., unknown reinforcers in the environment) would probably not be applied only to the target behavior (e.g., the first behavior in Figure 6.5) but more generally and therefore might influence a rate change in control behaviors. Under these conditions, the experimenter would have no way of knowing whether the treatment was powerful enough to generate rate change at all. Alternative explanations would leave the researcher in an equally confusing situation. Perhaps the treatment was so powerful that the observed base rate change in control behaviors was caused by generalization of influence. It may also be the case that the behaviors are too closely interrelated and that improvement in the first behavior will result in rate changes in the second and third. The behaviors must be sufficiently independent from one another to make such generalization unlikely. Regardless of which alternative actually occurred, change in rate when the baseline condition is in effect seriously weakens multiple-baseline experiments and leaves the researcher with uninterpretable results.

Failure of those behaviors that were previously control behaviors to exhibit rate change when they become intervention targets also presents the researcher with problems. Suppose, for example, that the rate of the second behavior did not increase when B (treatment) was applied to it. Again several possibilities might be operative. It may be that the treatment is effective only for certain behaviors (in this instance, the first behavior). This could simply mean that all the behaviors under study are not controllable with the same treatment. One essential assumption of the multiple-baseline design is that the target behaviors *are* all amenable to control by the experimental treatment. A second possibility might involve the absence of control of the treatment at the beginning. If the change in the first behavior was caused by some other coincidental influence and *not* the treatment, the treatment might also fail to change the second behavior. This possibility is somewhat remote, since it is doubtful that a coincidental influence would be so specific as to affect the first behavior and not the second or third, which were under baseline.

Despite the difficulties noted above with a multiple-baseline design, it is a powerful design for time series experiments. It is particularly useful when reversal is either undesirable or impossible because skill acquisition is involved. As with most basic designs, many variations can be developed to allow investigation in many situations. Such variations involve expansions as well as combinations of other design components. The example and discussion presented above involved multiple behaviors in a single participant. However, the basic design may also be used to study the same behavior across multiple environmental conditions or may be applied using multiple participants.

TRADITIONAL GROUP EXPERIMENTAL DESIGNS

Traditional group experimentation has held a position of prominence in behavioral research for a long time. Many of the basic design formats were developed in agricultural research and were subsequently modified or applied directly to other areas of investigation. Group experimental research is used in a broader range of investigations than time series designs, although the design concepts can be understood in terms of a few basic formats. Beyond this core of basic designs, nearly endless variations and expansions have been used in particular situations. This section presents an overview of group experimental designs.

Traditional group experiments are often characterized by a single measure or fewer assessments of a group of participants in contrast to the many measurements found in time series studies. When multiple measures are used for the same participants, they involve far fewer observations than time series studies. (More than two or three repeated measures is unusual.) As with time series research, group designs involve several distinctive formats.

Independent Group Comparisons

One of the most commonly used designs involves **independent group comparisons.** The term *independent*, in this context, simply refers to different groups of participants for each condition. For example, Group A is made up of different participants from Group B. Consequently, there is little reason to expect the scores in one group to be influenced by scores in the other, and they are, therefore, considered independent. This term is used primarily to distinguish the separate group designs from those in which more than one measure is recorded for the same group. When repeated measures are recorded on the same participants, such as in a pre-post design, the scores are not considered independent and the comparison is called "nonindependent."

Beyond group independence, the number of experimental variables is an essential determinant of design configuration. The experimental variable, of course, is that factor or question being studied. For example, if we were attempting to determine the effects of material meaningfulness on learning rate, the experimental variable would be *material meaningfulness.* Material meaningfulness is the variable that is being investigated, and it is the experimental variable. Figure 6.6 illustrates an example design for an independent group comparison with one experimental variable that is labeled material meaningfulness.

One Experimental Variable

The format illustrated in Figure 6.6 has one experimental variable (group comparison with one experimental variable, often called a *single-factor design*). This

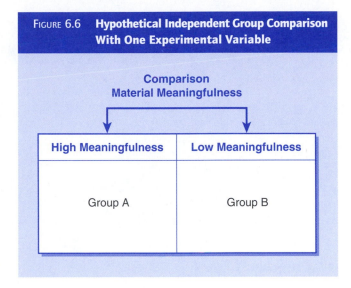

FIGURE 6.6 **Hypothetical Independent Group Comparison With One Experimental Variable**

Comparison
Material Meaningfulness

High Meaningfulness	Low Meaningfulness
Group A	Group B

example uses material meaningfulness as the experimental variable and illustrates a study in which two groups are compared: Group A received highly meaningful material, and Group B received material of low meaningfulness. Single-factor designs may include more than two groups; in fact, it is not uncommon for it to involve three, four, or more groups. Each of the groups or conditions within the experimental variable is called a *level* or *condition* (e.g., two levels or conditions of meaningfulness—high and low—are involved in Figure 6.6).

One basic assumption is essential to the independent group design regardless of how many levels or groups are being used: *the groups must be equivalent before the administration of a treatment.* The usual procedure is to constitute the groups and then to administer the experimental treatment, with different treatment conditions given to Groups A and B. The performance score is generated either as the treatment is administered or on some type of test given immediately after the treatment. If the groups of participants are equivalent before the treatment begins, then any differences between the groups can be attributed to the treatment. If groups are not equivalent before treatment, any differences observed in the performance measure may be a result of differences in group characteristics before the treatment rather than the intervention itself. Therefore, if the study is to actually investigate the effects of a treatment, the only difference between the groups *must be the treatment.* This is the important concept of control mentioned earlier. The various means of forming equivalent groups are primarily distinguished by the way in which participants are assigned to the respective groups. This was discussed in detail in Chapter 4. The independent group design with one experimental variable is an attractive design for action research because its simplicity makes it reasonably easy to implement in a field setting. The Research in Action box illustrates two action research studies using this design.

Two Experimental Variables

A researcher may be interested in investigating two experimental variables in the same study. This may be accomplished conveniently by using a format known as a *two-factor design.* (The number of "factors" refers to the experimental variables— e.g., a single-factor design has one experimental variable, and a two-factor design involves two experimental variables.) Figure 6.7 illustrates a hypothetical two-factor

RESEARCH IN ACTION

KEY POINTS IN THE CHAPTER REFLECTED IN THIS BOX:

- The manner in which similar design formats can be used to investigate very different topics
- How to control possible influences by assuring equivalency between comparison groups on all characteristics except the experimental variable
- Some differences between quasi-experimental and experimental designs

For more research in action tips visit www.sagepub .com/drewstudy

OBJECTIVES TO LEARN FROM THIS BOX:

- Understand how to control age, gender, and other factors except the experimental variable to help explain study results.
- Understand how to control age between two groups where the experimental variable is based on preexisting differences in ethnic background.
- Understand how the concept of control can be implemented in action research.

Below you will find two action research scenarios, one related to student engagement in reading and the second involving student self-esteem. In this box, the key points of the chapter regarding selecting criterion measures are addressed as follows: (1) controlling influences other than the experimental variable, and (2) determining the appropriate group experimental design. In each scenario, we will see a diagram of the study being planned. Like other steps in the action research process, planning ahead is important to determine variables that need to be controlled so that any effects can be attributed to the experimental variable. Action research requires a great deal of attention prior to beginning the study, in particular because the study is conducted in a field setting where the context is not tidy. You may also wish to think about how you would plan for control, and construct a diagram for your own action research study.

SCENARIO 1: ENGAGEMENT IN READING

Emily is working on a study manipulating the effects of engagement on how young students learn to read. She is using what is labeled as concept-oriented reading instruction (CORI) as a means of engaging the experimental group, and her comparison group is going to receive drill and practice (DAP) on words and sentences. Emily's experimental variable is teaching method, thus one group will receive the CORI method while the second will receive the DAP method. The diagram below pictorially summarizes Emily's design.

Emily needs to hold all possible influences equivalent between the two groups except her experimental variable. This means she will want to have the group characteristics similar in terms of age, ability, gender, and other factors that might influence her criterion measures. She will also need to have teachers for the two groups be as similar as possible as far as teaching experience, age, gender, and some of those seemingly intangible factors that are important like enthusiasm and teaching style. These control factors illustrate very well some of the challenges facing action research. It is important, however, to keep the two groups as similar as possible with the exception of the experimental variable. To the degree she can accomplish such equivalency, Emily will be more able to interpret any differences in scores as being due to the experimental variable.

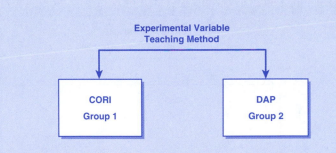

SOURCE: This action research scenario is roughly based on Swan, E. A. (2003). *Concept-oriented reading instruction: Engaging classrooms, lifelong learners.* New York: Guilford Press.

SCENARIO 2: STUDENT SELF-ESTEEM

Daniel is beginning a study to see if his students with learning disabilities have different self-esteem depending on whether they are of Latino or Caucasian descent. In this study, Daniel's experimental variable is ethnic background and his goal is to control or hold equivalent all other influences. This means that he doesn't want any differences between the groups in terms of intelligence (measured IQ), academic achievement, age, gender, or other group characteristics that might have some influence on self-esteem. If he is successful in this, then any differences in self-esteem scores can be attributed to his experimental variable of ethnic background. Of course, as he interprets such results he will need to do so with caution, acknowledging the fact that there may be unknown group characteristics that he hasn't been able to control.

   Daniel's study is an example of a quasi-experimental design because his groups were already existing and different before he began the study. Such a circumstance is fairly common in action research. Obviously, he cannot randomly assign participants to the Latino or the Caucasian groups. They come that way and they bring with them a long history of coming from different backgrounds. Since he is measuring self-esteem and what effects being Latino versus Caucasian has on self-esteem, this preexisting group difference is actually integral to the study. However, Daniel will need to be a little cautious as he draws interpretations from his results. The figure below is a diagram for Daniel's study.

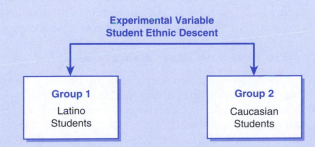

Think about this: For each of the action research studies in this box, what are the specific variables that need to be controlled? Write two lists that include the details of what is to be controlled for each study. For example, should age, academic ability, and gender be controlled between groups? Are some factors important in the reading study that are not in the self-esteem study and vice versa?

SOURCE: This action research scenario is roughly based on Rubin, D. (2000). *Race and self-esteem: A study of Latino and European-American students with learning disabilities.* Unpublished master's thesis, University of Utah, Salt Lake City.

FIGURE 6.7   **Hypothetical Independent Group Comparison With Two Experimental Variables**

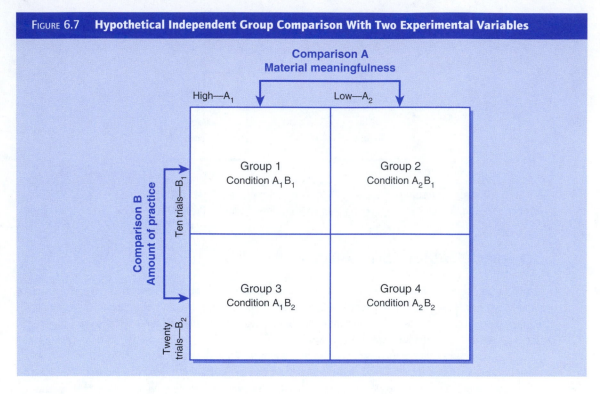

design. Note that this discussion is still focused on independent group comparisons, which means for the design in Figure 6.7 that the experimenter must constitute four different groups of participants. The experimental variables in Figure 6.7 are material meaningfulness and amount of practice. There are two levels of each variable (high versus low meaningfulness on Comparison A, and 10 versus 20 practice trials on Comparison B). This design is frequently labeled a "2 by 2" or "2 $\times$ 2," referring to the number of levels or conditions in each variable.

The two-factor design is flexible with regard to the number of levels in each factor. It is not necessary that the two experimental variables include the same number of levels; one may use three on A and two on B or any number of combinations (e.g., 3×2, 2×3, 3×4). The assumption of pretreatment group equivalence is also necessary for two-factor designs, as it is for group comparisons in general.

More Than Two Experimental Variables

More complex group designs may also be used if three or four experimental variables are studied simultaneously. These are simple, logical extensions of what has already been discussed and also may involve a variety of levels within the experimental variables (e.g., three-factor, $2 \times 4 \times 2$, $3 \times 3 \times 5$). If three experimental variables are involved (A, B, and C), the pictorial representation is three-dimensional, as in a representation of a cube. More complex designs, if used in a totally independent group-comparison format, require a large number of participants since each condition or cell has separate groups of individuals. More complex designs also present interpretation difficulties because of the complexity of results with several experimental variables. The challenge is to get clear about what the study is and interpret the results. Actual implementation is not difficult. Although complex designs can be useful on occasion, the simpler experiment often provides a more clear-cut demonstration of effect and is therefore preferable when possible.

Simulation

For additional simulations visit www.sagepub .com/drewstudy

Simulation 6.1

Topic: Concept of control: one experimental variable with independent groups

Background statement: The text has discussed the importance of what is known as the concept of control. This is one of the most essential factors in experimental investigations. See the diagram below, which refers to the study designed in a previous simulation that compared the self-concepts of learning disabled, emotionally disabled, and nondisabled children. Thus the investigation is actually a quasi-experimental design since the group differences exist before the study begins.

Task to be performed: Apply the concept of control to attempt the formulation of equivalent groups (except for the experimental variable of subject classification). Make specific notes regarding what factors you will want to control. How might you control the factors you have noted?

Write your response, then turn to page 164 for Simulation Feedback 6.1.

Repeated-Measures Comparisons

There are situations in which the experimenter either does not desire or is not able to compare independent groups of participants. In such a situation, the researcher may choose to record data on the same group under two or more different conditions. Because the same participants serve as the data source more than once, this type of experiment is known as a **repeated-measures design.** These designs are called nonindependent again because the scores are on the same participants, and the performance at Time 2 is certainly not independent of the performance at Time 1. Figure 6.8 illustrates a nonindependent comparison.

The Old Pre-Post Design

The general repeated-measures design may be used in several applications. Frequently, an experimenter will administer two different testing sessions with either a treatment or time lapse intervening between them. For example, this may take the form of a math computation pretest followed by an instructional treatment and then a posttest, with any difference in computational performance between the

FIGURE 6.8   **General Pre-Post Design Format**

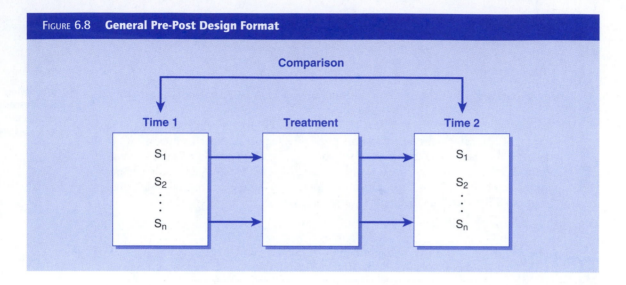

pre- and posttests attributed to the instruction. Known as a **pre-post design,** an example of this arrangement is shown in Figure 6.8. As indicated in the figure, the data (often mean scores) are compared between the pretest and posttest performance to determine if significant change has occurred. If there is a difference in the mean scores between administrations, the researcher might then attribute this difference to the intervening treatment, assuming nothing else changed between the two test times.

The crucial assumption underlying pre-post designs is that the treatment is the *only* influence that intervened between measurements. If this is actually true, the researcher may accurately infer that the treatment generated the performance change. This assumption, however, is somewhat difficult to substantiate. The only data usually available are the performance scores on pretests and posttests. The researcher often has little firm evidence that test scores would not have changed had no treatment been administered. In using the simple one-group pre-post design, there is always the unknown influence that may have occurred between tests to plague interpretation. There is also no evidence concerning how much improvement may have resulted from test practice. Problems that threaten the soundness of this design and suggestions for circumventing them are discussed in Chapter 9.

Beyond the Pre-Post Design

We are not limited to two data points in repeated-measures designs. It may be desirable to obtain multiple assessments over a longer period to trace performance change in a more detailed fashion than is possible with only two measures. The condition that occurs between measures may merely be time passage, or it may involve some active intervention such as the treatment suggested above. In either case, the repeated-measures design is still plagued by the same assumption weaknesses that were mentioned with the pre-post format. Depending on the actual circumstances surrounding an experiment, repeated measures with more frequent assessments may be more vulnerable to test practice than is the case with only two data points since there are more opportunities to practice the test.

Despite the problems confronting repeated-measures designs, they are an essential part of a researcher's toolbox. Frequently, the nature of the research question demands observation of performance change on the same participants. Many expansions and variations are used to circumvent the problems discussed above. Such variations may involve the addition of comparison groups, which permits measurements that will substantiate or assess the soundness of the basic assumptions.

Mixed-Group Designs

A **mixed-group experimental design** involves two or more experimental variables with independent groups on one or some of the variables and repeated measures on the remaining variable or variables. This type of design is called "mixed" because of the use of both independent groups and repeated measures (i.e., it "mixes" independent and nonindependent comparisons). Figure 6.9 illustrates a mixed two-factor design where material meaningfulness is the independent comparison and recall time is the repeated comparison. As illustrated in the figure, this merely means that two groups are formed with one being administered condition A_1 (highly meaningful material) and the other A_2 (material with little or low meaningfulness), and that both groups are tested for recall immediately and again after 24 hours (B_1 and B_2).

The mixed-group format is extremely flexible. If three experimental variables are being studied, the researcher may design the investigation with one independent variable and two repeated or with two independent and one repeated. Figure 6.10 illustrates both of these options. The same basic assumptions are operative with

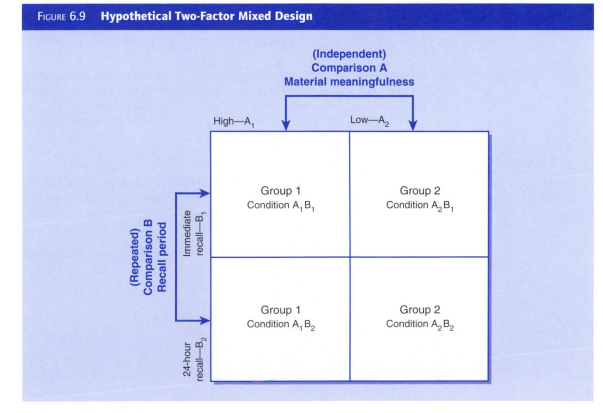

FIGURE 6.9   **Hypothetical Two-Factor Mixed Design**

mixed designs as with other group comparison formats. More complex designs may be used on occasion, although interpretation of results becomes more difficult.

Comments on the Design Alternatives

This chapter outlined a wide variety of options regarding experimental designs. There is no single answer to the frequently asked question, "Which is the best?" Each approach has its strengths and limitations as we will see in greater detail in later chapters. They serve different purposes and operate under different situations. Researchers must assess the conditions that are operating in an investigation being planned. The task then becomes selection and, more typically, modification of a basic design format to be used. All of the designs discussed in this chapter are used for difference questions. These designs compare participant performance before and after an intervention, between groups that receive different interventions or between groups with different characteristics, between a pretest and posttest, or between repeated performance measures over a period of time. Given the fact that all of these situations represent difference questions or comparisons, choosing which design to use depends on other circumstances related to the study. Does the study involve an intervention with one participant to try to improve interpersonal behavior? Or might the study be best conducted with a group of children who are tested on math computation, then receive an intense instructional session, and then are tested again to see if there was improvement? Answering these types of questions will lead you toward the selection of a design format, or it may mean you modify a design to fit your research circumstances. Table 6.2 summarizes single-subject and group designs, notes basic features for these designs, and outlines some of their prominent advantages and limitations.

AFTER THE DESIGN: ANALYSIS AND INTERPRETATION

After the design is selected (or more likely, assembled from various format choices), the study is begun. This implementation will typically involve a brief pilot study, using the exact procedures, with some individuals who are similar to the participants that will actually be in the study. This is an important step in order to avoid mishaps from failing to anticipate something and to be sure the participants can perform the task in the manner we thought they could. The pilot is very important in order to not make mistakes during data collection.

It is also important to plan ahead for data analysis as we are putting together the design. Planning for the data analysis requires that we lay out the details of each comparison involved in the study as well as determine the type of data we are collecting. In Chapter 10, we will discuss different data types ranging from ordinal scales (e.g., data from a rating scale of 1 to 5) to interval and ratio scales such as counting the number of correct answers on a math test. Different data types lead to different analyses, so it is essential to plan ahead for this step.

Once the data are analyzed, the results are interpreted. This interpretation is aimed at answering the original research question. The interpretation may relate to a theory if there was a theory involved in the conception of the study. In education and behavioral science, interpretation of the results will also likely draw implications for practice, which are suggestions about what the results might mean in terms of teaching students, assessing their progress, or some other element of the educational process. Interpretation attempts to close the research loop that we examined early in Chapter 2 (see Figure 2.1).

FIGURE 6.10   **Option Examples for Three-Factor Mixed Designs**

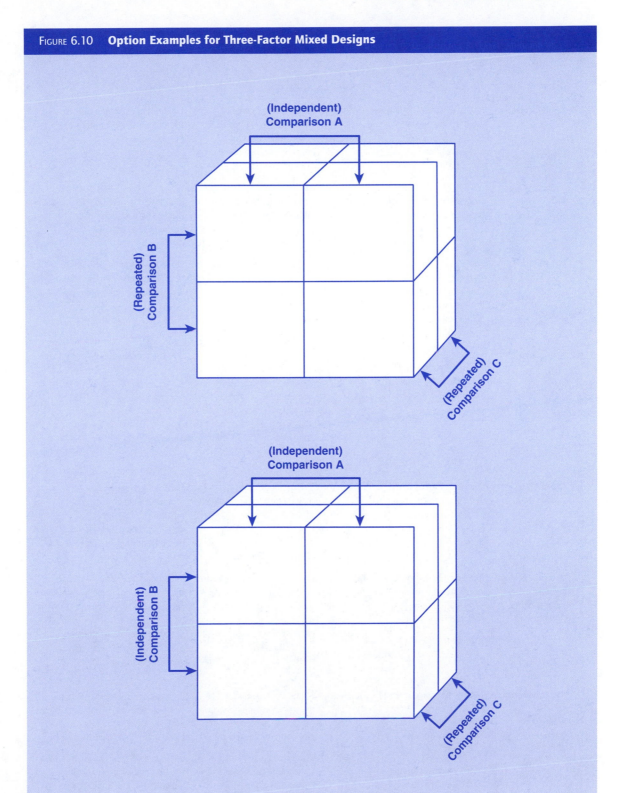

TABLE 6.2   Summary of Experimental Designs

Design Type	Features	Research Question	Advantages	Limitations
Single-Subject	Multiple sequential phases alternating between baseline and intervention, one or very few participants	Difference	Useful for implementing clinical interventions and also gathering data; recording many observations on same participant may allow observation of change	Limited generalizable results because of small numbers of participants
A-B	Simple, two-phases with baseline and intervention	Difference	Easy to understand because of design simplicity	Poor internal validity because using only two phases does not demonstrate adequate control
A-B-A-B	Three (A-B-A) or four (A-B-A-B) phases where baseline and intervention are sequentially implemented and reversed	Difference	Improved internal validity because condition reversal allows demonstration of control	Some limitation of application because certain behaviors not reversible, such as learning
Multiple-baseline	Multiple A-B phases where the target and timing are staggered to demonstrate control	Difference	Internal validity improved over simple A-B format because the staggered implementation allows demonstration of control; allows demonstration of control for behaviors that are not reversible like teaching content	Can be cumbersome to undertake
Group Experimental	Compares groups of participants receiving different interventions or having different characteristics	Difference	Use of many participants may promote generalizability of results.	Recording relatively few measurements on each participant may limit generalizability; participants' performance may be atypical if setting is nonroutine
One experimental variable, independent comparison	One variable under investigation with different participant groups for each condition	Difference	Simple study to execute with control being achieved by assuring the participants are equivalent on all characteristics except the one under study and all are treated similarly during the study	Because of the narrow focus of the study on one experimental variable, the study situation may not reflect participants' usual performance where influences are more complex—limiting generalizability of results
Two experimental variables, independent comparisons	Involves two experimental variables with different groups of participants for each condition	Difference	Allows the investigation of two variables simultaneously, which may enrich the information collected	Requires special attention so the two experimental variables studied are logical and potentially useful combinations of focus for study
Pre-post designs	Compares a group of participants' performance before and after a treatment or intervention	Difference	Permits comparison of the same participants' scores before and after the treatment or intervention	Sometimes difficult to assure that the treatment is the only influence between the pre- and posttests

TABLE 6.2 (CONTINUED)

Design Type	Features	Research Question	Advantages	Limitations
Mixed-group designs	Uses two or more experimental variables, combines independent and repeated comparisons on the variables	Difference	Allows simultaneous investigation of independent and repeated-measure comparison variables, which may enrich the information collected	Requires special attention so the two experimental variables studied are logical and useful combinations of focus for study with particular attention to the combination of independent and repeated-measure configurations
Quasi-experimental	Compares groups that are different prior to beginning the study	Difference	Permits the comparison of participants that are already known or thought to be different before the study	Sometimes difficult to be confident that the pre-study difference is the only dynamic influencing scores and therefore being able to accurately attribute results to the single known source of influence

Chapter Summary

+ One common method of controlling age between two groups receiving different reading instruction methods is to randomly assign participants to the two groups so the characteristics are *very* similar between the groups.

+ To control age between two groups where the experimental variable is based on preexisting differences in math skill levels, one procedure would be to define two potential groups of participants, one having a high level of math skills and the second having a low level. In the definitions of the two groups, age can be defined as the same (e.g., 10 to 12 years old). Then randomly sample participants from both groups and they will be similar in age levels but different in math skill.

+ More sessions of data collection are needed when greater variability is observed in the baseline. One rule of thumb is that for each 10% of variability, at least one other data collection session is warranted. Where there is 30% of variability between data points, you would need at least three data points in the baseline.

+ An A-B design is a single-subject design that involves two phases: A, in which the baseline data are collected before treatment is implemented; and B, in which data are recorded while treatment is underway.

+ The assumption underlying an A-B-A-B design is that if the treatment being studied is the influential or controlling variable (i.e., the factor influencing the behavior change in B_1) then removal of the treatment condition for A_2 ought to reestablish the behavior rate at the baseline level and demonstrate the treatment effect. This demonstration is not evident in the A-B design.

✦ Multiple-baseline designs are particularly useful when reversal is either unde-sirable for ethical reasons or impossible because skill acquisition is involved, such as instructional studies where learning occurs.

✦ Independent group experiments have different groups of participants in each group, whereas repeated-measures group designs have the same participants being assessed repeatedly.

✦ Mixed-group designs have one or more experimental variables that are inde-pendent, while other experimental variables involve repeated measures on participants. Totally independent group designs have different groups of par-ticipants being compared for each experimental variable.

✦ Planning ahead for data analysis should be done before the investigation is begun. Later in this text, you will learn that consideration needs to be given to the type of question, the type of data collected, and other matters.

Key Terms

A-B design. A single-subject design that involves two phases: A, in which the base-line data are collected before treatment is implemented; and B, in which data are recorded while treatment is under way. This design is not widely used because more sophisticated designs have been developed that provide stronger evidence.

A-B-A-B design. A single-subject design that involves four phases. The first A repre-sents the baseline before treatment is implemented. The first B represents initial application of the treatment. The second A designates removal of treatment and return to baseline conditions, and the second B represents a return to treatment conditions. This is also known as a reversal design.

Concept of control. The process of holding all possible influences constant except the experimental variable, which is what is being studied. For example, if the researcher is comparing the effectiveness of Reading Programs A and B, the reading programs should be the only factor that is different between the groups. All other influences (e.g., intelligence or age) should be equivalent between the groups.

Criterion measure. That which is being measured in a study. If, for example, a study were focusing on the height of a particular group of people, the criterion measure might be inches. *Criterion* measure is synonymous with the term *dependent variable*.

Experimental variable. That phenomenon that is under study; the factor the researcher manipulates to examine the effect. For example, if the researcher were interested in determining which of two teaching methods was more effective, the experimental variable would be the method of teaching. *Experimental variable is* synonymous with the term *independent variable*.

Independent group comparison. Group research designs in which different subjects are used for each group. A group of subjects receives only one treatment, and there-fore the scores in one condition are presumed to be independent of scores in another condition. This is distinguished from studies in which subjects may receive two or more assessments or treatments (repeated measures), and the scores in one condition cannot be considered independent of the scores in the other.

Mixed-group experimental design. Mixed-group experimental designs are traditional group investigations where two or more experimental variables are studied with independent groups on one or some of the variables, and repeated measures on the remaining variable or variables.

Multiple-baseline design. A single-subject research design in which data on more than one target behavior are simultaneously recorded. Phase changes from baseline to treatment are then staggered, with each behavior serving as the sequential control for the previously treated behavior, as in the diagram in Figure 6.5.

Pre-post design. A traditional group design where the researcher administers a pretest, then applies a treatment of some type, followed by a posttest assessment to determine the difference between the two testing sessions. There are also studies where the treatment between the assessments is a time period intervening between assessments rather than an active treatment.

Quasi-experimental design. A group study design in which the groups are formed from subject pools that are different before the experiment is begun, and this difference is the basis for the experimental variable. An example might be the comparing of groups from two levels of intelligence (Group A with an IQ range of 75–90 and Group B with an IQ range of 100–115). In this example, the level of intelligence is the experimental variable under study, and the two groups are pre-experimentally different. This is in contrast to a true experimental design in which both groups are formed from the same subject pool and become different after they are administered the respective treatments.

Repeated-measures comparison. A study design in which the researcher records data on the same subjects under two or more treatment conditions.

Reversal design. See A-B-A-B design.

Single-subject design. Single-subject experiments involve investigations where different phases of treatment are compared. The experiment compares a participant's performance without treatment (the baseline phase) and with treatment (generally termed "treatment phase" or labeled by the specific treatment).

Traditional group experimental design. Traditional group experiments are conducted by forming groups of participants for comparisons. These studies are often characterized by the different groups receiving different treatments (e.g., different teaching methods) and then being assessed regarding their performance for comparison purposes.

Student Study Site

The companion Web site for *Designing and Conducting Research in Education* www.sagepub.com/drewstudy

Supplement your review of this chapter by going to the companion Web site to take one of the practice quizzes, use the flashcards to study key terms, and check out the many other study aids you'll find there. You'll even find some research articles from the Sage Full-Text Collection and a step-by-step guide that will show you how to read an educational research article.

Simulation Feedback

For additional simulations visit www.sagepub .com/drewstudy

Simulation Feedback 6.1

All of the factors to be controlled will of course depend on the specific details of your study. You can, however, indicate certain standard areas that should receive attention. The experimental variable in this case is "subject classification" so as much as possible, you will want to hold other variables equal except subject classification. Initially you might attend to *subject variables*. Such factors as gender, age, IQ, and socioeconomic status should be equivalent. This would mean, for example, that you would want equivalent numbers of males and females in all three groups. This does not mean that they need to be split evenly with half males and half females, but it does mean that if one group has roughly one third females, all groups should have about the same proportion of females. In fact, one could ensure the concept of control by limiting the study to only one gender. Similarly, the groups should be equivalent in age and the other variables noted above. One way of accomplishing this is to use a specific type of random sampling known as stratified random sampling (discussed in Chapter 4), a particularly useful technique for quasi-experimental studies such as this.

A second area of attention involves procedural variables. All participants should be tested in the same manner, with the same test, roughly during the same time of day, and so on. Basically, implementing the concept of control on procedural matters relates to the same concept as above. All groups should be treated in an equivalent manner so that there will not be any systematic differences that might influence the results (in addition to the experimental variable).

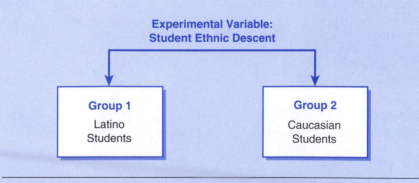

SOURCE: This action research scenario is roughly based on Rubin, D. (2000). *Race and self-esteem: A study of Latino and European-American students with learning disabilities.* Unpublished master's thesis, University of Utah, Salt Lake City.

7

DESIGNING NONEXPERIMENTAL RESEARCH

After reading Chapter 7, you should be able to do the following:

✦ Describe the purposes of experimental and nonexperimental research.

✦ Distinguish between independent variable and dependent variable.

✦ Describe the procedures used in collecting data in survey research.

✦ Discuss the strengths and challenges in conducting survey research, including questionnaire and interview investigations.

✦ Describe the process for planning and conducting quantitative observational studies.

DEFINING EXPERIMENTAL AND NONEXPERIMENTAL RESEARCH

By definition, the purpose of **experimental research** is to examine cause-and-effect relationships. In conducting experimental research, the investigator manipulates a *condition* (aka, **independent variable** or treatment) in order to analyze whether subjects who receive the treatment (experimental group) perform differently from those who do not (control group). Let's say a researcher wants to compare a newly developed middle school math program with a math program currently used at schools in a Los Angeles school district. Two groups of students are identified and matched based on age, grade level in math, socioeconomic background, and so forth. Through random assignment (a critical component of experimental research), one group will receive the new math program (treatment) and the other will receive the program currently in use (control). The **dependent variable** (how we measure the difference between the two groups) is a standardized achievement test in math that is given to both groups at the beginning and end of a school year. The results allow the researcher to analyze the differences in academic performance between the two groups with the purpose of determining whether there is a cause-and-effect relationship between the use of a specific math program (independent variable or treatment) and an increase in student performance (dependent variable). In order to determine this relationship, all extraneous variables (e.g., additional tutoring in math the students in the experimental group are receiving) must be controlled or they will compete with the independent variable in explaining the outcome.

In **nonexperimental research,** existing phenomena (e.g., middle school children's' *satisfaction* with a math program at William Tell Elementary school) are *described* without manipulating (changing) the treatment. The dependent variable (e.g., how we measure satisfaction) could be a survey of student responses or observations of student behavior during math instruction (McMillan, 2004; Salvia, Ysseldyke, & Bolt, 2007). In this chapter, we examine both types of nonexperimental research: surveys and observations.

SURVEY RESEARCH

Survey research involves asking questions of a sample of individuals who are representative of the group or groups under study. As is true with all research studies, there are steps to follow that will facilitate the success of your investigation (see

---

BOX 7.1   STEPS IN PLANNING AND CONDUCTING SURVEY RESEARCH

1. Distill the problem: Clearly specify the category of the survey research question you want to ask (descriptive, difference, or relationship).
2. Operationally define all your terms, activities, and measurements.
3. Plan how you are going to collect the data, including developing the questionnaire or interview protocols and identifying the target population.
4. Develop survey questions that are written clearly and in a fashion that minimizes the possibility of misinterpretation by your potential respondents.
5. Determine the method for collecting your data (e.g., mailed, hand-delivered, electronic, face-to-face interview).
6. Identify incentives that will facilitate the response rate to your survey (e.g., "Answer a few questions in this interview and your name will be entered in a drawing to go to Disneyland." Or, "Enclosed is a dollar just to say thanks for taking the time to complete the questions on this survey.").
7. Conduct a pilot test to iron out any potential problems (e.g., poorly written questions, too much time to complete) .
8. Analyze pilot data, revise questionnaire as needed, and distribute to population sample.
9. Once the questionnaires have been returned, analyze the report and discuss the results.

Box 7.1). Problem distillation is the first step in this process. Once distillation has been completed, the next step in designing a survey involves planning the procedures to be used in collecting data. This will include developing an instrument and determining the sample to be drawn. A variety of sampling techniques can be used, and each involves very specific procedures that must be carefully planned and executed.

Surveys typically use one of two procedures for data collection: questionnaires or interviews (Mertens, 2005). Questionnaires may be distributed by hand (e.g., in a group meeting or class session), mailed to the respondents, or made available through a Web site. Similarly, interviews may be conducted individually—face-to-face, by telephone, or via the Web. An interview may also involve a focus group. Essentially, focus groups are interviews where 5 to 10 people orally respond to questions presented to them by a moderator. Focus group sessions may last for as long as 2 hours and are intended to illicit spontaneous reactions and ideas among participants while the moderator records not only the discussion but the group dynamic as well.

The basic purpose of any survey is to obtain information related to the question(s) being studied from a sample of respondents. Although this sounds simple enough, it can often be a formidable undertaking. Great care must be exercised in planning a survey investigation to facilitate successful execution of the study. Surveys, whether they are written questionnaires or interviews, have strengths and weaknesses that must be considered by the researcher in selecting an appropriate technique (see Table 7.1).

Questionnaire Investigations

Mailed Distribution

Questionnaire investigations involve mailed or electronic distribution of the written instrument that asks questions of the participants. Mailed questionnaires facilitate access to geographically dispersed respondents and generally represent a relatively small financial investment depending upon sample size. The expenses for a mailed questionnaire are essentially postage; the paper needed for instrument reproduction; and the personnel costs involved in instrument development, reproduction, and mailing. However, the expense may be increased if the response rate is low and the researcher is forced to send out reminders or incentives (e.g., money) in order to increase participation.

TABLE 7.1   Strengths and Weaknesses of Questionnaires and Interviews

	Strengths	*Weaknesses*
Written Questionnaires	• Reduces interviewer bias by use of one instrument in collecting the data • Easily quantified • Convenient for respondents	• Questions must be developed carefully and pilot tested for clarity and objectivity • Lack of data from nonrespondents may create concerns regarding biased results • Possible low response rate if mailed out • Potentially high costs to ensure good response rate
Web-Based Questionnaires	• Questionnaire is easily accessible and seldom lost • Convenience and ease of response • Easily quantified • Reduced interviewer bias • Reduced response and return time	• Lack of comfort or knowledge regarding computers • Limited availability of computers and required operating system or software • Increased costs depending on security or software needs to develop, implement, and evaluate survey
Face-to-Face Interviews	• Allows for a variety of question formats, including closed and open-ended questions; lengthy questions with multiple responses • Responses can be probed by interviewer to illicit clarity or additional information • Data obtained and analyzed may be quantitative or qualitative	• Large sample size is labor intensive, which may increase overall cost in time and money • Responses may be open to interpretation, which increases probability of interviewer bias
Telephone Interviews	• Large samples may be contacted in short period of time • Allows for use of open and closed questions using prompts and/or probes • Data obtained are easily quantifiable	• Potential for low response due to limited respondent availability or interest • Limited time for each interview • Some potential for interview bias if using open-ended questions
Focus Groups	• Convenient format using multiple participants within a single time frame • Interactions among participants enhance quality and quantity of responses • Enhances opportunities to use open-ended questions and probes to illicit more in-depth responses	• Labor and material cost may be prohibitive if several groups are included in study • Potential for moderator bias • Difficult to quantify data given type and complexity of responses

Electronic Distribution

Electronic distribution may significantly reduce the distribution cost by eliminating the need for postage associated with mailed questionnaires. Participant accessibility is often a major consideration that favors electronic distribution. Clearly, if respondents are geographically scattered, the electronic questionnaire may be an excellent option. Surveys conducted via e-mail or the Web are instantly available to potential respondents. Whereas mailed or hand-delivered surveys reach respondents at different times or not at all, electronic distribution allows for the data to be collected and monitored in real time. Finally, electronic surveys eliminate manual data entry. Whereas printed survey responses must be manually tallied or rekeyed in order to enter data, electronic surveys can be programmed to completely eliminate manual data entry. This allows information to be organized and analyzed more quickly and efficiently.

Although electronic surveys have some definite advantages, they are not without their problems. It may be difficult for the researcher to access accurate and current e-mail addresses for respondents. In this electronic age, people often change e-mails, fail to read their e-mails in a timely fashion, or choose not to use e-mail as a means of communication. Other disadvantages include user technological capability and access to computers and upgraded software, as well as increased security costs to protect users from viruses and spam. All of these disadvantages are becoming less and less frequent but still exist.

Response Rate

Questionnaire studies may involve some challenges in increasing the percentage of respondents completing and returning the questionnaire. In fact, low response rate is an often-used argument against questionnaires distributed by mail or electronically. Related to this difficulty is slow response. Participants may take their time in returning the questionnaire, and the researcher has little means of controlling their behavior. Additional difficulties include a lack of control regarding the nature of participants' responses and the potential of receiving information from a biased or atypical sample (Hendricks, 2006; Thomas, 2004). It is difficult to argue against the idea that there is likely a difference between those participants who respond and those who do not. Most of the factors involved in careful design of mailed questionnaires focus on circumventing such problems. A synthesis of the factors that are particularly problematic with mailed distribution can be reduced to two major categories: (a) low response rate, and (b) the accuracy of the participants' responses. Clearly, a researcher has limited means of controlling the respondent once the study is underway. Consequently, all possible care must be taken before the study is initiated to circumvent difficulties related to accuracy and response rate.

There are challenges facing electronic distribution that are similar to mailed questionnaires in that potential respondents may discard or delete the survey without responding. Everyone knows the impact of e-mail boxes flooded with spam and other junk mail. For many of us, fear of infecting computers with a virus often means that we delete all e-mail that is not from someone we know personally. This lowers the possibility of response significantly.

Encouraging potential respondents to go to a Web site for questionnaire completion also has its problems. It is one more step for respondents to take in order to help us gather information. There has to be an inherent interest in the topic on the part of the respondent or an incentive from the researcher (e.g., "Complete this survey and you will have an opportunity to win a new car.") for the respondent to take the time to seek out a Web site and complete a questionnaire.

One final matter presents a challenge in electronic distribution of questionnaires— the only potential respondents are those with access to computers. Results from such a survey do not reflect the information or opinions of those without computer access.

In regard to low response rate, a question that often plagues beginning researchers is just how low it must be before there is trouble. Of course, answers to this question vary, but investigators begin with the basic assumption that what they really want is 100% of the respondents to return a completed questionnaire. This would be the best of all possible circumstances, but it seldom occurs. Some studies using mailed questionnaires have response rates as low at 10%, which is generally considered inadequate. Some authors suggest that any response rate below 60% makes researchers nervous, and that those at or above 85% are excellent although infrequent (Goodwin, 2005). It should be noted, however, that such guidelines represent subjective statements. There is no wide consensus among researchers indicating these figures are set in concrete.

There are certain factors related to response rate that warrant further examination. One of these factors is the length of the questionnaire. Respondents are more likely to complete a one- or two-page questionnaire than they are one that is four or five pages in length. There are no rules regarding optimum length for a questionnaire, but it seems clear that the shorter it is, the more likely you are to obtain a satisfactory response rate. There is also some evidence that money as an incentive for respondents increases response rate, although an optimal amount remains unclear (Jobber, Saunders, & Mitchell, 2004; Trussell & Lavrakas, 2004).

Another consideration regards the ease with which a respondent can complete the questionnaire. This relates to the length of the questionnaire, but there are other factors that also influence the effort required to complete the form. If there is little time and effort required, there will probably be a higher return rate (and perhaps more accurate and honest responses) than if the process is time-consuming and difficult. Part of this will be determined by the clarity of instructions provided for the respondent. Unclear instructions cause confusion regarding what is to be done and may even result in many participants discarding the questionnaire. Open-ended questions may have the same effect. Such questions take more time and effort because they require the respondent to write out the answers. Respondents should be asked to report or evaluate observable behavior rather than to make inferences. Such requirements will likely enhance response rate and improve accuracy (Wiersma & Jurs, 2005).

For additional simulations visit www.sagepub.com/drewstudy

Simulation

Simulation 7.1

Topic: Questionnaire studies

Background statement: Increasing the response rate for questionnaire studies is a challenge, but one that can be met if the researcher carefully takes into consideration factors that will encourage responses by the participants.

Stimulus information: You have recently been employed by the Washington Unified School District as a research associate. The school district has undertaken a major reform effort to improve early reading in elementary schools and has decided that they should become more aware of the views of parents and the community. You have been asked by the superintendent to analyze and draw recommendations from a questionnaire study that has been conducted on parent and community views on this new program. By way of background, you are told that the response to this questionnaire appears to be somewhat negative. The parents did not think that the new program would work and were concerned about the training of teachers to implement the program. Obviously, this is not what the superintendent wanted to hear, and so you are being asked to analyze the questionnaire and see if there were any flaws in either the development or dissemination of the instrument. Your analysis reveals that the questionnaire was six pages long, was mailed to respondents with no follow-up, and there was a 10% response rate among parents and community members.

Tasks to be performed: It is now time to advise the superintendent. What information would you give the superintendent regarding this questionnaire? What were the strengths and weaknesses of the questionnaire and its distribution to the intended population? What would you suggest in designing a new questionnaire study to ensure more accurate views from parents and community members?

Write your response, then turn to page 182 for Simulation Feedback 7.1.

Potential Challenges in a Questionnaire Study

There are some potential pitfalls that may threaten a questionnaire study if they do not receive attention during planning. For example, the questionnaire must be constructed in such a manner that it will extract accurate information from the participants. The questions must be written clearly and in a fashion that minimizes the possibility of misinterpretation by respondents. There are also certain factors to be considered in construction of a questionnaire that can either encourage or discourage responses by the participants.

One of the best procedures for circumventing the challenges above is to conduct a pilot test of the instrument. A pilot test would involve asking a few individuals to complete the questionnaire before the actual study begins. The pilot provides information regarding whether the instructions and questions are clear and whether the time and effort required on the part of the respondents is reasonable. It is very important that the pilot test be conducted with individuals who are similar to the respondents in the sample, otherwise it will tell little or nothing concerning how the actual respondents will react.

There is also a growing body of researchers who are investigating electronic survey approaches using the Web and e-mail. The initial evidence is promising, with suggestions of at least comparable response rates, respondent preference, and the ability to control data collection electronically (Leece et al., 2004; Ritter, Lorig, Laurent, & Matthews, 2004). Employing technology for surveys is certainly gaining increased attention by researchers and will change the manner of sampling, distribution of survey instruments, and participant response (Goodwin, 2005; Hutchinson, 2004; McMillan, 2004). However, such approaches still require careful attention to the construction of the survey instrument and matters of length, unambiguous questions, and simplified response requirements remain important.

A variety of other steps can be taken to improve the response rate in mailed questionnaire studies. It is a commonly accepted practice to include a self-addressed, stamped envelope for participants to use in returning a mailed questionnaire. The nature and tone of any cover letter or reminder cards are also important (Price, Yingling, Walsh, Murnan, & Dake, 2004). For instance, a letter that has a coercive tone is less effective than one with a more voluntary appeal to respondents. In addition, the body of the letter is important. A shorter letter results in a higher response than one that includes long and involved statements.

Respondents are more inclined to complete a questionnaire if they are convinced that the study has value. One factor that may influence this perception relates to organizational sponsorship of the investigation. A study being sponsored by a credible government agency, a university, or some other well-known and respected organization is likely to be viewed as more legitimate than one that is not. Participants are generally more responsive to an investigation with such sponsorship than a study with no apparent organizational affiliation. It is important to note, however, that not all organizational sponsorships may be looked upon favorably. Certain sponsors may be viewed with suspicion by respondents, such as those that may have a commercial motive (e.g., the salesperson appears at your door 2 weeks later). Although sponsorship of a questionnaire study is important in terms of response rate, an investigator must carefully consider the impact of the particular affiliation on the participants being sampled. It is important to see the study through the eyes of the participants.

Respondents are most likely to complete a questionnaire if they attend to it as soon as they receive it. Obviously, a researcher cannot look over the shoulder of each participant, but there are certain precautions that can be taken in terms of mailing. For example, response rates are reduced if the questionnaire arrives just before a major holiday or vacation time. Researchers should attempt to avoid these times or any other periods that may have a similar effect. Participants may be inclined to delay response until after the holiday has passed, and if it is an extended holiday, they may decide that it is too late to respond afterward, or they may have forgotten about it. Precise control is usually not possible because of many unknown influences (e.g., mail service, e-mail technical problems). An investigator must know a fair amount about the population being sampled to avoid potential problems. If school personnel are involved, it is better to sample in September than in May, although year-round school schedules complicate even that generalization.

Follow-up is also a step that may improve the return rate in questionnaire studies (McMillan, 2004). In general, three follow-up contacts are the optimum. Any more contact is often viewed by the respondent as harassment. The initial follow-up may simply be a reminder postcard. The second contact should be another reminder letter with the questionnaire attached. Finally, the third follow-up should be a telephone call. A number of specific issues require attention in deciding the nature of follow-up procedures (e.g., timing, protection of anonymity, content of the follow-up, etc.). The beginning researcher who anticipates undertaking a questionnaire survey should consult publications specifically devoted to this research method (e.g., Price et al., 2004; Tourangeau, 2004; Zoltan, 2003).

Interview Investigations

Interview investigations have the same basic purposes as questionnaire studies but simply use different data collection procedures. Interview studies use personal contact and interaction to gather data necessary to address the question(s) being studied (see Box 7.2). Such contact may be made on a face-to-face basis or by telephone. Each procedure has its strengths and weaknesses that must be considered as the researcher decides which approach to use (Goodwin, 2005; Hardy & Van Leeuwen, 2004; Khandelwal & Dhillon, 2004). Interview instruments should undergo pilot testing prior to being used in the actual investigation. Interviewers using such procedures should be careful to follow instructions in a consistent fashion to ensure standardization of the data collection process.

Face-to-Face Interviews

One challenge in conducting interview studies is the expense involved. If the interview is conducted on a face-to-face basis, costs can be high. An interviewer's compensation may be considerable and often includes travel and lodging expenses. This is one area in which the telephone offers a significant advantage over face-to-face procedures. Telephone interviews can be undertaken without travel expense and can be completed very quickly. The telephone interview greatly reduces expenses, but there are problems involved that may be so significant as to seriously limit its use.

The face-to-face interview also has other strengths and limitations. Generally speaking, the interview is a social interaction between people and is vulnerable to the influences that affect such interchanges (Cote & Ericsson, 2005; Tanofsky-Kraff, Yanovski, & Yanovski, 2005). Data recording might be substantially altered to the degree that an interviewer has a personal opinion regarding the outcome of the study. It may also be influenced by the perceptions of the interviewer in terms of the participant being interviewed. Suppose that the interviewer holds some bias regarding a particular political organization. If a respondent is encountered who belongs to that particular group, it is not unreasonable to suspect that the interaction with that individual may be different from that with individuals who are not so affiliated. Data may even be consciously altered in such circumstances.

Certain considerations must receive attention by the researcher to maximize the effectiveness of the interaction and facilitate an accurate interview. One factor involves the behavioral and personal characteristics of the interviewer. Interviewer behavior is an influential factor in the success or failure of the data collection process. One of the first tasks that must be accomplished is the creation of a favorable impression on the respondent. Such initial perceptions may set the stage for a successful interview, or lead to a complete refusal to participate. A respondent must

---

BOX 7.2   PLANNING AND CONDUCTING AN INTERVIEW

Planning for an Interview

- Develop a list of potential places where you are most likely to find people to interview about your topic.
- Develop a list of people who would be good candidates to interview about your topic. Write down their names.
- Of the places and people listed above, which ones would you most likely be able to contact and why?
- What is your plan to make this potential interview a reality? In other words, what efforts of yours could make it happen? List the steps.
- List at least five questions (ones that would result in detailed responses) that you could ask an interviewee. Always refer back to the questions that are guiding your research.

Conducting an Interview

- Contact the person you would like to interview and set up a time and place for the interview.
- Tape record (with written permission from the interviewee) or take notes during the interview.

---

be immediately convinced that the interviewer is legitimate and the study is of sufficient value to become involved. The interviewer should always present credentials and identification papers and provide an explanation of the purpose and nature of the investigation. An extremely important factor in the success of the interview is the clear establishment of rapport.

It is a commonly accepted fact that interactions between individuals of the same race or ethnic background are different from those that occur between persons of different races. This is the case in interview studies as well (Goodwin, 2005). If a study involves a particular racial or ethnic group, the researcher should be careful to use interviewers who are representative of this group. Accurate and honest responses are more likely to occur between individuals who share personal and behavioral characteristics. This is also true for social status. Respondents are more inclined to provide accurate and honest information to interviewers who are, or appear to be, from the same social class. This factor extends to matters of clothing, grooming, and social interactions. The interviewers should maintain a balance between attempting to be similar and appearing and behaving in a manner that legitimizes their role as professional interviewers.

Personal characteristics of age and sex are also important. In some cases, same-sex interviewers should be used, whereas in others the evidence is less conclusive and even confusing. A researcher must carefully consider the topic under study and the nature of the questions being asked when making this determination (e.g., are sensitive questions being asked for which a same-sex combination might be more effective, or does it seem inconsequential?). Concerning the age of the interviewer, in some cases the most effective interview can be conducted when the interviewer and the respondent are about the same age. At other times, the interviewer should be older than the sample group to provide credibility and maintain the legitimate role perception necessary for an accurate survey. If there is a question in the investigator's mind, the topic should be examined at length, either by reviewing the relevant literature or by undertaking a pilot study to provide empirical evidence related to this methodological concern.

Telephone Interviews

Telephone interviews offer an alternative to in-person interviews. Some of the challenges of face-to-face interviews are less evident on the phone, while other problems may surface. Perhaps the most difficult problem involved in telephone interviews is sampling bias. Obviously, the only respondents who can be contacted using this procedure are those who have telephones. Immediately, this makes the telephone survey less appealing for studies that need to sample a broader cross section of the population. This challenge must be considered as one examines the telephone survey as a potential means of data collection. Telephone interviews may also be plagued by the perception of the respondent regarding the motives or credentials of the interviewer. Everyone receives his or her share of telephone calls that appear to be suspect for one reason or another. The telephone has become a major instrument of burglars who want to determine if a person is home, as well as other scam artists. Callers may even obtain information regarding personal possessions through a fake interview. There are many reasons to be somewhat suspicious of telephone calls from unknown persons. These same factors greatly influence the type of data that can be obtained using a telephone interview. Although the telephone interview has certain advantages, these are often judged to be less compelling when balanced against the problems involved. Telephone surveys may result in a lower response rate than face-to-face interviews.

Focus Groups

This technique is commonly used as a means to test out new ideas and evaluate products and services. Focus group are also becoming commonly used in education for a variety of purposes, including generating ideas from parents or the community on how to improve a school, or asking faculty for their views on techniques for more effectively working together in a collaborative school culture. By definition, focus groups usually consist of 6 to 10 individuals who come together to respond to a question(s) and interact in a group dynamic.

When planning a focus group, the first thing to do is identify whom you want to participate and what you want to accomplish. Participants should be selected on the basis of their interest and background in the topic to be discussed, as well as similarity in age and social status. The researcher (moderator) should plan on having group participants respond to approximately five questions within about a 2-hour time frame. The setting should be comfortable and participants placed so that they can easily see and hear one another. The moderator should ensure that all members have the opportunity to participate in the group dynamic, but also keep the session moving so that participants don't get bogged down in one area if the intent is to cover several topics. It is best to record focus group sessions with a tape recorder or video camera in order to obtain an accurate record of the discussion. If this is not possible, then a person serving as an observer and recorder needs to be present.

An effective moderator for a focus group begins by explaining the overall goal(s) of the session and the ground rules for discussion (e.g., take turns, don't dominating the discussion, try not to interrupt someone who is speaking, no arguing). Moderators should clearly ask each question prior to facilitating the discussion, and then reflect back to the group a summarization of what was said.

OBSERVATION STUDIES

In this section, we discuss the process for planning and conducing **observation studies** of a quantitative nature. Several factors are important in planning an observation study, including participant identification, behavior to be observed, and time needed for observations. It is also important to remember that an observation study may take place in either a simulated (e.g., laboratory) or natural setting. In addition, the recording of observations in a given setting may be structured (e.g., counting specific behaviors using a checklist or rating scale) or unstructured (writing down field notes in a narrative form without a specific protocol). An examination of all

> **BOX 7.3   STEPS IN PLANNING AND CONDUCTING OBSERVATION STUDIES**
>
> - Determine the setting in which the study is to take place (natural or contrived) and the structure to be used in conducting the observations.
> - Identify who is to be observed and what behaviors will be under observation.
> - Determine how much time is needed to conduct the observations.
> - Determine the appropriate method (e.g., tally, duration, interval, time sampling) for recording observations.
> - Determine the process to ensure observer reliability (e.g., interrater reliability or correlational methods) in recording observations.
> - Observe the participants and target behaviors.
> - Code and record observations.

such possible variations is beyond the scope of this text. Consequently, this discussion will be limited to some basic considerations involved in developing a system of observation (see Box 7.3).

Identifying Participants

The first step in planning an observation study is to identify who is to be observed. This involves defining the types of individuals to be observed, such as young children with particular characteristics interacting on a playground or adolescents hanging out at the local shopping mall (Glotzer, 2005; Hadden & Von Baeyer, 2005, Matson, Dixon, & Matson, 2005). Regardless of the type of study, the basic aim is to precisely describe the participants who are included for observation. In doing so, the researcher must be careful not to identify individuals based on preconceived notions, stereotypes, or prior experiences, but on the basis of objective criteria. For example, if the population under study is to be children with intellectual disabilities interacting with students who are not disabled, then the criteria for identification is based on who the school has identified as a child with or without a disability, and not on the researcher's preconceived notion of what a child with a disability looks like or how he or she will behave.

The Behaviors to Be Observed

Another factor in the planning process the definition of what behaviors are to be observed. This task will require an operational definition of the actual focus of the observations.

   As such, the researcher must develop a system for categorizing and coding behavioral occurrences. For example, behavior could be roughly categorized into "aggressive" and "nonaggressive," with each being operationally defined. Specific behaviors should then be observed in each category and coded to facilitate recording by the observer. Clearly, there are many possibilities for aggressive and nonaggressive behavior, depending on the focus of the investigation. This might include physical and verbal behaviors. The coding of behaviors would obviously become very important if there were many different types of behavior to be observed, otherwise the actual recording procedure may become extremely cumbersome. In most cases, a carefully designed data sheet can be used so that the observer is only required to make a quick mark on the form if a particular behavior occurs. The researcher must decide what format is appropriate for the study. In some cases, an existing system will function very nicely. For others, the best approach may involve adaptation or development of a system that is specifically suited for that particular study. For example, a researcher may be studying the "aggressive behaviors" between 12-year-old males (Matson et al., 2005). In this context, the aggressive behavior to be defined may be both physical and verbal. In another study, an investigator may wish to observe the verbal communication between 19-year-old female students. A number of factors must be defined or described, especially if the observation is to be somewhat structured. The definition of behavior must be sufficiently precise so that an observer can reliably determine when it occurs. This means that the researcher must also attend to some other issues related to the behavior, such as defining any and all conditions under which the observations will be made. In what setting is the verbal communication between 19-year-old females to be observed? We know the females are students, but more details are still needed to implement the observation. Are they to be in small groups or large groups? Will the observation be in a natural setting such as the student union, or will it be a simulated setting such as a laboratory? What will be going on in the setting? In examining the communication between 19-year-old female students, the researcher will be primarily interested in studying communication (patterns, frequency, or duration) under conditions that would include a specific type of setting and activity. These conditions must be determined and defined prior to beginning this part of the study.

Some studies might be specifically designed to observe communication regardless of what was happening. If this were the focus of the study, controlling the activities would not be a part of the procedure. This should, however, be determined from the outset (and the question should always be addressed during planning).

Understanding the Time Needed for Observations

Time must also be a planning consideration in defining the conditions under which an observation study will be conducted. In this case, time should be thought of in at least two ways. First, the researcher may want to define the time (i.e., time of day, month, or year) when the data are collected. For example, the researcher may want to study communication patterns in 19-year-old females soon after waking up in the morning. Such a study might place a restriction on the time of day or time such as the first hour after rising.

The second view of time may involve a time *interval* for observation and data recording. In this situation, the researcher may be interested in observing the "frequency (number of occurrences) per hour" of a given behavior. Time must be specified so that there is a constant frame of reference. For example, two groups may interact the same number of times, but one may exhibit 47 interactions in 30 minutes, while another may have 47 interactions in 60 minutes.

Methods of Recording Observations

A variety of recording methods may be considered, depending on the nature of the investigation. These include the simplest procedure—the tally method—as well as duration and interval methods. In choosing which method is most appropriate, the researcher needs to keep in mind the procedures discussed above. Who are the participants, what behavior is being observed, and how much time is needed to conduct the observation?

Tally Method

The **tally method** is used to record the number of times that a particular behavior occurs. Once the behavior is clearly defined and coded, the observer tallies on paper (or with a hand counter) each time there is an occurrence. The observations must be recorded in relation to a time frame such as a session or a prescribed interval (e.g., 5 minutes). This permits the determination of rate: the frequency per session.

Duration Method

The **duration method** is a useful recording method for determining how much time a participant spends engaged in a behavior. In this case, the observer would probably observe an individual participant for a given period of time, starting and stopping a stopwatch as the behavior began and ceased.

Interval Method

Observations may also be recorded using the **interval method**. This procedure might be used if you were interested in whether or not a particular behavior occurred during a given interval. Using such a method, the observer would simply mark the interval on the recording sheet if the behavior occurs during that period. The behavior might be continuous throughout the interval, or it may carry over from a previous period and cease partway through the interval.

In each of the conditions discussed above, the interval would be scored as an occurrence. The interval recording method may be useful when it is difficult to count the individual occurrences of a behavior. A subcategory of interval recording is known as *time sampling*. Time sampling is useful when an observer cannot watch the participant continuously and, instead, samples the observations by looking at the participant on a systematic basis (e.g., at the end of a time interval). Sampling may permit observations on a group of participants simultaneously. If the target behavior is evident at the time the observer samples, it is recorded as an occurrence.

Observation Reliability

Every collection procedure will include a certain amount of error, whether a machine or a human does the recording. A machine recorder may be calibrated incorrectly and, thus, not accurately represent what actually occurred. Clearly, a human recorder may also make errors—a behavior might be overlooked or recorded inaccurately. Consequently, observation studies must include certain precautions that attempt to determine observer reliability. This is typically accomplished by using two or more observers (either continually or on a periodic, spot-check basis) and calculating the degree to which they agree. Such procedures are known as determining **interobserver reliability.**

Interobserver Reliability

There are a variety of methods for calculating interobserver reliability, and the circumstances related to the investigation will dictate which should be used. One commonly used procedure involves determining *percentage agreements* (including simple percentage agreement, effective percentage agreement, as well as other variations). Percentage-agreement methods are conceptually simple and easily computed, which has a certain appeal in terms of convenience and interpretation (O'Malley et al., 2003). This procedure is a measure of reliability commonly used in intervention programs. It asks the question, how much (what percentage) of the time did the two observers agree regarding the data recorded? Despite the advantage of simplicity, percentage-agreement methods have certain limitations.

One potential limitation pertains to the number of observations recorded. In particular, if there are very few observations (opportunities for agreement), percentage-agreement methods may provide a very imprecise picture of interobserver reliability. For example, if there was only one opportunity or observation and both observers agreed, the reliability would be represented by a 100% estimate. On the other hand, if there was one agreement out of two opportunities, the percentage agreement estimate of reliability would be 50%. Consequently, there is a great deal of variation with small numbers of observations, and the reliability estimates might be very misleading when compared with the same behaviors observed many more times.

Correlational Methods

Correlational methods may be used, as well, to estimate interobserver reliability (Betz, Hammond, & Multon, 2005; Wilson, Rosenthal, & Austin, 2005). The use of correlational techniques for this purpose is conceptually similar to asking any relationship question. The purpose is to determine the degree to which factors relate or vary together. Thus, if we have a positive correlation between two observers' recorded data, they tend to vary in the same direction. As Observer A records an increased frequency, Observer B also tends to record an increased frequency, which is some indication of the degree to which they agree or are reliable. The degree to which they agree is represented by the correlation coefficient. Correlational methods of assessing interobserver reliability have certain strengths not evident in percentage-agreement procedures. For one, correlational measures are not influenced by chance agreement in the same fashion as percentage-agreement methods. In addition, correlation coefficients have a definite mathematical interpretation regarding variation between observers. Correlations may also be used for further statistical analysis if this is desired in the particular investigation being planned. Correlation estimates are not, however, without problems. First, they are more difficult to interpret from a statistical point of view. Second, there are problems with correlational procedures when occurrences are infrequent (opportunity for agreement or disagreement). Third, if there is little variation in the data recorded, the correlation coefficient obtained becomes less precise. In summary, the correlation method overcomes certain problems but is limited in other respects. A researcher must determine the type of interobserver reliability method to be used based on the characteristics of the study. Reliability is important to provide credibility for the results obtained.

COMMENTS

In this chapter, we addressed the purpose and scope of two types of nonexperimental research: surveys and observations. The purpose of survey research is to ask questions of a sample of individuals who are representative of a group that is under study. Surveys typically use two procedures for data collection: questionnaires and interviews. Questionnaires may be distributed by hand, mailed to the respondents, or be accessible on the Internet. Similarly, interviews can be conducted face-to-face, by telephone, via the Internet, or in focus groups. Each of these approaches has advantages and disadvantages in terms of accessibility, response rate, cost, and time. In addition, there are potential pitfalls that may threaten the validity of survey studies, including clarity of the questions, time needed to complete the questionnaire or interview, and researcher bias. Each of these can be overcome through careful planning and thoughtful implementation of the study.

There are also several factors in conducting observation studies that require thoughtful planning on the part of the researcher. These include defining and identifying the participants and their behaviors that are to be observed, as well as ensuring adequate time to conduct the investigation. It is important to remember that an observation study may take place in either a simulated (e.g., laboratory) or natural setting. In addition, the researcher must pay close attention to the method used to record the observations (e.g., tally, duration, or interval). Finally, the researcher must ensure the reliability of the observations. This may involve any one of several procedures, such interobserver reliability or correlational methods. The following Research in Action box describes an action research study in which some elements of the research involved nonexperimental methods. This illustrate some of the complexities that can be encountered in such investigations.

RESEARCH IN ACTION

KEY POINTS IN THE CHAPTER REFLECTED IN THIS BOX:

- The need to develop a template for types of student questions and conversations
- The need to develop a specific and detailed protocol within the template that will allow observers to record occurrences easily, quickly, and accurately
- The importance of training observers and conducting interobserver reliability tests
- The importance of developing an organizational spreadsheet so this researcher can track her observers because of the complexity of her action research implementation

For more research in action tips visit www.sagepub .com/drewstudy

OBJECTIVES TO LEARN FROM THIS BOX:

- How to develop a template for types of student questions and conversations
- How to develop a working protocol within the template that will allow observers to record occurrences easily, quickly, and accurately
- How complex the implementation of an action research study can be

Emily is planning to use observation as one of the measures in her study of reading instruction. She is comparing two approaches to instruction, one involving student engagement through emphasizing concepts of interest to the students (CORI) and the other method using drill and practice on words and sentences (DAP). One measure involves assessing the engagement itself and for that she will use observation to collect the data.

Students who are engaged in the concepts surrounding an academic subject are often very excited about it. They are active and animated. They talk eagerly about the concepts with their classmates. They ask questions about the topics they are reading, both from their teachers and their peers. They share information about their reading and their conversations often revolve around these subjects. These are the behaviors that Emily wants to observe. The exact topics will vary depending on what the students are reading about. It will be necessary to determine topics for each group of students so an observer can observe, listen, and count the number of times students mention and ask questions about their reading topics. Formulating a template will be possible as Emily determines some categories of engaged behaviors. Following this, she is will need to develop very specific protocols based on the template since each site will involve variations in topics and conversations among the participants. Emily will also be very busy organizing her observers, training them, and conducting interobserver reliability checks. She will help them prepare their observation recording sheets for each session of data collection. She will also develop a spreadsheet to organize observer deployment and data collection at the different sites.

Emily's observations will occur in the classrooms where the students are being taught. The observers will be introduced to the class environment over a period of time before they begin to collect data. This will allow the students and teachers both to become more acclimated to the observer presence and reduce the impact of observer presence on behavior. Emily will outline the details of target behaviors for observation but she will likely also leave some other elements available on the observation sheets to capture spontaneous but important behaviors by the students. Engagement in classrooms is often spontaneous.

Think about this: For the action research study in this box, what are the types of student questions and conversations that need to be in the general template? From the general template, try drafting specific protocol sheets that will allow the observers to record data. Why is it important to train Emily's observers and to test for interrater reliability?

SOURCE: This action research scenario is roughly based on Swan, E. A. (2003). *Concept-oriented reading instruction: Engaging classrooms, lifelong learners.* New York: Guilford Press.

Chapter Summary

✦ The purpose of experimental research is to examine cause-and-effect relationships. In experimental research, the investigator manipulates a condition (independent variable) in order to analyze whether subjects who receive the treatment (experimental group) perform differently from those who do not (control group). The dependent variable in experimental research is the method used to measure the difference between the experimental and control groups.

✦ The purpose of nonexperimental research is to describe a phenomenon (e.g., a treatment) without manipulating or changing it.

✦ Survey research involves asking questions of a sample of individuals who are representative of a group or groups under study.

✦ Survey research typically uses two procedures for data collection: questionnaires and interviews. The basic purpose of survey research is to obtain information from a sample of respondents regarding a question or questions being studied.

✦ Questionnaire investigations may involve mailed or electronic distribution. Challenges to this type of survey research include low or slow response rates and lack of control regarding the nature of participant responses and the potential of receiving information from a biased or atypical sample.

✦ Interview investigations have the same purpose as questionnaires but different data collection procedures, including personal contact and interaction to gather data. Interview studies may include face-to-face interactions, telephone interviews, or focus groups.

✦ Several factors must be considered in planning and conducting an observation study, including participant identification, behaviors to be observed, and time needed for observation.

✦ Observations may be recorded using several methods: tally method (records the number of times that a particular behavior occurs), duration method (records how much time a participant spends engaged in a behavior), or interval method (records whether or not a behavior occurs during a given interval [e.g., a 10-minute period of time]).

✦ Observation studies must include precautions to determine the reliability of the observer(s) in collecting data. Interobserver reliability involves determining the percentage of agreement among observers (What percentage of time did the observers agree?). Correlational methods estimate interobserver reliability by determining the degree to which factors relate or vary together. A positive correlation among observers means they tend to vary in the same direction.

Key Terms

Dependent variable. That which is being measured in a study. If, for example, a study were focusing on the height of a particular group, the dependent variable might be inches. *Dependent variable* is synonymous with the term *criterion measure*.

Duration method. A procedure for recording observations in which the observer records how much time a participant spends engaged in a behavior.

Experimental research. In experimental research, an investigator *manipulates* a condition (aka, independent variable or treatment) in order to analyze whether participants who receive the treatment (experimental group) perform differently from those who do not (control group).

Independent variable. That phenomenon that is under study; the factor that the researcher manipulates to determine the effect. For example, if the researcher wanted to determine which of two teaching methods was more effective, the independent variable would be the method of teaching. *Independent variable* is synonymous with the term *experimental variable.*

Interobserver reliability. A procedure to determine the reliability of the observer(s) in collecting data. Interobserver reliability involves determining the percentage of agreement among observers (What percentage of time did the observers agree?). Correlational methods estimate interobserver reliability by determining the degree to which factors relate or vary together.

Interval method. A procedure for recording observations in which the observer records whether or not a behavior occurs during a given interval, such as a 10-minute period of time.

Interview investigations. These have the same purpose as questionnaires but have different data collection procedures, including personal contact and interaction to gather data. Interview studies may include face-to-face interactions, telephone interviews, or focus groups.

Nonexperimental research. In nonexperimental research, existing phenomena (e.g., middle school children's' *satisfaction* with a math program) are *described* without manipulating (changing) the treatment.

Observation studies. Observation studies involve the recording of observations in a given setting that may be structured (e.g., counting specific behaviors using a checklist or rating scale) or unstructured (writing down field notes in a narrative form without a specific protocol).

Questionnaire investigations. These involve mailed or electronic distribution of a written instrument that asks questions of the participants.

Survey research. Survey research involves asking questions of a sample of individuals who are representative of a group or groups under study. Survey research typically uses one of two procedures for data collection: questionnaires and interviews.

Tally method. A procedure for recording observations in which the observer records the number of times that a particular behavior occurs.

Student Study Site

The companion Web site for *Designing and Conducting Research in Education* www.sagepub.com/drewstudy

Supplement your review of this chapter by going to the companion Web site to take one of the practice quizzes, use the flashcards to study key terms, and check out the many other study aids you'll find there. You'll even find some research articles from the Sage Full-Text Collection and a step-by-step guide that will show you how to read an educational research article.

Simulation Feedback

For additional simulations visit www.sagepub .com/drewstudy

Simulation Feedback 7.1

In discussing the questionnaire with the superintendent, it would be important to address the length of the questionnaire (probably too long). Did the school district need that much information? If not, it is likely that length contributed to the low response rate. The other major difficulty was the lack of follow-up. As you recall, your text suggested that the use of appropriate follow-up procedures might increase response rate as much as 20%–30%. However, this would only raise the response rate to a maximum of 40%. That is still too low. There is another, even more delicate issue that relates to who is conducting the study. How might the Washington Unified School District letterhead influence response rate? It might be better if the study was conducted by a university or independent research organization that did not suggest conflict of interest.

8

Introduction to Qualitative Research and Mixed-Method Designs

After reading Chapter 8, you should be able to do the following:

+ Describe the general purposes and uses of qualitative research methods.

+ Determine when to appropriately use qualitative methods.

+ Distinguish between the emic, etic, and negotiated perspectives.

+ Describe various interview techniques and considerations.

+ Describe various observation techniques and considerations.

+ Discuss ethical issues in qualitative methods.

+ Describe the advantages and disadvantages of mixed-method designs.

+ Compare the types of mixed-method designs.

AN OVERVIEW OF QUALITATIVE RESEARCH

The beginning researcher should be familiar with all the major approaches to research, so that he or she will be able to determine the appropriate methods for each research question and develop a better understanding of his or her own view of knowledge. Qualitative research designs vary considerably along many of the same principles that distinguish among other kinds of research—e.g., experimental control versus realism, internal versus external validity. Qualitative researchers also differ in their beliefs about the unique nature of social experiences, debating whether any social situation and event involving a unique person or group of people can ever be replicated (Denzin & Lincoln, 2005; Neuman, 2006; Sofaer, 2005). Qualitative research often does not share the assumptions that typically drive experimental research (i.e., studies are primarily prompted by theory and test hypotheses, and should be generalizable).

Any scholar seeking an appropriate research design must pay attention to the research context because he or she faces the temptation to let a preference for methods rather than the nature of the study shape his or her choices. It is very important to remember that the nature of the research question should be what drives the selection of methods and design. The design must emphasize the logic that links the data to be collected and the conclusions drawn to the initial questions of the study. Research questions inform the sampling frame, direct where the researcher goes to get answers, suggest with whom one talks and what one observes, and set the conceptual framework into action (Mertens, 2005; Sofaer, 2005). Thus, careful identification of the questions is critical, and the choice of research design then flows from the nature of the research questions.

Different educational researchers using qualitative methodologies (or other methodologies) differ from each other in their approaches to conducting research. Consequently, readers and research consumers should take care not to assume that all scholars using qualitative methods share the same assumptions about the nature of knowledge and ways of knowing. The scholar designing qualitative research must be very clear about where he or she stands in order to assure the accuracy and trustworthiness of results and the integrity of communicating findings to readers. This not only forces the researcher to be cognizant of this issue, but also provides the reader with the information in order to judge the researchers' success at achieving neutrality. This stand is a value and belief judgment, and researchers who avoid clarity of perspective risk the danger of bias by cloaking value judgments with names such as objectivity, truth, and science. In this chapter, qualitative research approaches commonly used in educational and social science research are introduced that represent a variety of perspectives. Details are discussed regarding the scholarly traditions of qualitative inquiry, the planning and execution of qualitative studies, methods for data collection and analysis, and the applications of qualitative research to understanding research problems.

Also discussed in this chapter is an approach to educational and social science research called mixed-method research. As mentioned in Chapter 1, mixed-method designs incorporate aspects of qualitative and quantitative designs to address the research questions—generally to capitalize on the strengths of each type of design. Some mixed-method designs even encompass conducting simultaneous qualitative and quantitative studies! However, just as it is important for the researcher to meet the assumptions of the design when conducting a qualitative or quantitative study, he or she must attend to the assumptions of *both* designs when conducting the mixed-method study. This creates additional work in the design and planning phase, but allows for great rewards in the interpretation of data once those assumptions have been addressed. Just as there is great variability in quantitative designs and in qualitative designs, there is great variability within both the quantitative and qualitative components of mixed-method designs. It is important for the researcher to provide (and for the reader to look for) detailed descriptions of why each component was conducted the way it was, as well as how the components connect. A big part of this connection is determining when to use the different methods.

When to Use Qualitative Methods

The methods of qualitative research have their roots in anthropology, a social science primarily devoted to the study of unique human cultures. So-called **thick descriptions** that render a clear and accurate picture of the nature of each culture form the basis of anthropological studies. No assumption that these descriptions, and analyses of more specific relationships within the culture, are generalizable or even transferable to other cultures is part of this scholarly tradition. However, accumulating rigorous qualitative studies contributes to the development of general concepts or theories about human culture. Cultural or sociological concepts that appear across cultures provide the foundation for social science theories even though the details of the cultures differ dramatically. The main features of qualitative research therefore make it generalizable to theory rather than generalizable to different research populations.

Qualitative methods are specifically suited to studies seeking to answer questions that do the following:

- Require natural surroundings
- Examine unfolding events
- Focus on a broad analysis of an entire phenomenon or context
- Require the exploration of *reasons* for behavior and the ways in which behavior unfolds
- Need exploration, explanation, description, and illustration
- Lack global settings or have a small sample size

Natural Surroundings

Qualitative methods provide an answer to the challenge to learn more about how people behave in their typical surroundings (i.e., their natural setting). Educational settings, like other social situations, are very complex. Children react to each other;

respond to their friends sitting next to them; and complete (or fail to complete) problems and assignments for many reasons that spring from their personal lives, environments, and interactions with peers. For example, research on African-American and Mexican-American children suggests that the pressure not to achieve in school and not to "act white" is at times intense for some inner city children of color. These pressures seem to extend to racial and ethnic groups who seek aggressively to establish an identity and sometimes make the line between identity and exclusion difficult to distinguish (Bergin & Cooks, 2002). To study these children's achievement and failure patterns, scholars must study them in the place where the pressure occurs and record their perceptions and interpretations in their own words. Qualitative methods are appropriate, therefore, for researchers who seek to understand how people make sense of their surroundings and the circumstances that shape their lives—i.e., their cultural context (Denzin & Lincoln, 2005; Silverman, 2004).

Unfolding Events

Qualitative methods enhance the researcher's ability to study events as they naturally occur. The critical variables affecting unfolding events are not known in advance but must be discovered and observed as they occur. Much as a detective carefully exposes the critical facts and events as he or she investigates events in the past, a qualitative researcher observes and describes events as they occur. As such, a characteristic of qualitative designs is that they maintain **design flexibility.** Because the researcher is observing and describing as events occur, additional variables or people to observe, settings to observe in, or methods of observing or recording data may need to be added (or removed). In qualitative designs, it is important for the researcher to be able to "follow the data" wherever it may take him or her. When examining contemporary social processes as the focus of study, qualitative methods are generally preferred over other designs (Creswell, 2005; Neuman, 2006).

Broad Perspective

Qualitative methods are also well suited for situations where the researcher wants to focus on a phenomenon from a global or holistic perspective. Because the research is conducted in the natural setting with events unfolding as they naturally do, the research often cannot focus on one (or just a few) aspects of the setting because it would mean a loss of data. All events and behaviors within a context are linked (whether we like it or not). In order to get the most accurate description of the focus of the research, it is vital to allow for the inclusion of any and all data that may come up in the data collection.

Reasons for Behaviors

Another situation where qualitative methods are well suited occurs when the researcher seeks to understand the reasons why behaviors occur as they do and how these behaviors occur. A long tradition of research affirms that human beings' behaviors often are shaped by their interpretations and beliefs as strongly as by "objective" events around them. Even the source of information, the social status of the person who conveys information, and the acceptance and beliefs of others in the group have been shown to shape people's choices (Punch, 2005). An aspiring gang member may consequently choose to believe what his homies[1] say about the intentions and motives of a teacher who tries to befriend him or her rather than believe the teacher. Whether the teacher is truly supportive or not, the student's beliefs about that support may determine how he or she chooses to act. Contemporary,

---

[1]According to the National Center for Education, Disability, and Juvenile Justice, this is the current terminology for other members of one's gang.

real-life phenomena and the reasons that shape them are best studied using qualitative methods (Neuman, 2006).

Some approaches to qualitative research include not only the participants' interpretations and perspective, but also those of the researcher. Because the researcher has direct contact with the participant(s), he or she develops unique personal insights through his or her own experiences, culture, and perspective. As such, it is important for the researcher to retain **empathic neutrality.** This is different from objectivity in that there is no assumption of a lack of opinion or perspective. With empathic neutrality, the researcher can and should have his or her own perspective and values. However, these should be used in a nonjudgmental way; they can be used to illuminate an issue or clarify a description, but should not be used to make a value judgment about the behaviors, values, or experiences of the participants.

Details of Behavior

The need to explore, explain, describe, or illustrate behavior and interactions to better understand them as well as uncover poorly understood variables also provides situations in which qualitative methods are appropriate. For example, a researcher may seek to explore the strategies that fourth graders typically employ when solving story problems in mathematics. The question is not, "Which logarithms or methods work best when children use them?" but rather, "How do nine-year-old children typically think about math problems?" A design that allows the children to talk about what they are thinking and doing as they work on a math problem gives the researcher a view about what the children are doing, choices they make as they seek to solve a problem, and their rationales for making these choices. Later on in a research agenda, after the researchers know more about the strategy use of fourth graders, specific teaching methods that teach mathematics more effectively can be developed and tested using experimental designs (or the two could be linked in a mixed-method design).

Sample Size

Finally, researchers often need to conduct their inquiry when small sample sizes and few global settings exist. Qualitative methods allow the researcher to approach the subject, probe the setting, and describe it in a natural fashion and in great depth (Neuman, 2006; Silverman, 2004; Sofaer, 2005). This holds true whether one is working with large groups of participants or very small ones. Unlike group quantitative designs, which require moderate to large sample sizes (greater than 20–30), and single-case designs, which require small sample sizes (8 or fewer), qualitative designs can be equally effective for small or large numbers of participants.

Topics range widely from social and spousal relationships, to children's experiences in school, to community and cultural practices related to classroom learning (Foster, Lewis, & Onafowora, 2003; Langhout, Rappaport, & Simmons, 2002; Walzer & Oles, 2003). Some subjects of interest to lay populations, such as gangs and violence, are receiving considerable investigation using qualitative procedures (Cepeda & Valdez, 2003; Lane, 2002; Totten, 2003). Qualitative investigations are being increasingly used to probe a wide variety of topics in education.

Some texts on research design provide a typology of different kinds of qualitative research; however, no matter how the kinds or designs are grouped, there are more similarities between them than differences. The similarities involve the details of conducting the research such as data collection methods, data types, and analysis methods. Where the differences lie is in the preparation of the report of the research results because this is where the researcher is concerned with answering the research question. In Chapter 14, we will discuss the different forms that qualitative research reports may take, which is related to how the data are analyzed. How the data are collected, and the basics of qualitative methods, is the focus of this chapter.

Data Collection

Because the data used in qualitative research come in the form of researchers' and participants' words, some important principles affect the technical soundness of a research design using qualitative methods. These soundness principles relate directly to the general validity or trustworthiness of qualitative research. First, researchers should seek data from a variety of sources, using different collection methods, and possibly from different perspectives. This process of checking data sources, methods, and perspectives is often called **triangulation.** A researcher can triangulate data by drawing upon different sources of data (usually three or more, hence the term), different methods of data collection, or by utilizing a design involving multiple researchers (Neuman, 2006; McMillan, 2004). A design may involve interviews with people having very different points of view (teachers, students, parents, administrators), the gathering of existing documents that provide multiple perspectives (school board minutes, faculty meeting minutes, school records), or spending extended time in the field observing and recording behavior as it occurs.

Before discussing the actual collection methods, it is important to note that the data collected can have different perspectives: emic, etic, or negotiated. The **emic perspective** is how the participant(s) view the phenomenon being described or analyzed. For example, a study seeking to describe elementary school students' use of recess time might contain data from an emic perspective such as the students' descriptions of what they do at recess and how much they enjoy it. The **etic perspective** is the viewpoint of the researcher as an outsider—possibly his or her interpretation of the participants' perspective. From the example of students' use of recess, this might include data of the researcher describing the students' activities or making judgments of their enjoyment or attitude. Lastly, the **negotiated perspective** involves both the emic and etic perspectives, but requires that the researcher and participant(s) discuss each perspective and the differences between them. For example, one of our students may state that he really enjoyed playing dodgeball today (emic), yet the researcher says he didn't look like he was since he was crying for half of the game (etic). The resulting discussion may lead to a settled perspective of "well, I really like the game of dodgeball, but I didn't like getting hit in the face," which resolves the differences in perspective by incorporating aspects of each.

The researcher also must practice questioning, listening, observing, and recording data. You will recall from our earlier discussion of the research process that we require all our research students to practice the procedures and processes they will use to carry out their studies before conducting the actual research activities. This can mean testing a survey on a group of people similar to the participants, rehearsing an interview protocol, practicing with recording devices in settings similar to the research setting, or any other activity on which the research depends. In several contexts, we have referred to the qualitative researcher as the research *instrument.* This comparison is appropriate because the quality of data is absolutely dependent on the quality of data recorded and it takes practice and care to acquire these skills. Consequently, we ask our students to practice taking field notes and developing expanded field notes from audio and video tape, to write "thick description," and to prepare practice cases. As noted earlier, thick description is narrative description that provides a clear and accurate picture of the nature of the phenomenon being described. Practice makes perfect is trite but true. However, it is important to note that if you practice something the wrong way, when you actually go to perform, you won't do it properly. It is important to make sure your practice is every bit as accurate and reliable as when you are doing the actual data collection. These practice techniques help prepare the qualitative researcher to collect research data. The three most common methods of data collection used in qualitative research are interview, observation, and reviewing existing documents or archival research.

Interview

The interview is one of the most commonly used methods for gathering qualitative data. Interviews can be highly structured or completely open-ended, depending on the purpose of the interview, the researcher's familiarity with and knowledge about the setting, and the exploratory or confirmatory nature of the study. When designing an interview study, it is important to keep in mind critical issues about the relationship between the research, the interview guide or protocol, and the respondent.

Simulation

Simulation 8.1

Topic: Preparing an interview guide

Background statement: The quality of data acquired through the interview process in large part depends on the congruence between the interview's purpose and design and on the quality of the researcher's preparation. An interview guide or protocol carefully constructed to elicit the maximum amount of data with the minimum amount of participation by the interviewer is part of this important preparation.

Tasks to be performed: As an experienced researcher, you have been called by the chair of the resource education team at a large middle school in your community for help with a puzzle. The standardized tests used to diagnose student problems have failed to provide adequate information about students' educational needs. Several students the team thought would do very well are failing miserably and others in the program whose disabilities seemed more serious are thriving. The resource team suspects that differences in the students' homes may hold clues to the surprising performance of some students. Parents have agreed to talk about their parenting styles and skills, and the team has asked you for advice about the design and conduct of the interviews. What would you advise the team as they design their parent interview study?

Write your response, then turn to page 207 for Simulation Feedback 8.1.

For additional simulations visit www.sagepub .com/drewstudy

Interviews require both questions and answers. Consequently, the interview process is highly interactive, and good interviewing techniques take considerable practice (see Table 8.1). New researchers should not be discouraged, however, because a relaxed manner, asking questions well, note taking, appropriate use of follow-up probes, establishing trust, and keeping track of responses become easier with time and practice. The important thing for each new researcher to remember is that research interviewing is a way of gathering data and differs substantially from less formal interviewing he or she may have done in the past—interviewing a job applicant, for example. Detailed records, careful attention to the substance and affect of responses, and unfailing politeness will go a long way toward improving the quality of the interview process and of the data gathered.

Interview techniques. When designing research that involves interviews, researchers can ask themselves some simple questions that protect the quality of the process. These questions help the researcher prepare, ask good questions, record the data appropriately, and attend to the social context of the interview to assure the highest quality of data possible.

TABLE 8.1 **Advantages and Disadvantages of Interviews**	
Advantages	*Disadvantages*
Flexible—can be more or less detailed to accommodate information needed	Expensive—can require a lot of travel as well as hours of training for assistants and development of interview protocol
Personal perspective of the respondent is provided. Meaning or feelings can be detailed.	Time-consuming—often require travel or one-on-one format. Also require time to transcribe and interpret
Dialogue to clarify questions or responses is possible (and generally encouraged). This includes follow-up questions.	Vulnerable to manipulation by the respondent
Provide for greater depth of information.	Require great skill and expertise of interviewer—intense concentration; the ability to listen, write, and anticipate questions; strong interpersonal interaction skills; note taking; maintaining neutrality while encouraging cooperation (i.e., not biasing respondent).
	Not appropriate for broad surveying of general attitudes or beliefs

When getting ready to conduct an interview, one should ask the following questions: Who will conduct the interview? Should the principal investigator or someone else interview respondents? Is there a same-gender or different-gender (or race, class, etc.) interviewer issue that needs to be addressed because of the social setting, beliefs of the respondents, or topic of the study? Is trust or a preestablished relationship important? Are there reasons for seeking an outside interviewer such as preserving anonymity of the respondents?

Anonymity refers to keeping the identity of the respondent from being known by the researcher. This could be important if the respondent is acquainted with the researcher and there is the potential for negative consequences. For example, take a situation in which a college instructor is conducting interviews about undergraduates' attitudes toward their faculty advisors. If this instructor were to interview one of his or her advisees, a power differential would exist that would threaten the quality of the responses. Besides the researcher, others to consider who may become involved include someone to interview, someone to record, interviewers representing constituent groups (i.e., teachers, administrators, parents, students), and friends and confidantes of the respondent.

No matter if anonymity is necessary or not, **confidentiality** is of the utmost importance. Especially when discussing topics that are sensitive or may have repercussions for the respondent, all personally identifying information should be somehow masked to prevent repercussions or negative consequences of others knowing the information. For a more detailed discussion of the need for confidentiality, see Chapter 3 on ethics.

Another important question in the preparation process is this: Who should be interviewed? This is not an idle question. The researcher may need to seek the answer in the original research questions or in the setting itself. One might ask an insider informant to help determine with whom the researcher should talk. Constituent groups should be represented, as should a broad range of opinions. If insufficient variability in responses seems to occur, the researcher should ask participants if there is anyone he or she should interview who does not agree with the majority in order to check the representativeness of responses. But the researcher should also constantly use the resources and knowledge of people within the research setting to make sure people with important information or representing important points of view are included. The researcher should also seek a variety of perspectives; deliberately search for outsiders who represent important points of view or power sources; and seek multiple sources for the same information to check for its confirmability. The researcher can systematically sample people's views on various organizational levels and with responsibilities relevant to the research question. To protect the reliability of the data, an interviewer must be especially careful to ask respondents only for data about which they have firsthand knowledge and that they can provide freely and candidly. Unlike experimental designs, qualitative research designs using interview techniques often allow the sample of people to be interviewed to evolve naturally as more is learned, the researcher follows hunches, and hypotheses and patterns suggest new directions for discovery.

After selecting an interview sample, the researcher should decide explicitly how interviews will be conducted. As we discussed earlier, individual interviews yield the most personal and possibly the most unique data, but they are costly in time and effort. Some alternatives can include interviewing members of groups in pairs or in groups. These decisions should take a number of important issues into account: reliability, candidness, the protection of respondents' confidentiality and protection of the respondent from possible negative effects for participating, the threat of "group think" in a group interview, stimulation of ideas by others—spontaneity and liveliness, and time constraints.

The researcher should select a time and place for interviews and make appointments with respondents that can be meticulously kept. Respondents are doing the researcher a favor by giving their time and information and should be treated with the utmost consideration and respect (Creswell, 2005; Mertens, 2005). Interviewers can count on some participants missing or forgetting appointments; this is simply part of the reality of field research.

Careful preparation in other areas is also important. A researcher should gather background data on the setting, selected respondents, and topics of interest and use existing documents and records, written accounts by others, or other interviews already conducted to prepare for each interview. This preparation can take a number of forms. First, as just noted, the researcher should make substantive preparation in order to avoid asking people what can be found out more efficiently in other ways. Asking people such things is a waste of people's time and makes the interviewer appear too lazy to do important background work. Second, careful preparation provides stimulus for questions and the opportunity to be organized and informed. Third, the interviewer should practice each specific interview protocol and develop interviewing skills to avoid wasting the respondent's time, repeating questions or appearing unorganized, and failing to record good information. An interviewer who knows the subject and the interview protocol will be relaxed, friendly, and expeditious in the interview process instead of fumbling for his or her notes and checking for the next question while only half listening to an answer.

This planning process also includes the questions to be asked. The researcher should plan so that he or she asks good questions and does not "shoot from the hip." Most institutional review boards ask a researcher to either provide preplanned interview guides; sample questions; or (at the very least) the topics, tactics, and directions all interviews will take. If open-ended or naturalistic interviews are planned, these must be accurately described beforehand so that the logic of discovery is justified. In most cases, a specific interview guide should be prepared in advance. This careful planning is important for several reasons: (1) The interview will be planned to fit the person and the situation; (2) important questions will not be forgotten or overlooked; and (3) the time the interview will take can be planned and respondents informed in advance how long the interview should last. Table 8.2 describes five general formats for interviews.

TABLE 8.2   Formats for Interviews

	Topic Addressed	Wording of Questions	Order of Questions	Form of Questions
Unstructured	May or may not be prespecified	Impromptu	Impromptu	Open-ended
Partially Structured	Prespecified	Prespecified	Impromptu	Open-ended
Semistructured	Prespecified	Prespecified	Prespecified	Open-ended (essence of response is coded)
Structured	Prespecified	Prespecified	Prespecified	Open-ended (exact response is coded)
Fully Structured	Prespecified	Prespecified	Prespecified	Forced choice (e.g., true–false, multiple choice)

Several simple procedures can help make this advanced planning pay off with a successful interview:

1. Most researchers leave space directly on the interview guide for note taking and plan explicit follow-up questions if the responses are stilted or not forthcoming or questions need clarification. If an interviewer asks follow-up questions that are not included in the guide, he or she should write down the questions so that the interviewer will know exactly what was asked that elicited a specific response. Audiotape recordings (and sometimes videotapes) provide verbatim records, but they are not always possible, and researchers sometimes do not have sufficient resources to transcribe all tapes.

2. A good interview often begins with a broad, open-ended question that allows the respondent to answer however he or she chooses. This offers the opportunity for respondents to talk openly and at length, puts them at ease, and elicits high-quality information without the interviewer prompting or unduly influencing the form and content of the data. This tactic requires careful listening skills and familiarity with the interview guide in order to avoid asking questions later in the interview that the respondent already has answered. Starting with questions about less sensitive topics may also help to put the respondent at ease. Once he or she is comfortable with the interviewer and the interview process, the more difficult or uncomfortable questions can be introduced.

3. Make certain interview questions use everyday language that is completely familiar to the person being interviewed. Research jargon is deadly in an interview.

4. Ask unambiguous questions that have been tested on people like those in the research population. Any time spent explaining questions is time wasted—it irritates the respondent and degrades the relaxed and trusting atmosphere of the interview.

5. Ask only one question at a time. Like survey research, interviews must give the respondent the opportunity to answer a given question leaving no doubt about the connections between question and response. In addition, when two or more questions are asked at the same time, respondents may be distracted or ramble, trying to think of what they are going to say next. Sometimes they may even be unsure whether they have answered the question or may leave out a part of their response so that the question must be asked again or rephrased.

6. Do not ask leading questions. The researcher's task when interviewing is to find out what the respondent believes or knows, not to tell them what they think or feel. For example, "How do you feel about X?" is a better, less leading format than "How much do you like X?" even though they address the same general topic.

7. Anticipate places in the interview where respondents might need help thinking through an answer, and plan probes or follow-up questions in advance to prevent fumbling and uncertainty. Probes can provide clarification, elaboration, and encouragement. However, researchers should also learn to use silence—three seconds or more when waiting for an answer—to encourage lengthier and more complete responses and to avoid prematurely cutting off a respondent who is thinking through a response. When an interviewer jumps in with the next question prematurely, the response to the previous question will be incomplete.

8. Interviewers must also think fast on their feet and construct follow-up questions in the interview as they go. As a series of interviews is conducted, the researcher will begin to see patterns in the guide that require specific follow-up questions to improve the interviewing process. The researcher should always ask respondents at the end of the interview if it would be all right to get back to them if further questions arise or if clarification is needed later. Of course, this is only possible if the participants have given their consent for their identity to be recorded in association with the data. If the interviewer has promised total anonymity (as distinguished from confidentiality), then no record identifying respondents may be kept. Anonymity is sometimes necessary in settings where the safety or well-being of the respondents is unacceptably threatened by any existing record.

9. Questions should be posed in a context or setting that reminds, draws out, and increases the memory of the respondent. This also provides recognition and recall and improves the detail of responses. This is why the interviewer should travel to the respondents' environment rather than asking respondents to come to an office or classroom if at all possible.

10. Save the most difficult questions for the middle of the interview, and end on a less stringent note. Record the affect or tone of the interview and note any hostility, friendliness, reluctance, reticence, or general discomfort on the part of the respondent. The trustworthiness of the data depends on the interviewer's ability to assess the quality of the data provided. Table 8.3 summarizes the various steps that are important in conducting a qualitative research interview.

Recording the data from an interview. As we noted previously, interview data can be recorded in a number of ways. Some important guidelines will help assure the accuracy and usefulness of recorded data. First and foremost, researchers should take copious notes. This requires the ability to listen, think, and write at the same time. Although this process often is very accurate, it does leave room for disputation or controversy if only one person is in the room in addition to the respondent. However, note taking is less obtrusive than tape recording. Many interviewers are beginning to use laptop computers to record responses. People are becoming increasingly comfortable with their presence, many prefer them to tape recorders, and the respondent can see immediately what the researcher has written if they would like to review an exact sentence or phrase. This approach requires excellent typing skills or else you run the risk of interrupting the flow of the interview and affecting the respondent's answers. It also can be advantageous to use one interviewer and one note taker, but trust, confidentiality, and spontaneity are more difficult to achieve under these circumstances.

TABLE 8.3   **Conducting a Qualitative Interview**

Getting Ready

- What do you need to know?
- Is this the best way to learn what you need to know?
- Who will be interviewed?
- Who will do the interview?
- Where will the interview take place?
- How will the interview be conducted?
- Has enough time been planned to cover the questions, and is the interview a reasonable length?

Asking Good Questions

- What adjustments in questions might be necessary for this particular situation? To the person being interviewed?
- How should the questions be ordered? Why is a particular order best in this situation?
- Are the questions unambiguous and do they contain only one question?
- What follow-up questions or probes might be needed to get the most complete information?
- Do the questions suggest an answer the interviewer would prefer? Do they put words in the respondent's mouth?

Keeping Track of Responses

- How will responses be recorded?
- What impact might the recording method have on the people being interviewed?
- Is the recording method acceptable and ethical in the situation?
- How does the recording method serve the best interests of the inquiry while protecting the respondent?
- What are the trade-offs between different recording methods in this particular situation?
- Does the interview guide apply to all the people you wish to interview? What adjustments might need to be made for people in particular roles and with different responsibilities?
- Does the interview guide provide sufficient flexibility?

Understanding Your Effect/Affect

- Does my relationship with this person inhibit his or her ability to be candid?
- Am I open and relaxed?
- Is a relationship of trust and rapport in place?
- Is the purpose of the interview clear to the respondent?
- What signals do I send the person being interviewed through eye contact, nonverbal cues, and verbal reinforcement?
- Does the person being interviewed believe that the information will be kept confidential? Will it?
- Can I expect to finish the interview without distractions? Will I prevent interruptions if possible?
- Can I compensate for the effect of distractions?
- Can I listen to what is said and keep the respondent's statements free of distortions?

Audiotapes are a common method for recording interviews. They are accurate and indisputable, but they can be very intimidating to some respondents. Tape recording sometimes dampens candor, requires greater trust, and often requires assurances that the tape will be destroyed after the inquiry is completed, because voices can be recognized. Experienced researchers often recount experiences where respondents ask them to turn off the tape recorder before they will answer a particularly sensitive question, or they open up at the end of the formal interview when the tape recorder is turned off. The transcription of tapes is very expensive, so researchers often request permission to tape an interview and then take copious notes that later can be expanded or developed into systematic field notes by checking sections of a tape. In addition, when something goes wrong with the tape recorder, it often is not discovered until the researcher is at the point of transcribing the tape—which unfortunately may be weeks or months later. One of us had the experience of audiotaping several interviews with school staff across a few weeks only to discover that the built-in microphone was malfunctioning. The full 2 weeks of interviews had to be completely reconducted—which most likely affected the respondents' candor and cooperativeness since they now had to double their commitment of time and energy and most felt excessively "put out" by the research.

Interviews are human interactions, and the interviewer directly influences the quality and quantity of data gathered. It requires practice to create an open and relaxed atmosphere during interviews. This atmosphere may depend on where the researcher and respondent sit, level of privacy, body language, or small talk.

The trust and rapport necessary for a successful interview often are a function of current or past interactions, but they can be notably affected by careful planning by the researcher. For example, some parents find the school an intimidating or even hostile place and are reluctant to go there. The school would be an inappropriate place to interview parents who might not be comfortable there. Whenever possible, it is good practice to get the respondent's input about a good place to conduct the interview.

A researcher also should be careful to make the purpose of an interview or conversation clear to the respondent. If possible, respondents should have the assurance of confidentiality. They also should have confidence that the interviewer will use discretion and their responses will be free from distortion. If confidentiality is not possible, the respondent should know this at the outset before giving permission to be interviewed. Respondents have every right to immediately halt any interview that extends beyond the topic or scope they have agreed to and refuse to answer any or all questions (see informed consent discussion in Chapter 3). The researcher communicates the importance of the person being interviewed by assuring privacy, freedom from distractions, and respect. When respondents feel confident their rights are being respected, they will be more likely to give useful and trustworthy responses.

Finally, you must not "lead the witness." The interviewer must be careful about communicating attitudes to the respondent through eye contact, nonverbal encouragement and responses, or verbal reinforcement to responses. This "leading" may be completely unintentional and nonverbal and does not require that you say something as obvious as, "Don't you think mainstreaming is a superior way to educate children with moderate intellectual disabilities?" Interviewing is a very personal process and can be successful or not depending on its verbal and nonverbal, interpersonal aspects. If researchers signal by their behavior that they are in a hurry, that interruptions are more important than the person being interviewed, or that they value the response they are getting, and so on, they will influence the nature of the information in one direction or another.

Studies relying primarily on interview data can take the form of journalistic reporting, oral histories, anthropological life histories, or folklore and storytelling. This discussion is a very brief introduction to a highly developed data-gathering technique. We suggest that you consult other volumes for more complete discussions of interviewing techniques and their application to qualitative methods (e.g., Powell & Amsbary, 2006; Rubin & Rubin, 2004).

Observation

Interviews provide a method for collecting data imbedded in the interpretations, perceptions, and experiences of respondents. However, observation provides a direct method for qualitative researchers to record human behavior and events as they occur—by watching. Observation for qualitative research is often divided into participant and nonparticipant observation. In participant observation, the individual conducting the investigation actually participates in the setting or activity being observed. As the term suggests, in **nonparticipant observation,** the investigator plays an outsider role and does not actively participate in the setting or activity. The lines between these two kinds of observation are not as clear as this dichotomy suggests. An educational anthropologist might join in the daily activities of an elementary school as a form of participant observation. Depending on whether the staff and students know his or her position can influence the degree of participation or nonparticipation. Other disciplines in the social sciences also experience the fuzzy line between participant and nonparticipant observation. However, the level of detachment or involvement shapes much of the data, so researchers should be acutely aware of the differences and variations in these two techniques.

Participant observation. **Participant observation** is a commonly used technique in anthropology and is less common in education and other social and behavioral sciences. This is due to the fact that when engaging in participant observation, the researcher must primarily act as a participant in the group under study, which is difficult in circumstances where an observer's personal characteristics make him or her stand out from the participants. For example, adults in elementary classrooms or playgrounds stand out unless they are part of the school staff and are routinely present in those settings. While it may be possible to enlist adult insiders in schools to conduct observations, it is likely that they will have a difficult time performing their other professional responsibilities while engaging in the intense activities associated with participant observation. It would also be nearly impossible for them to participate from the student perspective. In addition, participants face a major emotional and psychological challenge. It may be difficult for them to remain sufficiently disengaged from the children to record objective data. Box 8.1 presents a study in which participant observation was possible in the field of education. In the fall of 2002, Rebekah Nathan (2006), a professor of anthropology, became a freshman student to better understand student life in college.

BOX 8.1   WHAT LIFE IS LIKE FROM A STUDENT'S VIEWPOINT

Faculty in colleges and universities often see student behaviors and attitudes as disinterested in learning and distracted by other life events. Rebekah Nathan (a pseudonym) was a cultural anthropologist at a large public university and decided to go undercover to find out about student life from their point of view. She became a freshman in 2002 and enrolled as an undergraduate student. In her fifties, Professor Nathan used her experience in ethnographic research methods to interview, live, and go to school with the students that she saw in her classes. Her book, *My Freshman Year: What a Professor Learned by Becoming a Student* (2006), outlines a fascinating story of college life that illuminates a complex set of influences seldom imagined by those who are no longer students. As a participant observer, Professor Nathan found that a very high percentage of her fellow students worked hard, played hard, and had more options for extracurricular activities than they could use. The students often visited about relationships and alcohol and drugs, but not politics or academic matters. Content did not often influence what classes they took, but convenience did.

Professor Nathan found her class work challenging and finished her year with a 3.1 GPA. She has significantly altered the way she teaches based on what she learned, and this book provides an excellent example of how participant observation can be used effectively as a research tool. It also demonstrates the challenges of qualitative methodology and the intensity of work involved.

SOURCE: From Farrell, E. F., & Hoover, E. (2005). "Getting schooled in student life: An anthropology professor goes under cover to experience the mysterious life of undergraduates." *The Chronicle of Higher Education*, (vol), A36-A37. Reprinted with permission from The Chronicle of Higher Education.

Depending on the purpose and context of a study and the researcher's level of access to the setting, participant observation can provide an in-depth opportunity for cultural analysis. The participant observer spends extensive time in the setting waiting for particular core events to reoccur. The research can slightly alter the focus of analytic attention, each time attending to certain features of what is occurring, and then focus on rereading and analyzing field notes and iterative experiences with observation and reflection to develop an interpretive model for the study. The participant observer, through active participation, can then test emerging models by trying them out.

Nonparticipant observation strategies include nonreactive, unobtrusive research. The researcher is not directly engaged in central behaviors and activities within the situation under study. The observer is acknowledged by participants but is not involved. Research using nonparticipant observation includes studies of behavior in natural settings such as classroom interaction, descriptions of social behavior in a variety of settings, a number of studies focusing on educational evaluation, and others (Janesick, 2004; Silverman, 2004). Nonparticipant observation is often used when the researcher does not want to or cannot reasonably include him- or herself in the group being observed. For example, when conducting a study on social interactions among kindergarteners, the researcher would probably have trouble being fully accepted as one of the students—both by the other kindergarteners as well as the teacher. Table 8.4 summarizes advantages and disadvantages of both participant and nonparticipant observation.

TABLE 8.4   Advantages and Disadvantages of Participant and Nonparticipant Observation

Participant Observation	Nonparticipant Observation
Advantages	*Advantages*
Depth of understanding and immersion available to the researcher	Objectivity/neutrality. Easier to remain emotionally unattached
Allows for personal testing with behaviors, attitudes, and experiences	Data can be recorded immediately.
Less time needed to distinguish commonplace from unusual in a setting	Observer can also interview participants—especially as follow-up on observations.
Increased access to cultural patterns that explain participants' sense of their own behaviors and culture	Can be less time-intensive
Disadvantages	*Disadvantages*
Tendency to focus on frequently occurring events	Does not provide for as in-depth or natural an experience.
Potential for sampling bias	Lack of first-person insider insights to cultural patterns, attitudes, beliefs, etc.
Loss of objectivity through emotional attachment	Does not allow for personal testing
Potential for settling too early on a particular theory about the setting	Potential to focus on frequently occurring events
Need for deception/informed consent	Potential for sampling bias (although not as great as with participant observation)
Temptation to accept others' explanations too readily or miss subtle features that are taken-for-granted by insiders	
Data often cannot be recorded immediately	

Recording data from an observation. Data collection during observation can take many forms, including structured observation protocols and the use of mechanical devices such as videotapes and audio recordings. However, the most common method remains the taking of in-depth, comprehensive field notes. The structure of field notes depends on personal preferences of the researcher, but generally includes the same three categories as field notes taken during an in-depth interview: a detailed description of the setting, events, statements, and actions observed; a record of affective aspects of the observation, including observer responses and attitudes; and reflections and preliminary sensemaking. See Figure 8.1 for an example of a field note recording form.

As with an interview, detailed observation takes practice. Many new researchers find it demanding to record the many events and stimuli surrounding them in a research setting, and they report that it is surprisingly difficult to decide what to record. Careful sampling of people, events, and locations within the study's parameters helps alleviate the novice's tendency to be overwhelmed by the press of too much information and data during observation research while protecting the reliability of data gathered. If you decide to undertake an observation study, be sure to spend time practicing data recording and ask an experienced researcher to read and critique your field notes. The quality of data collected once the actual study begins will be well worth the time spent in preparation.

Existing Documents, Videotapes, and Audiotapes

In all literate societies, written (and sometimes audio and visual) records exist in archival form. By reviewing these records, the qualitative researcher can tap the history of the social group, culture, organization, or events that are central to the research. These records include such things as minutes of faculty meetings, newspaper and magazine articles, diaries, videotapes of teaching events, audiotapes of counseling sessions, memoranda, and correspondence. Archival records contribute data that are independent of the researcher's presence, interpretation, or preexisting theories. These sources provide different perspectives and cross-checks on forms of data gathered more directly. Materials prepared by and for others serve as an important resource for field research that complements data obtained directly.

When examining existing records, it is important to remember that the individual or individuals who did the initial recording (whether it is written, audio, or video) had their own perspective and biases. This makes it especially important to not only be aware of your own perspective and those of the person(s) of interest, but also the perspective of this new, third party. The importance of triangulation and the other steps to defend against the threats to validity cannot be stressed enough.

Ethical Issues in Qualitative Research

Ethics play such a critical part in qualitative research approaches that they deserve revisiting. In addition to those issues raised in Chapter 3, the depth of qualitative researchers' knowledge and engagement in a research setting place particular stress on the need for confidentiality and discretion. Qualitative researchers may be in a situation where they have particular challenges because they may know more about their participants (Brinkmann & Kvale, 2005; Haverkamp, 2005; Trimble, 2006). This discussion provides a beginning for qualitative field researchers by emphasizing the obligations of all involved. The researcher's primary responsibility is to the participants and emerges from the personal interactions involved in fieldwork. However, conflicting commitments do arise, and researchers must constantly be on

FIGURE 8.1   Sample Recording Form for Field Notes

Observation Notes

Teacher Name: _____   Date: _____

*Write detailed notes of entire observation including everything the **teacher says and does**. In addition, be sure to include: **Time** (minutes of activity), **Grouping** (whole class, pairs, independent, etc.), **Materials** (books, word cards, pencil and paper, etc.), and **Description** (what they are doing). Any relevant thoughts or reactions you have as an observer should be recorded under the **Reflective Notes**.*

Grouping	Materials	Time	Detailed Description of All Teacher-Directed Activities	Reflective Notes

guard to question their own actions. They must intrude minimally as they collect data while they are trying to understand the world they are studying. They must affect the setting as little as possible and assume a neutral role as much as possible. While unique relationships and trust must be formed to acquire high-quality, truthful data, the balance between "friend" and "stranger" roles must be maintained.

The way in which information is obtained and how it is disclosed also present challenges. We encourage you to read the research ethics chapter (Chapter 3) frequently as a reminder of the need to continually question procedures and their effects on those being studied.

MIXED-METHOD DESIGNS

There are a number of circumstances in which researchers can investigate different aspects of the same problem using elements of both qualitative and quantitative methods. These approaches are termed **mixed-method designs** (Creswell, 2005; Mertens, 2005; Punch, 2005). As we have seen before, features that are considered strengths of some methods may be characterized as limitations of others. Many researchers believe that mixed-methods approaches allow a researcher to capitalize on the strengths of the various methods (Tashakkori & Teddlie, 2002; Johnson & Onwuegbuzie, 2004). However, mixed method designs are not just the use of a quantitative and a qualitative design at the same time. Recent work develops specific mixed-method designs that incorporate elements of both qualitative and quantitative research (Creswell, 2005; Gay et al., 2006).

The basic reason for using mixed-method research is to capitalize on the strengths of each approach and to minimize the limitations or weaknesses. One point to keep in mind, however, relates to the time and expertise needed to conduct rigorous mixed-method investigations. These are challenging on both fronts. As we will see, the time and effort involved in mixed-method studies is often significant. Likewise, mixed-method investigations require knowledge about multiple methodologies and how they can be effectively implemented. This often leads to a team of researchers working together, both to expand the knowledge base of multiple investigation methods and to expand the capacity for data collection.

Approaches to Mixed-Method Design

As will be explained in a later section of this chapter, the extent and specifics of each aspect of the mixed-method design depends on the research question(s) being asked; however, there are a few general approaches that can be described. In general, the three types of mixed-method designs depend on where the qualitative and quantitative portions fall in the process: simultaneously (the data accuracy or validity approach), quantitative before qualitative (the enhancing the explanation approach), or qualitative before quantitative (the testing the explanation approach).

Data Accuracy or Validity

Mixed-method approaches may involve using one type of data as a source of triangulation for the other data type. Using this approach, both qualitative and quantitative data are collected from the beginning with both viewed as equivalent sources of information about the question being asked. Then, during the analysis phase, researchers examine both types of data to see if they seem to tell the same story. An example of this might involve interviewing students about how they behave during study periods. At the same time, researchers may be observing the students during study period using a structured observation checklist. Examining both the qualitative interview data and the quantitative observation data, the investigator is able to see if students behave in the same way that they say they do. In this fashion, one type of data serves as a check for the other type of data. Researchers analyze the qualitative data collected during interviews to see if students report the same or similar study period behavior that is observed.

Mixed-method investigations that use one type of data as a check on the other present some interesting challenges. For this approach to serve its basic purpose, it is necessary for the researcher to be able to do significant translations between the data types. We must be able to agree about how to interpret behavioral observations (quantitative data) and the statements students give (qualitative data) in order to draw conclusions. How do we know when the two data types are telling the same story so that we can meaningfully say that both agreed with each other and therefore provided strength to the interpretation? Generally, this is up to the reader or reviewer to determine. When this is done well, the use of one type of data to provide support for interpretation of the other is a tremendous strength. However, the challenge is found in integrating and translating across data types.

Enhancing the Explanation

A second mixed-method approach involves collecting quantitative data as a priority and subsequently using qualitative data to more fully explain the quantitative results. This approach consists of a two-phase data collection process. First, the investigator collects quantitative data and analyzes the results. Then, he or she initiates a second phase of the study in which qualitative data are collected to explain or further probe one or two of the quantitative results.

This type of study is useful to enhance the answer to *why* something happened. This approach would have been very helpful in an early study (Welch & Drew, 1972) of the effects of certain rewards on student behavior. The quantitative results indicated that students didn't perform as well as the researchers thought they should under one of the reward conditions. It was speculated that this lowered performance was due to the fact that the students became anxious to the point that it was detrimental to their performance. This was, however, only speculation. It would have been helpful to follow up with a qualitative phase to ask students about how they were feeling. This would have been a nice application of the mixed-method study where the qualitative phase seeks to explain some of the quantitative results.

Studies where qualitative data are used to further explain selected quantitative results provide a strong application of mixed-method investigations. This helps to solve one of the long-standing frustrations of quantitative researchers—why did that result happen? Analysis of quantitative data is very helpful for determining what happened but is sometimes rather limited in terms of illuminating *why* it happened. Thus, being able to follow those types of questions with a second qualitative probe is a strength of substantial proportions. The limitation is found in the details. It is not always an easy task to determine which part of the quantitative results should receive follow-up with qualitative probing. Mixed methods are used in the action research study found in the following Research in Action box as an approach to help explain quantitative data.

Extending the Results

A third mixed-method approach uses qualitative investigation as the first phase with quantitative data to explain or extend the qualitative results. In this method, qualitative data are collected first to explore a particular area or participant group of interest. This is followed by a second phase where quantitative data are gathered to support the qualitative findings or to see how they can be generalized. We also might have used this approach in the reward study above. We might have conducted a qualitative interview of students and found that they felt anxious in certain academic

RESEARCH IN ACTION

KEY POINTS IN THE CHAPTER REFLECTED IN THIS BOX:

- The manner in which this study used mixed methods by collecting qualitative data and quantitative data
- How the qualitative data may be used to enhance the explanation of quantitative results
- The need to use nonparticipant observation in this circumstance over participant observation

For more research in action tips visit www.sagepub.com/drewstudy

OBJECTIVES TO LEARN FROM THIS BOX:

- Understand how to use mixed-method approaches to help explain study results
- See how the qualitative and quantitative elements of this study complement each other to provide more complete information than either would singly
- See how one approach to observation becomes a logical choice in the context of the study setting
- Consider the implications of method selection and determining what effects such a choice might have on the data

Emily is planning to use nonparticipant observation as one of the measures in her study of reading instruction. Viewed in total, her study is one employing mixed methods. Her overall design is an experimental one, employing a comparison of one reading method to another. One group intervention involves student engagement through emphasizing concepts of interest to the students (CORI) and the other method using drill and practice on words and sentences (DAP). Although her overall design is experimental, one measure involves assessing the engagement itself and she will use nonparticipant observation to collect the data.

Emily's selection of nonparticipant observation to collect data on engagement is a natural choice over participant observation. Her observers will need to be inserted into the environment and cannot effectively become part of the natural environment. The only other adults in the classroom are the teacher and the teacher's aide. Both of these individuals are fully involved in implementing the instructional techniques. Although she will sacrifice some of the natural environment, research evidence suggests that the effects of inserting nonparticipant observers will become negligible quite rapidly as the children and adults in the classroom become accustomed to the observers and the addition of the extra adult (Gelfand & Drew, 2003). From an observation standpoint, this is her only choice, it has minimal limitations, and with appropriate observer training will likely produce high-quality and reliable data. The qualitative data collected by the observer will be an invaluable complement to test score data and may provide enormous insight regarding how and why the engagement group (CORI) differed from the comparison group receiving drill and practice (DAP).

Think about this: For the action research study in this box, what elements of the study make it a mixed-method approach? Why is nonparticipant observation a good choice and the most logical choice for collecting the qualitative data? How are the qualitative data collection elements adding to the results of the study and thereby enhancing the explanation possible beyond what might be the case if Emily had measured only reading test scores?

SOURCE: This action research scenario is roughly based on Swan, E. A. (2003). *Concept-oriented reading instruction: Engaging classrooms, lifelong learners.* New York: Guilford Press.

TABLE 8.5	**Elements of Different Research Methods**
Method	*Elements*
Quantitative	Prefers explicit definitions and hypotheses
	Prefers explicit procedure description
	Data in numerical scores
	Attention to assessing data and score reliability
	Attention to design validity
	Prefers design or statistical variable control
	Prefers design control of procedural bias
	Prefers random sampling to obtain representative information
	Prefers statistical summary of results
	Prefers dividing phenomena into parts for analysis
• **Experimental**	Manipulates study conditions to observe participant responses
	Imposes treatment or intervention
	Explicitly defines procedures, samples, and conditions for data collection
• **Nonexperimental**	Often studies conditions as they exist in natural environment
	No imposition of treatment or intervention to determine participant reaction
	May use numerical or narrative data
Qualitative	May prefer hypotheses and definitions to emerge in context as study develops
	Data in narrative description form
	Achieves validity by cross-checking data sources (triangulation)
	Prefers narrative & literary procedure description
	Prefers logical analysis for control or accounting for variables (describing what else is going on)
	Relies on researcher to detect & minimize procedure bias
	Prefers expert information samples
	Prefers narrative results summary
	Prefers holistic description (describing the whole picture)
	Prefers not to tamper with natural setting
Mixed Methods	Employs elements from multiple other methods such as collecting both quantitative and narrative information
	Quantitative data may serve as a source of triangulation for the qualitative data, and vice versa
	Qualitative data may be able to investigate why a particular quantitative result was evident
	Quantitative data may be able to provide support for a particular qualitative result

TABLE 8.6   Example Strengths and Limitations of Selected Research Methods

Method	Strengths	Limitations
Quantitative	Participant performance is recorded as a quantity, which can be done reliably	Numerical representation of performance may tell incomplete story of participant behavior
	Analysis promotes examination of component parts of participant performance	May be difficulties generalizing results to nonresearch environment; the world does not operate in component parts
	Detailed preplanning encourages control of extraneous variables in order to determine influences of the target variable under study	Some extraneous variables difficult to control and when they are controlled, the environment is changed from outside world
	Analysis can be accomplished in a relatively short time period	Analyzed results can be difficult to understand and interpret
	Useful for collecting information about large groups of people	Results may be somewhat general or abstract and difficult to apply to specific settings or people
• Experimental	Manipulates interventions or treatments to study effects on participant responses	Often creates artificial environment; participant behavior or performance may be influenced
	Allows determination of the impact of treatment/intervention on participant behavior	Influence of that treatment or intervention may be distorted because of isolated manipulation
• Nonexperimental	Gathers data from participants without altering environment	Accuracy and reliability of data may be questioned because participants provide it in uncontrolled setting
Qualitative	Participant behavior recorded in natural setting with complexities of environment operating	Environmental influences may be so complex, it is difficult to understand what is transpiring
	Some definitions and hypotheses allowed to emerge as study develops	Integrity of definitions and hypotheses may be less clear as they emerge under during an ongoing study
	Useful for in-depth study of a limited number or small group of people	Results may not be generalizable to other groups
	Reports of results can be quite dramatic, interesting, and easy to understand	Analysis of data is typically very time consuming
Mixed Methods	Capacity to capitalize on the strengths of multiple methods	Mixed-method research requires significant understanding of multiple methodologies. Translating and integrating both types of data may be difficult
	Qualitative data may be useful to help explain or elaborate on quantitative results	Determining which element of the quantitative data to pursue with qualitative data may be challenging, and significant time and skill are needed to collect both types of data
	Quantitative data may be useful to further explore initial qualitative results	Determining which element of the qualitative results to pursue with quantitative data may be challenging, and significant time and skill are needed to collect both types of data

situations. In fact, there were quite a few students who indicated this anxiety became so strong that they believed it got in the way of their academic performance. We might then have followed up with the quantitative study to see if their performance was actually affected negatively when we put them in anxiety-provoking situations.

Selection of the Best Method

All methods have applicability in appropriate situations, and combining methods bring up concerns about appropriate research training (e.g., Dittman, 2004; Kersting, 2004; Moghaddam & Finkel, 2005). Selection of an appropriate method should primarily depend on the question under study and the setting in which the research is being conducted (see Tables 8.5 and 8.6). This type of reasoning is not always employed, however. In some cases, the choice of methodology is made based on what skill set the researcher possesses.

Related to the above point is the significant time and knowledge involved in all applications of mixed methods. As we described the different approaches to mixed-method research, it was evident that they may require more time than using a single methodology. Time may not be something that the researcher has to spare. However, the strengths of the approach may be worth the extra time. The knowledge or skill set required for mixed-method research may also be difficult to find. Unfortunately, it is still rare for a single academic department to teach both quantitative and qualitative methodologies beyond a superficial introduction—generally the faculty strengths lie with one or the other approach. Therefore, most departments currently offer little of the alternative approach.

Chapter Summary

+ Qualitative methods are as varied as quantitative methods.

+ Qualitative methods rely on widely divergent assumptions about the nature of social reality.

+ Only three main kinds of data are collected for qualitative research—observation, interview, and archival data—even though the final reporting of the research may emphasize different aspects (e.g., teacher behavior versus student behavior) of the situation under study.

+ Mixed-method designs can serve as a synthesis of qualitative and quantitative designs—using the strengths of one to make up for the limitations of the other.

+ Depending on how the two designs are being used to answer the research questions, the mixed-method study could be equally qualitative and quantitative, primarily qualitative, or primarily quantitative.

+ All three approaches to mixed-method designs can strengthen the overall study design and provide a wealth of data.

+ The beginning researcher should plan to study and practice the techniques of qualitative research as systematically and carefully as he or she might prepare for any other form of rigorous research. This enhances the probability of making the study worth doing and the results worth reading.

✦ This preparation is especially important with mixed-method designs because of the need to conduct both a quantitative and a qualitative study (or portion of the study). It is important that both portions are similarly well-carried out, otherwise the final product will only be as good as the weaker section.

Key Terms

Anonymity. Refers to keeping the identity of a respondent from being known by the researcher.

Confidentiality. Refers to keeping the identity of a respondent from being known by anyone other than the researcher.

Design flexibility. Adding or removing methods of collecting, recording, or analyzing data while the data are being collected (rather than after they have been collected). This provides the researcher the advantage of being sensitive to changing events.

Emic perspective. How the participant(s) views the phenomenon being described or analyzed.

Empathic neutrality. Empathic neutrality is often presented as an alternative to objectivity; however, rather than assuming the researcher has no opinion or perspective, the researcher's opinion or perspective is openly acknowledged and described. In doing this, the researcher must also be willing to suspend that view and not make judgments on the views of participants that may differ from his or her own.

Etic perspective. The viewpoint of the researcher as an outsider.

Mixed-method designs. Research designs that incorporate aspects of both quantitative and qualitative research methods that capitalize on the strengths of each while minimizing the weaknesses.

Negotiated perspective. A blend of both the emic and etic perspectives that is discussed and agreed upon by the researcher and participant(s).

Nonparticipant observation. An approach to observation wherein the researcher is not a full, active member of the setting or group being observed.

Participant observation. An approach to observation wherein the researcher is a full, active member of the setting or group being observed. It often involved deception in that the other participants cannot know the observer is actually observing.

Thick description. Narrative descriptions that provide a clear and accurate picture of the nature of the phenomenon being described.

Triangulation. A process of using a variety of different sources, collection methods, or perspectives to check the consistency or accuracy of research conclusions.

Student Study Site

The companion Web site for *Designing and Conducting Research in Education* www.sagepub.com/drewstudy

Supplement your review of this chapter by going to the companion Web site to take one of the practice quizzes, use the flashcards to study key terms, and check out the many other study aids you'll find there. You'll even find some research articles from the Sage Full-Text Collection and a step-by-step guide that will show you how to read an educational research article.

Simulation Feedback

Simulation Feedback 8.1

For additional simulations visit www.sagepub .com/drewstudy

The advantages of the interview are (1) it is flexible and can uncover information about the setting that the interviewer did not know; (2) it can convey the meaning of events for those participating; (3) it provides a way to gather detailed information about the situation from the participant's point of view, revealing personal perspectives that are unique to the individual; and (4) it can clarify the responses to questions emerging from other data, provide information not available elsewhere, and offer the opportunity for elaboration and explanation.

The interviewers should design their questions so that the parents can provide information about the students that the educators cannot get anywhere else. Questions should ask about the importance of school in the family and the students' feelings about school. They should elicit what a test means to the child, if the child has talked about tests, homework, assignments, or other activities with his or her parents, and how the child has described these experiences to the parent. Questions should address reading, conversation, sleep, eating, and other family patterns that are known to affect student performance and should ask for the parents' feelings about these family patterns in relation to the child's schoolwork. Finally, the interview questions should provide a way to ask parents specific questions related to their own children and their work. Examples of schoolwork accompanied by questions about what the parents think a child might have meant in a response, portrayed in an artwork, or assumed from a question in the schoolwork will give the researchers a personalized view of the world from the child's family's perspective.

The researchers also should carefully determine who will conduct the interview for each family. If racial, religious, or social class tensions exist in the neighborhood, or if gender bias might cause parents to respond in a particular way, interviewers should be adjusted to the family to secure the most trustworthy responses. Parents should be treated with all the respect of any research respondent, including requests for permission to tape, assurances of confidentiality, and reminders that the parent is not required to answer every question and may halt the interview at any time if he or she wishes.

Before each interview, the researchers should gather all data available about the child at the school and read and review the data. Questions should be carefully personalized to child and parents whenever possible. Reviewers must take care not to ask the parents for information about the child that the school already has or should have.

Finally, the procedures for each interview should be carefully laid out—who will interview, how will the interview be recorded, and so forth.

RESEARCH DESIGN PITFALLS

After reading Chapter 9, you should be able to do the following:

✦ Define design validity and describe the two primary types of validity.

✦ Discuss the following threats to internal validity in the context of various research designs:
  ★ History
  ★ Maturation
  ★ Test practice
  ★ Instrumentation
  ★ Statistical regression
  ★ Hawthorne effect
  ★ Bias in group composition
  ★ Experimental mortality

✦ Discuss the following threats to external validity in the context of various research designs:
  ★ Population sample differences
  ★ Artificial research arrangements
  ★ Pretest influence
  ★ Multiple treatment interference

✦ Describe the primary issues that researchers must attend to in order to preserve rigor.

✦ Identify the threats to rigor and how to defend against them.

Thorough planning is an essential component in developing a sound research project, whether it is a quantitative or qualitative investigation. Without thoughtful planning prior to beginning an investigation, the results of the study may lack validity and therefore have no meaning or usefulness in the world at large. In this chapter, we examine several of the most common pitfalls encountered by researchers in the design of a study.

TYPES OF DESIGN VALIDITY

Design validity is defined as the technical soundness of a given study—in other words, a study's rigor and scientific merit. A study has scientific merit if it accurately distinguishes knowledge from ignorance. It is the responsibility of a researcher to find the most trustworthy information (truth) available regarding a statement, hypothesis, or explanation of a phenomenon. As an investigator designs a study, careful attention is given to two primary types of validity (internal and external) to safeguard against using data collection procedures that may prevent meaningful implications being drawn from the results.

Internal Validity

Internal validity is about credibility. It is defined as the extent to which all extraneous influences, other than the variable(s) under study, have been accounted for (controlled) and the observed effect can be attributed to this variable(s) (also called the independent or experimental variable). For example, in an experimental study, let's say a researcher wants to compare the effectiveness of a new reading program that we'll call "Read to Learn" with an existing program, "Basic Elements of Reading," for first-grade students at Walt Whitman Elementary School. In designing the study, the researcher randomly assigns the students into two groups that are "matched" by age, grade level, reading achievement scores, and socioeconomic

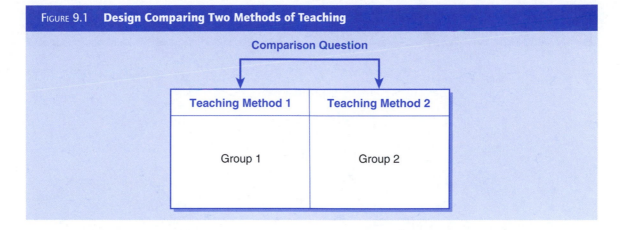

FIGURE 9.1 **Design Comparing Two Methods of Teaching**

status. Group 1 (experimental group) receives the new "Read to Learn" program and Group 2 (control group) continues in the "Basic Elements of Reading" program. To ensure that the study is internally valid, the researcher must try to account for (control) all "influences" on the two groups other than the fact that one group is receiving the new reading program and the other continues in the existing program. Some possible outside influences could be differences in the years of experience for the two classroom teachers who are instructing the students; additional tutoring in reading for some children in one group but not the other; or time of day that the two programs are taught (one group receives instruction in the morning while the other group receives instruction after lunch). Figure 9.1 illustrates the research design that would be involved in this study.

As indicated by the double arrow in Figure 9.1, the research question involves comparing the effectiveness of Teaching Method 1 (Read to Learn) with the effectiveness of Teaching Method 2 (Basic Elements of Reading) as measured by student scores on a standardized achievement test. The differences between Method 1 and Method 2 are systematic differences in the sense that one group is systematically treated with Method 1, whereas the second group is systematically treated with Method 2. In order for the researcher to say that the systematic difference between the two groups is a direct result of using "Read to Learn" versus "Basic Elements of Reading," all other systematic differences between Groups 1 and 2 must have been eliminated.

This same basic principle for internal validity applies to quantitative, nonexperimental research when comparisons are involved. An example may be found in a survey study in which the researcher wants to determine whether there is a difference between student achievement scores in a school in which average annual parent income exceeds $50,000 and one in which more than 80% of the students are receiving reduced or free lunch (parent income is below poverty level). In this case, the researcher would try to ensure internal validity by accounting for all influences other than parent income level.

External Validity

External validity refers to the circumstances under which the results of a study can be generalized (transferred) to a population beyond the participants in the study.

External validity speaks directly to how much the study methodology (including participants, research environment, measures, and manipulated variables) is similar to the world in which the researcher wants to add new knowledge and trustworthy information. Figure 9.2 illustrates the nature of external validity.

FIGURE 9.2   **External Validity Questions Generalizability of Results to the World Outside the Investigation**

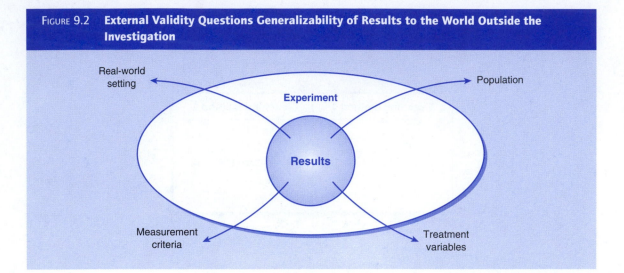

The arrows in Figure 9.2 illustrate the research questions. How well do the results of a given investigation represent the population and the environment under study? Further, does the treatment, as well as the measures to collect data on the treatment, represent performance criteria in the world beyond the research setting? If a treatment (independent variable) is under study, does it represent something that may serve as a treatment in the outside world? If survey research is involved, are the respondents asked questions that are relevant to the world outside the interview or questionnaire setting? For example, "What do you see as the most important challenge facing public schools in America today?" This question is clearly relevant beyond the individual responding. In addition, the manner in which the question is asked allows for a response that can be generalized to a larger population (e.g., local, state, or national).

THREATS TO EXPERIMENTAL DESIGN VALIDITY

As we examine various threats to design validity, the purpose is to maximize strengths (internal and external validity) and minimize limitations. Internal threats include extraneous variables (any variables other than the one under study). Extraneous variables include history, maturation, practice, instrumentation, statistical regression, the Hawthorne effect, bias in group composition, and experimental mortality. External threats involve population sample differences, artificial research arrangements, pretest influence, and multiple treatment interference. The following is a list of threats to design validity, each of which will be discussed in detail below.

Threats to Internal Validity

- History
- Maturation
- Test practice
- Instrumentation
- Statistical regression
- Hawthorne effect
- Bias in group composition
- Experimental mortality

Threats to External Validity

- Population-sample differences
- Artificial research arrangements
- Pretest influence
- Multiple-treatment interference

Threats to Internal Validity

In the following discussion, the various threats to internal validity will be examined in the context of several research designs. As you read through this chapter, two points should be kept in mind. First, it is important to avoid as many threats as possible in order to conduct the most rigorous study feasible given the circumstances. Second, it may not be possible to eliminate or control all other variables other than the one under study; nearly every study conducted has some area in which it could be strengthened. When the researcher has been rigorous and eliminated or controlled as many potential threats as possible given the circumstances of the study, the threats remaining must be "lived with" and acknowledged in the interpretation of results.

History

History refers to an uncontrolled event (extraneous variable) that occurs during the study that may have an influence on the observed effect other than the variable under study. As suggested by this definition, history is a threat to internal validity when the researcher is obtaining more than one observation (repeated measures) on the same participants. History is a threat to internal validity that may be difficult to circumvent, because the researcher is often not aware of extraneous events and there may be little that can be done in advance to prevent their occurrence. For example, in the study discussed previously on comparing the effects of a new reading program with one that is already in use in a school, one potential "history" threat occurs if one of the group of students is receiving additional tutoring after school but not the others.

"History" threats may also have an impact on pre-post designs in group experiments. They may also be a challenge in time series experiments if the event occurs at approximately the same time as the intervention. Suppose an investigator is conducting an experiment concerned with the effects of certain exercises on overall physical fatigue. The study is being conducted with sixth graders and involves the administration of a pretreatment measure followed by the exercises, which, in turn, are followed by the posttreatment measure. Figure 9.3a represents a visual diagram of the experimental design. This investigation is asking a difference question. Represented by the double arrow in Figure 9.3a, the researcher will be comparing the pretest scores with the posttest scores to determine if there is a difference.

On the surface, it appears that the only major event occurring between these two measures is the treatment, which in this case involves certain physical exercises. Assuming that the study is internally valid, any differences between pretest and posttest performance should primarily be a result of the treatment. However, an extraneous variable (historical event) could threaten the internal validity of the study. Suppose the time required for this experiment is about 2 hours. The experiment begins at 9:00 AM and proceeds through the pretest and the treatment by 10:30. At this time, recess is scheduled and the children go to the playground, where a serious fight erupts. The fight involves several children from the experiment and continues for 10 minutes before it is broken up. At the end of recess, the children in the experiment return and take the posttreatment fatigue test. In analyzing the data, the researcher finds that the measures on the posttest show significantly greater fatigue than the pretest scores. If the researcher is unaware of the playground fight, it might be logical to conclude that the physical exercises involved in the treatment

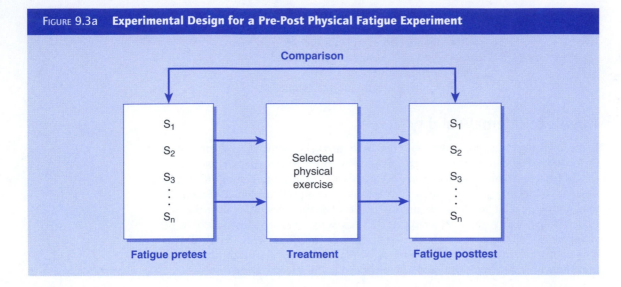

FIGURE 9.3a   **Experimental Design for a Pre-Post Physical Fatigue Experiment**

Comparison

| Fatigue pretest | Treatment | Fatigue posttest |

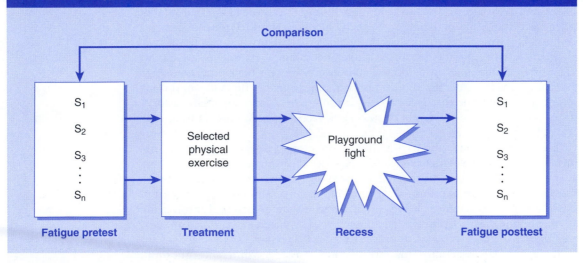

FIGURE 9.3b   **Experimental Design for a Pre-Post Physical Fatigue Experiment With a History Threat**

Comparison

seem to produce a significant general fatigue effect in sixth-grade children. Naive concerning the history threat, the researcher assumes that the design in Figure 9.3a is what happened when, in fact, the data are more likely the result of the design represented in Figure 9.3b. The treatment, the fight, or the effect of both could have caused the resulting difference in scores. Interpretations that the selected exercises generated the observed general fatigue may be in error.

History threats may also be a potential contaminator in quantitative, nonexperimental studies. For example, it may cause a problem when an "incident" occurs between two interviews with the same participants. Perhaps the factor under study was merely the passage of time between the two interviews (*but,* something traumatic also occurred during that time).

History may also threaten the internal validity of time series experiments like those often used in behavior modification studies. Time series experiments are

FIGURE 9.4   **Example of a Data Display From a Hypothetical Experiment Using an A-B Design**

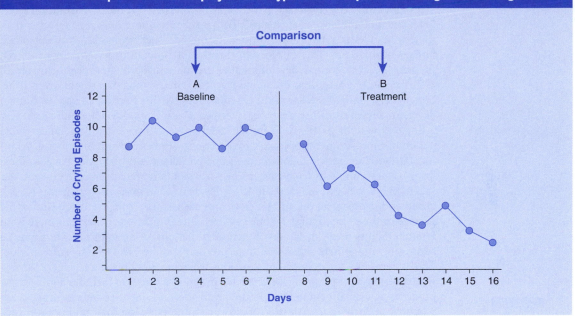

characterized by various data collection phases. Data are collected before the treatment or intervention to establish the baseline rate (Phase A) of the behavior being studied. After the researcher is satisfied with the reliability of observation and stability of behavior frequency, treatment is initiated in Phase B. Figure 9.4 illustrates a hypothetical experiment using the A-B design.

This type of study is asking a difference question as suggested by the double arrow indicating comparison. Did the treatment make a difference? Is there a difference between baseline behavior frequency and the recordings after the intervention was initiated? The intervention may have been some aversive stimulus or reinforcement condition. The researcher, who is interested in the effect of the *independent variable* (intervention), is assuming that the treatment under study was the cause of the change in behavior frequency. If some specific event other than the treatment occurs simultaneously with the intervention, it may threaten internal validity. The change in behavior frequency evident in Figure 9.4 may be a result of the intervention, the specific history event, or a combination of the two.

The researcher may do several things to guard against this threat in time series experiments. First, this type of experiment is often replicated numerous times before a researcher begins to draw practice implications from results. It is fairly unlikely that an outside event would systematically occur in close proximity to the intervention over a series of studies. Often a researcher will reverse experimental conditions (using an A-B-A-B design) after behavior has stabilized. Here again, the chances of a specific event either reversing or in some other way occurring simultaneously with both intervention and reversal are small. In addition, the use of multiple-baseline procedures has resulted in lowering the threat of history. The multiple-baseline design allows us to study treatment effect on a given participant using several target behaviors. The probability of accidental historical incidents occurring at staggered intervals that coincide with all phase changes in a multiple-baseline design is very small. However, the researcher should avoid (if possible) scheduling interventions close to high-risk times when confounding variables are more likely to occur.

Maturation

Distinct from the challenges associated with "history" variables, **maturation** refers to factors that influence participants' performance *because of time passing* rather than specific incidents. Maturation influences include such things as growing older, hunger, and fatigue. This category of threat is of concern in longitudinal research such as studies on human development where the actual growth process is involved.

Behavioral researchers often observe the effects of a treatment over time. Longitudinal designs are one of the two major approaches to research used by human development investigators; the other is termed *cross-sectional*. In longitudinal studies, a single sample of participants are repeatedly observed or tested over an extended period of time—sometimes years. Cross-sectional studies attempt to gather developmental data but not by following the same participants over time. Cross-sectional investigators sample different groups of participants representing several age levels (e.g., 3 to 5, 6 to 8, 9 to 11, and 12 to 15). They then test or observe participants in each group and compare across groups. Both approaches draw conclusions regarding the passage of time (e.g., aging). If time passage is the primary variable, then there is no internal validity problem. However, there are situations where an investigation may be addressing a treatment other than time, but may still involve a lengthy study period. This is common, for example, in situations where a school district is experimenting with a new type of program. Often such a program evaluation includes a pretest, the program as a treatment, and a posttest with the time involved representing a full school year. Such an investigation could encounter many internal validity problems, including maturation. The study involves a pre-post design similar to the one diagrammed in Figure 9.3a, with a long treatment period. If the researcher proceeds with a single group, administering the pretest, treatment, and posttest, a difference question is being asked. The research question may be stated as, "Is there sufficient difference between pretest and posttest performance on the treatment to be significant?" The interpretation involves the amount of change between the two measures. The researcher is attempting to attribute any difference between the two performance measures exclusively to the treatment. There may, however, be maturational influences that render this interpretation invalid.

Suppose that Figure 9.5 illustrates a graph of the data obtained in the above study. If the investigator draws the inference that the performance change is attributable to the treatment (experimental program), then such an interpretation may be invalid. Why? Because the investigator doesn't know whether the performance change was caused by the treatment or by participant maturation. A full academic year is involved and it would be expected that as the children grow older, they perform better on most academic tasks due to maturational influences not associated with the treatment. This interpretation would be particularly true with younger children. Thus, the treatment and/or the participants' maturation could be associated with the performance change.

How should a researcher avoid or circumvent the maturation threat, such as the one just described? In order to explain the amount of change that occurred as a result of the program, the investigator must first have an estimate of how much growth is expected simply as a result of natural growth and development. For example, let's say the children can be expected to improve by 20 correct responses on the spelling test merely as a function of their growth and development. If this is true, improvement beyond that amount could be attributed to the treatment.

In reality, avoiding a maturation threat is quite difficult. First, the necessary evidence regarding untreated growth and development is seldom available. Even if it is available, what reason is there to think that the participants in the study are like those from which the evidence was obtained? Fortunately, there are more technically sound approaches to minimizing the maturation threat.

The use of multiple experimental groups is one way to avoid a maturation threat. The study might compare a new school program with a program currently in use. Figure 9.6 provides a visual representation of this design. In this type of design, difference questions are asked, but some additional elements have been included.

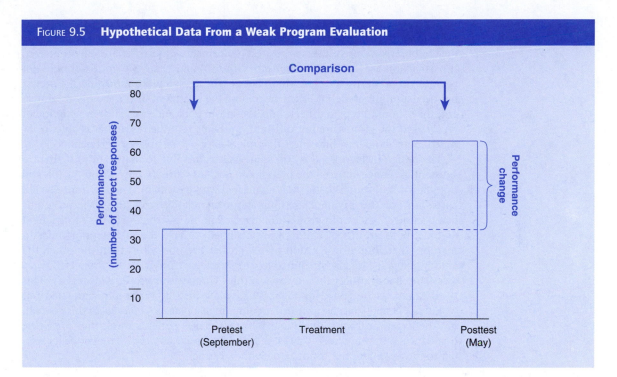

FIGURE 9.5   **Hypothetical Data From a Weak Program Evaluation**

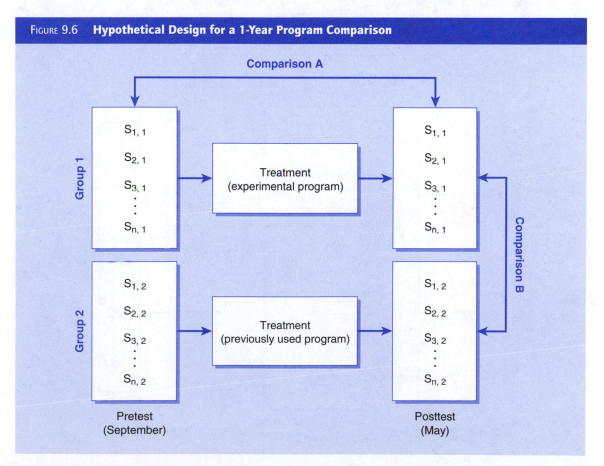

FIGURE 9.6   **Hypothetical Design for a 1-Year Program Comparison**

The design represented in Figure 9.6 has changed from that shown in Figure 9.5., so that the effects of two instructional programs are being compared. As indicated by the double arrows, pretest versus posttest performance differences are still of interest. If participants are randomly assigned to Groups 1 and 2, the two groups should not be different on the pretest. This should be confirmed as a precaution after the pretest has been administered, but before beginning the treatment. If the groups are different, they should be placed back into the larger pool and the random assignment repeated. If the groups are not different on the pretest, the researcher is able to say much more about any differences that might exist on the posttest performance.

The design in Figure 9.6 is still somewhat vulnerable to maturation. If there is substantial change between the pretest and posttest scores (Comparison A), it is still not known how much change was associated with treatment. There is a more solid basis, however, for saying something about the relative strength of the programs being studied. Since both groups are involved in the treatment for the same length of time, both groups of children are assumed to have the same opportunity to mature. Therefore, if one group makes greater pre-post gains than the other, the amount of gain could be attributed to a more effective program. To more effectively assess the maturation gain, however, a third comparison group is necessary. This third group, as suggested by Figure 9.7, would also be randomly generated but would not actually receive a treatment other than a placebo. *Placebo*, in this context, has the usual meaning—the "sugar pill" that makes patients think they are being treated when they are not—that is, they would receive an activity that appears similar to the treatment but is not actually the treatment.

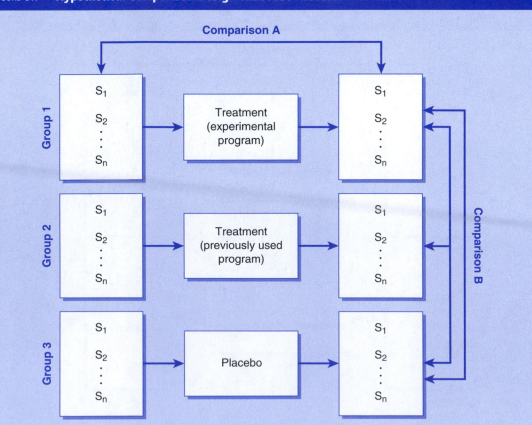

FIGURE 9.7   **Hypothetical Comparison Design That Also Assesses Maturation**

The design represented in Figure 9.7 is effective because it compares the new experimental program with the previously used program and simultaneously permits an estimate of how much change is caused by maturation. This is accomplished by using two types of difference comparisons: Comparison A looking for pre-post differences within groups and Comparison B looking for differences between groups on the posttest. Group 3 receives a placebo as a treatment. The nature of this placebo activity is critical in that it must be similar but unrelated to the treatment. Comparison A differences occurring in Group 3 can be assumed to be caused by maturation. Any "Comparison A" differences that occur in excess of the Group 3 changes could then be attributed to a treatment for either Group 1 or Group 2. Thus, it is possible to infer how much change is due to maturation and how much is caused by instruction.

It is necessary to address the practical considerations of conducting such a study in a school. For example, a problem may occur if the three treatment conditions (experimental, previously used, and placebo) have to be implemented by three different teachers. In such a situation, performance differences between groups might be a result of differences in teacher effectiveness. It might be more advantageous to have all three groups taught by one person for the portion of each day involving the treatment. Even this approach would require careful training to minimize differences caused by the person's preference for one treatment over the others.

Maturation also presents a threat to internal validity in studies where a pre-post design is not used. In a group experimental design with only one performance measure, the question asked is, "What is the difference between these groups?" For whatever reason, a researcher may find it most convenient to test one group of participants and then move to the next group for testing. By conducting the study in this manner, an investigator may be systematically introducing a difference between the groups in addition to the experimental treatment. If, for example, Group 1 is tested in the morning and Group 2 is tested in the afternoon, maturation (e.g., fatigue) may be a threat to internal validity.

Survey research is also subject to maturational threats. For example, consider the situation where a researcher wishes to conduct a survey on high school students' views regarding leisure time activities. In this instance, sophomores and seniors are being compared. It is most convenient to use a questionnaire that can be distributed personally, completed, and returned immediately (e.g., in a study hall period). It is also convenient to collect data from the seniors during the Wednesday morning study hall and the sophomores during the Friday afternoon study hall. Differences between the groups could be associated with the intended comparison (seniors versus sophomores), the differences in views of leisure activities between Wednesday morning and Friday afternoon, or both. It is important to eliminate the *systematic* way in which these variables influence one group differently from another.

To focus on the systematic dimension of influence, it is necessary to spread any effect of fatigue or hunger as equally as possible among all groups. To do this, a researcher will want to gather data on an equal number of participants from each group in the morning and in the afternoon. The impact of the differing times would thus presumably be spread evenly between the groups.

Studies using time series designs may also be vulnerable to a maturation threat. Such investigations are asking a difference question such as, "Is there a difference between baseline and postintervention behavior when using time-out procedures in a fourth-grade classroom?" or, "Does the intervening time-out program make a difference in behavior?" Maturation in a physiological growth sense may threaten the design if the duration of the experiment is sufficient that growth might be expected. If an experiment's duration is sufficient to permit physical growth and development, a researcher may incorrectly interpret this change as due to the intervention.

Many time series studies are of such short duration that physiological maturation is not a problem. These studies are, however, subject to threats from maturation in the form of fatigue or hunger. If, for example, an experiment lasts for a day with the baseline being established in the first part of the morning, intervention and continued measurement might proceed throughout the remainder of the day but without sufficient time for reversal of the treatment conditions. Fatigue, hunger, or some other influence, occurring because of time passing, may well affect performance *in addition* to the treatment. The strongest safeguard against maturation in this situation is replication (i.e., repeating the experiment).

If the purpose of the study is to examine time passage as an experimental variable, then maturation, in that sense, is the topic under study and is not a threat to internal validity. However, there are other difficulties that may threaten internal validity. Assume that aging is the topic of study. The typical longitudinal study involves repeated administrations of a measure during that period. In this case, test practice will influence changes in performance (Gelfand & Drew, 2003; Nadelman, 2004). This would alter the average scores between comparison points in addition to the experimental variable. In addition, many developmental studies are conducted over a period of years. As such, a number of participants may be lost during the time period in which the study is being conducted. Consequently, comparisons between beginning performances (of groups) and ending performance may be altered because the groups represent different participants. Cross-sectional investigations circumvent the difficulty of participant attrition because they assess a number of different groups at the same time.

Cross-sectional differences may be interpreted as representing developmental changes or trends similar to those in longitudinal studies. Such interpretations must be made with caution as there may be other factors affecting performance differences between groups. It may be that development (e.g., aging) is not the primary contributor to differences. Social changes and influences between the groups may have a significant impact. For example, there may be half a decade or more between the youngest and oldest group, meaning that these individuals may have grown up in very different environments (e.g., social mores, approaches to schooling). Differences between the groups may be due to developmental factors and/or differing environments.

Test Practice

Test practice is a threat to internal validity when the effects of participants taking a test influence how they score on a subsequent test. In other words, a participant takes a test and in the process learns some of the test material. To illustrate, participants are given a math test, receive math instruction (treatment), and then take a second test to determine the effects of the instruction. However, having taken the first test may influence their results on the second test.

Test practice is a threat to pre-post designs. It occurs in studies where a researcher administers a pretest, followed by a treatment, and then a posttest on the same participants (the same is true for interviews, questionnaires, etc.). The basic format of this design presumes the researcher is assessing the difference between pretest and posttest performance, with a purpose of interpreting differences due to the treatment. However, a portion of the change from pretest to posttest performance levels may be caused by test practice. This is particularly true if the measurement represents a new and unique experience for the participants, so that they may have a great deal to learn about how to perform. For example, if the participants have never encountered an achievement test before, their pretreatment performance might partially reflect their lack of experience at taking such tests as well as their knowledge of content. The process of taking the pretest may teach them how to take the test as well as teach them some content, all of which would be reflected on their posttreatment scores.

To circumvent a test practice threat, a researcher may take one of two approaches. If participants clearly have a background that includes experience on the measurement instrument, an investigator may assume that test practice will

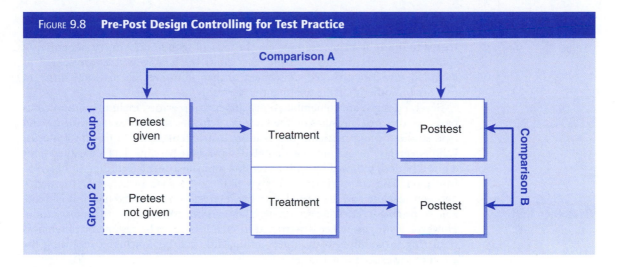

FIGURE 9.8   **Pre-Post Design Controlling for Test Practice**

generate less performance change and therefore be less of a threat. Another alternative would be to actually give participants the experience with a preexperimental warm-up. Using this approach, the researcher provides practice on the task before the first measure, which establishes at least some pretest to posttest similarity in terms of participant experience. Such procedures are somewhat weak, however, because they do not control or assess the amount of improvement due to additional test practice. Although participants have experience, they still may improve with more practice. A more valid procedure would involve a comparison group that does not receive the test practice, only the treatment.

To implement such a multigroup study, a researcher would initially draw a sample of participants at random. If the plan involved having 20 participants in each group, the sample would include 40 participants who would then be randomly assigned to the two groups (20 to Group 1 and 20 to Group 2). Group 1 would then receive the pretest, but Group 2 would not. Since Group 2 participants were randomly assigned from the same sample as Group 1, there is little reason to believe that they are different (see Figure 9.8). Presumably, the scores that Group 2 *would* have obtained on the pretest, if one had been administered, would not differ from those obtained by Group 1. From that point on, both groups receive the same treatment and posttest. Any differences between the groups on the posttest should be a result of test practice, since the opportunity to learn from the pretest is the only difference between the two groups. Figure 9.8 suggests that two questions may be addressed. Comparison A indicates performance change from the pretest to the posttest, whereas Comparison B estimates the amount of test practice. The difference between the pre and post mean scores for Group 1, minus the difference between Groups 1 and 2 on the posttest, presumably provides an estimate of the effect due to treatment.

Instrumentation

As a threat to internal validity, **instrumentation** represents influences on scores due to calibration changes in any instrument used to measure participant performance, whether they are mechanical changes or changes in the observer. In terms of mechanical calibration, suppose a researcher was using an audiometer to gather data on children's hearing. If something occurred midway through the experiment that changed the calibration of that instrument, all data collected from that point would be systematically different from data gathered before the change. Those systematic differences might mistakenly be attributed to some treatment when, in fact, they are partially due to the machine having been adjusted.

In education and behavioral science, most data are collected with human instruments such as observers and scorers. The same fundamental problem discussed in regard to the audiometer example may be present with human instrumentation. If something occurs during the study that alters the way responses are scored or recorded, any data obtained subsequent to that point are systematically different (for reasons other than the treatment under study).

Several designs are vulnerable to instrumentation errors, including group comparisons, repeated measures on the same participants, time series experiments, and field studies using participant observation. Instrumentation as a threat to internal validity can also be examined in an A-B design where baseline data are gathered for a given period, followed by an intervention and subsequent recording of observation data. The comparison of interest is the difference in behavior frequency between baseline and the period after the intervention was introduced. It is desirable to be able to attribute any changes in behavior frequency to the intervention. However, if the researcher is restricted in such inferences by systematic differences occurring in addition to the intervention, little can be concluded regarding the effect of the experimental variable.

The most serious problem occurs if the change in addition to the intervention occurs close to the timing of the instrumentation change. Under these conditions, the influence of the contaminating factor may appear to be a part of the experimental effect. In terms of instrumentation problems, the difficulty is presented by changes in the observer who is recording behavioral data. For example, perhaps the researcher, either knowingly or unknowingly, alters his or her mental set for data recording because change is expected as a function of the intervention. What occurs on the data sheet is some change in behavior frequency as a result of the intervention per se and/or change as a result of the observer's altered manner of recording data. Since all that has been recorded is behavioral frequency, no one knows how much of the difference may be attributed to the intervention and how much to instrumentation changes in the observer.

Several approaches may be used to circumvent instrumentation problems. Replication may help, although if the same observer is used, there is little reason to expect much assurance of control. In addition, if other observers are used, they may also be subject to bias similar to that influencing the first observer. One approach, which is more cumbersome but may provide more assurance of stable instrumentation, is a technique borrowed from medical research. This approach, referred to as a *double-blind technique,* uses a procedure where the person recording the data would not be aware of the time that the intervention was introduced. Thus, a person other than the observer performs the treatment manipulation. This would mean that the observer would not know precisely when intervention occurred except through actual changes in behavioral frequency.

Experiments in which groups are compared may also be vulnerable to instrumentation threats. The difficulty in this type of experiment is primarily logistical (e.g., having to do with the manner in which the experiment is executed) rather than an integral part of the study design. If, for example, the objective is to compare Group 1 with Group 2, the researcher must focus on minimizing systematic differences between groups that occur in addition to the experimental variable under study. Instrumentation presents the greatest potential threat of generating such differences when all the participants in one group are tested and the researcher then moves to the next group. Because of a variety of possible influences on the researcher (e.g., fatigue, practice, or unconscious mental set), one group may be systematically treated differently from another. To control for this type of problem, the researcher must focus on spreading such influences as evenly as possible among groups and thus remove the systematic dimension that may make groups different. This may be done by randomly testing participants from all groups such that the participants in different groups are alternated in the order of testing.

Statistical Regression

Statistical regression occurs if participants have been assigned to a particular group on the basis of atypical or incorrect scores. Under such circumstances, a participant's placement in a group may be in error, since the score is atypical. That individual's typical performance may be more like that of the participants in another group. If the misclassified participants then regress toward their average performance during the experiment, internal validity may be threatened (groups thought to be equivalent turn out not to be, or those thought to be different are actually not).

Statistical regression may create a problem in research designs where group comparisons are being made. This should not be taken to suggest that all group comparisons are equally vulnerable. However, if groups are being formed that represent preexisting participant classification differences, statistical regression may well present a serious challenge. For example, if a researcher wishes to compare performance by participants representing two levels of intelligence, a regression problem may be encountered. There may be a portion of one group whose IQ scores are atypical. Results of the comparison, thought to be attributable to level of intelligence, may in fact be a function of another factor. The researcher believes there are only two specified levels of intelligence within the two groups, when in fact, because the scores are atypical for one group, the investigator may not actually have the types of groups expected. Consequently, the performance or scores may appear more like that of the actual intellectual level at which the participants usually operate rather than the atypical score. In this sense, the performance may "regress" toward the average level of functioning.

The notion of statistical regression from an atypical score is also relevant as a threat to time series designs. A fairly common procedure called a "probe" is often used to establish the level of baseline skill. This technique is usually characterized by presenting the participant with a task to be performed and assessing the ability to perform it. Based on the results of such a probe, the modification of behavior is planned and implemented. If, for some reason, a participant's response to a given probe is atypical, then a statistical regression may occur. In somewhat the same fashion as a group design, a series of probes will provide some insurance against the atypical response being viewed as average. Time series experiments are generally less vulnerable because of the greater number of measurements usually recorded before an intervention or other phase change.

Hawthorne Effect

The **Hawthorne effect** refers to a change in sensitivity or performance by the participants that may occur merely as a function of being in an investigation. Due to the experimental environment (e.g., a laboratory), a change in routine caused by the study, or any other fashion by which participants are made to feel special, their performance may be different from how it would be if were they not participants. Such an influence becomes a threat to internal validity with group comparisons. Under such circumstances, the members of one group (e.g., experimental group) might perform better because they feel "special," whereas the members of another group (e.g., control group) might not have the "special" feeling and not perform as well. This creates a potential performance difference between the groups in addition to the experimental variable(s).

The Hawthorne effect is clearly a challenge when conducting an experimental study in which groups are compared. However, other types of research designs, such as time series experiments, are also vulnerable to the Hawthorne effect. As an illustration, refer to the A-B paradigm illustrated by Figure 9.9. As the intervention occurs, it is almost certain that the participant will be aware that the routine has changed. An observed change in postintervention performance may, therefore, be a result of the altered conditions under investigation (e.g., reinforcement schedule)

FIGURE 9.9   **Example of an A-B Time Series Data Display**

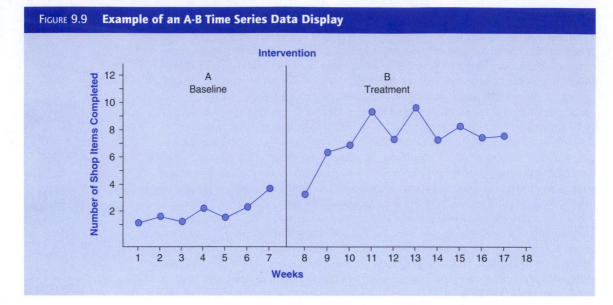

and/or the participant may have changed performance level because of the change in routine (Hawthorne effect).

Controlling for the Hawthorne effect essentially means that the systematic *difference* between the groups (in addition to what is being studied) needs to be removed or minimized. It is difficult to control the Hawthorne effect by removing it from the experimental group. The basis for the concept of control is to remove systematic differences (except the one under investigation) by making the groups as equal as possible. If the Hawthorne effect cannot reliably be removed from the experimental group, the most effective control method would be to "Hawthorne" both groups equally. This might be interpreted to mean that the members of the control group are treated in a fashion that will make them feel equally special, but not actually given the experimental treatment per se. Since the question focuses on the effects of the treatment, or differences between a group that receives the treatment and one that does not, "Hawthorning" both groups does not interfere with this comparison. The absolute level of performance by groups is not as important as the relative performance derived from comparing two or more groups. This type of control for the Hawthorne effect has contributed to a decline in the use of terms such as *experimental groups* and *control groups*. Many researchers prefer the term *comparison groups* to avoid the misconceptions concerning what a control group adds to an experiment and how it ought to be treated.

Some researchers using studies with very small numbers of participants may respond by saying, "Why bother?" This type of research has been characterized by a pragmatic philosophy. From that standpoint, one might simply assert that it is of no consequence whether the Hawthorne effect was occurring in addition to the intervention. If the behavior can be modified, from an instructional point of view, that is important and that should be the primary focus. Many researchers accustomed to using a small number of participants, as well as those coming from more traditional group design backgrounds, would take a somewhat different stance on this issue. They would prefer a more analytical approach that at least attempts to separate the influences of the Hawthorne effect from those of the intervention. A number of operations may be helpful in this regard.

One challenge involves the collection of baseline data. The question being addressed is essentially a difference question, comparing baseline performance with postintervention performance. If baseline data are gathered in a setting that primarily represents routine for the participants (e.g., a classroom) and the intervention involves a nonroutine setting (e.g., another classroom or individualized instruction), the potential influence of the Hawthorne effect is immediately evident. In some cases, the nature of the intervention necessitates a nonroutine environment (e.g., a small room with reduced stimuli). When this is the case, it is wise to also gather baseline data in the intervention environment. The Hawthorne effect may still be a problem when the intervention is implemented even if baseline and experimental settings are the same. There is little that can be done to eliminate the Hawthorne influence under these conditions, primarily because the same participant is experiencing preintervention and postintervention conditions (e.g., change in reinforcement contingencies). Most researchers will not, however, assess the influence of their intervention until the behavior rate has stabilized. Reference to Figure 9.9 reveals that the performance is much more erratic immediately after intervention. The Hawthorne effect is likely to be most potent immediately after the participant's routine is disturbed. The influence of the Hawthorne effect might be expected to decline as the participant becomes acclimated (i.e., as a new environment becomes routine). Thus, the stable rate of performance is assumed to reflect the intervention to a greater degree than rates observed immediately after intervention. The guideline for stable data presented by Gelfand and Drew (2003) is useful in such circumstances to determine how much additional data should be collected.

Bias in Group Composition

Bias in group composition is a threat to internal validity occurring when there are systematic differences in the composition of groups *in addition to* the treatment under study (experimental group). This threat is relevant to both experimental and quasi-experimental designs. As mentioned earlier in the book, an experimental design is one in which a single population of participants is identified and sampled prior to the study. Groups are then formed in a manner that promotes equality before the beginning of treatment (e.g., random assignment). Therefore, in an experimental design, the groups do not become different until treatment begins. A quasi-experimental design differs in that the groups are not formed from the same single participant pool. The group composition, which reflects the research question, may be based on a preexisting condition such as levels of intelligence. The diagram in Figure 9.10 portrays such an investigation. Quasi-experimental designs are particularly vulnerable to internal validity threats from bias in group composition. These designs are used in many areas of behavioral science. They have considerable value, providing essential information to many disciplines such as comparative and abnormal psychology, special education, and so forth.

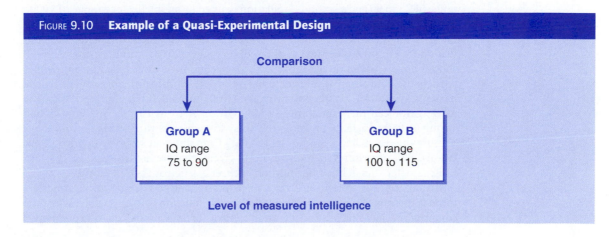

FIGURE 9.10   **Example of a Quasi-Experimental Design**

Comparison

Group A	Group B
IQ range	IQ range
75 to 90	100 to 115

Level of measured intelligence

The challenge in using quasi-experimental designs is to control systematic differences between groups *with the exception of the one under study.* In Figure 9.10, the experimental variable is intelligence, and to maximize internal validity it is desirable to diminish or eliminate other systematic differences between the groups. A quasi-experimental design raises a red flag because there is a higher probability of differences occurring in addition to the one under study. The presence of possible bias in group composition inhibits the meaningful interpretation of results. Precautions may be taken, however, to minimize the probability of group composition bias in quasi-experimental designs. First, the research question must be clearly articulated. If the experimental variable is intelligence, for example, then factors such as socioeconomic status, race, sex, or age must be controlled or held constant between groups.

Working with a quasi-experimental design presents a considerable challenge regarding controlling potential bias between groups. Since a researcher cannot make use of the power of random assignment, other alternatives must be used. In the absence of random assignment, an investigator is faced with the task of determining which factors are important to control. This task is challenging because of the potential for error. Not only might a researcher inadvertently omit control for some factor that is known to be influential, it is also possible that many variables have not yet been identified as important to control. One obvious question is, "How do you decide which factors need to be controlled?" These decisions are generally based on both previous research and logic. For example, if the task involved had been previously used and results indicated that performance was influenced by different stages of child development, the investigator would be remiss if chronological age were not held constant between groups. Similarly, if gender, socioeconomic status, or other factors had been shown to influence task performance, they should likewise be controlled. In the study illustrated in Figure 9.10, intelligence was the variable under investigation. If the variables mentioned above were known to influence performance on whatever task was being used, Groups A and B should be equivalent in chronological age or socioeconomic status and should have about equal numbers of both sexes or only one sex represented in the study.

To facilitate control in a quasi-experimental study, it is useful to turn to the sampling procedure, since assignment is already predefined. Recalling the example in Figure 9.10, the research question involved comparing the performance of two groups with different levels of intelligence. Suppose for the moment that it has been determined that chronological age and socioeconomic status, as well as visual, central nervous system, and health impairments have been identified as being important for control. The question then becomes one of how to best accomplish such control.

With a quasi-experimental design, the researcher is essentially working with two participant populations distinguishable on the basis of the experimental variable. In this example, there will be one participant population defined by an intelligence range of 75 to 90 and a second population defined by an intelligence range of 100 to 115. A method of controlling other factors is to define both populations as having the same characteristics on those other factors. Thus, although the participant population for Group A is defined in different IQ ranges than Group B, Groups A and B should have a common age range and socioeconomic status. In addition, neither participant population would include any people with identifiable visual, central nervous system, or health impairments. Given these defined characteristics, the investigator can then randomly sample Group A from Participant Pool A and Group B from Participant Pool B. This is known as *stratified random sampling* because the researcher is randomly sampling from different strata or defined populations. This procedure generally results in groups that are not different on the control characteristics defined in common between participant populations.

An experimental design involves a single participant pool from which groups are formed, presumably with no differences before the initiation of treatment. Bias in group composition does not present the same level of threat as in the quasi-experimental design because of the single participant pool and thus an absence of preexisting systematic differences. As a precautionary measure during sampling, it is often wise to eliminate potential participants who may encounter difficulties in performing the task (assuming such difficulty is not part of the normal deviation in performance). With the advantages offered by a single participant pool, group composition becomes a relatively simple matter. The primary concern is to form groups that are equal before the treatment. One of the most powerful procedures (and easily performed) involves randomly assigning participants to experimental conditions or groups. Earlier methodological approaches often emphasized experimental matching as a means of equating groups. In addition to challenges inherent in experimental matching, the procedure does not take advantage of the fact that group performances such as means are compared in group studies, not individual scores. Using random assignment acknowledges the fact that group performance is the focus and aims at making pretreatment *groups* equal rather than individual participant *pairs*.

Action research in the field often involves complex situations where the researcher cannot use a quasi-experimental design or an experimental design that *purely* has a single source of participants. The following Research in Action box describes such a situation.

Experimental Mortality

Experimental mortality becomes a threat to internal validity when there is a differential loss of participants between comparison groups. It is not uncommon for a researcher to lose a certain number of participants for a variety of reasons. Perhaps they are absent from school on the test day, and timing is important, so they cannot be tested at a later time. On other occasions, an error in research procedures might compromise the data from a given participant, requiring deletion of that data from the study. In general, experimental mortality presents no serious difficulty regarding internal validity as long as the loss is approximately equal between groups. The usual procedure employed (as long as the participant loss is approximately equal) involves randomly selecting replacement participants from the same participant pool initially used to compose the groups. Researchers should therefore form their original participant pool so that a certain number of potential participants remain as a replacement pool after groups are formed.

A threat to internal validity arises when groups lose participants in *different proportions*. A researcher may be unaware of the exact characteristics of the participants who are lost, in particular those characteristics that either related to or caused the loss. Consequently, whatever the characteristics, they have been deleted to a greater degree from some groups than others. If the lost participants are then replaced by randomly selecting from the replacement pool, the researcher may be building in systematic differences between the reconstituted groups. Using a hypothetical situation from a psychology learning laboratory, suppose that an experiment involves white rats as participants. Because of qualities in the participants (unknown to the researcher), a substantially greater proportion of one group dies. Although the exact reasons for death may be unknown, it is possible that the participants who were physically weak were more vulnerable to death. If replacement is accomplished by randomly selecting from the replacement pool, it is likely that about as many strong rats will be chosen for replacement as weak rats. Thus the replacement participants may include more strong rats than were in the group for which they are substituting. Since differential group loss requires more replacements in one group than the other, the addition of more potentially strong rats to that group may result in built-in differences between the groups. Appropriate procedures for equalizing groups may have been implemented initially, but the mortality threat presents itself after the experiment is under way.

RESEARCH IN ACTION

KEY POINTS IN THE CHAPTER REFLECTED IN THIS BOX:

- The importance of minimizing bias in group composition
- How action research presents challenges because it is conducted in field settings
- One example of circumventing a design pitfall in an action research study

For more research in action tips visit www.sagepub .com/drewstudy

OBJECTIVES TO LEARN FROM THIS BOX:

- How to think flexibly about circumventing design pitfalls in action research

Emily is conducting a study manipulating effects of engagement on how young students learn to read. One of her conditions is labeled as concept-oriented reading instruction (CORI) and her comparison group is going to receive drill and practice (DAP) on words and sentences. Emily's experimental variable is teaching method and the diagram below pictorially summarizes Emily's design.

Emily needs to hold all possible influences equivalent between the two groups except her experimental variable. She will want to have the group characteristics similar in terms of age, ability, gender, and other factors that might influence her criterion measures. In order to avoid bias in group composition on these factors, Emily will need both groups to be similar on these variables. These control factors illustrate very well some of the challenges facing action research. She cannot randomly assign participants to the conditions because the school district assigns students to classrooms so she will define her control factors (e.g., age, ability) and then assign classrooms to the CORI or the DAP groups. Because she has a large number of classrooms, the overall group composition (the CORI group and the DAP group) is unlikely to be different in terms of participant characteristics. On top of this she will layer another selection process that will minimize teacher differences between groups. These two components will make her comparison reasonably clean and help her in attributing any differences to the experimental variable.

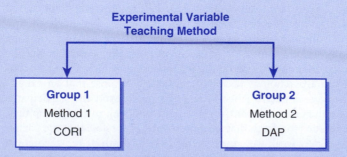

Think about this: For the action research study in this box, what other design pitfalls might surface? How can these pitfalls be minimized as threats to internal validity?

SOURCE: This action research scenario is roughly based on Swan, E. A. (2003). *Concept-oriented reading instruction: Engaging classrooms, lifelong learners.* New York: Guilford Press.

Experimental mortality also presents difficulties in designs other than group comparisons. A vulnerable design involves an investigation in which repeated measures are administered to the same group of participants over a long period of time. This refers to pre-post or longitudinal repeated measures designs. The repeated measures design is more vulnerable under some conditions than others. Experimental mortality is not problematic in situations where the duration of an investigation is fairly short and the researcher actively implements both pretreatment and post-treatment measures. However, such control is not always possible. For example, nonexperimental investigations called "follow-up studies" are often vulnerable to experimental mortality.

Follow-up studies are frequently used to evaluate the ultimate effectiveness of a treatment program. In a follow-up study, program entrance (admission) records often serve as the first or pretreatment data point. Because of these circumstances, such studies are occasionally called "post hoc" in the sense that existing data are used. A researcher may or may not actually see the clients during their treatment and may have only the pretreatment records for identification of participants. Experimental mortality becomes a serious issue when the investigator attempts to locate participants for follow-up assessment. Experience has shown that this is perhaps the most difficult type of study to conduct, and experimental mortality is the primary source of difficulty.

Depending on certain decisions by the researcher, several practical questions and issues may be considered. First, just how different do the mortality rates have to be before the researcher should be concerned? This varies from one type of research to another, and decisions are based on the experience and clinical judgment of the investigator. This is the type of decision best made before beginning an experiment. For example, based on what has been written in earlier research, an investigator may decide that any differential of more than 10% is going to be considered a threat to internal validity. Thus, if Group A lost 10% of its initial participants, whereas Group B lost 20% or 25%, the preset caution point would have been exceeded (i.e., the differential would be 10 to 15%). The question then becomes what can be done about the threat. This may be one situation in which, after carefully examining the information available, the researcher decides to proceed but to mention the loss as a potential weakness in the findings. The investigator may, however, decide that an internal validity threat is so imminent and potentially devastating to interpretation that the study should be discontinued with this sample of participants. The researcher may choose to start over with a totally new sample of participants.

Threats to External Validity

External validity involves how well the results of a particular study apply to the population, treatment variables, and measurement criteria in the world beyond the investigation.

Although internal and external validity are not in direct conflict, one may be applied to the disadvantage of the other. This is an area in which a researcher may have to decide to concentrate attention on one type of validity, while potentially sacrificing rigor with respect to the other. The value of research should not be determined on the basis of a given study, but rather in terms of programs of research with a cumulative purpose. As knowledge accumulates establishing the effectiveness of a given method used in a study (internal validity), the researcher may then become more concerned with its influence in the real-world environment (external validity). This change in focus will require increasing attention to external validity, perhaps sacrificing a bit of internal control. Ultimately, as a scientist approaches the real world, he or she has accumulated data not only on how the factor operates in a laboratory setting, but also on its influence as it interacts with environmental conditions. When generalizability is the focus, the researcher must avoid threats to external validity.

For additional simulations visit www.sagepub .com/drewstudy

Simulation

Simulation 9.1

Topic: Internal validity

Background statement: This simulation presents a time series experiment and asks that you critique and circumvent any threats to internal validity.

Tasks to be performed:

1. Read the following material. Note difficulties as well as the experimenter's explanation.
2. Determine the soundness of the experimenter's interpretation. Do you agree with the explanation? Why or why not?
3. What would you suggest as a means of circumventing any threats to internal validity?

Stimulus material: A time series experiment was conducted on a young boy who was identified by his teacher and his parents as being hyperactive. The investigator believed that the hyperactive behavior could be brought under control by positively reinforcing the child for remaining in his seat and staying "on task" while ignoring (thereby not reinforcing) any out-of-seat occurrences or "off-task" behavior. Since the researcher suspected that the hyperactive behavior was being reinforced and maintained in the classroom, it was decided that a time series A-B-A reversal design would be used. The data collected appeared as in the illustration below.

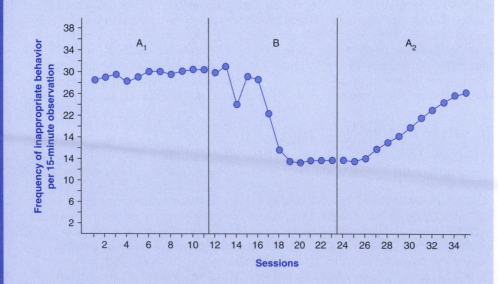

In viewing the above data display, the researcher became excited since it appeared that the treatment (positive reinforcement) was effective in reducing inappropriate behavior. The baseline appeared to be stable (consistently high rate) and a change was

(Continued)

evident under Phase B. The rate stabilized nicely and showed a somewhat gentle but convincing reversal under Phase A_2. Thus, the researcher suggested that the treatment has an effect on the inappropriate behavior.

Then some new information came to the researcher's attention. The mother had long been frustrated by the child's behavior and had consulted her local family physician, who prescribed medication to control the hyperactivity. This medication was begun on the day that Phase B was initiated. The medication rather than the reinforcement contingencies could have generated the behavior change in Phase B. The researcher, however, maintained that the treatment was effective as evidenced by the reversal when reinforcement contingencies were changed back to baseline conditions.

Do you agree or disagree with the interpretation? If so, would you use this interpretation for the same or different reasons from those expressed by the researcher? If not, why not? How would you change the design or in some other way test the interpretation?

Write your response, then turn to page 239 for Simulation Feedback 9.1.

Population-Sample Differences

An entire population is rarely available for a researcher to conduct a study. Even if the whole population were available, expense and time involved in recording data on an entire group are usually so great that it is unfeasible to do so. Consequently, researchers use samples of participants selected from the larger population. **Population-sample differences** are a threat to external validity because the participants in a study are not representative of the population to which generalization is desired.

One dimension of external validity concerns the degree to which the participants in a study represent the population to which generalization is desired. If there are substantial differences between participants and the larger population, it is likely that the participants will respond differently on the task from the larger group. If researchers are unaware of such differences, they may interpret the results as being applicable to the population when, in fact, they are not. Population-sample representation relates directly to the way in which participants are selected.

An important issue in sampling is how well the researchers know the characteristics of the population and the participant pool. As researchers proceed to define the population, it is unlikely that a thorough knowledge of all characteristics of the population is available. To the degree that there is confidence concerning the importance of those known characteristics, researchers can control external validity. This speaks specifically to the approach the researchers take with regard to defining the population. One view is that it is better to define the population in a restricted fashion but to have confidence in the knowledge concerning a restricted set of characteristics. The alternative position requires a much less rigorous definition of characteristics. Generalization under these conditions is viewed as an inference from the participant(s) in the experiment to "a population similar to those observed." The crucial factor is that the type of interpretation is clear. Researchers need to be aware of whether the population knowledge and resulting level of confidence concerning generalization are reliable.

Artificial Research Arrangements

A second threat to external validity involves the research arrangements chosen for the investigation. **Artificial research arrangements** are a threat to external validity when participants' behavior or performance is altered because the research setting deviates from their usual routine. Essentially, this phenomenon is the Hawthorne effect operating as a threat to external validity. To the degree that a research setting deviates from the routine the participant is accustomed to, it is likely that the participant's responses are changed. If a group of children have their daily classroom routine altered by being tested in a "small, distraction-free room," their performance may be either boosted or depressed because of the nonroutine setting. Participants' performance may be different from how it would be if they were to perform the task in a routine setting. If participants are responding differently because of the setting, their performance does not represent the original participant pool from which they were drawn. A researcher may have initially gone to great lengths to sample participants that are representative of a given population to enhance generalization. Although the participants may have been representative at that time, they become a select, nonrepresentative group as soon as the investigation is begun if the research environment is substantially artificial. Nonexperimental research may be equally vulnerable to the degree that participants are placed in a nonroutine situation. An interview may create an artificial environment depending on how and where it is conducted. In all cases, an investigator must judge the degree to which external validity is threatened by artificial research arrangements.

When participants are individually treated, which is often the case in many interviews and psychological experiments, it is difficult to imagine that the research arrangements are routine. The degree to which external validity is threatened depends on the situation *to which generalization is desired.* If, for example, a researcher is studying a new method of individualized instruction, considerable generalizability might be possible. True, the results may not generalize to the classroom from which the child came, but it should be remembered that the researcher is exploring individualized instruction.

Pretest Influence

It is not uncommon for a researcher to use a pretest activity or warm-up task before starting actual experimental procedures. This is done for a variety of reasons, but in general the purpose is to ensure that when participants begin the experiment, the performance reflects the participant-task interaction and not the participants' "learning to respond" behavior. Although useful for purifying examination of the participant task interaction, such a pretest or warm-up may threaten external validity. **Pretest influence** is a threat to external validity when a pretest activity or warm-up task results in "learning to respond" behaviors that may influence a participant's response during a study. For this reason, instructional and psychological procedures used in the field are seldom preceded by warm-up procedures. Consequently, the "learning to respond" behaviors are usually a part of the participant's performance in a real-world setting.

Multiple-Treatment Interference

Multiple-treatment interference becomes a threat when more than a single treatment is administered to the same participants. The subsequent treatments have potential cumulative effects from the first treatment and therefore may not be similar to the outside world—thereby threatening generalization. Because the effects of prior treatments are often not dissipated by the time later treatments are administered, participants may have a depressed or increased performance on a second or third research task. To the degree that these participants' sensitivity is altered for the second or third treatment, the generalization of results from these treatments is reduced. This, of course, assumes that a sequence of multiple treatments is not the usual procedure in the population sampled.

To avoid multiple-treatment threats generally requires making reasonably certain that the participants receiving subsequent treatments remain experimentally naïve. In some situations, researchers may depend on the passage of time to accomplish this. However, the effectiveness of such an approach is uncertain, and the researcher may be depending on a weak assumption. Alternatively, if sufficient time passes between treatments, often the research appears more like two distinct studies than two treatments within one.

STANDARDS OF RIGOR

As is true with other research designs, qualitative researchers must also ask specific questions regarding the research process in order to assure the *trustworthiness* of a study. Certain steps in the design, data gathering, and data analysis process can help researchers avoid pitfalls and maintain trustworthiness (Denzin & Lincoln, 2005; Mertens, 2005; Silverman, 2004). The two main issues researchers must face to preserve rigor are reliability and validity.

The concept of reliability in qualitative designs (often referred to as dependability) has much the same general meaning as it does in quantitative designs: consistency. However, whereas in quantitative designs, reliability more often refers to the consistency of the instruments used to collect the data, with qualitative designs reliability refers more to the consistency of the procedures for collecting the data. A question to ask yourself is this: If I collected these data at a different point in time, or using different methods, or if someone else collected them, how similar would the data be? Unlike the reliability coefficient produced in quantitative designs, reliability in qualitative designs provides a descriptive answer to the questions the researcher asks of the data collection.

There are a few actions a qualitative researcher can take to protect reliability. First, he or she could use low-inference descriptors. For example, when observing a fourth-grade student complete a page of math problems, the observer should make a note of what the student actually did (e.g., worked diligently on the sheet of math problems) rather than on what he or she might have thought or felt (e.g., she seemed frustrated by the task). When looking for insights into what a person thought or felt, a low-inference measure would involve asking the person rather than inferring from his or her behavior.

Along with low-inference measures, mechanical or electronic recording devices should be used whenever possible. This allows the researcher to go back and reexamine the raw data (rather than a secondary version) to determine how well it was recorded or interpreted. This enables the maintenance of an *audit trail*—a record of data that can be followed by another scholar from conclusions back to the raw data—allowing for inspection of procedures to determine where bias may have affected data collection and interpretation.

Validity in qualitative research contains both internal and external aspects. Internal validity captures the accuracy or truthfulness of the findings. Qualitative researchers refer to this feature as trustworthiness, credibility, confirmability, or authenticity (Denzin & Lincoln, 2005; Mertens, 2005). Regardless of terminology, the standards for quality are crucial to how much confidence one can have in the research, which is the crux of internal validity. As with all standards of rigor, specific features of a research design can help protect the validity of a qualitative study. To begin with, the duration and intensity of data gathering should assure that many of the important events and details are recorded over time, involving the important participants in the group, and in many different situations and combinations. This prevents unique or unrepresentative events from receiving unwarranted attention and importance in the analysis. In quantitative designs, these unrepresentative events would be noted as outlier data, perhaps as a lone point separated from other observation points on a scatter plot. Probability protects statistical analyses of quantitative data while time in the field and multiple, in-depth records of events protect qualitative analyses of data.

Thick, rich, and supportive data from a variety of sources improve the likelihood that a researcher will be able to create a valid description and complete a valid analysis. Consequently, qualitative researchers often practice "thick (or rich) description"— the detailed, accurate, and vivid description of settings, people, and interactions similar to the skilled work of an essayist, 19th-century naturalist, or art or theater critic. Thick description challenges a scholar's writing skills, demanding accurate and vivid, not flowery prose. Beginning researchers sometimes have difficulty keeping the "purple prose" out of their vivid descriptions, but, as with all writing, care, practice, and numerous revisions can hone the qualitative researcher's writing skills.

For qualitative researchers, external validity suggests the ability to generalize concepts across and between sites. This is often referred to as generalizability or transferability (Gay et al., 2006). The purpose is to study similar target topics in multiple places or sites (or at different times, or by different researchers). Using information gathered in different sites, such as comparative case studies, researchers should be able to describe patterns existing in broader social environments and describe more abstract or general concepts related to specific research findings. While not all qualitative investigators subscribe to this concept, many do as a part of rigorous design and methodology (e.g., Neuman, 2006; Silverman, 2004). This is the feature referred to earlier as theoretical generalizability.

Threats to Rigor and How to Defend Against Them

A rigorous qualitative research design must include safeguards against common threats to validity. These can threaten both internal and external validity depending on how the threat affects the interpretation of the data. The threats to validity in qualitative designs fall into two broad categories: threats to trustworthiness and researcher effects. Of the following list, the first six of these deal with trustworthiness and the last two concern researcher effects:

Incompleteness of the information collected—makes a clear connection between the data and the conclusions difficult due to gaps

Inadequate interpretation of findings—can occur if sufficient information is not presented

Inconsistencies in the data that are not discovered or addressed (i.e., statements at one point in the report that contradict those in another section)

Inadequate use of metaphors, diagrams, or direct quotations—these are all techniques that can facilitate the reader's understanding of the researcher's interpretations

Participants' views not fully integrated into the report—can lead the report to be too heavily influenced by the researcher's perspective rather than that of the participants

Failure to disqualify alternate explanations for findings or interpretations—all empirical work should stand up to testability or falsifiability

Observer effects (i.e., presence of the observer changes the behavior of some participants)

Observer bias (i.e., observer treats some participants differently from others or inserts his or her own values without acknowledging them as such)

Some of the above threats may be manifested subtly, but others may be quite obvious. No matter how easy to identify and address, each of these potential threats must be acknowledged and dealt with. There are many steps that can be taken to protect against these threats, such as the following:

Spending extended time in the setting will allow the participants to become accustomed to the presence of the researcher. A sufficient amount of time (which will depend on a number of factors) should be spent so that the researcher is not a disruptive presence.

Maintaining contact with all participants in the setting will also reduce disruption and help to avoid isolation.

Disengaging from or leaving the site during final analysis can reduce potential bias in interpretation.

Deliberately seeking disconfirming evidence of negative cases as conclusions begin to coalesce allows the researcher to disqualify alternate explanations.

Keeping a research journal (or memos) that describes the research process in detail and the researcher's feelings and affective responses is an important part of the audit trail mentioned earlier.

Clearly specifying the researchers' status or position, so that readers know exactly what point of view drove the data collection, is known as *reflexivity*.

Meticulously describing the informants, how and why they were selected or chosen (maintaining confidentiality), the context or setting boundaries and characteristics, the specific conceptual frameworks used in the design and deductive analysis of the study, and the data collection and analysis procedures, is necessary for others to make determinations on every aspect of the research including the reliability and validity (both internal and external).

Having someone who was not involved in the initial research (e.g., colleagues and peers) examine and review the data, and audit emerging findings and conclusions to see if they follow logically backward to the data, is called an *external audit* or a *data audit*. Someone who is external to the project is less likely to have the same biases (if they exist) and will be able to provide an additional perspective on the accuracy of the findings.

Using the strategy of triangulation—corroborating evidence across different (a) researchers/observers, (b) methods of data collection, or (c) theories or perspectives. By using multiple sources or methods and reaching similar conclusions, the researcher's confidence that the findings are credible (i.e., internally valid) will be much greater.

Having some participants look over the report so that they can judge the accuracy of the descriptions and interpretations is called *member checking*. This gives the researcher feedback as to how well he or she was able to record, convey, and interpret the data.

In summary, standards of rigor in qualitative research rely on processes that protect the reliability and validity of the study as surely as they do for other research methods. The principles of confirmability, dependability, and credibility are firmly grounded in rigorous qualitative research. Transferability also is a principle of qualitative research

TABLE 9.1   Standards of Rigor for Qualitative Research

Truth value or internal validity   => Credibility
Generalizability or external validity => Applicability
Consistency or reliability   => Auditability
Neutrality or objectivity   => Confirmability

SOURCE: From Guba, E. G., & Lincoln, Y. S. (1989). *Fourth generation evaluation.* Newbury Park, CA: Sage. Reprinted with permission from Sage, Inc.

that encompasses certain premises of positivism, based on assumptions about the replication of patterns in social science and theory development.

Gelfand and Drew (2003) noted that qualitative standards of rigor have not become as widely accepted in psychology and education, although the fundamental principles of science must be evident. An acceptable qualitative investigation must explicitly attend to the study's truth value, applicability, consistency, and neutrality. Truth value or internal validity leads to credibility, external validity or generalizability leads to applicability, consistency or reliability leads to a clear audit trail (a traceable chain of logic), and neutrality or objectivity provides confirmability. Table 9.1 summarizes some helpful analogies between terminologies.

What beginning researcher would not want his or her study to be credible, applicable, consistent, and neutral? Issues of rigor should be planned for both in advance and during the design phase in qualitative research, just as they must be addressed during the design phase in quantitative designs. Rigor is more difficult to rescue in the middle of the study when the researcher is enthusiastically involved in a setting with interesting and valued people engaged in socially valuable and admirable activities. Rigor also cannot be recovered during analysis if the data are fundamentally flawed by poor design and execution (Myers & Well, 2003).

COMMENTS

Planning or conceptual design is a vital consideration in beginning any research study. We have examined a broad array of threats to validity in this chapter, and we have explored these threats in various contexts. Our purpose has been to illustrate some of the pitfalls a researcher may encounter in designing or planning research and to suggest some approaches to avoiding them. As researchers become more experienced with scientific approaches to gathering information, they begin to anticipate limitations and threats to data accuracy. The careful and thoughtful examination of a research design, with consideration of what influences might detract from interpretation, is a powerful tool.

To summarize, internal validity refers to the technical soundness of an investigation. A study is internally valid to the degree that influences beyond the variable under investigation have been removed or minimized as systematic effects. External validity, on the other hand, speaks to generalizability. An investigation is externally valid to the degree that the arrangements, procedures, and participants are representative of the outside setting, thereby allowing the results to generalize or transfer.

External and internal validity may sometimes be at odds with each other. The logistics involved in designing an internally valid experiment occasionally work against achieving as much generalizability as is desirable. Research studies that exercise a great deal of environmental control (e.g., some laboratory experiments) may have great internal validity but may be less externally valid because of the artificial setting. Other experiments may have greater external validity if the environment remains more natural (e.g., an intact classroom), but internal validity may be reduced to some degree.

Meaningful research must be thought of in terms of *programs* of research that often involve a series of related studies, each perhaps investigating a slightly different part of the puzzle. Experiments conducted in the initial phases of a research program may sacrifice some degree of external validity to more accurately study the variables involved. Alternatively, later phases of a research program may sacrifice some degree of internal validity to achieve a better perspective of how the phenomena being studied operate in the world outside the laboratory. The cumulative evidence obtained in such a program of research is more likely to result in meaningful information and changes in practice. Researchers must use their best judgment when deciding exactly where it is most critical to exercise the tightest control and where they can best afford to live with less rigorous control. Decisions of this nature often depend on experience as a practicing researcher and the specific circumstances of a study.

Chapter Summary

Design validity refers to the technical soundness of the research study—its rigor and scientific merit. The two primary types of design validity are internal and external. There are several threats to internal validity that can be eliminated or controlled in the design of the study:

+ *History:* An uncontrolled event that occurs during the study that may have an influence on the observed effect other than the variable under study.

+ *Maturation:* Factors that influence a participant's performance because of time passing rather than specific incidents.

+ *Test practice:* The effects of participants taking a test that influence how they score on a subsequent test.

+ *Instrumentation:* Influences on scores due to calibration changes in any instrument that is used to measure participant performance, whether those are mechanical changes or changes in the observer.

+ *Statistical regression:* Problem that occurs when participants have been assigned to particular group on the basis of atypical or incorrect scores.

+ *Hawthorne effect:* Change in the sensitivity or performance by the participants that may occur merely as a function of being a part of the research study.

+ *Bias in group composition:* Systematic differences between the composition of groups in addition to the treatment under study.

+ *Experimental mortality:* A differential loss of participants between comparison groups.

There are several threats to external validity that can be eliminated or controlled in the design of the study:

+ *Population-sample differences:* The degree to which the participants in a study are representative of the population to which generalization is desired.

+ *Artificial research arrangements:* The degree that a research setting deviates from the participant's usual routine.

✦ *Pretest influence:* A pretest activity or warm-up task that results in "learning to respond" behaviors that may influence a participant's response during a research study.

✦ *Multiple-treatment interference:* More than one treatment is administered to the same participants and results in cumulative effects that may not be similar to the outside world and may threaten generalization of the results.

Threats to the rigor of a study may include information that is incomplete; inadequate interpretation of findings; inconsistencies in data; inadequate use of metaphors, diagrams, or direct quotations; failure to fully integrate participant views; failure to disqualify alternate explanations; observer effects; and observer bias.

Specific steps can be taken to assure the trustworthiness (rigor) of a study. These include focusing on reliability and validity. The concept of reliability may be referred to as dependability (qualitative studies) or consistency (quantitative studies). The concept of internal validity may be referred to as the trustworthiness, credibility, confirmability, and authenticity (qualitative studies) or the accuracy of the findings (quantitative studies).

Key Terms

Artificial research arrangements. A threat to external validity based on the fact that participant's behavior or performance is altered because the research setting deviates from the participant's usual routine.

Bias in group composition. A threat to internal validity occurring when there are systematic differences between the composition of groups in addition to the treatment under study.

Design validity. Refers to the technical soundness of the research study, its rigor and scientific merit. The two primary types of design validity are internal and external.

Experimental mortality. A threat to internal validity occurring when there is a differential loss of participants between comparison groups.

External validity. Refers to how much the research setting is like the world that the investigator wishes to generalize to; the degree to which the results can be generalized

Hawthorne effect. A threat to internal validity occurring when there is a change in the sensitivity or performance by the participants that may occur merely as a function of being a part of the research study.

History. A threat to internal validity that is an uncontrolled event occurring during the study that may have an influence on the observed affect other than the variable under study.

Instrumentation. An instrumentation threat to internal validity involves the influences on scores due to calibration changes in any instrument used to measure participant performance, whether those are mechanical changes or changes in the observer.

Internal validity. An internally valid experiment successfully controls (or accounts for) all *systematic* influences between the groups being compared, *except* the one under study. This allows the researcher to attribute any differences to the experimental variable.

Maturation. A threat to internal validity involving factors that influence a participant's performance because of time passing rather than specific incidents.

Multiple-treatment interference. A threat to external validity occurring when more than one treatment is administered to the same participants and results in cumulative effects that may not be similar to the outside world and may threaten generalizability of the results.

Population-sample differences. A threat to external validity involving the fact that participants in a study are not representative of the population to which generalization is desired.

Pretest influence. A threat to external validity when a pretest activity or warm-up task results in "learning to respond" behaviors that may influence a participant's response during a study.

Statistical regression. A threat to internal validity occurring when participants have been assigned to particular group on the basis of atypical or incorrect scores.

Test practice. A threat to internal validity involving the effects of participants taking a test that influence how they score on a subsequent test.

Student Study Site

The companion Web site for *Designing and Conducting Research in Education* www.sagepub.com/drewstudy

Supplement your review of this chapter by going to the companion Web site to take one of the practice quizzes, use the flashcards to study key terms, and check out the many other study aids you'll find there. You'll even find some research articles from the Sage Full-Text Collection and a step-by-step guide that will show you how to read an educational research article.

Simulation Feedback

Simulation Feedback 9.1

For additional simulations visit www.sagepub .com/drewstudy

The researcher's observations about the reversal in A_2 are based on the basic assumption of the design (that if withdrawal of the treatment results in reversal, the treatment may be viewed as generating the effect). These arguments are not, however, entirely convincing. For the moment, suppose that the medication generated the behavior change in Phase B. It is possible that physiological adaptation occurred after a period of time and the medication was no longer as effective as it was initially. If this adaptation began to occur at about the time that A_2 was instituted, the gradual change under the reversal condition may have been a result of a lessening effectiveness of medication (rather than a withdrawal of the reinforcement contingencies). Thus the data in Phase A_2 could support a medication influence as well as reinforcement contingencies.

Circumventing this threat would best be accomplished by a replication of the entire experiment and by studying the effects of the reinforcement without medication being involved. If the researcher had known of the problem before terminating the experiment, some strength could have been gained by adding a B_2 condition (making it an A-B-A-B design).

Part III
DATA ANALYSIS AND RESULTS INTERPRETATION

Part III completes the research loop by exploring statistics, data tabulation, and analysis and interpretation of results. Chapter 10 begins with a discussion of what statistics are and why we use them. Categories of statistical tools are examined including descriptive and inferential. The process of selecting an appropriate statistical tool is discussed, beginning with the type of research question and an exploration of which kind of statistics are appropriate for the different types of data that may be collected. As always, the underlying principle is planning ahead to maximize a study's strength.

Chapter 11 discusses the various components of data aggregation and tabulation as well as how and when to use tables and graphs. Chapter 12 covers descriptive statistics including central tendency and dispersion. The emphasis is on how to select a descriptive statistic appropriately. Chapter 13 moves ahead to inferential statistics, beginning with a background discussion of what statistical significance is and why it is important. Inferential statistics are examined, starting with the broad categories of difference questions and relationship questions and exploring how the research question determines choices of inferential statistics. This discussion proceeds through varying design configurations with the continuing emphasis on selecting the appropriate inferential statistic. Chapter 14 examines the analysis of qualitative data, moving from preliminary analysis to post data-gathering analysis. This discussion covers both the processes employed as well as the outcomes derived from qualitative analysis.

Chapter 15 completes the last leg of the research loop with a focus on interpreting results. Within the framework of research as an integrated procedure, this exploration describes the process of translating data back to the research question and drawing inferences for theory, practice, and future research. The emphasis in this stage is drawing meaning from the results obtained.

10

STATISTICS CHOICES

After reading Chapter 10, you should be able to do the following:

✦ Describe what statistics are and what they are used for by researchers.

✦ Discuss why statistics are important.

✦ Discuss and differentiate between descriptive and inferential statistics.

✦ Discuss how different statistics are appropriate for different types of research questions.

✦ Discuss how the type of data is important in selecting which statistical analysis to use.

STATISTICS: WHAT AND WHY

This chapter will examine topics that are crucial to determining the appropriate statistical analyses to be used and also the process of selecting an appropriate statistical tool.

It is not the intent to provide a detailed discussion of how to calculate statistical tools. This has been accomplished in a variety of textbooks that focus solely on statistical methods (e.g., Goodwin, 2005; Murphy & Myors, 2004; Nadelman, 2004). The purpose of this portion of the book is to introduce the area of statistical analysis and indicate how these techniques fit in the overall scheme of the research enterprise.

What Are Statistics?

The term **statistics** is colloquially used to label a set of analysis procedures commonly applied in quantitative research. The word has some additional, more technical meanings but when graduate students and faculty are discussing research methods, the term generally refers to quantitative analyses (Best & Kahn, 2006; Craighead & Nemeroff, 2004; Gay et al., 2006). These analyses are applied to the data collected through observations of participants' performance on the task or instrument presented to them (whether that is a test they take or some activity they carry out). Researchers perform these analyses so they can determine what occurred and whether their treatment was effective.

As noted above, statistical analyses are limited to investigations that have collected quantitative data, or converted part of the data into numerical format. It is not unusual for studies that use qualitative methodology to also supplement the descriptive information with some quantitative data, which may be summarized using statistical analyses. Mixed-method studies (i.e., studies employing both quantitative and qualitative procedures) are becoming more popular as researchers recognize their utility and become increasingly comfortable crossing the methodology boundaries (e.g., Mertens, 2005). Qualitative analyses will be examined in Chapter 14. The current chapter will discuss matters that are relevant as you prepare to select the appropriate statistical analysis for quantitative data.

Why Statistics Are Important

We noted above that researchers use statistical analyses so they can determine what occurred and whether their intervention or treatment was effective. The way this occurs is that the investigator summarizes the scores for all of the participants. For example, if the researcher was comparing two types of reading programs, one group might have been taught using Program A while a second group was taught using

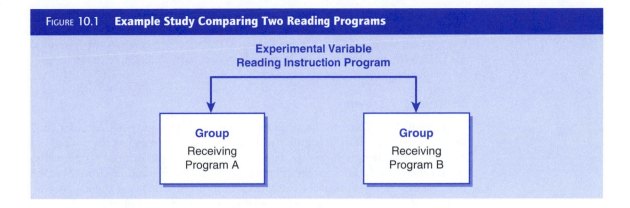

FIGURE 10.1   **Example Study Comparing Two Reading Programs**

Program B. This is a difference question, since we want to see if there is a difference between the effectiveness of the two reading programs. The task of the researcher here is to summarize the participants' performance in each condition (probably obtaining a mean of their respective correct responses) and compare those two group means. A diagram of the study might look like the one in Figure 10.1.

The researcher will use statistical analysis to make the comparison between mean scores of the two groups. This analysis will determine whether the difference is statistically significant. If, for example, this analysis indicates that the group receiving Program A scored significantly better than the group receiving Program B, the researcher can say with some confidence that Program A is more effective than Program B under these circumstances. In more technical terms, if the differences in scores reach statistical significance, there is little likelihood that such differences would have occurred by chance. This allows the researcher to attribute the differences to his or her treatment (the reading program), which is why the study was undertaken. Most often you will see such results reported in a statement that might say, "Results indicate that the students receiving Instructional Program A performed at a significantly higher level than those receiving Instructional Program B ($P < .05$)." The information in parentheses at the end of the statement means that the probability that these differences might occur by chance is less than 5%, indicating that there is more than a 95% probability that these differences are due to the treatment. This level of support makes the researcher pretty confident that his or her treatment is effective.

Categories of Statistical Techniques

We have emphasized repeatedly that the research process should be conceived as a series of vitally interrelated parts. We need to underscore this fact again by noting that there is a crucial relationship between the purpose and design of a study and the statistical tools used. For each type of research question, there is a family of statistical analyses that may be used. There are statistical tools available for nearly every conceivable research purpose or question. Two broad purposes are generally involved in behavioral research—descriptive and inferential. Different statistical procedures are designed to facilitate the functions of descriptive and inferential studies. These general categories of statistical techniques are broadly identified as descriptive statistics and inferential statistics.

Descriptive Studies

This kind of study allows the researcher to describe performance or scores on a group of individuals. Descriptive studies address descriptive research questions. The description may involve annual income, average height, educational achievement, or any of a number of different dimensions. These studies usually do not intend to go beyond the process of providing a picture of the group that is being investigated. Such studies provide a summary of the data from which a description can be made (e.g., average height or range of intelligence). **Descriptive statistics**—analyses used for descriptive questions—make it possible to conveniently examine characteristics or performance (see Chapter 12).

Inferential Studies

Inferential research, on the other hand, has a different purpose. An inferential investigation may describe a group of participants, but it also has the purpose of drawing implications from the data about some comparison or relationship. Inferential studies address either difference or relationship questions. It may be that the researchers are testing the soundness of some psychological theory, making some predictions regarding student academic success, or determining which of several treatment approaches is more effective. In accomplishing this purpose, they are inferring beyond the data to some abstract concept or some generalized situation. This inference goes beyond a reporting of "what is" and is the major characteristic of inferential research that distinguishes it from descriptive research. **Inferential statistics** have a different purpose in that they allow interpretation or inference related to comparing groups or examining relationships, perhaps about some theory (see Chapter 13). Some investigations address both descriptive and inferential purposes to some degree—they are not limited to one or the other.

The Decision Tree: Moving From the Question to the Analysis

Once data are collected by testing performance or observing participants, the researcher's next series of tasks is to examine the scores, analyze data, draw conclusions concerning the participants' performance, and interpret the data in terms of the original research question. To interpret the data, it is necessary that the researcher have a way of looking at scores that will provide a clear picture of what happened in the experiment. Seldom can this be accomplished by merely examining the numbers or performance scores. This is particularly difficult when groups are used (if only one participant is studied, it is a bit easier). Visual examination of raw scores usually permits attention to only loose questions, and answers to such questions are frequently vague. It may be possible to determine that George scored about as well as most participants, or that Sally obtained the highest score in all groups, but little can be determined about group performance. Groups are often the basis for a research question, such as "How well can this group be expected to perform on Task X?" or "Which is more effective, Treatment Method A that Group 1 received or Treatment Method B that Group 2 received?" The researcher has to be able to speak in terms of group performance if the group represents the basis for answering the research question. Statistics represent summary and analysis procedures that permit the researcher to determine group performance characteristics in a manner that is far more precise and convenient than visual inspection of the raw data.

Statistics are used to perform research functions that cannot be accomplished without them. In descriptive research, statistics provide a convenient and precise data summary that allows the researcher to describe "what is" or "what happened" in situations where mere visual inspection of the data would be insufficient. The process of selecting an appropriate analysis involves several decisions that need to be addressed in a cumulative fashion. This process is like a branching decision tree in that one starts at a given point and moves sequentially through several decisions.

The beginning point should not be a surprise to you by now: we start with the research question.

Decision One: What Type of Question?

The first decision relates to what type of research question is being asked. As we have said before, it is quite possible that you may have multiple research questions and that is often the case. What is important, though, is that you know what question or questions you are asking so that you can apply the correct analysis to the relevant question.

The general types of questions include descriptive, difference, and relationship. For each of these types of question there is a family of statistical analyses that can be appropriately applied. For descriptive questions, we use descriptive statistics; for difference questions, we use statistics that allow us to compare; and for relationship questions, we use statistics that are generally referred to as correlations, which determine the degree of relationship.

So a very early decision relates to what type of research question is being studied. If our study involves some preliminary description of the participants, followed by a major focus on difference questions, then the statistics should reflect that configuration. That would mean that we would use descriptive statistics to summarize what our participants look like and then turn our major focus to comparison statistics for the difference questions. In fact, this is often what an investigation will involve. Readers will always ask you what your participants looked like (i.e., their characteristics), and that will be accomplished by summarizing their average age, reading scores, or whatever other piece of demographic information is relevant to your study. This is important so your readers can know about the students that you studied and what characteristics they had. Your readers may also include other researchers who want to follow up on your study, which means they will need to know about the participants' demographics. After the descriptive part of the study is accomplished, you will need to select the appropriate statistical analysis for the comparisons you want to make.

Once you have determined the type of research question, there are a few subsequent decisions that need to be made. These decisions are somewhat different for each question, as we will see. Table 10.1 summarizes our decision tree and the elements or questions that must be addressed.

TABLE 10.1   Decision Tree for Selecting Statistical Analysis

Decision One: Research Question Type	Decision Two	Decision Three	Decision Four	Decision Five
Descriptive Question	Central Tendency	Data Type	Distribution & Accuracy	
	Dispersion	Data Type	Distribution & Accuracy	
Difference Question	Type of Comparison			
	Independent	Number of Data Points (or groups)		Data Type
	Nonindependent	Number of Data Points (repeated tests)		Data Type
	Mixed (only for two or more experimental variables)	Number of Data Points (or groups)	Number of Experimental Variables	Data Type
Relationship Question	Same or Different Data Type			
	Same	Data Type		
	Different	Data Types		

Decision Two and Thereafter

As we see in Table 10.1, the second and subsequent decisions in selecting a statistical analysis differ for various types of question. Consequently, we will examine each separately. The discussion in each case is a brief sketch, as we will come back to each point in more detail as we proceed through the text.

Descriptive Question

The second column for descriptive questions in Table 10.1 shows central tendency and dispersion. In this case, we are not deciding *between* central tendency and dispersion since we will need to use both in order to obtain a complete description of our participants. It is important to realize that you will need both types of summaries in order to determine an accurate picture of your participants.

The third decision relates to what type of data is being collected. This is important because some descriptive analyses require arithmetic (notably the mean and standard deviation), and such calculation is dependent on the data type.

Finally, in the fourth decision you need to be alert to the distribution of scores and accuracy issues pertaining to various descriptive statistics. For example, certain descriptive statistics become quite inaccurate if the distribution is skewed or substantially different from being bell-shaped. More details will be examined relating to these matters in Chapter 12 as we proceed toward selecting the descriptive analysis for particular situations.

Difference Question

Decision two for difference questions is also found in the second column of Table 10.1. Here the researcher needs to determine what type of comparison is being made and there are three options: independent, nonindependent, and mixed. Each of these types of comparison will use a different analysis, as you will see in the more detailed discussion in Chapter 13. Decision three involves the number of data points or groups to be compared (e.g., two, more than two). In the case of nonindependent comparisons, the number of data points refers to the number of repeated tests, such as pretest versus posttest or pre, mid, post. These will result in selecting different statistical analyses. The fourth decision on difference questions, the number of experimental variables, will also lead the researcher to selecting particular analyses over others. Finally, in the last column we encounter our last point on the decision tree: what type of data has been collected. The matter of data type is found in several points on the table, and the remainder of this current chapter examines different data types and how they relate to selecting a statistical analysis.

Relationship Question

The second column of Table 10.1 indicates that the second decision for relationship questions pertains to the type of data for the two measures that are collected in this type of question. The basic question is whether the two are both the *same* (e.g., are both interval or is one interval and the other ordinal). This is important for the *type* of correlation analysis to be used. Finally, in the third column, we want to know *what* the data type is—is it nominal, ordinal, interval, or ratio? These two decision points are important, and different answers to the questions lead us to selecting different analyses. The details on these matters are also found in Chapter 13.

For additional
simulations visit
www.sagepub
.com/drewstudy

Simulation

Simulation 10.1

Topic: Research question and analysis selection

Stimulus material: The research question to be studied reads as follows: Compare the effectiveness of different methods of teaching reading.

1. What type of research question is this likely to be?

2. What steps might you take in selecting a statistical analysis on Table 10.1?

Write your response, then turn to pages 256–257 for Simulation Feedback 10.1.

THE IMPORTANCE OF DATA TYPE IN SELECTING STATISTICS

Different types of data lead us to selecting different statistical analyses for each of the three types of research question. This is an important common element for making analysis selection. For that reason, we now turn to an examination of data types. Statistics play a critical role in the overall process of quantitative research. They represent vital tools for quantitative researchers to use. It is important, however, to keep statistical tools in perspective along with other tools. The research process involves a *series* of necessary components, with statistics representing only one. Many statistical tools are available to researchers for various questions. To select the appropriate analysis, certain considerations must receive attention. The remainder of this chapter will focus on one of the most basic factors a researcher must consider in selecting the statistic to be used—the different types of data that may be collected.

Properties of Numbers

Selecting an appropriate criterion measure is crucial to the success of a study. The researcher must consider several factors that relate both to the research question and to the type of statistical tools that may be used. Criterion measures represent a means of describing real-world events or occurrences (e.g., a child's behavior or performance). It is essential that the criterion measure or data accurately represent the performance or activity, otherwise the research question intended for investigation may not be what is actually studied. In addition, the researcher needs to consider what data properties are present as the criterion measure is selected. Here we will examine the data properties of identity, order, and additivity and see how they are important to keep in mind as a researcher selects a criterion measure and a statistical tool (Goodwin, 2005; Nadelman, 2004).

Identity

An activity, behavior, or a performance level should be reflected in the way the measure is recorded, and therefore, the form that the numbers are in. For example, numbers have the property known as **identity.** A number is unique and is not exactly the same as any other number. If a number is used as the criterion measure representing an event, the event should also have the property of identity. That is, there should be reason to believe that the event designated by a number is unique from other events (and numbers).

Order

Numbers also have the property of **order.** One number is less than or greater than another on some continuum. Likewise, the events, behaviors, or performances to which this type of measure is applied should also have order. If one event is represented by a given number (e.g., six) and a second event is represented by a higher number (e.g., seven), there should be a sound basis for believing the second event is larger or greater on some continuum than the first. This may be exemplified by ranking the relative heights of basketball players. By lining the team up in order from the shortest to the tallest, it is possible to rank each individual in terms of height relative to the others on the team.

Additivity

Numbers are also characterized by the property of **additivity.** That is, by adding together two numbers, one can obtain a third number, which is also different or unique. This last property is important for most of the arithmetic operations performed in statistical analysis. If the data type being analyzed does not have the property of additivity, arithmetic operations should not be performed because that arithmetic will not accurately reflect the performance (see discussion below). Data properties of identity, order, and additivity are important to keep in mind as a researcher selects a criterion measure and a statistical tool (Goodwin, 2005; Nadelman, 2004).

Not all of the behaviors or performance levels studied in behavioral science have all three properties of identity, order, and additivity. Different activities have some properties but not others. This does not mean that they are unfit topics for investigation or that data cannot be recorded on them. It does, however, emphasize the necessity of specifying a criterion measure that parallels the observed phenomenon. Different types of data can be used with different types of analysis. It is very important that a beginning researcher become acquainted with measurement scales to make appropriate decisions in selecting the statistical tool needed.

Types of Data

As we saw in Table 10.1, the decision tree for all of our research questions leads through data type at some point. The matter of what type of data is being collected relates to how we count or record performance. For example, if a researcher is measuring reading comprehension, it is important to realize that there are various ways to record that criterion measure. One could say that a student either does or does not exhibit reading comprehension. However, this is not a very accurate way of assessing it. Obviously, a student's academic performance will reflect *more or less* of the measure rather than just showing that he or she has or does not have it. The way we measure performance and record the scores relates to the type of data collected and is very important with regard to the statistical analysis selected.

Nominal Data

The first type of data to be discussed is called **nominal data,** also termed categorical or classification data. Nominal data represent the most primitive type of measurement. They are useful when all that can be accomplished is the assignment of events to categories. For example, an item on a questionnaire may require a "yes" or "no" response from the participant. Under such circumstances, all that can be determined from the data is whether a participant's response falls into one or the other of two categories—the yes or the no. Other examples are found in biological classification systems, psychiatric diagnostic categories, and many other areas both within and beyond the boundaries of science. Nominal data have the property of identity, since presumably each category is completely different from the other categories.

The essential element to be noted with regard to nominal data is that the information is in the form of categories. These categories may be participant responses, attributes of people, or characteristics of people or events. The data categories are distinct and mutually exclusive, *without an apparent underlying continuum*. If numbers are used to designate categories (e.g., Response Type 1 or Response Type 2), they serve only as identification labels. Such numbers do not reflect or represent any magnitude of something, or order continuum. Numbers used to label the categories could be replaced with any symbol that would conveniently and effectively discriminate one category from another (e.g., Group A or Group B). If numbers are used, it is important to know that they cannot be added, subtracted, or otherwise manipulated with arithmetic. It makes no more sense to use arithmetic on nominal numbers than other labels like A, B, or C.

Ordinal Data

The second type of data to be discussed is known as **ordinal data** or rank order data. Ordinal data move measurement from the qualitative discrimination between events to a more quantitative basis of assessment. Ordinal measurement is characterized by the ability to rank order events on the basis of an underlying continuum. Thus, the ranks denote "greater than" or "less than" on the dimension being assessed.

A variety of situations exemplify ordinal data. The earlier ranking of basketball players with regard to relative height would result in ordinal data. Likewise, ordinal data may be generated by the frequently used Likert or 1 to 5 scale. A Likert scale is often used in various forms as a way of roughly approximating the degree to which a characteristic is found in a person's performance or behavior. Likert-type scales often use 1 to 5 scales or 1 to 7 scales depending on the preference of the researcher and the situation. Recall the yes-no questionnaire response example mentioned under nominal data. It is possible that this dichotomous response option could be transformed to a Likert scale with an underlying continuum representing relative degree of agreement. This could be accomplished by following the stimulus statement with a response format such as the following:

Highly disagree	Disagree	Neutral	Agree	Highly agree
1	2	3	4	5

Respondents provide much more information about how they view the stimulus statement with this type of format than by merely selecting a dichotomous response of yes-no or agree-disagree. With this type of data, the researcher is able to discriminate between those participants who are only mildly in disagreement with the statement and those who are firmer in their position.

Instruments with rating scales are often used in action research such as the scenario portrayed in the Research in Action box. Such instruments are typically referred to as Likert-type scales even though they may employ a different approach to applying the numerical reference. For example, the instrument in the Research in Action box uses a 1 to 4 scale on selected questions and a 1 to 5 scale on others.

RESEARCH IN ACTION

Key points in the chapter reflected in this box:

- How Likert-type scales can be used to assess self-esteem
- How different types of data can be collected in one study
- The importance of data type in selecting descriptive statistics
- The importance of data type in selecting inferential statistics for difference questions

For more research in action tips visit www.sagepub.com/drewstudy

Objectives to learn from this box:

- How to identify different types of data
- Why different data types are appropriate for various statistical analyses

Daniel is using instruments with Likert-type scales to measure self-esteem in his study of Latino and Caucasian students with learning disabilities. His goal is to find out if there are differences in their self-esteem with the intent to identify areas that he can attend to as he teaches the students. Daniel believes that self-esteem is important to the students' classroom performance and that enhancing their self-esteem may result in academic improvements in the long run. However, his action research focuses on the first step of identifying potential differences between his Latino and Caucasian students.

Daniel has identified instruments that are aimed at measuring self-esteem. He will use the Rosenberg self-esteem scale as well as selected further measures designed to assess subclasses of self-esteem labeled as public self-esteem and private self-esteem. Daniel will also collect demographic information on his participants so he can describe what their characteristics are like (e.g., age, grade levels, IQ).

Daniel's measures of self-esteem use Likert-type scales. They are designed with a 1 to 4 scale on several questions (1 = strongly agree, 2 = agree, 3 = disagree, and 4 = strongly disagree). Other questions provide response options of 1 to 5 (1 = completely satisfied, 2 = mostly satisfied, 3 = satisfied, 4 = partly dissatisfied, and 5 = completely dissatisfied). Daniel's demographic data are all rather typical for matters like age, grade, and GPA. He also collected family information on socioeconomic status, which involved parent income and parent education level in years.

Daniel is using his demographic data to present a description of his participants. For this he will use descriptive statistics and the choice regarding which ones will depend on the type of data collected. For his major research questions comparing Latino and Caucasian students, he will use statistics that will compare their self-esteem scores. Selection of which statistical analysis to use for these questions will also depend heavily on the type of data collected.

Think about this: What type of data is Daniel collecting for his demographic information? What descriptive statistics can be appropriately used for these data and why? What type of data is Daniel collecting for his difference questions? What inferential statistics can he appropriately use for these data and why?

SOURCE: This action research scenario is roughly based on Rubin, D. (2000). *Race and self-esteem: A study of Latino and European-American students with learning disabilities.* Unpublished master's thesis, University of Utah, Salt Lake City.

The relative firmness of the viewpoints is all that may be determined, however. The actual amount of difference between any two response possibilities is not known. One cannot say that the difference between any two responses represents an equal interval (e.g., the amount of difference in agreement between 1 and 2 is not known to be the same as that between 3 and 4). While the serial order of responses may be determined so that a response of 4 is relatively more in agreement with the statement than a response of 3, we still do not know what the actual interval is. Ordinal data have both the properties of identity and order but, since the interval is unknown, additivity is not present. Because of this, arithmetic operations cannot be performed on ordinal data scores.

Interval Data

The third type of data to be examined is called **interval data.** Interval data have all the properties of nominal and ordinal data, plus added information concerning the interval units. When interval measurement is possible, the researcher is working with known and equal distances between score units. With interval data, the researcher can determine greater than or less than as can be done with ordinal data. However, the researcher can also determine the magnitude of a difference in the underlying continuum of what is being measured. If, for example, the differences between scores are equal (i.e., the differences in score units generated by subtracting 10 from 25 and 20 from 35 are both 15), then there is a corresponding equivalence in property magnitude differences. Interval data are characterized by all three number properties: identity, order, and additivity. The property of additivity allows arithmetic to be performed on interval data.

Common examples of interval data include calendar time and temperature as measured on centigrade and Fahrenheit scales. Differences in the score units on these measures represent known and constant magnitude differences in the factor being measured. The example measures also involve another characteristic of interval data: an arbitrary zero point. Temperature exemplifies this characteristic easily. Temperature measured as 0 degrees on the centigrade scale reads 32 degrees on the Fahrenheit scale, whereas 0 degrees F is the same as −17.8 degrees C. Therefore, the zero point is arbitrary, attained at different points depending on which scale is used, and in neither case does 0 degrees indicate the complete absence of temperature. (Absolute 0 degrees in temperature is on the Kelvin scale.) Likewise, the calendar time or numbering of years was rather arbitrarily begun on the Christian calendar with the birth of Christ.

Measurement in behavioral science does not achieve interval status as frequently as it does in the physical sciences. For example, data generated in cognitive psychology and education are often recorded in the form of the number of correct responses or the number of errors committed (as measures of, say, learning or forgetting). The researcher seldom knows whether the units represented by such measures are equal amounts learned. This makes it difficult to say with certainty that interval data are being obtained. Usually the behavioral researcher will assume that the units approximate equality unless the data are obviously ordinal or nominal. This assumption, if reasonably in harmony with the properties of what is being measured, provides more latitude in terms of statistical methods that can be used.

Ratio Data

The fourth and final type of data to be discussed is known as **ratio data.** Ratio data have all the properties of interval data but are distinguished by the fact that the zero point is not arbitrary. A zero score on a ratio scale *does* signify total absence of the property being measured.

Examples of ratio data are primarily found in physical measurement and seldom in behavioral science. As noted in the previous section, temperature measured on the Kelvin scale (also known as the absolute zero scale) conforms to the characteristics of ratio measurement. Likewise, height, weight, and time (to perform) are examples of ratio scale data. Educators and behavioral scientists may be interested in time (e.g., response latency) or some other measure that appears to be a ratio scale like counting the number of correct answers on a test. However, it is not uncommon for educational studies to be conducted using nominal, ordinal, or interval scales. Fortunately, there are few statistical procedures that require ratio data characteristics, and consequently the primary focus in this text will be on the first three types of data.

Using Different Statistics for Each Data Type

The major point of considering data type for statistical selection relates to whether or not arithmetic is required on the scores. If arithmetic is required, then the data must be an interval level at a minimum (considering nominal to be the data you can do least with, moving to interval and ratio where you can compute arithmetic). Both interval and ratio data permit arithmetic on the scores because of the property of additivity. This is not a minor point. Arithmetic is needed to calculate many statistics that we use in daily life. For example, determining a mean or average score requires arithmetic. This means that to determine an average score, you need to have interval data.

It is important to know that there are *very* useful statistics for each type of data, so just because you can't compute arithmetic for a particular type does not mean all is lost. As we proceed through the rest of this text, we will find statistical tools that work well for ordinal and nominal data as well as those that are useful for interval and ratio data. We will find a statistical analysis for each type of research question (remember—descriptive, difference, and relationship questions), different types of data, and a few other considerations. Selection of the appropriate statistic for the given circumstance is crucial for the success of your study.

For additional simulations visit www.sagepub .com/drewstudy

Simulation

Simulation 10.2

Topic: Action research data and statistics selection

Background statement: On page 252, Daniel's action research study involved multiple types of data. He is measuring self-esteem with Likert-type instruments using both a 1 to 4 scale and a 1 to 5 scale. The difference in scales is not a problem because the 1 to 4 scale is being used for one part of the self-esteem measurement (global self-esteem) and the 1 to 5 scale for other components (public self-esteem and private self-esteem). What type of data is being collected? What properties do these data have and how is this relevant for selecting statistical analyses?

Daniel is also collecting demographic data on his participants. The demographic data are being measured in terms of age, grade level, GPA, socioeconomic status (parental income), and parent education (years of schooling). What type of data is being collected? What properties do these data have and how is this relevant for selecting statistical analyses?

Write your response, then turn to page 257 for Simulation Feedback 10.2.

Chapter Summary

✦ Statistics is a label for a set of analysis procedures commonly applied in quantitative research. These analyses are applied to the data collected from participants' performance on a task or instrument presented to them (e.g., a test). Researchers compute statistics so they can determine what occurred, such as whether one treatment was more effective than another.

✦ Statistical analyses are important because they allow us to summarize data in order to determine what happened in the study, such as which reading program was more effective in teaching reading skills.

✦ Descriptive statistics are used for descriptive research questions. Such description may involve average height or educational achievement, for example. Inferential studies address either difference or relationship questions, which are termed inferential questions. This inference goes beyond examining "what is" and distinguishes it from descriptive research. Inferential statistics allow interpretation about comparing groups or examining relationships.

✦ Descriptive statistics are used for descriptive questions, whereas difference statistics are used for comparisons or difference questions. Relationship statistics (also called correlations) are used for relationship questions.

✦ Different types of data lead us to selecting different statistical analyses for each of the three types of research question. Some analyses require arithmetic and such calculation is dependent on the data type. To use arithmetic operations on the scores, a researcher must have either interval or ratio data. For nominal or ordinal data, nonparametric statistical analyses should be used. Nonparametric analyses are a general type of statistic that can be properly used with nominal and ordinal data.

Key Terms

Additivity. A number property that permits arithmetic on the scores. By adding together two numbers, one can obtain a third number that is different or unique. Data with additivity reflect direction and quantity of the property being measured.

Descriptive statistics. Analyses used for descriptive questions.

Identity. A number property that distinguishes each number as unique and not exactly the same as any other number. Identity merely reflects distinction among numbers and does not indicate greater or lesser amounts of the property being measured.

Inferential statistics. Analyses used for difference and relationship questions. Difference statistics are used for comparisons or difference questions, and relationship statistics (also called correlations) are used for relationship questions.

Interval data. Interval data have all three number properties of identity, order, and additivity. When interval measurement is possible, the researcher is working with known and equal distances between score units and arithmetic can be used on the scores. The zero point on interval data is artificial and does not reflect an actual absence of the property being measured.

Nominal data. Nominal data are also called categorical or classification data and represent the most primitive type of measurement. Nominal data only have the number property of identity and are useful when all that is needed is the assignment of events to categories.

Order. A number property that indicates one number is less than or greater than another on some continuum. If one number is higher than another number (e.g., six and seven, with seven being the higher), the higher number reflects a larger amount of the property being measured but the exact quantity is not reflected.

Ordinal data. Ordinal data are known as rank order data and have the number properties of identity and order. Ordinal data move measurement from the discrimination between events to a more quantitative basis of assessment. Ordinal measurement provides the ability to rank order events on the basis of an underlying continuum, and the ranks denote "greater than" or "less than" on the dimension being assessed.

Ratio data. Ratio data have all the number properties of identity, order, and additivity. For ratio data, the zero point is not arbitrary and a zero score on a ratio scale signifies total absence of the property being measured.

Statistics. A set of analysis procedures commonly applied to the data in quantitative research. Researchers compute statistics so they can determine what occurred, such as whether one treatment was more effective than another.

Student Study Site

The companion Web site for *Designing and Conducting Research in Education*
www.sagepub.com/drewstudy

Supplement your review of this chapter by going to the companion Web site to take one of the practice quizzes, use the flashcards to study key terms, and check out the many other study aids you'll find there. You'll even find some research articles from the Sage Full-Text Collection and a step-by-step guide that will show you how to read an educational research article.

Simulation Feedback

For additional simulations visit www.sagepub .com/drewstudy

Simulation Feedback 10.1

Research ideas often emerge as multiple types of questions. However, this one is more straightforward than others.

Question 1: This is formatted as a difference question. Think about the following points:

a. Begin with the statement we have, which is, "Compare the effectiveness of different methods of teaching reading." Since this indicates we are comparing methods of teaching reading, we can think of it as a difference question and draw a diagram of the study.

b. The experimental variable is *teaching method*. Generally the researcher has a couple of specific methods in mind, but the term *teaching method* works as well as the specific methods being compared for our purposes. The diagram for this study might appear as shown below. If you can diagram it like this, it is definitely a difference question and we can move on to Table 10.1 on page 247 for analysis selection steps.

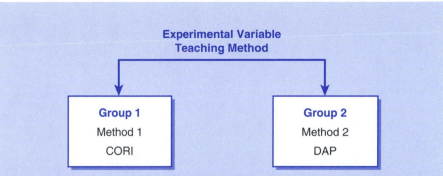

Experimental Variable
Teaching Method

Group 1	Group 2
Method 1	Method 2
CORI	DAP

Question 2: Reference to Table 10.1 under the difference question moves us to the second column (since we already know the type of question). Decision two requires determining the type of comparison. In this case, it is an independent comparison since the diagram indicates "Group 1 and Group 2," so we have two different groups. Decision three (Table 10.1, Column 3) involves determining the number of data points—which is two in this case since we are comparing two groups. Finally, the last decision in this case relates to the number of experimental variables—which is one (that experimental variable is "Teaching Method"). This is a substantial advancement toward selecting a statistical analysis. You may want to try your hand at actually choosing an analysis on Table 13.2 on page 312 and ask your instructor if you are correct.

Simulation Feedback 10.2

It is not uncommon for researchers to collect different types of data, and that is certainly the case in this study. The self-esteem data generated by all of the Likert scales are ordinal. These data have the properties of identity and order but do not have additivity, so the statistical analysis cannot involve arithmetic. The demographic data are different. All of these measures fit into interval or ratio scales and all have the properties of identity, order, and additivity. For these measures, arithmetic can be used in the statistics for descriptions of the participant demographics.

11

DATA TABULATION

After reading Chapter 11, you should be able to do the following:

+ Rank a set of raw data.

+ Group a set of raw data using intervals.

+ Construct tables to present data.

+ Judge good and bad table use.

+ Determine when it is appropriate to use a graph rather than a table or narrative.

+ Distinguish between different types of graphs. Convert tabular data to graphs.

Summarizing the data is one of the first tasks to be done after the data are collected. The current chapter examines this summary process in the form of data tabulation and some aspects of presenting the data. Much of this relates to formats that are appropriate for data aggregation and presentation for publication purposes. However, we have found that this process is very useful for writing the research report because it helps visualize what happened.

AGGREGATING DATA

It is difficult to determine how well participants performed by simply inspecting the raw data. Usually you need to summarize the data in some form to help with analysis, interpretation, and presentation to the research consumer. We will examine a number of procedures that are useful for data tabulation and presentation.

Ranks

A first step that may be helpful in examining the data is to place participants in **rank order** according to their performance scores. For example, suppose you had 24 participants with scores such as those found in Table 11.1. It is difficult to interpret what the participants' performance represents when the raw data are presented in this manner. However, participants' performance scores can be more easily interpreted when they are ranked such as in Table 11.2.

Reviewing Table 11.2, we see that Eugene and Kent performed the best of all participants and Sherry had the poorest performance. This table also illustrates that there may be tied scores for participants. Both Eugene and Kent scored 110 on the task and their ranks are therefore 1.5 (split between 1 and 2). The next participant (Alice) receives the rank of 3 since 1 and 2 have already been used. Researchers seldom use raw performance scores from participants for presentation in a report or publication for several reasons. To begin with, including the participants' names in such a report would violate confidentiality. Most institutional review boards require that investigators delete participants' names after the data collection is complete. Aggregating data in the form of tables like Table 11.2 is very useful in preparation for data analysis. However, you would never allow such a table to be open for public inspection with identifying information.

The Research in Action box presents an action research study using a table structure that summarizes data comparing reading engagement between two groups. You will note that the third column of the table also presents statistical comparisons between the groups of students, indicating where significance was obtained in the comparisons.

TABLE 11.1	**Unranked Participant Performance Scores**			
Participant	Score		Participant	Score
Robert	91		Terry	60
Myrna	84		Carl	103
Ralph	84		Kay	105
John	97		George	102
Sally	108		Carole	107
Sherry	59		Phil	105
Eugene	110		Don	100
Andy	106		Walt	106
David	67		Bonnie	101
Earl	85		Kent	110
Laurie	82		Anita	99
Maurice	95		Alice	109

TABLE 11.2	**Ranked Participant Performance Scores**	
Participant	Score	Rank
Eugene	110	1.5
Kent	110	1.5
Alice	109	3
Sally	108	4
Carole	107	5
Andy	106	6.5
Walt	106	6.5
Phil	105	8.5
Kay	105	8.5
Carl	103	10
George	102	11
Bonnie	101	12
Don	100	13
Anita	99	14
John	97	15
Maurice	95	16
Robert	91	17
Earl	85	18
Myrna	84	19.5
Ralph	84	19.5
Laurie	82	21
David	67	22
Terry	60	23
Sherry	59	24

RESEARCH IN ACTION

KEY POINTS IN THE CHAPTER REFLECTED IN THIS BOX:

- How tables may be used to summarize data
- How tables can easily present statistical comparisons

For more research in action tips visit www.sagepub .com/drewstudy

OBJECTIVES TO LEARN FROM THIS BOX:

- How to summarize group data in tabular format
- How to present a table that reflects the experimental groups and the study design

Emily is conducting a study manipulating the effects of engagement on how young students learn to read. One of her conditions is labeled concept-oriented reading instruction (CORI) and her comparison group is going to receive drill and practice (DAP) on words and sentences. One of her measures involves reading comprehension scores with two subtests: word knowledge and correct sentence structure. The table below summarizes the data and comparisons between groups.

Table 1
Mean Word Knowledge and Sentence Structure
Scores by Students Taught Using CORI and DAP Instruction

	CORI Students	DAP Students	Significance
Word Knowledge	8.21	3.79	P < .01
Sentence Structure	15.08	9.04	P < .001

Think about this: Why did Emily combine data on her groups with the statistical comparison summary in a single table?

SOURCE: This action research scenario is roughly based on Swan, E. A. (2003). *Concept-oriented reading instruction: Engaging classrooms, lifelong learners.* New York: Guilford Press.

Grouping

If the list of responses is long (e.g., 120 participants), the researcher can shorten it by grouping. Grouping can be accomplished in a variety of ways, but the most common method is to use intervals or common content.

Intervals

Grouping using **intervals** is for quantitative data only. It involves condensing the full set of scores into a smaller, more manageable number by collapsing all scores in a certain range into a single score.

One factor to be considered in grouping raw data is determining the *size* of score intervals. This is established based on two "rules of thumb" that have evolved over the years. The first is that the number of intervals should generally not exceed 20 or be fewer than 10 (the number of intervals is typically between 10 and 15). With a smaller number of intervals, there will obviously be fewer to contend with in any inspection or analysis. However, the smaller number of intervals will obviously require a larger interval size. A larger interval causes more error since any given score may be more units away from the **midpoint** score than if the interval were smaller. This means that the score used (the midpoint score) is farther from the actual score when the interval is larger—it is this distance that increases the error associated with the score (see below for more on midpoint scores). Using a larger number of intervals results in smaller interval size, reducing the error by making all scores closer to the midpoint. A large number of intervals, however, may be somewhat more cumbersome. Most sets of data can be grouped appropriately with 10 to 15 intervals.

A second rule of thumb for determining the size of intervals is that certain score ranges are preferred for intervals. There is some difference of opinion regarding exactly what these intervals are. For the most part, however, intervals of 2, 3, 5, 10, and 20 are seen as being the most preferred. While these intervals cover most sets of data, there are some that are more convenient than others. If a researcher is using an interval of 2, for example, he or she has not grouped the data a great deal *unless* there is a very small range in the scores and a rather high frequency at each interval. Therefore, an interval of 2 is likely to be useful only in rare situations. In addition, intervals with an odd number of score units are more convenient to use than those with an even number. It is easier to understand and establish the midpoint of an interval of 3 or 5 than one of 4 or 6 since the midpoint of those units is a whole number. Refer to Table 11.3 where we see, for example, an interval of 60 to 64. This is a 5-unit interval including scores of 60, 61, 62, 63, and 64 which makes the midpoint very easy to establish.

The examples used above involve whole numbers. If the scores used can include decimals, the rules are the same, except that there is one more point to consider. When including decimals, the *exact* limits of the interval 60 to 64 are actually 59.5 to 64.5 and consequently any scores falling between these exact limits are considered to be in the interval. You need to make sure that all possible instances of your data can be placed in one, and only one, interval. If two consecutive intervals are 55 to 59 and 60 to 64, any whole number between 55 and 64 will be placed in one interval or the other. However, if one participant had a score of 59.4, which interval would he or she be placed in? If we consider the intervals as having exact limits of 54.5 to 59.4 and 59.5 to 64.5, then we know where 59.4 is included. It is important that the decision rules (i.e., the limits) for the intervals used include the same number of decimal places as the scores being placed into those intervals. Otherwise some scores will fall outside the range of intervals and will make for some confusing situations. With minor modifications on the earlier interval examples, one can cover most data sets and employ intervals that are all constituted with odd-numbered score units (e.g., 3, 5, 9, 19).

Another factor to be considered in grouping data is where to begin and end the intervals. There is no reason to begin far below the lowest participant's score or continue much beyond the highest participant's score. Therefore, if our participants' scores ranged from 23 to 79 on some hypothetical task, it makes little sense to begin with an interval of 0 to 4 and end with an interval of 85 to 89. Several of the intervals on either end of the range would have a frequency (represented by *f*) of 0 and therefore be useless (even if the scores that were *possible* on the task ranged from 0 to 100). Moreover, in beginning the intervals it is most natural to start with a score unit that is a multiple of the interval. This would suggest that if the interval is 5, the interval might begin with 15, 20, or some other multiple of 5. For our hypothetical task, we have a range of 23 to 79, or 56 score units. If we used an interval of 3, we would have too many intervals (56 divided by 3 equals 18.67). However, an interval of 5 will result in an appropriate number of intervals (56 divided by 5 equals 11.2 or 12 intervals). Therefore, we will use an interval of 5, beginning with 20 to 24 and ending with 75 to 79. Table 11.3 illustrates how data from a set of scores may be grouped using intervals.

TABLE 11.3   **Hypothetical Example of Data Grouped by Interval**

Score Interval	X	f
60–64	62	2
55–59	57	1
50–54	52	6
45–49	47	10
40–44	42	20
35–39	37	18
30–34	32	19
25–29	27	16
20–24	22	13
15–19	17	9
10–14	12	2
5–9	7	3
0–4	2	2
		$N = 120$

The left column shows the score intervals used to group the data. The other pieces of information are included to describe these intervals. X is the midpoint of each respective interval. For example, notice that the interval 60–64 has a midpoint of 62. As stated before, intervals with an odd number of points included have whole-number midpoints (this is also the median of the interval range). The f refers to the frequency with which scores fall into a given interval (e.g., a score of 63 would be given a value of 62—the midpoint—and there were two scores assigned that value). It would have been quite tedious to list each score individually for the data in Table 11.3. Of course, each score was listed originally as the researcher aggregated the data; however, for purposes of inspecting the data, the format in Table 11.3 is more informative and convenient.

For additional simulations visit www.sagepub .com/drewstudy

Simulation

Simulation 11.1

Topic: Grouping data

Background statement: Raw data collected on a large group of participants are frequently difficult to use without further tabulation. Grouping raw data often facilitates inspection and further analysis. This frequently involves taking the data set in the form it was collected and transferring it to a sheet that summarizes it in a manner that is usable. In performing this operation, there are certain matters that require attention (e.g., number of intervals, interval size).

(Continued)

Tasks to be performed:

1. Review the stimulus material below.

2. Select intervals that are appropriate for grouping the data set presented in the stimulus material. Indicate why you selected the intervals you did.

3. Present the data in tabular form similar to that illustrated in Table 11.3, including the midpoint and f columns.

Stimulus material:

You have been employed for the summer as a research assistant in the psychology learning lab. Some of the work in the beginning involves data that were collected in a learning experiment conducted earlier. As the junior research assistant in the lab, you have been given the job of tabulating the data in preparation for descriptive analysis. The criterion measure was the number of errors committed by participants in learning the task.

Data Set

Donald B.	13	Robert B.	13	Fred R.	34
Jay T.	34	Robyne A.	33	Sara F.	23
Thomas B.	42	James R.	6	Lowell B.	10
Donald R.	26	Jane Z.	31	Tom L.	14
Laura B.	63	Linda P.	23	Dan B.	46
Fred A.	3	Scott E.	21	Sandy S.	43
Myrtle R.	37	David B.	62	Joe S.	14
Bob D.	51	Vern L.	48	Sallie P.	29
George J.	38	Archy T.	36	Ray J.	31
Ellen C.	63	Barbara B.	43	Bonnie S.	20
Ann T.	8	Grant W.	39	John A.	17
Connie M.	9	Lloyd S.	46	Robert W.	33
Randy L.	41	James D.	5	Cyrus R.	14
Larry B.	27	Jeanne G.	13	George L.	23
Anne L.	22	Diane B.	42	James V.	61
Mike B.	36	Ben E.	16	Anne R.	30
Bruce W.	18	Ed P.	25	Claude G.	26
Marla D.	28	Jane F.	30	Mike R.	33
Hans P.	34	Billy W.	35	Danny K.	36
Hal H.	38	Michelle K.	41	Randall C.	43
Mark E.	47	Dan P.	56	Susan P.	58
Toby L.	18	Dean M.	25	Harry B.	28
Mike H.	30	Winston M.	34	Kathy R.	35
Mary A.	36	Margie S.	41	Nancy S.	43
Carl A.	47	Carl T.	56	Charles P.	25
Earl T.	28	Lee I.	34	Clara P.	41
John M.	43	Bill M.	47	Bob W.	28
Bob C.	47				

Write your response, then turn to page 285 for Simulation Feedback 11.1.

Common Content

Another method of grouping data is one that is more prominent with the use of qualitative data. Grouping data for common content allows the researcher to organize the data into themes or groups. This will actually be discussed in much greater detail in Chapter 14, "Analyzing Qualitative Data," but a brief treatment is included here for illustrative purposes.

Suppose we asked 120 people, "Which subject do you think is the most important one taught in schools today?" and used an open-ended format (thought we left interview formats back in Chapter 8, didn't you?). We might get a variety of answers (up to 120 seemingly different ones), which could make it difficult to summarize and interpret. Therefore, we want to group them. We might take different answers such as "reading," "decoding," "comprehension," "language arts," "literacy," and "enjoyment of reading" and call them all "Reading." Then we can count how many of the different answers fall into our category of "Reading." An example of these data is presented in Table 11.4. Comparing Tables 11.3 and 11.4, notice that with common content grouping, no midpoint is included. Since we are not using scores on a common metric, it doesn't make much sense to try to identify a midpoint of "reading," "decoding," "literacy," and so on. Therefore, we only need to report the categories themselves and the number of responses in each category.

TABLES

Tables are used in research reports to summarize data that cannot conveniently or effectively be presented in the narrative of the text. Tables are more expensive to prepare and publish than text and therefore should be used only when they enhance the presentation (American Psychological Association, 2001). An appropriately constructed table supplements rather than duplicates textual material and can save space in circumstances where a lengthy or complex narrative would be otherwise required. However, tables must be carefully planned and constructed or they may detract from a reader's understanding of the data.

Constructing Tables

The general rule in constructing tables is that they should be as simple and clear as possible while still presenting all the information necessary to complement the text.

TABLE 11.4 Hypothetical Example of Data Grouped by Common Content	
Group (or Theme)	*f*
Reading	22
Math	25
Writing	10
Science	12
History	19
Art	9
Music	9
Physical Education	14
	N = 120

In general, tables should read from top to bottom and left to right. They are numbered consecutively using Arabic numerals in the order they appear in the text (e.g., Table 1, Table 2). This numbering system is modified somewhat for most textbooks where tables are numbered consecutively for each chapter (e.g., Table 11.1, 11.2, and so on for Chapter 11). The researcher preparing a manuscript should indicate where a table is to appear in the text with instructions to the editor and printer. The table should be placed as close as possible to the first reference to it in the text. For example, if we were to refer to Table 3 in this sentence, we would follow this paragraph with instructions like those below, and continue the text again below where the table will go. Although tables usually appear between paragraphs, if necessary they may be placed in the middle of a paragraph. The researcher prepares the actual table on a separate manuscript page and places it at the end of the manuscript for submission to the editor of a journal or textbook.

[**Insert Hypothetical Table 3 About Here**]

Tables included in other types of reports are often included within the text. For example, when you write your thesis or dissertation, you will include the tables in the text where they should be read rather than on a separate page at the end of the manuscript. See Figure 11.1 for an example of how a table in a dissertation might look.

For the most part, tables should be constructed so they can fit the width of a journal page. Only in rare cases should a table be constructed that requires it to be placed sideways on a page. In extremely rare cases, when alternatives such as dividing a table into multiple tables are not feasible, a table could be included that covers more than one published page. One should make certain to consult the publishing requirements and characteristics of the journal or publishing organization for specific space limitations.

For the beginning researcher, it is important to keep in mind that tables should augment, clarify, or save space in the text. The reader should not use them unless they are necessary or facilitate understanding. If information can be conveniently and effectively incorporated into the narrative, a table is probably not necessary or appropriate. As usual, a researcher preparing tables for a report should consult the intended publishing outlet for unique or specific details regarding format (e.g., the *Publication Manual of the American Psychological Association*). Each publisher is somewhat different with respect to requirements. We have presented information that pertains only to the general preparation of tables.

Table Explanations

A table must be able to stand alone and therefore should be clearly labeled. The title should be sufficiently descriptive and complete that a reader can understand what is contained therein by simply inspecting the table. Abbreviations should not be used in a table unless they are commonly understood or parenthetically explained. Some explanations may be placed below the table, although they should be kept to a minimum. These explanations, usually termed "notes," come in three types.

General Notes

General notes provide explanations or qualifying statements regarding the whole table. These notes appear at the foot of the table and may include the *source* of a table if it was reprinted from another publication, or they may provide the reader with other information pertaining to the table in general. (See Figures 11.1 and 11.2 for examples of general notes.)

Specific Notes

Specific notes are used to explain or elaborate information about a particular part of the table contents. These are designated by using a lowercase letter superscript such as "a" or "b" beside the specific part of the table being explained, and the same superscript letter preceding the explanation at the foot of the table (see Figure 11.3 for an example).

FIGURE 11.1   **Example of Table in Dissertation**

they are the largest race/ethnicity group in the U. S.), the implicit assumption is that the

odds or rate of identification for White students is appropriate or accurate. When using

this method of denominator, it may be important not to assume direction of causation or

effect. A discrepancy between the identification rates for African-American and White

students may be an indication of *over*representation of one group or *under*representation

of the other. It should only be considered the first step in the investigation, with further

steps examining the effect of intervening variables.

This third method of calculating the denominator is what is used by the National

Research Council (NRC; Donovan & Cross, 2002). Table 1 provides a comparison of the

composition index, risk index, and rate ratio. The figures are based on data from the U. S.

Department of Education's Office of Special Education Programs (OSEP) for the 1998-

1999 school year.

Table 1

1998 OSEP Data for All Students with Disabilities Disaggregated by Racial/Ethnic
Group: Composition Index, Risk Index, and Rate Ratio

Race/ethnicity	Composition Index	Risk Index	Rate Ratio
African-American	20.03%	14.28%	1.18
American Indian	1.24%	13.10%	1.08
Asian/Pacific Islander	1.72%	5.31%	0.44
Latino	13.93%	11.34%	0.94
White	63.08%	12.10%	1.00
Total	100.00%	11.96%	----

Note: This table is adapted from Donovan, M. S. & Cross, C. T. (Eds.) (2002). *Minority students in special and gifted education.* Washington, DC: National Academy Press.

SOURCE: From Hosp, J. L. (2002). *Disproportionate representation of minority students in special education: Academic, economic, and demographic predictors.* Unpublished doctoral dissertation, Vanderbilt University, Nashville, TN. Reprinted with permission from John L. Hosp.

Table from Donovan, M. S. & Cross, C. T. (Eds.), (2002). *Minority students in special and gifted education.* Washington, DC: National Academies Press. pp. 57–59. Reprinted with permission of the National Academies Press.

FIGURE 11.2   Example of Single-Column Table From a Journal Article

THE JOURNAL OF SPECIAL EDUCATION VOL. 37/NO. 2/2003 **75**

TABLE 2. Characteristics of Included Subsamples

Variable	n	%
Publication type		
Journal article	8	18
Dissertation	2	5
Technical report	34	77
Publication year		
1978	1	2
1983	3	7
1990	1	2
1994	32	73
1995	1	2
1996	1	2
1997	2	5
1998	1	2
1999	2	5
State conducted in		
New York	32	73
Other than New York	12	27
Length of study (in months)		
11	41	93
24	1	2
Setting		
Elementary school	6	14
Elementary & middle school	33	75
All levels	5	11
Predominant racial group		
Caucasian	16	36
African American	15	34
Hispanic	13	30

Note. Due to rounding, some percentages may not add to 100.

of interest (in this case, predominant racial group) because the unexplained variability (i.e., the error) is controlled for.

With this accounted-for variability (within-$Q = 49.19$, $p = .18$), the between-groups effect was found to be nonsignificant (between-$Q = 1.42$, $p = .49$). The referral rate of African American students, as compared to Caucasian students, was not significantly influenced by which racial group was predominant in the population under study. Examination of the overall effect, however, revealed a significant discrepancy between the referral rates of African American and Caucasian students ($M = 1.32$, $p = .0005$).

Hispanic to Caucasian Comparison

Visual inspection of the plots was used to determine that the effect sizes were approximately normally distributed. The 35 subsamples with Hispanic and Caucasian frequencies yielded a fixed-effects model mean effect size of 1.05 (confidence interval from 1.02 to 1.09). An analysis of homogeneity, however, yielded a Q of 410.61 ($p < .0001$). Attempts at partialing out

the Q by means of an analog to the ANOVA using predominant racial group was unsuccessful (within-$Q = 391.46$, $p < .0001$). As a result, a random-effects model was adopted that accounted for the within-group variability ($Q = 38.82$, $p = .19$) but yielded a nonsignificant between-group difference ($Q = 1.97$, $p = .37$). Examination of the overall effect size also revealed a nonsignificant difference ($M = 1.06$, $p = .49$). The referral rates for Caucasian and Hispanic students were found to be similar.

Discussion

The results indicated that the referral rates of racial groups vary significantly. The initial fixed-effects models indicated that the rate of referral was greater for both African Americans and Hispanics as compared to Caucasians. Because no intervening variables were identified that mediated these referral rate differences, the variability within each set of comparisons was statistically accounted for (i.e., random-effects models were used). Although the random-effects African American to Caucasian comparison was significant despite the larger confidence interval, the Hispanic to Caucasian comparison was not.

Compared to the national rates for eligibility stated previously, the referral rates identified by the present analysis indicate higher rates for both African American and Hispanic students. The OSEP-reported eligibility rate for African American students, compared to that for Caucasian students, was 1.18 versus a mean referral rate of 1.32. For Hispanic students compared to Caucasian students, the OSEP-reported eligibility rate of .89 was lower than the mean referral rate of 1.06. For example, these rates indicated that for every 100 Caucasian students who are referred for assessment or intervention, 132 African American students and 106 Hispanic students are referred. In contrast, for every 100 Caucasian students found to be eligible for special education, 118 African American students and 89 Hispanic students are found to be eligible. This indicates that (a) more African American students and a similar number of Hispanic students are referred for special education and (b) more African American students but fewer Hispanic students than Caucasian students are found to be eligible for special education.

Because the operational definition of referral for this analysis included referrals for assessment *or* intervention, students who ultimately were provided with services through means other than special education (e.g., Title I, Bilingual or English Language Learner [ELL] services) appear in the referral data but not in the special education classification data. Differences in referral and eligibility rates may be explained by disproportionate numbers of African American and Hispanic students served by Title I and ELL, respectively (MacMillan & Reschly, 1998). For example, consider the referral rate of 100 Caucasian students versus the referral rate of 132 African American students. If the base eligibility rate (from the referred sample) for Caucasian students were 60%, the corre-

FIGURE 11.3   Example of Multiple-Page Table From a Journal Article

School Psychology Review, 2002, Volume 31, No. 1

Table 3
Estimated Hours per Week in Five School Psychology Roles by Census Region

Variable		NE	MA	SA	ESC	ENC	WSC	WNC	Mtn	Pac	Overall	F	n
		Mean (Standard Deviation) by Region											
Current Assessment[a]	M	18.9	18.8	23.3	26.5	24.2	19.5	22.5	19.8	24.1	22.2	5.56***	972
	SD	(10.3)	(10.6)	(10.6)	(15.5)	(10.9)	(12.3)	(10.3)	(10.4)	(12.5)	(11.0)		
Preferred Assessment[b]	M	12.4	10.8	13.2	15.7	13.5	12.4	13.1	12.6	12.9	12.8	2.35*	911
	SD	(6.3)	(6.5)	(7.1)	(8.7)	(7.3)	(9.1)	(7.1)	(6.8)	(7.8)	(7.2)		
Current Intervention[c]	M	8.9	9.9	6.5	6.9	6.8	9.0	7.4	8.0	7.2	7.6	4.04***	973
	SD	(6.6)	(7.5)	(6.2)	(7.5)	(5.7)	(7.7)	(6.3)	(6.1)	(6.6)	(6.5)		
Preferred Intervention	M	12.1	12.1	10.8	12.2	11.2	12.7	11.6	10.6	11.1	11.4	1.03	906
	SD	(6.2)	(6.3)	(5.9)	(7.4)	(5.6)	(7.6)	(6.2)	(5.2)	(6.0)	(6.0)		
Current Consultation	M	8.0	7.6	6.3	4.9	6.3	7.0	6.5	6.9	6.3	6.6	1.87	963
	SD	(6.9)	(6.1)	(5.1)	(4.4)	(4.5)	(5.1)	(4.9)	(4.7)	(8.3)	(5.9)		
Preferred Consultation	M	8.7	9.6	8.9	8.0	9.0	9.0	8.9	8.8	8.7	9.0	0.55	899
	SD	(4.9)	(5.7)	(4.7)	(4.1)	(4.5)	(5.8)	(4.8)	(4.5)	(4.9)	(4.8)		
Current System Consultation	M	2.7	2.4	2.3	2.1	2.5	3.9	2.6	3.2	2.9	2.6	0.96	952
	SD	(4.0)	(3.8)	(4.4)	(3.1)	(4.0)	(8.1)	(3.9)	(4.0)	(4.6)	(4.3)		

Table 3 continues

FIGURE 11.3   (Continued)

Regional Differences in School Psychology Practice

Table 3 continued

Variable		NE	MA	SA	ESC	ENC	WSC	WNC	Mtn	Pac	Overall	F	n
Preferred System	M	4.3	4.1	3.9	3.5	4.0	6.6	3.9	5.3	4.2	4.3	2.44*	891
Consultation[d]	SD	(4.0)	(3.8)	(4.2)	(2.3)	(3.8)	(8.3)	(3.7)	(6.0)	(3.9)	(4.2)		
Current	M	0.5	1.1	1.6	0.9	0.8	1.5	1.0	1.0	0.6	1.0	1.41	932
Research	SD	(0.9)	(3.9)	(5.4)	(2.0)	(2.1)	(3.8)	(2.1)	(2.4)	(1.5)	(2.9)		
Preferred	M	2.7	3.2	3.7	2.8	2.5	3.9	2.6	2.5	2.6	2.9	1.76	875
Research	SD	(5.2)	(4.6)	(5.9)	(2.4)	(2.6)	(5.1)	(2.7)	(2.5)	(2.8)	(3.8)		
% Time in													
Eligibility	M	55.7	56.3	55.7	65.5	65.6	50.8	62.4	58.0	65.1	60.0	3.19***	1015
Services[e]	SD	(29.3)	(29.6)	(32.5)	(30.7)	(27.2)	(38.0)	(29.0)	(29.4)	(30.3)	(30.0)		

Mean (Standard Deviation) by Region

*$p < .05$. **$p < .01$. ***$p < .001$.

[a] ESC, ENC, Pac, SA > Mtn, WSC, NE, MA; WNC > NE, MA (ES range = .33-.66). [b] ESC > SA, Pac, Mtn, NE, WSC, MA; ENC, SA, WNC, Pac > MA (ES range = .30-.69). [c] MA > Mtn, WNC, Pac, ESC, ENC, SA; WSC, NE > ENC, SA (ES range = .27-.50). [d] WSC > NE, Pac, MA; WSC, Mtn > ENC, WNC, SA, ESC (ES range = .28-.53). [e] ENC > Mtn; ENC, Pac > MA, SA, NE, WSC; ESC, WNC > WSC (ES range = .27-.50).

SOURCE: From Hosp, J. L. & Reschly, D. J. (2002). "Regional differences in school psychology practice." *School Psychology Review, 31*, 11–29. Reprinted with permission.

Probability Levels

The third type of table note typically used in educational research involves **probability levels**. These are employed when the table presents statistical analysis results and use asterisks in the body of the table with corresponding explanations at the foot of the table (e.g., $^*p < .05$, $^{**}p < .01$; see Figure 11.3 for an example). (Probability statements such as these will be discussed more completely in Chapter 13.) If more than one type of note is used for the same table, they should appear beneath it in order from general to specific to probability (American Psychological Association, 2001).

Good and Bad Table Use

A point to remember is that tables should enhance the reader's understanding of the report or manuscript. As such, any "good" table is one that accomplishes this—it facilitates understanding of the material being presented. Conversely, a "bad" table is one that is confusing, difficult to read, or does not contain information that is helpful. The main "causes" of this are (1) including too much information, (2) including too little information, or (3) poor organization of the content.

So much information can be included in a table as to make it difficult to interpret. In general, if a table cannot be contained on a single page, there is too much information. In this case, you should try to divide the information into multiple tables that each display a portion of the information. Since tables are two-dimensional (represented by rows and columns of data), it is generally good practice to include only two sets of variables. For example, the columns in Table 11.2 relate to three separate variables—each participant's name, his or her score, and his or her rank. Each row represents the data from a single participant.

Similar to a table containing too much content, having too little information can be confusing rather than illuminating. Tables with too little information are probably better explained as narrative rather than presented in tabular form. Tables that only contain one column or row are probably better as text. Also, if the information in a table can be summarized in one or two sentences, it is better to use the sentences than the table. For example, the information in Table 11.5 could be summarized as, "The participants earned a mean score of 94.79 ($SD = 15.36$)."

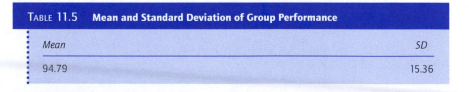

TABLE 11.5	Mean and Standard Deviation of Group Performance
Mean	*SD*
94.79	15.36

The third way a table can be confusing or difficult to understand is if the contents are poorly organized. Poor organization is any system that others could not identify or which uses an organizing variable that is not important or should not be emphasized. Therefore, when organizing a table, make sure to structure it around the information you want to emphasize or clarify. Table 11.2 does this by ordering the cases (i.e., each participant) by his or her rank (or score, since the ranks are based on the scores). This is the information that is intended to be emphasized. Another method could be to order the participants alphabetically. This is shown in Table 11.6. This makes the core information (i.e., the data that need clarification or enhancing) more difficult to examine because it is not arranged in some type of order. For example, if the results in Table 11.6 were rank ordered, the reader could quickly determine the maximum and minimum scores as well as the range. When they are listed alphabetically by participant name, these descriptive statistics are not as easy to determine and should be provided for the reader.

TABLE 11.6   Alphabetical Participant Performance Scores

Participant	Score	Rank
Alice	109	3
Andy	106	6.5
Anita	99	14
Bonnie	101	12
Carl	103	10
Carole	107	5
David	67	22
Don	100	13
Earl	85	18
Eugene	110	1.5
George	102	11
John	97	15
Kay	105	8.5
Kent	110	1.5
Laurie	82	21
Maurice	95	16
Myrna	84	19.5
Phil	105	8.5
Ralph	84	19.5
Robert	91	17
Sally	108	4
Sherry	59	24
Terry	60	23
Walt	106	6.5

While tables can be useful in enhancing the reader's understanding of the information being presented, sometimes it is not enough. For some types of information, enhancement needs to come in the form of a visual representation—such as **graphs, charts,** or **plots**.

GRAPHING DATA

It is widely accepted that visual representation of data is an extremely useful tool in research. If the old adage "a picture is worth a thousand words" holds true, then graphs are a valuable way to save time and text (and therefore space) in a research report. Graphs often provide a dramatic statement of the results where narrative or tabled data are difficult to comprehend. Graphs attract a reader's attention, clarify points or results, and in some cases save space in a publication (which can be very expensive). There is no single type of graph that serves every purpose in research. This section will examine a variety of factors pertaining to the utilization of graphs.

When to Graph

Graphs serve several purposes in the overall research process. Many investigators find graphs to be extremely valuable as they are examining the data in preparation for writing the research report. **Working graphs** are constructed in order to provide a visual representation of how participants performed. Often these working graphs help the writer to explain what seemed to happen in the study. Such graphs may or may not appear in the final publication of the report, depending on how clearly and succinctly the authors were able to express the results in narrative form. Experience has shown that using working graphs (often in rather crude form) in this fashion is particularly helpful for beginning researchers, although more experienced researchers may use them, too.

The decision to use a graph in a report (particularly for publication) must be made with great care. Simply adding graphs capriciously to a report is inappropriate. With respect to publication, it should be remembered that figures (all illustrations other than a table are called **figures**) are typically quite expensive to prepare and reproduce. The most important point to consider is whether or not the graph is really necessary. The *Publication Manual of the American Psychological Association* (APA, 2001) states that

> Figures are more expensive than tables to reproduce, and both [tables and figures] are more expensive than text to compose, so reserve them for your most important data and situations where their use enhances your ability to communicate your findings. (p. 21)

Therefore, you should only employ graphs in reports when they are needed to clarify or augment the text, or when they will save space by eliminating the need for lengthy narrative. Determining the need for a figure primarily rests with the author, although journal editors will not hesitate to require inclusion or deletion of figures as the manuscript is reviewed. It is always good practice to have a colleague read your report in manuscript form to receive feedback regarding the clarity of the narrative as well as potential need for figures. Often an investigator is so close to the study that important points are inadvertently omitted or expressed poorly.

Types of Graphs

There are a variety of ways to graphically represent data, and different data (or different types of data) are better suited to explanation through different types of graphs. The types of graphs explained in this section are the most common ones used in education. They can be helpful during the analysis phase of research by helping the researcher summarize and interpret the findings. They can also be useful in reporting the results of research by helping the reader understand the data the researcher is conveying.

Bar Graphs and Histograms

Bar graphs and histograms are used to express data on the frequency of certain responses or events. The bars on these types of graphs can be shown either vertically or horizontally, but are usually shown vertically because taller bars demonstrate a higher frequency. Figure 11.4 is an example of a bar graph. Each bar represents a different response to the question, "What do you want to be when you grow up?" asked of 82 kindergarten boys. Notice that the responses are ordered alphabetically across the horizontal axis. The vertical axis is used to denote the number of responses for each category. The graph shows us that "fireman" was the most common answer (26 boys said they wanted to be firemen) while "lawyer" was the least common (only 1 boy gave this answer).

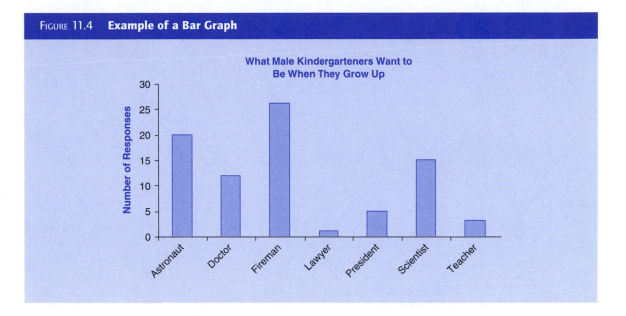

FIGURE 11.4   **Example of a Bar Graph**

Also notice that the bars do not touch each other. This is common when the different bars represent different categories or separate answers—as in the example—and it differentiates bar graphs from histograms. A histogram is a specific type of bar graph in which the horizontal axis is a continuous variable (i.e., interval or ratio-level data). In a histogram, the bars are allowed to touch each other because they are adjacent points on a continuum. Figure 11.5 shows the number of students who read a certain number of words correctly in one minute in the spring of third grade. Just as values on the vertical axis increases from the bottom to the top, values on the horizontal axis increase from left to right. Also, since these are ratio data, notice that the mean and standard deviation are included to the right of the graph. These statistics are used to describe the data (see Chapter 12 for further discussion of descriptive statistics).

Line Graphs

Line graphs are similar to bar graphs except that they use lines instead of bars to represent the data. Any instance that uses a bar graph could use a line graph instead. Another common use of line graphs, however, is to plot changes in data over time. Figure 11.6 shows a typical line graph that does this. The vertical axis is labeled as the dependent variable and it increases from bottom to top. In Figure 11.6, this is the number of words a student reads correctly in one minute. The horizontal axis is used to display the measure of time—in this case it is the number of weeks. The figure thus shows that the student's performance increased over the 6 weeks of intervention. Line graphs are the most common type of display used in single-subject research designs (see Chapter 6 for further discussion).

Area Graphs

Area graphs are any type of display that uses the area of the graph to demonstrate magnitude rather that a single direction on a single axis of a plot (e.g., bar and line graphs use—each axis is used to represent a separate variable, one of them generally being frequency of response). While bar and line graphs are best used to demonstrate the frequency of responses at certain levels of a variable, area graphs are best used to show the relative percentages of the total that each level of a variable

FIGURE 11.5   **Example of a Histogram**

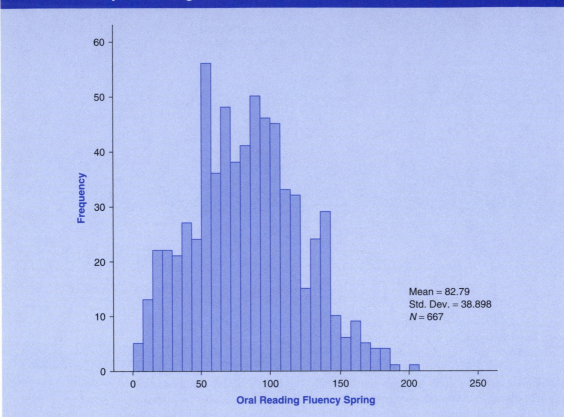

FIGURE 11.6   **Example of a Line Graph**

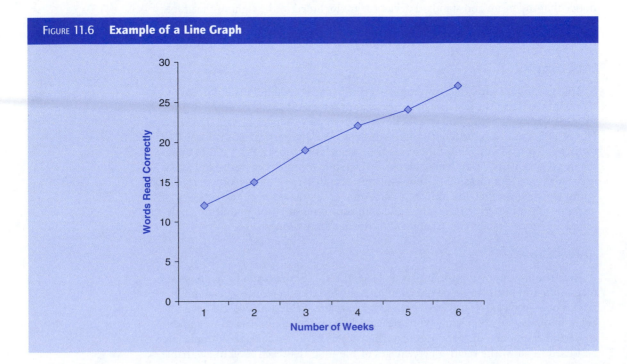

represents. There are ways to combine the two (e.g., adding area to a line graph), but these aren't used as often as a simple area graph.

The most common area graph is a pie chart. If you've ever read *USA Today*, you are familiar with pie charts. Pie charts (like the one in Figure 11.7) are made up of a circle that is divided into sections that represent the different categories being expressed. The larger the "slice" of the pie, the greater the frequency of that category or its percentage of the whole. For example, Figure 11.7 shows the percentage of instructional time dedicated to different literacy activities by a group of kindergarten teachers. Each slice of the pie is color-coded to denote which literacy component it represents. The greater the percentage of the pie, the more time spent on that activity. As the figure shows, the greatest amount of time was spent on Word Study/Phonics—27% of the instructional time. The next greatest was Comprehension at 21%, and so on. Area graphs are best used to describe results from a single variable—especially those that are nominal (or categorical) in nature.

Scatter Plots

At first glance, scatter plots look somewhat like line graphs in that they use similar horizontal and vertical axes. However, whereas line graphs are used to depict frequency counts (or performance) along different levels of a variable (which could be time), scatter plots are used to display the relation between two variables. Each variable is plotted along one axis, from the intersection (bottom left corner) out, in

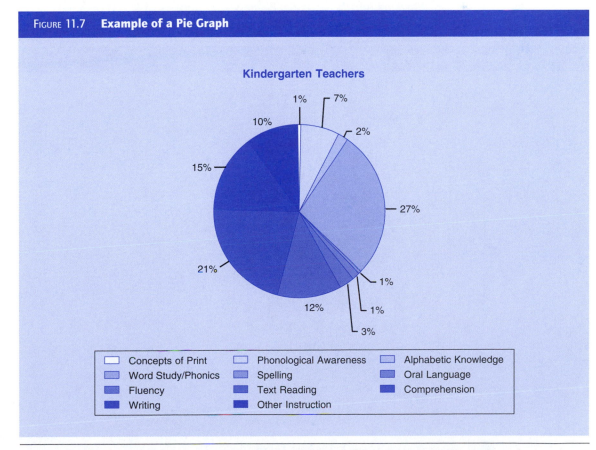

FIGURE 11.7   Example of a Pie Graph

Kindergarten Teachers

Concepts of Print
Phonological Awareness
Alphabetic Knowledge
Word Study/Phonics
Spelling
Oral Language
Fluency
Text Reading
Comprehension
Writing
Other Instruction

SOURCE: From *Reading First Teachers' Use of Instructional Time and Its Relation to Reading Achievement* by M. Hosp, J. Hosp, & J. Dole (2005). Paper presented at the Society for the Scientific Study of Reading, Twelfth Annual Meeting, Toronto, Canada.

increasing values—that is, the bottom left corner of the scatter plot is the low value for each variable, usually zero. Every case, whether it is students, schools, or states, has a value for each variable. These are plotted along each axis to provide a single point for each case. These are the dots shown in Figure 11.8. Each case is assigned one dot that represents its value on both variables. This way the pattern demonstrated by the relation between the two variables becomes evident. For example, Figure 11.8 shows the relation between students' performance on a measure of their oral reading fluency in the fall and again in the spring of the same year. This pattern shows that there is a strong relation between fall scores and spring scores. This relation can also be calculated and presented statistically as a correlation (see Chapter 13 for a discussion about correlations). Especially for correlational research where the researcher is comparing two continuous variables, scatter plots can be very useful in identifying the relation and expressing it to the reader.

Box Plots

Box plots, sometimes referred to as box-and-whisker graphs, are used to compare performance among groups on a continuous variable. Each group gets its own box that describes its performance using the median and interquartile range (see Chapter 12 for a discussion of these). This allows a comparison of groups on both central tendency and dispersion (the two characteristics that describe a distribution). Figure 11.9 shows a graph of box plots. It compares performance on a measure of oral reading fluency for four groups of differing language proficiency. Each box describes the group performance with the bottom of the box signifying the 25th percentile and the top indicating the 75th percentile. The line in the middle of the

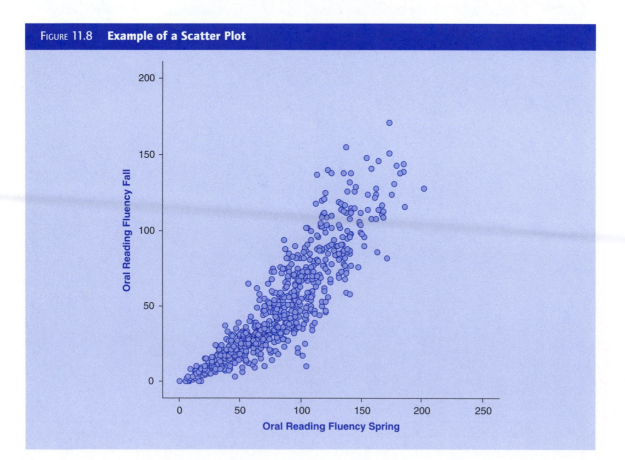

FIGURE 11.8   **Example of a Scatter Plot**

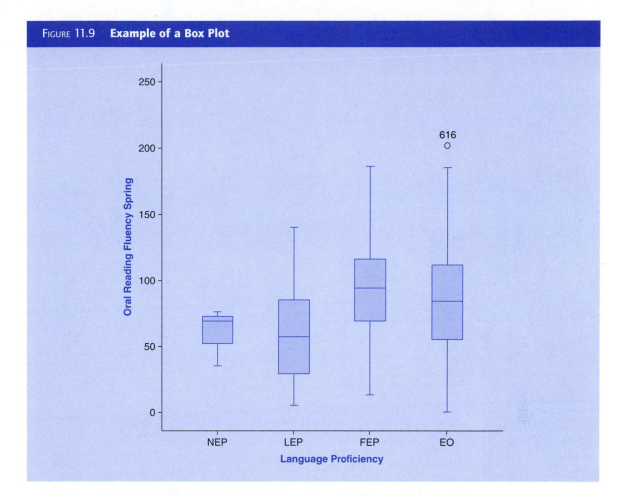

FIGURE 11.9   **Example of a Box Plot**

box is the 50th percentile. The stems off the ends of the box (also referred to as the whiskers) extend to the 10th and 90th percentiles. If any score falls outside of that range, the data point is added to show how far outside it falls (and is usually labeled with the case number).

The box plots in Figure 11.9 show that the non–English proficient group (NEP) is not as variable as the others—i.e., the box is not as elongated. We can also see that the fluent English proficient group (FEP) and English-only group (EO) have similar medians, which both appear to be higher than those for the NEP and limited English proficient group (LEP). Also, the EO group had one member perform above the 90th percentile.

Converting Tables to Graphs

As shown in the previous section, there are many different types of graphs used in education. Figure 11.10 illustrates a variety of different approaches to graphing the same data. This experiment investigated the types of errors committed by participants with intellectual disabilities by learning stage on an associative learning task.[1] Errors were classified into four types: (1) extralist intrusions

---

[1] Participants of average intelligence were also studied, but those data are not presented here to conserve space.

FIGURE 11.10 **Subjects' Mean Errors by Type and Learning Stage**

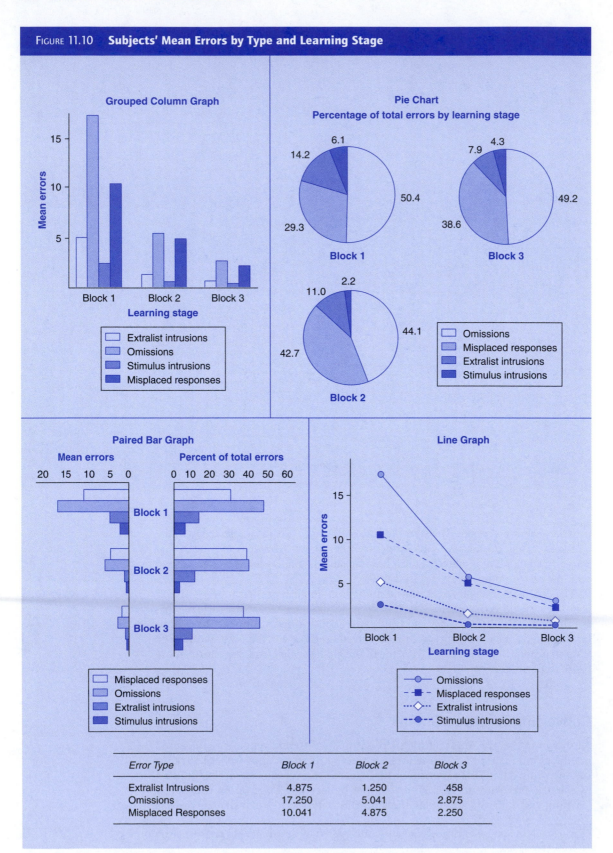

Error Type	Block 1	Block 2	Block 3
Extralist Intrusions	4.875	1.250	.458
Omissions	17.250	5.041	2.875
Misplaced Responses	10.041	4.875	2.250

(responses that were not on the list of material to be learned), (2) omissions (failure to respond), (3) stimulus intrusions (participants giving a stimulus word instead of a response word as an answer), and (4) misplaced responses (participants answering with a response that was supposed to be paired with another stimulus). Learning stage was divided into three blocks, each containing several trials.

Each type of graph presents the data in a somewhat different manner, and the choice of which approach to use would depend on the nature of the narrative. The author(s) might select one over another based on the theoretical basis for the study, which may largely direct the line of reasoning and writing. Bar graphs are simple and very flexible in terms of how they may be used. Line graphs are also very flexible but are typically used to depict change over time such as in time series studies or those involving repeated measures on the same participants. Pie graphs are often used when percentages are employed as the criterion measure (percentages may also be portrayed with other graph formats). Graphs such as the paired bar example are useful when multiple criterion measures need to be visually compared. The example formats presented in Figure 11.10 are illustrative rather than exhaustive.

Preparation of Graphs

There is considerable variation in the manner in which graphs are prepared in education. Much depends on the particular journal or publishing house involved in producing the printed document. However, there are certain general guidelines that are customarily followed. The APA (2001) provides a list of standards for figures as follows:

The standards for good figures are simplicity, clarity, and continuity. A good figure

- augments rather than duplicates the text;
- conveys only essential facts;
- omits visually distracting detail;
- is easy to read—its elements (type, lines, labels, symbols, etc.) are large enough to be read with ease in the printed form;
- is easy to understand—its purpose is readily apparent;
- is consistent with and is prepared in the same style as similar figures in the same article; that is, the lettering is of the same size and typeface, lines are of the same weight, and so forth;
- is carefully planned and prepared. (p. 177)

As noted, these standards are quite general and there are a number of other preparation factors that are common practice. In general, a graph should read from left to right and bottom to top. The independent variable is plotted on the horizontal axis, and in cases where it represents a comparison between differing magnitudes of the variable (e.g., years—1982, 1983, 1984; age—10, 12, 14; dosage—5cc, 10cc, 15), the format should proceed in an increasing manner from left to right. The dependent variable is plotted on the vertical axis and should read from bottom to top. Where feasible, the vertical scale should be arranged so that zero shows at the bottom of the vertical axis. If it is not practical to include the full scale on the vertical axis, the axis should be broken with a double slash as shown in Figure 11.11. A double slash may also be used to break the horizontal axis if the graph might be misinterpreted based on the absence of a zero on the experimental variable. This is also illustrated in Figure 11.11.

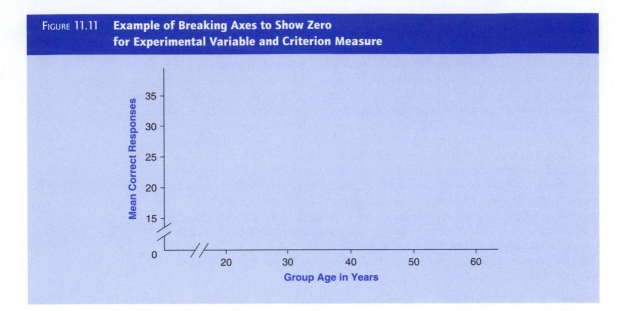

FIGURE 11.11   **Example of Breaking Axes to Show Zero for Experimental Variable and Criterion Measure**

Graphs may be prepared in nearly any size as long as they are easily read. Most editors will either reduce or enlarge the figure to fit their publishing format. However, greater clarity is generally achieved by reduction of a graph that is too large rather than enlarging one that is too small to fit the format. From the standpoint of proportion, the vertical axis should be about two-thirds the length of the horizontal axis. It is always prudent to consult the specific guidelines of the particular publisher (or institution) for details concerning size and proportion requirements before the graph is prepared for the final manuscript or report (see APA, 2001, for general manuscript guidelines).

It is important to clearly label all aspects of a figure. A graph should be able to stand alone, which makes this labeling crucial. The title of the figure should be complete so that a reader knows what information is being presented. Both vertical and horizontal axes should be clearly labeled (e.g., learning stage, age, treatment sessions, mean errors, IQ, mean correct responses) and the calibration provided on both axes (e.g., Block 1, Block 2, Block 3; 0, 5, 10, 15). Without complete and clear labels, a figure is often unintelligible. With respect to placement of figures (and tables for that matter), the researcher writing the report will need to indicate where they should appear in the manuscript. This is usually accomplished by breaking the text as soon as possible after reference to the figure is made in the narrative, and inserting instructions to the editor and printer. Such instructions should be very simple. For example, if we were to refer to Figure 2 in this sentence then we would insert the following in the text.

[Insert Hypothetical Figure 2 About Here]

Obviously, there is a great deal of latitude with respect to the preparation of graphs. Once again, specific details are usually available from the organization or publisher that produces the publication. It is also helpful to review some manuscripts that have been published by your colleagues to see how graphs were prepared.

Graphing Faux Pas

Many of the errors committed in graphing data have received attention in the guidelines presented above. However, there are some additional points that need to be mentioned. The cardinal rule for graphing data is that the graph should be *clear and not misleading*. This requires that a graph be as simple as possible. An overly complex graph is no easier to understand than a lengthy narrative or a complex set of numbers. Simplicity and complete labeling will usually solve problems of clarity.

Graphs may also be misleading if they are not carefully conceived and prepared. It was noted in the preceding section that the vertical axis should be about two-thirds the length of the horizontal axis in most cases and that calibration of the vertical axis should go to zero if practical. This rule of thumb creates a commonly accepted proportion between the two axes. When these guidelines are not followed, the result may be a visually misleading graph. For example, the two graphs in Figure 11.12 use the same data. Because the vertical axis of the top graph only goes from 0 to 30, the individual appears to be making good progress over time—i.e., the trend of her progress is quite steep. However, when we look at her progress on the graph with the vertical axis that goes from 0 to 130 (the bottom graph), her progress does not look so good. Since the measure used as the dependent variable uses a scale of 1 to 130, the bottom graph is a more accurate depiction of the student's performance. Also in this case, what is needed is some type of standard for comparison (a criterion-referenced goal line or one plotting the performance of a peer comparison group).

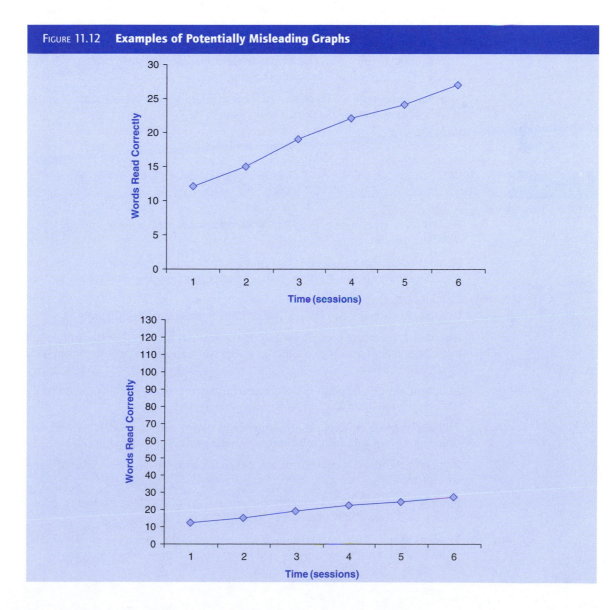

FIGURE 11.12   **Examples of Potentially Misleading Graphs**

We all commit graphing errors from time to time. The researcher is usually so completely immersed in the project that he or she may understand a figure that is confusing or unintelligible to a reader who is approaching the topic "cold." One of the most useful precautions against making such an error is to have the graph and manuscript reviewed by a colleague who has not been involved in the study.

Chapter Summary

✦ Using a variety of methods to present and summarize data can help the reader to understand them. It can also be useful for the researcher in reaching conclusions and summarizing the data him- or herself.

✦ Tables and graphs can be used for similar purposes or quite different ones.

✦ Different types of tables and graphs have different strengths, which can affect the decision to use one over another.

✦ The beginning researcher should be familiar with each type of table and graph in order to decide which one is best for the purposes of the study being conducted and to judge which is best for enhancing the explanation of the data collected.

✦ It is important to be familiar with how to interpret each type of table or graph and what some of the pitfalls of each might be.

Key Terms

Figures. Any type of graphical display of data, other than a table, included in a report or manuscript.

General notes. Notes for a table that provide explanations or qualifying statements regarding a whole table rather than a specific portion (see entry for "specific notes").

Graphs, charts, plots. Interchangeable terms for different types of figures.

Intervals. A process of grouping scores that assigns a common score (the midpoint) to all cases falling within a certain range of performance. Not to be confused with interval-level data.

Midpoint scores. The point in the center of an interval or range of scores. It is usually represented by an X.

Probability levels. An application of inferential statistics that provides levels of decision making based on the probability of finding a result of that magnitude.

Rank order. Ordinal-level data that are ranked from first to last on the basis of some characteristic.

Specific notes. Specific notes are used at the bottom of a table to explain or elaborate on the information contained in the table.

Working graphs. Displays of data that are used to aid the researcher in interpreting results, but may not necessarily be used in reporting those results to others.

Student Study Site

The companion Web site for *Designing and Conducting Research in Education* www.sagepub.com/drewstudy

Supplement your review of this chapter by going to the companion Web site to take one of the practice quizzes, use the flashcards to study key terms, and check out the many other study aids you'll find there. You'll even find some research articles from the SAGE Full-Text Collection and a step-by-step guide that will show you how to read an educational research article.

Simulation Feedback

Simulation Feedback 11.1

For additional simulations visit www.sagepub .com/drewstudy

Our first task in selecting intervals for this data set involves determining the number and size of intervals to be used. The data indicate that we have a score range of 60 units, with the lowest number of errors being 3 and the highest, 63. Recall that it would be easiest if we could use an interval with an odd number of units. You will also recall that we would not like to exceed 20 and would prefer to have somewhere between 10 and 15 intervals. Dividing our score range by a potential interval size of three, it appears that we will need 20 intervals. Actually, an interval size of three will only get us to a score of 59, so we would have to add two more intervals to include the highest error score of 63. This would result in 22 intervals, which is more than is desirable. A potential interval size of five score units will result in 12 intervals plus one in order to include the high error score of 63. Thus, if we use an interval of five, we would have 13 intervals, which appears to be appropriate. A seven-unit interval size would result in 10 intervals, which is at the lower limit in terms of the number commonly used in behavioral science. For our purposes, an interval size of five seems to be the most serviceable option. The table of grouped data may appear as follows:

Hypothetical Grouped Data Table

Score Interval	X	f
60 to 64	62	4
55 to 59	57	3
50 to 54	52	1
45 to 49	47	7
40 to 44	42	11
35 to 39	37	10
30 to 34	32	14
25 to 29	27	11
20 to 24	22	5
15 to 19	17	4
10 to 14	12	7
5 to 9	7	4
0 to 4	2	1

12

DESCRIPTIVE STATISTICS

CHAPTER OBJECTIVES

After reading Chapter 12, you should be able to do the following:

+ Describe what central tendency measures are and what they do.

+ Distinguish among the three measures of central tendency and when they are used.

+ Describe what dispersion measures are and what they do.

+ Distinguish among the three measures of dispersion and when they are used.

Once the data have been collected and raw scores tabulated, a researcher usually has several operations to perform. In nearly all cases, the first process is data compilation in some form that describes the group performance. Compilation or data summary in descriptive form involves the use of descriptive statistics. Descriptive statistics are tools for data analysis that allow the researcher to determine how well the participants performed on the task. For example, using descriptive statistics as a summary tool, the researcher can see what the average score was on a math test. Descriptive statistics permit the researcher to see how much variation there was in the group—that is, whether many of the participants scored above the average or just a few. They allow the researcher to see a summary of the participant group's scores. This type of summary is very helpful because it tells the researcher far more about his or her participants' performance than just examining a listing of individual scores or seeing that a particular student answered all but two of the questions correctly. Descriptive statistics truly describe how the participants performed.

CATEGORIES OF DESCRIPTIVE STATISTICS

Two general categories of descriptive statistics are commonly used—**central tendency measures** and **dispersion measures.** Central tendency measures provide an index of where the scores tend to bunch together or the typical score in the group of scores. Dispersion measures, on the other hand, describe the amount of variability among the scores in the group (Best & Kahn, 2006; Salkind, 2007; Sirkin, 2006). As evident in Chapter 11, measures of central tendency and dispersion are frequently used in graphs and tables. Consequently, these two chapters are interrelated as far as data description.

One preliminary note should be made regarding the researcher's objective in compiling a descriptive data summary: if the primary intent of an investigation is to describe the group, the researcher may well terminate analysis with the computation of descriptive statistics. Such statistics will provide the information necessary for the goal of group description. It is possible, however, that the investigation's purpose goes beyond describing the group. Perhaps the researcher wants to determine if females perform better than males on a reading comprehension test. This would represent an *inferential* purpose in which the researcher wants to infer about the comparative performance of males and females. Such a study would go beyond group description and might interpret gender differences in terms of some theory about teaching reading. If this is the case, descriptive statistics would allow preliminary computation necessary to perform further data analysis using inferential statistics, which will be discussed in Chapter 13. Descriptive statistics are commonly computed regardless of whether the investigation is a descriptive or inferential study. In the first case, the descriptive statistics are probably terminal operations, whereas in the latter case, they are preliminary operations in preparation for further analysis. The Research in Action box presents an example of action research in which descriptive statistics were used to summarize participant characteristics prior to making comparisons of Latino and Caucasian students.

More often than not, the actual computation of statistical analysis is accomplished using a computer. A variety of software programs are available that will perform both descriptive and inferential analyses, and even print out tables and graphs of the data in draft form (Frankfort-Nachmias & Leon-Guerrero, 2006). Two widely used computer programs include the Statistical Package for the Social Sciences (SPSS)

RESEARCH IN ACTION

KEY POINTS IN THE CHAPTER REFLECTED IN THIS BOX:

- How different types of data should be treated for measures of central tendency
- How different types of data should be treated for measures of dispersion
- The importance of data type in selecting descriptive statistics

For more research in action tips visit www.sagepub .com/drewstudy

OBJECTIVES TO LEARN FROM THIS BOX:

- How to identify different types of data
- Which measures of central tendency and dispersion are appropriate for different types of data

Daniel is conducting an action research study on Latino and Caucasian students with learning disabilities. He is collecting demographic data to describe his participants and also using instruments with Likert-type scales to measure self-esteem. His major goal is to see if there are differences in their self-esteem with the intent to identify areas that he can attend to as he teaches the students.

Daniel has different types of data. His demographic data includes ordinal data on parental education level, and he also has student data on age, grade level, IQ, and socioeconomic status, which are considered interval. All of his data on self-esteem are considered ordinal. Because of the different types of data, Daniel used means and standard deviations on his interval data because he could compute arithmetic on the scores. For his ordinal data, he used medians and semi-interquartile ranges to avoid arithmetic computations on the Likert scale scores.

Think about this: Why did Daniel select the measures of central tendency he did for both demographic data and self-esteem data?

SOURCE: This action research scenario is roughly based on Rubin, D. (2000). *Race and self-esteem: A study of Latino and European-American students with learning disabilities.* Unpublished master's thesis, University of Utah, Salt Lake City.

produced by SPSS Science in Chicago, and SAS/STAT by the SAS Institute in Cary, North Carolina. Such programs have become nearly standard tools for researchers in all areas and greatly reduce some of the more tedious aspects of data analysis. Desktop computers can typically perform the analyses necessary for the vast majority of research projects in education and the social sciences. It is vital, however, that researchers understand which statistical analyses are appropriate for particular types of questions and designs. Computer technology cannot select a particular statistical analysis for a given question. Occasionally a department of educational psychology (or other department that teaches statistics) will use advanced graduate students as statistical consultants. However, depending on such statistical consultants is very risky. These consultants frequently know a lot about statistics and how to operate the computer programs, but they may know little about research design. *You* should know what analysis or analyses you need for your study and ask the consultant (if you are using one) to compute *that* analysis (occasionally they may have to be convinced, but it is your study).

Central Tendency Measures

Data may be summarized and presented in a number of ways. Frequently, it is desirable to be able to characterize group scores with a single index that will provide some idea of how well the group performed. This requires a number that is representative of the group of scores obtained. One type of index commonly used for such group description involves numbers that reflect the concentration of scores, known as central tendency measures. Three measures of central tendency are generally discussed: the **mean,** the **median,** and the **mode.** Each measure has slightly different properties and is useful for different circumstances.

The Mean

Probably the most familiar measure of central tendency is the **mean.** To obtain the mean, or arithmetic average, simply add together all the participants" scores and divide this total by the number of individuals in the group. In a spelling test, the mean might be 25 correctly spelled words. These data might appear like the example in Table 12.1.

TABLE 12.1	**Hypothetical Raw Scores on Spelling Text**
Participant	*X*
1	33
2	6
3	25
4	35
5	10
6	30
7	25
8	32
9	35
10	19
	Total = 250 $\bar{X} = 25$

Raw data scores. The example just given involves a mean calculated on actual raw data scores. This procedure becomes somewhat laborious if many individuals are serving as participants. An alternative is to compute a mean on data that are grouped into intervals, as discussed in Chapter 11 and in the example in Table 12.2. Because each score does not have to be summed individually, the computation is considerably easier. In Table 12.2, we find one additional column over what we saw in a similar table in Chapter 11—fX. The values in the fX column are generated by multiplying the midpoint value (X) by the frequency (f) (e.g., 6 times 52 is 312). The fX values are then totaled and the mean is obtained in the same manner as before, by dividing the total scores (fX total) by the number of individuals (N can be obtained as indicated in the table by adding the f's together, since each f represents a participant). The mean for this example turns out to be 33.29.

Introducing errors into the computation. As you might expect, using the grouped data approach for calculating means introduces a certain amount of error into the computation. This error occurs when scores are assigned the interval midpoint value. Although not serious in most cases, it must be kept in mind when data are being summarized. Because of this potential for error, it is usually preferable to compute raw data means unless the number is so large that the process is simply too cumbersome. If grouped data means are used, the researcher must remember that some error may be present in the means. As noted in Chapter 11, greater error is likely with larger intervals than with smaller intervals since the midpoint of the smaller interval is likely to be closer to a given exact score. Of course, if intervals are reduced considerably, the computation task becomes more laborious, somewhat like with the use of raw data.

Distribution of scores. The mean has occasionally been likened to the fulcrum on a seesaw. This analogy places the mean at the center of gravity or "point of balance" in a distribution of scores (Best & Kahn, 2006; Salkind, 2007). Consider the first example of a mean as presented in Table 12.1. If this distribution of scores were

TABLE 12.2   Hypothetical Example of Grouped Data Approach Used in Computing Means

Score Interval	X	f	fX
60–64	62	2	124
55–59	27	1	27
50–57	52	6	312
45–49	47	10	470
40–44	42	20	840
35–39	37	18	666
30–34	32	19	608
25–29	27	16	432
20–24	22	13	286
15–19	17	9	153
10–14	12	2	24
5–9	7	3	21
0–4	2	1	2
		N = 120	Total = 3,995

FIGURE 12.1   Center of Gravity Effect of Deviations Around Mean

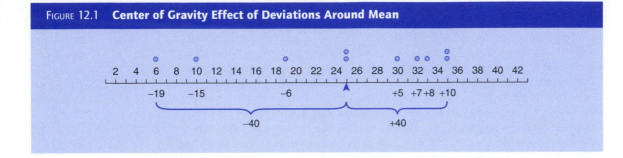

placed on a seesaw, it might appear somewhat like Figure 12.1. The mean of 25 is positioned as the fulcrum with the individual scores represented as weights placed at the appropriate distances from the center. The score deviations away from the mean are then noted as plus and minus values on their respective sides of the fulcrum. These deviations are then summed for each side, and the total minus deviations is equal to the total plus deviations (+40 plus −40). This is characteristic of means as a measure of central tendency and is essentially the formal definition of a mean: *the total signed deviations around a mean equals zero* (+40 added to −40 equals zero).

The Median

A second measure of central tendency is the **median.** The median is a point in the distribution that has exactly the same number of scores above it as below it when all scores are arranged in order. The specific point at which the median exists in a given distribution is slightly different depending on whether the number of individuals in the group (*N*) is odd or even. If *N* is even, then the median is a hypothetical score value midway between the two scores that occupy the midpoint in the distribution. Suppose one wished to determine the median in the series of scores that follows: 3, 5, 6, 9, 10, 12, 14. Because there is an odd number of individuals (N = 7), the score that occupies the midpoint in the distribution becomes the median; in this example it is 9. In another series of scores, determining the median is slightly different. Consider the following: 3, 5, 6, 9, 10, 12, 14, and 16. There is now an even number of scores (*N* = 8), which places the median midway between the two middle scores. In this case, the interval between 9 and 10 is one unit on the scale. Midway between the two would be half of that interval, or 0.5. The median is therefore 9.5.

TABLE 12.3   Illustration of Grouped-Data for Median Determination

Score Interval	f
30–34	2
25–29	1
20–24	6
15–19	10
10–14	9
5–9	2
0–4	2
	N = 32

Grouping by interval. The examples and discussion of medians thus far have involved raw data scores. Medians may also be obtained with data that are grouped by interval. The process is essentially the same. For example purposes, look over Table 12.3. Since N is 32, the median will be at a point where 16 scores fall above and 16 below. Counting individuals up from the bottom in the f column yields $2 + 2 + 9 + 10 = 23$, which is beyond the median point. To obtain exactly 16, some but not all of those cases that fall into the score interval of 15 to 19 must be taken. Looking at the next lower interval, $2 + 2 + 9 = 13$, which is only 3 short of the 16 needed for the median. Therefore, take 3 of the 10 cases in the score interval of 15 to 19. For computation purposes, those 10 scores must be assumed to be spread evenly throughout the interval even though they probably are not in reality. With this assumption, the median point can be determined by proceeding 3/10 of the distance into the interval. Since the interval distance is 5 units, 3/10 of that equals 1.5 units. The 1.5 units must now be added to the lower limit of the score interval of 15 to 19 to obtain the median.

It is important at this point to recall interval limits, which were discussed briefly in Chapter 11. The *exact* limits of any interval are actually midway between the intervals that are usually specified. In Table 12.3, the exact limits for the specified median interval (15 to 19) would be 14.5 to 19.5 (29.5 and 34.5 for interval 30 to 34, 24.5 and 29.5 for interval 25 to 29, and so on). Thus, if 1.5 units are added to the exact lower limit of the median interval (14.5), a score of 16 is obtained, which is the median for this example. (Note that in this example, the median *score* was 16 and that it was also necessary to find the *point* at which 16 scores were above and 16 below—the definition of a median. The two 16s are a coincidence, and obviously other examples might result in differences between the median score and the number of cases needed to obtain that median.)

The grouped data procedure for determining the median is useful when a large number of participants are involved in the study. This approach is considerably easier than ordering the actual scores for many individuals.

The Mode

The third measure of central tendency to be discussed is the **mode.** The mode is simply an indicator of *the most frequent score or interval.* For raw data or actual score distributions, the mode would be defined as that score that occurred most frequently (i.e., more participants obtained that score than any other score). For data grouped into intervals, the midpoint of the most frequently occurring interval is considered to be the mode. For example, in Table 12.3, more scores fell into the interval of 15 to 19 than any other interval. Since the midpoint of that interval is 17, this is considered to be the mode.

Modal frequencies. Occasionally more than one score or interval will appear with high frequencies that look like modes or are close to being modes. If two scores (or intervals) occur more frequently (and with equal frequency) than other scores, a distribution is said to be "bimodal." This term is used somewhat loosely on occasions when the two modes are not precisely equal; the score that occurs most frequently (between the two) is distinguished as the "major mode," whereas the less frequent score is called the "minor mode." A distribution with only one most frequently occurring score is termed "unimodal."

Comments on Central Tendency Measures

As might be expected based on this discussion, the mean, median, and mode have a variety of different properties and are useful in different situations. The type of data collected has a very important influence on which measure is preferred or can be used. Remember our discussion of different data types in Chapter 10? Those major points are operating here as we examine descriptive statistics. If nominal data have been gathered, the mode is the only central tendency description that may be used. Ordinal data, on the other hand, will permit the use of the median as well as the mode. Interval and ratio data, since they both include additivity, permit the computation of a mean in addition to the other central tendency measures.

Some difference of opinion exists regarding firm statements about data types and statistical analyses like those just presented. Over the years, some statisticians have been willing to compute arithmetic on data that do not have additivity, while others have been more reluctant to do so (Gelfand & Drew, 2003; Nanna & Sawilowsky, 1998). Irrespective of where one stands on these matters, a researcher must be concerned about the meaningfulness of the central tendency measure selected. It makes little sense to present a median or mean when categorical data are being scrutinized. Even if numbers are used to designate the categories, they are merely serving as labels and could easily be replaced by letters (e.g., A, B, C) or by any other convenient designation that would permit discrimination. The numbers, therefore, do not say anything about the properties being observed except that they have identity and one can be discriminated from another (there is no underlying continuum of quantity). While you *could* perform arithmetic operations on the label numbers, such manipulation would have no meaning with regard to the property. For example, suppose there are two categories, male and female, designated with numbers 1 and 2. It makes little sense to obtain an arithmetic mean. (What does 1.5 mean in terms of these particular categories?)

Ordinal data do not present such a clear situation as nominal data. Mean ranks found in research literature may or may not be appropriate depending on the situation. Ordinal data varies considerably in terms of how nearly the ranks represent amount or magnitude as well as order. In some cases, the data fit into a lower-level ordinal scale and represent only gross directionality. In such situations, a median is the preferred measure of central tendency. On other occasions, the ranks may represent considerably more concerning magnitude even though exact interval equivalence is not a certainty. Under these circumstances, the use of a mean is meaningful in terms of the property being measured to the degree that magnitude statements have some meaning. Again, researchers must remain cognizant of their purpose— that of being able to say something meaningful about the topic. Just manipulating numbers does not fulfill this purpose.

The mean (average) is the most frequently used measure of central tendency and there are several reasons why. One important reason involves research purposes other than description. If a researcher is conducting an inferential study, he or she will likely want to compute additional analyses on the data. The mean is useful for further arithmetic manipulation and is therefore more useful for many of the additional operations necessary in inferential statistics. The median and mode, on the other hand, are more often terminal descriptive statistics. It should be noted that because of the arithmetic operations involved in computing a mean, interval or ratio data are preferred for this measure of central tendency, since they have the property of additivity.

Depending on the shape of the distribution, the three central tendency measures may have the same or different score values. If the distribution is shaped like the example in Figure 12.2, the mean, median, and mode will have the same score value. This unimodal, symmetrical distribution results in all three central tendency measures being at the same point in the curve.

The distributions that are not both unimodal *and* symmetrical result in a different picture of the central tendency measures' placement. For example, Distribution A in Figure 12.3 is symmetrical but *not* unimodal. In fact, this distribution appears to have the double-hump appearance of a bimodal distribution. Distribution A therefore is characterized by two modes, which makes it impossible for the three central tendency measures to have the same score value. However, the median and

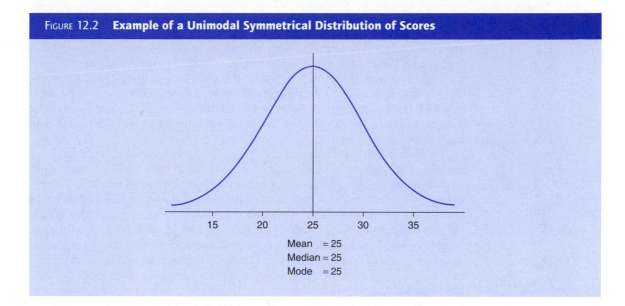

FIGURE 12.2   **Example of a Unimodal Symmetrical Distribution of Scores**

Mean   = 25
Median = 25
Mode   = 25

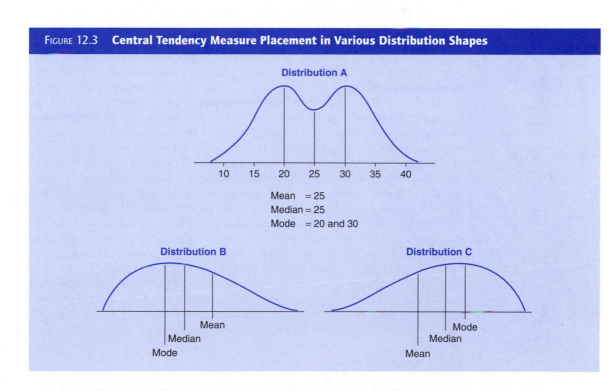

FIGURE 12.3   **Central Tendency Measure Placement in Various Distribution Shapes**

Distribution A

Mean   = 25
Median = 25
Mode   = 20 and 30

Distribution B

Distribution C

mean in Distribution A still have the same score value. This is to be expected when symmetry exists in the way that the scores are distributed.

Distributions B and C in Figure 12.3 represent a different central tendency picture than either of the other examples. Both of these distributions are characterized by being asymmetrical in shape. When distributions are asymmetrically shaped (scores occurring very heavily on one end, tailing off on the other end), they are known as *skewed* distributions. (The direction of the skew is referenced toward the tail or point of the curve.) Distribution B illustrates what is called a positively skewed distribution, whereas Distribution C is an example of a negatively skewed set of scores. Since measurement scales commonly read from left to right in an ascending fashion, the term *positive* is used when the tail is toward the upper end of the scale and *negative* is used when the tail is toward the lower end. Note the positioning of the central tendency measures in skewed Distributions B and C. Such a skew in distributions tends to generate different score values for each of the measures. The mode, as usual, is positioned at the hump or most frequent score. The median is in the middle of the distribution, whereas the mean is nearer the tail than the other measures.

It is evident from the discussion above that all three measures of central tendency may vary from sample to sample with regard to the exact score value that each represents. This will occur because of the way the scores are distributed as well as individual differences in the scores, regardless of distribution shape. The mean tends to be less likely to substantially change position than the median and mode. This greater stability increases the desirability of the mean as a measure of central tendency in most samples. There are, however, occasions when this is not the case. If a particular sample includes a few atypical or extreme scores, the mean may give a distorted picture of the distribution. For example, suppose a sample of individuals is being described in terms of annual income. Say the sample includes primarily those individuals in the middle-income bracket, with the exception of one person who has a multimillion-dollar yearly income. In this case, the mean will show a much higher average income than is actually typical for this group. If such extreme scores are involved in a distribution, the median will provide a more adequate description of central tendency than the mean. It is often advisable to examine more than one measure of central tendency if accurate description is essential. This is particularly important if distributions are skewed as in Distributions B and C in Figure 12.3.

The choice of which measure of central tendency to use depends on what the researchers want to do and how they wish to describe their sample. If the investigators want to guess a given participant's score and to be *exactly correct* for most of the others, the mode is the best score to pick. This is because more participants obtained that score than any other score in the distribution, which raises the likelihood that the researchers would guess exactly right. For purposes of purely descriptive research, the median is a very functional measure. Despite the fact that it is somewhat less stable than the mean, the median is not so affected by extreme scores; therefore, it is often more descriptive of the typical score. In addition, it is easily communicated. Beyond the purpose of descriptive research, if you have inferential purposes as a part of the study, a mean is usually preferred over the median or mode. It uses the data more fully and is used in many further analyses that are often employed in inferential research. As with other areas of the research process, selection of a central tendency measure must be accomplished on the basis of research purpose (Salkind, 2007; Sirkin, 2006). It is inappropriate to rigidly use only a particular measure of central tendency.

Dispersion Measures

Describing a set of scores with central tendency measures furnishes only one description of a distribution, where the performance levels tend to be concentrated. In performing this function, the central tendency measure, whether it is the mean, median, or mode, attempts to characterize the most typical score with a single score.

A second important way of describing scores involves measures of dispersion. Dispersion measures provide an index of *how much variation there is in the scores*—that is, to what degree individual scores depart from the central tendency. By determining where the scores concentrate and to what degree individual performances vary from that concentration, a more complete description of the distribution is provided. In fact, in the absence of a dispersion measure to accompany the central

Simulation

For additional simulations visit www.sagepub .com/drewstudy

Simulation 12.1

Topic: Central tendency measures

Background statement: Descriptive statistics are frequently useful for summarizing group performance. Central tendency measures provide a single index that is representative of the concentration of scores or where the scores tend to be bunched. One of the determining factors in the choice of which central tendency measure should be used is the type of data collected.

Tasks to be performed:

1. Review the stimulus material that follows.

2. Answer the following questions:
    a. What type of data are involved in the example?
    b. What central tendency measure should be used and why?
    c. What score represents the central tendency measure?

Stimulus material: You are a teacher for the sixth-grade science team. The school district has developed an instrument that is supposed to assess your team members in terms of their probability of science fair success. This instrument involves a paper-and-pencil test that has a score possibility of 1 to 7 with 1 being the best possible score and 7 being the worst. These scores are based on ratings of performance by a highly qualified science fair judge who has several years of experience. Your varsity team takes the test, and scores are transmitted to you in the following form:

Name	Score
Peggy	2
Joseph	5
Roberta	7
John	4
Judy	1

Respond to the three questions in the "Tasks to be performed" section.

Write your response, then turn to page 304 for Simulation Feedback 12.1.

tendency, knowledge about any set of scores is limited. An example will illustrate this point. Assume that two groups of students are practicing seriously for a spelling contest. During the last month of practice before the spelling bee, they keep a record of their scores to determine averages that reflect their new skill level. Figure 12.4 illustrates the distribution of scores for both teams. Both teams have the same average (mean) score of 193, yet their spelling performances are considerably different. Team Jordan has an extremely consistent performance (teams adopted their captain's name). They can be relied on to spell about the same number of words correctly each session. They seldom score below 180 but likewise they have seldom

FIGURE 12.4   **Hypothetical Distribution of Spelling Scores for Two Spelling Teams**

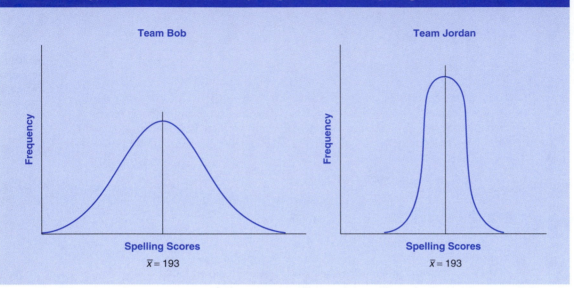

spelled more than 206 words correctly. Team Bob's scores, on the other hand, are all over the place. Although they have the same average score of 193, team performance is erratic. When they are performing well, their score runs well up into the 200s, but during an off session they are fortunate to break 100. During the last month when scores were recorded (for purposes of this book, of course), they scored a 282 the first session and followed with a second session of 104.

Information provided by the central tendency measure in this example is limited. In discussing indicators of variability, three measures of dispersion will be examined: the **range,** the **semi-interquartile range,** and the **standard deviation.** Each provides somewhat different information.

The Range

The range is the simplest and most easily determined measure of dispersion. As suggested by the term, the **range** refers to *the difference between the highest and lowest scores in a distribution.* In our example of the students' spelling bee, the range for Team Jordan would be between 180 and 206, or a 26-word range. Team Bob's range would be between 104 and 282, or a 178-word range.

This example illustrates how easily the range in a set of scores may be determined. The range provides a quick index of variability, which gives additional information beyond the central tendency measure. Unfortunately, the usefulness of the range is somewhat limited because it uses little of the data available in a set of scores. It is determined entirely by the two extreme scores. Since the extreme scores may be highly variable, the range may fluctuate a great deal. Its usefulness is mostly limited to preliminary data inspection. Extreme scores may be due to a number of factors that are not very representative of the participant's usual performance (e.g., physical or emotional trauma or irregularities in circumstances).

The Semi-Interquartile Range

The second measure of dispersion to be examined is the **semi-interquartile range,** which circumvents some of the difficulties noted regarding the range. Before exploring this measure, however, certain related items require attention. First, it is necessary

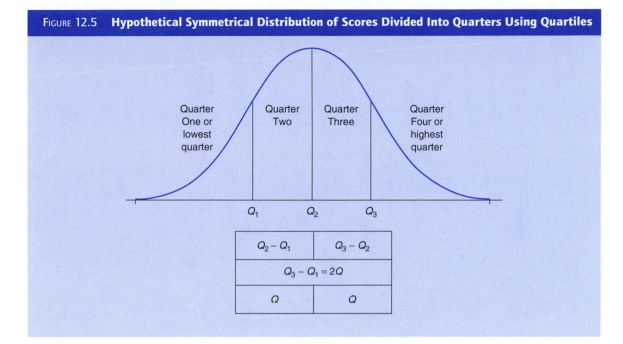

FIGURE 12.5   **Hypothetical Symmetrical Distribution of Scores Divided Into Quarters Using Quartiles**

to distinguish between *quartiles* and *quarters*. The hypothetical distribution illustrated in Figure 12.5 is divided into four sections, or quarters. The *points* used for this division, designated Q_1, Q_2, and Q_3, are known as quartiles. Thus, the *quartiles are points on the measurement scale that serve to divide a distribution of scores into four equal parts.* A participant's score may fall *in* a given quarter or *at* a given quartile, but not in a quartile, since the quartile represents a point on the scale.

Strictly defined, the semi-interquartile range is *half the range in scores represented by the middle 50% of the scores.* Look again at Figure 12.5 to examine this definition more closely. The middle 50% of the scores in this distribution represents those scores between Q_1 and Q_3. To establish the first and third quartiles, a simple counting procedure is involved. Q_1 is determined by counting up from the bottom of the distribution until a fourth of the scores have been encountered. If there were 48 participants in the total group, then a fourth of that would be 12. The 12th score up from the lowest would be at the first quartile. Similarly, the 12th score down from the highest would be at the third quartile. Midway between these two points is the second quartile or Q_2. Note that since Q_2 is the middle-most score in the distribution, it is also the median. The semi-interquartile range is represented by Q_1 minus Q_3, divided by two, or

$$\frac{Q_3 - Q_1}{2} = \text{Semi-interquartile range}$$

For example, if Q_1 was at 36 in the hypothetical distribution of scores and Q_3 was at 92, then the semiinterquartile range would be $92 - 36 = 56/2 = 28$ score units. The semi-interquartile range is generally represented by Q, therefore in the example $Q = 28$.

If the distribution is symmetrical like the one in Figure 12.5, the semi-interquartile range is the same as either $Q_2 - Q_1$ or $Q_3 - Q_2$. This changes, however, if an asymmetrical or skewed distribution exists as exemplified by Figure 12.6.

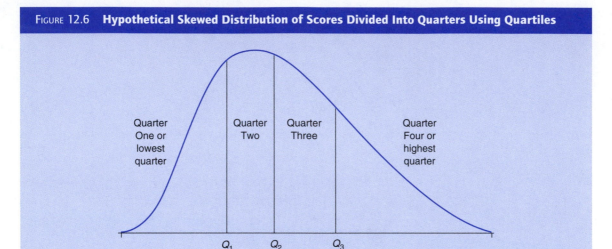

FIGURE 12.6 **Hypothetical Skewed Distribution of Scores Divided Into Quarters Using Quartiles**

The semi-interquartile range is a measure of dispersion that is easily determined and does not involve complicated computational operations. It is superior to the range as a dispersion index. It is a more stable measure, primarily because it uses more of the available data than the range. As such, it provides a much more complete picture as to how the scores are distributed along the scale of measurement.

The Standard Deviation

The third measure of dispersion to be discussed is the **standard deviation** (*SD*). By far the most commonly used index of variability, the *SD* involves somewhat more complicated computational procedures. The *SD* may be thought of as *a measure of variability in the scores around the mean.* The mean is therefore the reference point, and the *SD* provides a description of the distribution of individual scores around that point. In fact, the actual deviation of each score from the mean (mean − *X*) is used in calculating the *SD*. The *SD*, in one sense, might be thought of as an average of all the deviations from the mean. Let us turn to Figure 12.7 for an illustration to facilitate this discussion.

The *SD* is expressed in score units and represents a width index along the measurement scale. The width of this index becomes greater when the scores are more variable and narrower as the scores are more concentrated around the mean. Referring back to our spelling contest example, the *SD* of Team Bob's scores will be considerably larger (wider) than that of Team Jordan's scores. Team Bob's distribution looks like the illustration in Figure 12.7, whereas Team Jordan's scores are much more concentrated. Although this example involves two distributions of scores in two groups, it is obvious that several measures recorded on an individual would also result in a distribution of scores and can be conceived in the same fashion. Variation of a group of people is called interindividual variability, whereas variation of scores on one student is termed *intra*individual variablility.

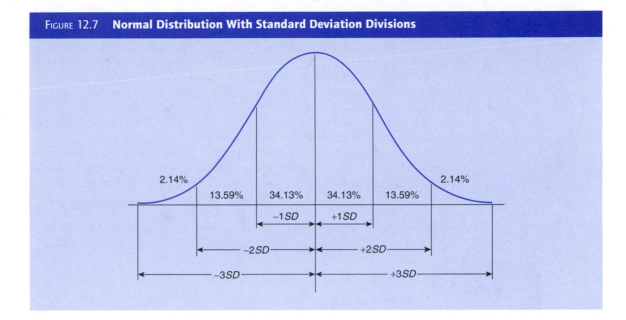

FIGURE 12.7   **Normal Distribution With Standard Deviation Divisions**

Figure 12.7 represents a set of scores that are normally distributed. The term *normal* in this context should not be viewed literally with other distribution shapes being thought of as abnormal. It is actually defined in terms of certain mathematical properties that determine the distribution's shape and was not developed as a description of actual events in the real world. A more descriptive term might be "bell-shaped" distribution. Note the percentages indicated for each standard deviation in Figure 12.7. These percentages remain constant for any set of normally distributed scores. For a normal distribution, about 68% of the scores will fall between +1 and −1 *SD*. (This also translates into 68% of the area under the curve.)

Comments on Dispersion Measures

Several issues are involved in the selection of a preferred measure of dispersion. If a quick and easily computed index is needed, the order of preference is range, semi-interquartile range, and *SD*. However, using convenience as the sole criterion for selection is questionable. The most stable and reliable index of dispersion is the *SD*, followed by the semi-interquartile range, with the range being the least stable measure. Likewise, if additional statistical computation beyond description is needed (e.g., inferential studies such as group comparisons) and the type of data permit, the *SD* should be the choice.

Somewhat like the mean, the *SD* is affected by a few atypical, extreme performances (highly skewed distribution). When such a situation exists, the *SD* does not provide as accurate a description of score dispersion as the semi-interquartile range. Therefore, if an extremely skewed distribution is obtained, *Q* is preferable over the *SD*. *Q* is frequently viewed as a natural dispersion companion when the median is used for central tendency.

Consideration must also be given to the type of data collected when selecting a measure of dispersion. If the *SD* is to be used, data must have the property of additivity. This would limit the use of the *SD* to interval and ratio data. The range and *Q* may also be used with interval and ratio data, but the *SD* requires at least interval data. If ordinal data are collected, range and *Q* may be used. Nominal data, however, present a rather different situation, since the only property present is identity. Since measures of dispersion assess variability along some assumed continuum, they are not useful for data without such a continuum. There is no continuum of measurement in nominal data and so a measure of dispersion does not make sense. Therefore, when working with nominal data, descriptive summaries are best accomplished using the mode and thereby determining which category(ies) received the concentration of responses. Beyond this, description can probably best be done using frequency graphs for each category.

Although guidelines have been presented here concerning which dispersion measure may be used under what conditions, considerable judgment is required on the part of the researcher. As in other areas of the research process, rigid rules are not applicable. If the *Q* will provide a more accurate description than the *SD* (despite available interval data), then it should be used. The basic purpose of *accurate description* must be kept in mind when determining which tool to select.

Simulation

For additional
simulations visit
www.sagepub
.com/drewstudy

Simulation 12.2

Topic: Descriptive statistics

Background statement: You have been asked to analyze data obtained from a class evaluation completed by university students. The form provides several items to which the student must respond on a 1 to 7 scale. The descriptive anchors for the scale are as follows: 1 = not much, 7 = very much. What type of data is involved? What descriptive statistical tools would you use and why?

Write your response, then turn to page 304 for Simulation Feedback 12.2.

Chapter Summary

✦ Measures of central tendency are statistical computations that describe where the scores are concentrated or tend to bunch together.

✦ The mean is probably the most familiar measure of central tendency and is the arithmetic average of all the scores. The median is a point in the distribution that has exactly the same number of scores above it as below it when all scores are arranged in order. The mode is the most frequently occurring score. The mean requires interval or ratio data since arithmetic is used on the scores. The median is well suited for ordinal data but may also be used on interval or ratio data. The mode can be used for nominal, ordinal, interval, or ratio data.

✦ Measures of dispersion are statistical computations that describe the amount of variability among the scores in the group.

✦ The range is a measure of dispersion that reflects the difference between the highest and lowest scores in a distribution. The semi-interquartile range is half the range in scores represented by the middle 50% of the scores. The standard deviation is a measure of variability in the scores around the mean. The standard deviation is a companion dispersion measure when the mean is used and requires interval or ratio data because arithmetic is used in computation. The semi-interquartile range is a natural companion for the median, and is useful for ordinal data but can also be used with interval or ratio data. The range may be used with ordinal, interval, or ratio data.

Key Terms

Central tendency measures. Statistical computations that describe where the scores tend to bunch together.

Dispersion measures. Statistical computations that describe the amount of variability among the scores in the group.

Mean. The arithmetic average of all the scores.

Median. A point in the distribution that has exactly the same number of scores above it as below it when all scores are arranged in order.

Mode. The most frequently occurring score.

Range. A measure of dispersion that reflects the difference between the highest and lowest scores in a distribution. The range may be used with ordinal, interval, or ratio data.

Semi-interquartile range. Half the range in scores represented by the middle 50% of the scores. The semi-interquartile range is a natural companion for the median, and is useful for ordinal data but can also be used with interval or ratio data.

Standard deviation. A measure of variability in the scores around the mean. The standard deviation is a companion dispersion measure when the mean is used and requires interval or ratio data because arithmetic is used in computation.

Student Study Site

The companion Web site for *Designing and Conducting Research in Education*
www.sagepub.com/drewstudy

Supplement your review of this chapter by going to the companion Web site to take one of the practice quizzes, use the flashcards to study key terms, and check out the many other study aids you'll find there. You'll even find some research articles from the Sage Full-Text Collection and a step-by-step guide that will show you how to read an educational research article.

Simulation Feedback

For additional simulations visit www.sagepub .com/drewstudy

Simulation Feedback 12.1

The data presented are ordinal data since they are generated from a rating scale that does provide evidence of greater than and less than but does not provide information concerning the interval between any two scores. This is the type of example that was used in discussing ordinal data in Chapter 10 as well as in previous simulations.

The central tendency measure of choice for these data is the median. This choice is based on the fact that the median does not require arithmetic operations such as adding, subtracting, or dividing. These operations generally should not be performed on ordinal data since the property of additivity is not present. The median is preferable over the mode for ordinal data, although both may be used.

The score representing the median in this example is 4.

Simulation Feedback 12.2

The data can be considered no more than an ordinal-level measurement. This is particularly true with the loose anchoring of the two ends of the scale and only vague terminology. Ordinal data have the properties of identity and order, and the statistical tools of choice would probably be the median and the semi-interquartile range. You would probably be in error to compute means and standard deviations because of the obvious lack of the property of additivity in the data. Certainly a mode and range could also be obtained, although they would not tell as much as the median and the semi-interquartile range.

13

INFERENTIAL STATISTICS

After reading Chapter 13, you should be able to do the following:

✦ Describe what statistical significance means for the researcher.

✦ Describe when parametric statistics can be used and when nonparametric statistics are used.

✦ Describe the types of considerations involved in selecting statistical analyses for difference questions.

✦ Describe the types of considerations involved in selecting statistical analyses for relationship questions.

General Background of Inferential Statistics

As noted earlier, many quantitative studies have a purpose beyond mere description. Commonly called *inferential studies,* they have a goal of interpreting the data and inferring about some setting, participants, or materials other than those that were directly involved in the completed study. Some of these studies are testing the application of a theory, model, or body of knowledge in a new setting or with participants that have not previously been investigated. In other cases, studies may be investigating the effectiveness of one or more treatments or instructional techniques. Such studies are often called inferential because of the suggestions that are generated or inferred from the results.

Certain issues like those examined with descriptive statistics also warrant discussion for inferential statistics. One of the first involves what they are and what they do. Inferential statistics, like those used for descriptive research, are tools for analyzing data in a way that will answer the question being asked. The questions asked by inferential studies are often placed in the form of hypotheses. The researchers will formally or informally state a hypothesis, for instance, about whether or not there are likely to be differences in performance between students receiving two different types of instruction. For this reason, these statistics are also used for hypothesis testing. They are used for determining whether there is a significant difference between groups (in the case of a difference question) or whether there is a significant relationship (in the case of a relationship question).

It was mentioned early in this book that three types of questions are typically studied in behavioral research—descriptive, difference, and relationship. Chapter 12 explored statistical procedures used for descriptive studies. This chapter will focus on the two remaining types of questions—difference and relationship. These general categories of research questions are often involved in inferential research. You will find that a wide variety of specific research questions may be studied within these two types.

Defining Statistical Significance

The statistical techniques used for inferential research essentially tell a researcher whether the results obtained are different from those that might have been obtained by chance. Stated a different way, these statistical tools tell the researcher what the probability is that chance could have generated the results. This is an important piece of information since the investigator would like to infer or interpret that the treatment generated the observed performance. For example, suppose a researcher is comparing the effectiveness of three instructional methods—A, B, and C. Students in the group receiving Method C performed better on the test than did those receiving either A or B. It is important to know whether the difference was most likely caused by the treatment or whether it represents normal variation in performance due to chance. If the differences are sufficiently dramatic to suggest a low probability (5% or less) that this result was caused by chance, then the differences are called **statistically significant.** Since the probability of chance is low, the researcher is inclined to infer or interpret that significant differences are the result of the effectiveness of the instructional methods. To determine what the probability of chance is, the investigator applies a statistical test to the data. Thus, in inferential research, statistics are the means researchers use to examine their data and determine whether chance or the treatment probably generated the results. This cannot be established by merely inspecting the raw data visually.

Chance of Probability

We mentioned that a chance probability of 5% or less is usually considered to be statistically significant, but a brief expansion on this statement is appropriate here. You may have seen notation like $P < .05$ and $P < .01$ in reading research reports. The "P" refers to probability, and the statement as a whole means that the probability is less than 5% (5 times out of 100) that the obtained results are caused by chance (or 1% if $< .01$ is used). The flip side of that statement is that results such as these will be due to the treatment 95% of the time, or 95 times out of 100.

Use of 5% as the cutoff point for statistical significance is actually arbitrary. This level was used early in the development of statistical procedures in behavioral science and has continued more out of tradition than because of any specific logic. Some researchers have asserted that a more logical basis should exist for determining what is and is not considered statistically significant. Despite these arguments, however, the 5% probability level of chance persists as the generally accepted upper limit for results to be considered statistically significant in most behavioral sciences.

Several statistical techniques are used in inferential studies. At times it may seem that the number and variety of statistical tests is never ending, particularly to the beginning student. Since there are so many different research questions that can be studied, many different tools are needed for these different problems. Just as the mechanic cannot make a screwdriver turn a nut, the researcher cannot make an inappropriate statistical test fit the question. To take the analogy a step further, the mechanic cannot remove *only* screws and expect to disassemble an automobile. Likewise, researchers cannot ask *only* those particular research questions for which they have statistics and expect to fully investigate a problem. In both cases, a full range of tools must either be in hand or within reach (whether it be the toolbox or the reference book).

For the most part, many statistical tests merely represent variations on a few basic themes. This chapter will essentially focus on the basic themes of statistical tests and indicate what types of variations are appropriate under what conditions. Only the more commonly used analyses will be discussed. The interested student may consult any one of many statistical texts for specifics regarding a particular technique that is not fully detailed in this volume.

Parametric and Nonparametric Issues

Two general categories of statistics are used in inferential studies: parametric and nonparametric tests. Both of these types of analyses are used to determine whether the results are likely to be due to chance or to the variable(s) under study. The same types of research questions may be studied using parametric or nonparametric statistics. Thus, parametric or nonparametric analyses may be used for studies that investigate either relationship questions or difference questions. Selection of the appropriate statistical analysis as far as parametric versus nonparametric tests depends on the nature of the data being collected (i.e., nominal, ordinal, interval, or ratio), the size of the sample, and certain assumptions about the population. **Parametric statistics** represent a general category of analyses that involve selected assumptions about the population of scores, generally use arithmetic and therefore require interval or ratio data, and typically need more participants than do nonparametric analyses. **Nonparametric statistics** represent a second general category of analyses that include fewer assumptions about the population of scores, can often be computed with ordinal or nominal data, and may be used with fewer participants than required by parametric analyses.

Assumptions

When a researcher collects data on participants, the data involve recording one or more scores on each individual. These scores represent a sample of all such possible scores in the universe. For example, recording the scores of 30 different participants would result in 30 different scores. This might be the case, for example, if you had groups of students competing in a spelling bee. These 30 scores represent a sample of all possible different spelling scores in the population. The population scores have certain characteristics or values such as a mean and a standard deviation (*SD*), and they are distributed in a particular manner.

Parametric statistics require a number of assumptions about the nature of the population from which the sample scores were drawn (Miles & Banyard, 2007; Salkind, 2007). For example, a given parametric statistic may require that the scores be normally distributed in the population. For that particular statistic to be appropriate, this assumption must be met or true, otherwise results of the computation may not be accurate. The population values (e.g., mean, distribution, and *SD*) are known as parameters, and because this category of statistics requires assumptions about these values, they are called parametric statistics.

Due to the fact that all the scores in the population are not recorded, a researcher has no way of verifying what the precise parameters are. Consequently, parameters or population values usually exist only in theory. Unless there is other information available (e.g., some massive study that previously recorded scores on the entire population), these values are truly assumptions. They are assumed to exist in a particular form that is in harmony with the requirements of the statistic that the researcher wishes to use. If, however, there is reason to believe (either based on logic or previous information) that the population values do not conform to the requirements of a given statistic, the researcher would be in error to use that analysis.

The above statements should not be interpreted to mean that a researcher may capriciously choose a statistical analysis and decide that the assumptions are met by the data. These assumptions must not only be reasonable but also supportable. If the soundness of any assumption is questionable, then a given statistical analysis should not be used. For this reason, the use of nonparametric statistics is very helpful in certain circumstances. Nonparametric statistics require fewer assumptions regarding the nature of the population from which the scores are drawn. It is not that no assumptions at all are involved, but rather that the nature of the population from which the scores were sampled is less frequently important. Requirements for nonparametric statistics more often involve the type of data and make fewer references to the population than parametric analyses.

One of the differences between parametric and nonparametric statistics involves the assumptions that must be met. For parametric statistics to be appropriate, a researcher must be able to reasonably assume that certain characteristics are true about the population from which the scores were drawn (Miles & Banyard, 2007; Salkind, 2007). Specific assumptions necessary for particular analyses will be noted later in this chapter as specific tests are presented. Nonparametric statistics do not, in general, require as many or as rigorous assumptions.

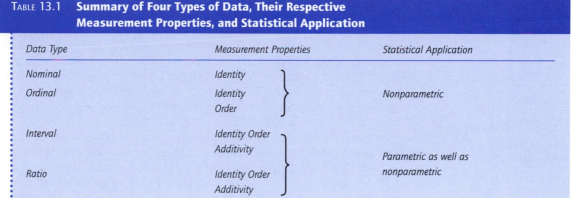

TABLE 13.1   **Summary of Four Types of Data, Their Respective Measurement Properties, and Statistical Application**

Data Type	Measurement Properties	Statistical Application
Nominal	Identity	Nonparametric
Ordinal	Identity Order	
Interval	Identity Order Additivity	Parametric as well as nonparametric
Ratio	Identity Order Additivity	

Nature of the Data

An additional difference between parametric and nonparametric statistical analyses involves the nature of the collected data. Four types of data were discussed in Chapter 10: nominal, ordinal, interval, and ratio. Each of these types of data was described as having different measurement properties. Nominal data have the property of identity; ordinal data have identity and order; and interval and ratio scales have identity, order, and additivity. These properties are important in terms of what statistical analyses can be appropriately performed (Dowdy, Wearden, & Chilko, 2004; Urdan, 2005). Table 13.1 presents the four data types with their respective measurement properties and indicates the appropriate application of parametric and nonparametric analyses.

As indicated in Table 13.1, the use of parametric statistics is limited to data that are either interval or ratio in nature. This limitation is dictated by the arithmetic operations involved in the computation of parametric statistics. These analyses require math manipulations on the actual score values such as addition and subtraction, as well as others that require the property of additivity. Without this property such arithmetic is meaningless, as the math computations are not an accurate representation of real-world events. For example, a student's ranking in class can show how he or she performs relative to classmates, but adding the ranks of students together makes no sense because the resulting number does not represent an actual performance level. Nonparametric statistics can be used with ordinal and nominal data, because they do not require such arithmetic manipulation on the actual score values. They may also be used with interval or ratio scales, as these data types satisfy the computational requirements of these analyses. If, however, other necessary characteristics are present in interval or ratio data samples (e.g., distribution assumptions, adequate sample size), parametric statistics are generally preferred as they are more powerful and make more efficient use of data.

The type of data recorded is, therefore, important in determining selection of the statistical analysis to be used. If a researcher collects data that are nominal or ordinal (e.g., yes-no or male-female categories; ranking or 1 to 5 rating scales, respectively), nonparametric analyses should probably be used (Miles & Banyard, 2007; Salkind, 2007; Urdan, 2005). If interval or ratio data are available, either parametric or nonparametric statistics may be employed. The decision in the latter case is made on other factors such as distribution assumptions (previously examined in a general fashion) and sample size.

Sample Size

As suggested by previous comments, the sample size is also important when selecting a statistical analysis. If few participants are used for experimentation (e.g., $N = 6$ to 8), there is little alternative—nonparametric analyses are more appropriate. Such a small number of participants does not represent much of a sample of behavior. With this limited sample, the mathematical operations required by parametric statistics (e.g., computation of means) become very questionable as to accuracy. Unless replicated several times with only six participants, there is the distinct possibility that an atypical sample has been drawn and that the performance is not at all representative. Although this is always a problem, the use of parametric statistics may suggest a false sense of security regarding the accuracy of the portrayal.

This raises an immediate and practical question. What is an adequate sample size for using parametric statistics? If a definitive answer were available, this section could have been much shorter. However, judging from the massive amount of literature available in the statistical area, such an answer is not possible. It has been our general rule of thumb that groups (n's) of less than 12 or 14 are questionable in terms of using parametric statistics for comparisons. This means that if two groups are being compared (Treatments A and B), then each group should contain minimally 12 to 14 participants before parametric tests may be used confidently. Certainly using 15 and even 20 per group increases the comfort with which the parametric mathematics may be performed, but the concern here is minimums. "Rules of thumb" are, of course, not hard and fast rules. Researchers must use their best judgment and consultation resources. The fact remains that with n's smaller than those noted above, the confidence in parametric analyses is substantially reduced, and nonparametric statistics are preferred.

Thus far, parametric and nonparametric statistical analyses have primarily been discussed in terms of group studies that use traditional experimental designs. This type of research has historically made greater use of statistical analysis than have investigations using single-subject experimental designs or many nonexperimental studies. There is, however, a continuing interest in the application of statistical procedures that are not traditional group studies (e.g., Anderson, 2002; Lall & Levin, 2004; Maris & Maris, 2003). The interested student may wish to consult these references for more detailed information regarding the use of statistical analyses in single-subject investigations.

Comments on Parametric and Nonparametric Statistics

As noted above, three general areas are important in selecting parametric versus nonparametric analyses: (1) assumptions about the nature of the population distribution, (2) the type of data that are collected, and (3) the sample size. In all of these areas, parametric statistics have been the standard and have been more rigorous in terms of requirements. *Parametric analyses require more stringent assumptions about the population distribution of scores, necessitate more sophisticated data, and require larger sample sizes.* This does not, however, imply that nonparametric analyses are a panacea for researchers who do not wish to attend to these factors. Nonparametric statistics do not represent tools that may be applied in a capricious manner, with an expectation of the same outcome.

The main advantage of nonparametric statistics involves the characteristics already described. They may be used in situations in which knowledge is lacking concerning the population distribution or in which the necessary assumptions for parametric analyses cannot be met. They may also be used in studies in which small samples are drawn and with more primitive types of data. If, however, *the necessary requirements for parametric statistics are met, they are preferred over nonparametric analyses* for a variety of reasons. Parametric statistics are more powerful than nonparametric analyses when they can be used. More *powerful* means that parametric statistics are more likely to detect a significant difference when there is one, or a significant relationship if there is one, than nonparametric statistics. Moreover, they make more efficient use of data. If the data are interval or ratio in scale, nonparametric analyses do not effectively use the information (Dowdy et al., 2004; Goodwin,

2005; Urdan, 2005). One further advantage offered by parametric statistics involves greater flexibility with regard to the types of research questions to which they may be applied. This is particularly evident with more complex studies in which more than one variable is under investigation. Thus, when it is possible to satisfy the requirements for parametric analyses, they should be favored over nonparametric statistics. When this is not possible, the use of nonparametrics provides the researcher with an alternative that is much more powerful than visual inspection of the data.

DIFFERENCE QUESTIONS: WHICH STATISTIC AND WHEN?

From the beginning of this text, a distinction has been made between difference and relationship questions. By way of review, difference questions are involved in studies that *compare*. Such comparisons may be made between the performances of two or more groups (e.g., where the groups receive different treatments or where the groups are compared on a survey regarding something like annual income), within a group but between different conditions (e.g., pretest-posttest experiments or answers to questions before and after an election), or within a single participant but between different treatment conditions (e.g., baseline–treatment–reversal comparisons). Relationship questions, on the other hand, explore the degree to which two or more phenomena relate or vary. This type of investigation might ask, "As intelligence varies, what *tends* to happen to reading ability?" As intelligence increases in a group, does reading ability tend to also increase, or does it tend to decrease? (Another example mentioned earlier involved length of marriage, perhaps measured in years, and annual net income measured in dollars.) Relationship studies involve recording data from two or more measures on a sample of participants (e.g., both intelligence and reading scores). With these two measures on each individual, the researcher then computes a correlation coefficient to determine how the two variables relate in the group. It is important to emphasize that the researcher is determining how they relate, *not* comparing them to each other.

Difference questions and relationship questions require two distinctly different types of statistical approaches. The purpose of the present section is to discuss difference questions and the type of statistical analyses employed for their data analysis. (Relationship statistics will be presented in a subsequent section of this chapter.) Many variations and combinations of difference questions may be asked. For nearly any type of difference question that can be invented, there are statistical techniques that may be appropriately applied. In the course of this discussion, both parametric and nonparametric analyses will be noted.

As we proceed we will refer repeatedly to Table 13.2, a summary of inferential statistics used for difference questions. This is a very important chart that you will need for simulations and as a reference throughout the rest of the discussion in this chapter. It is also a handy tool when you need to select statistical analyses in other situations like your thesis or dissertation. You will see that Table 13.2 is arranged in several columns. The left-hand column is labeled "Type of Analysis" and includes points related to (1) how many data points or groups are being compared (i.e., two groups, more than two groups), (2) types of data and parametric versus nonparametric statistics, and (3) the number of experimental variables in the study. The term data points is used to designate the number of groups compared because you won't always be comparing means—in some cases you will be comparing groups or *data points* where medians are used or some other summary. The other three columns have a general label of "Type of Comparison" with specific labels for each of the three columns—"Independent," "Nonindependent," and "Mixed." We discussed these types of designs before, and now we find that different analyses are needed for the

TABLE 13.2	**Summarized Inferential Statistics for Difference Questions**		

	Type of Comparison		
Type of Analysis	*Independent*	*Nonindependent*	*Mixed*
Two data points			
Parametric	z test t test for independent means	t test for nonindependent means	
Nonparametric			
Nominal data	Fisher exact probability test Chi-square test	McNemar test for significance for changes	
Ordinal data	Median test Mann-Whitney U test	Sign test Wilcoxon matched-pairs signed-ranks test	
More than two data points			
One experimental variable			
Parametric	One-way ANOVA (indep.)	One-way ANOVA (repeated measures)	
Nonparametric			
Nominal data	Chi-square test for k ind. comparisons	Cochran's Q test	
Ordinal data	Median test Kruskal-Wallis test	Friedman test	
Two experimental variables	Two-way ANOVA (indep.)		Two-way ANOVA (mixed)

independent comparisons (e.g., where you have different groups), **nonindependent comparisons** (e.g., repeated-measures comparisons), and mixed comparisons (designs that have both independent and repeated comparisons). Using Table 13.2 is easy: you determine how many groups or data points are being compared in the left column, then you move to the right to the appropriate column for independent, nonindependent, or mixed comparisons. After you have done that, you answer several questions about the study, like what type of data are collected (nominal, ordinal, interval, or ratio), and select the specific test inside the chart (like a t test for independent means, or a Mann-Whitney U test). Using the chart in Table 13.2 takes a little practice but becomes very easy after a few simulations.

Comparing Two Data Points

The first type of difference question to be examined involves comparing two data points or groups (left column in Table 13.2). Once again, the term *data point* refers to a performance record, or summarized scores, such as a group mean or a median. The two data points could be summarized performance records on two groups (e.g., mean correct responses by Groups A and B, median ranking by Groups A and B), two performances by the same group (e.g., in a pre-post investigation), or two summaries of performances by a single participant (e.g., baseline performance mean compared to postintervention performance in a behavior modification experiment). There are obviously several variations on these types of arrangements from our earlier design plans and from what you see in Table 13.2. We will move inside Table 13.2 as we actually choose which analysis to compute.

Independent Comparisons

Throughout this book, examples of two group comparisons with one experimental variable have been used. (Group A receives one treatment, Group B receives a second treatment, and the experimental variable is the method of treatment.) This is one of the simplest types of experiments and has a single focus: "Is there a difference in effectiveness between Treatment Method A and B?" Other things being equal, this question becomes, "Does Group A perform differently from Group B?" The term *independent* indicates that the scores under Condition A are not affected by or do not affect those in Condition B. For practical purposes, this means different participants constitute the two groups (not the case with, say, a pre-post investigation). If you have two different groups in your study, it is pretty safe to assume the performances are independent. If you have pretest and posttest scores on the same group, they are probably not independent because the scores being compared are from the same subjects with measures at two different times. The Research in Action box presents an example of action research where the researcher uses inferential statistics to compare two independent groups that are receiving different reading instruction.

Two groups may be compared in studies where the researcher has a weaker data scale (nominal or ordinal measurement) or few participants per group or both. As mentioned earlier, either the data (nominal, ordinal) *or* the small number of participants (fewer than 12 to 14 per group) will require the use of nonparametric statistics. Under other conditions in which interval data are approximated, the required distribution assumptions are reasonable, and if a more adequate sample is tested, parametric analyses are appropriate.

Parametric analysis. For comparison studies where interval or ratio data are recorded, it is common to compare the mean of the scores obtained by Group A with the mean of Group B. This process is testing for differences between two independent means. Since means are being specified, it is assumed that the appropriate data have been recorded that will permit the necessary mathematical manipulations.

Two parametric statistics are available for this situation: the z test and the t test for differences between independent means. The z test is useful for samples with group sizes of more than 30 individuals. The t test is similar to the z test except that it is also applicable for groups equal to or less than 30. Since the t test is more flexible in terms of the number of participants (e.g., $n = 12$ to 30 or above), it is almost always used to compare two means.

The t test requires interval or ratio data and group samples (n's) of about 12 or more. In addition to these requirements, the t test assumes that the criterion measure scores are normally distributed, and that both groups also have equal variation in terms of the criterion measure. If these assumptions are reasonable (or if there is little reason to believe that they are drastically violated), the t test for differences is a powerful and convenient analysis for comparing two independent means. It is simple to compute, and formulas may be found in nearly any statistics text (e.g., Dowdy et al., 2004; Salkind, 2007). Remember that the test to be used is the t test for differences between independent means. The reason for this emphasis becomes obvious later as another type of t test is examined.

Nonparametric analysis. Nonparametric statistical analyses may be used under certain conditions in which parametric statistics cannot be applied. For situations in which two independent data points are to be compared, there are analyses that can be used with both nominal and ordinal data. Two nonparametric analyses will be mentioned for investigations in which nominal data have been recorded. Recall that nominal data are characterized by categorical representation of events. For example, yes-no responses on a questionnaire and performances that are scored as pass-fail or successful-unsuccessful would be considered nominal data.

RESEARCH IN ACTION

KEY POINTS IN THE CHAPTER REFLECTED IN THIS BOX:

- Consider the type of question, the type of data, and the sample size as major elements in selecting an inferential statistical analysis.
- Different statistical analyses may be used for different elements or questions within a single action research study.

For more research in action tips visit www.sagepub .com/drewstudy

OBJECTIVES TO LEARN FROM THIS BOX:

- The usefulness of a diagram in conceptualizing a research question and determining which statistical analysis to use
- The cumulative process of decision making in selecting a statistical analysis

Emily is conducting an action research study that compares two approaches to reading instruction, one that emphasizes student engagement called concept-oriented reading instruction (CORI) and a second that focuses on drill and practice (DAP). She views her research question as a difference question that compares students who are engaged with those who are not engaged and sees this as a comparison of two groups of students. A diagram for Emily's action research study is shown below. She is collecting a variety of types of data but one type that is very important to her is reading test scores. Her research will need to answer the question of how well the students perform on reading tests if it is to effectively translate into action in the classroom. The data for reading scores involves the number correct on a test, which is probably ratio and certainly interval data. Emily has finished collecting data with 30 participants per group, which is a healthy *n* for her study. Because of her data type, her *n*, and her question, Emily will use a t-*test for comparing independent means* as an inferential statistic for this particular question. Her basic study design portrayed in the diagram below is a constant in her study. She will use this same design with other elements of her overall study, and the statistical analysis may change depending on the type of data collected for each subquestion.

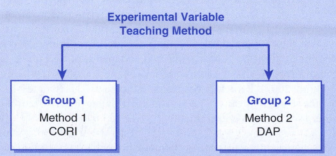

Think about this: How do the elements of type of question, data type, and number of participants become important in the decision-making process of selecting an inferential statistical analysis?

SOURCE: This action research scenario is roughly based on the work of John Guthrie at the University of Maryland and Emily Anderson Swan at the University of Utah (Guthrie & Anderson, 1999; Swan, 2003).

TABLE 13.3	Example of How Comparisons Might Be Made Using the Fisher Exact Probability Test	
	Performance Categories	
Groups	Pass	Fail
A	n	n
B	n	n

If a small number of participants are used (total N less than 20), a useful statistic for comparing two groups is the Fisher exact probability test. This test might be used in comparing, say, Groups A and B if the data collected involved categories (scores) such as pass versus fail. Table 13.3 illustrates how such a comparison might be made. Fisher's test is simple to compute (Urdan, 2005). If the sample is large, however, the computation becomes laborious for calculations by hand. In situations in which N is greater than 20, it is much easier to use the chi-square (X^2) test for comparing independent samples.

The chi-square test for two independent samples, like Fisher's exact probability test, is used with nominal data. The previous example (Groups A and B that had performance categorized as either pass or fail) also works well as an illustration for the chi-square test. The question is stated as follows: "Does Group A differ from Group B in terms of how many participants passed as opposed to how many failed?" The chi-square test is preferred when N is greater than 20. This test requires a cell (group) size (n) of at least five. Therefore, in Table 13.3 none of the categories (e.g., Group A, passed; Group B, failed) should have less than five individuals categorized like that if the chi-square test is to be used. If this occurs, such as Group B having only three individuals who passed, Fisher's test should be applied instead. Computational procedures for the chi-square may be found in a number of statistics texts (e.g., Goodwin, 2005; Urdan, 2005).

Using Table 13.2, both the Fisher exact probability test and the chi-square test are found in the second column under "Independent Comparison." To find the vertical coordinates, look in the far left column at the listing for "Nonparametric." The first line under that listing is for nominal data and the two tests just discussed are found to the right under the "Independent" column. This is a good example of using Table 13.2. You are comparing two data points—Groups A and B—(look in the left column), your data are nominal (move down the left column to where you find nominal data for comparing two data points); and finally, your comparison is independent because the two groups are different participants. Move your finger over to the second column, which represents Independent comparisons, and there you find the Fisher exact probability test and the chi-square test.

Two nonparametric analyses will also be mentioned briefly for studies where ordinal data have been collected. Remember, ordinal data are characterized by the ability to rank order events on the basis of an underlying continuum. The ranks indicate greater than or less than on the dimension being assessed—a property that is not necessarily characteristic of categories. The example of a rating scale of 1 to 5 is often used for ordinal data. You may wish to refer back to Chapter 10 for additional review and examples.

When data are in an ordinal scale, two groups may be compared using the median test. Using the previous example again, this analysis addresses the question of whether there is a difference between the medians of Group A and Group B. The median test may be used with a variety of sample sizes. Individuals interested in computational procedures should consult any of the nonparametric texts that provide details on this technique (e.g., Levin & Fox, 2006).

A second nonparametric analysis that is useful for comparing two independent samples of ordinal data is the Mann-Whitney U test. This is a powerful nonparametric analysis for comparing two groups for which rank-order data have been collected. This test also may be used with a variety of sample sizes and with different sample sizes in each group (e.g., Group A, with $n = 1$, and Group B, with $n = 3$, up to group n's of 20). Beyond group n's of about 20, the Mann-Whitney U test becomes somewhat laborious if computed by hand. Readers who need to use this test in such situations can consult a number of sources for computing procedures (e.g., Best & Kahn, 2006; Levin & Fox, 2006).

For additional simulations visit www.sagepub .com/drewstudy

Simulation

Simulation 13.1

Topic: Parametric versus nonparametric statistics

Background statement: Selection of the appropriate statistical tool is an essential first step before the data are analyzed. It will do no good to perform computations correctly if the incorrect analysis has been used. The choice between parametric and nonparametric statistics rests essentially on three factors as noted in the text of this chapter: assumptions, nature of the data, and sample size. Because the assumptions exist primarily in theory (unless evidence exists that suggests a problem), your practical decision may have to be based primarily on the latter two factors.

Tasks to be performed:

1. Review the following stimulus material.

2. Indicate whether you would be inclined to use parametric or nonparametric statistics and why.

Stimulus material: You are conducting a study in which two reinforcement techniques are being compared to determine which is most effective. Two groups of children have been formed by random assignment with 20 participants in each group. The data are collected that rate behavior on a scale of 1 to 7 with 1 representing nondisruptive and 7 representing highly disruptive behavior.

Simulation 13.2

Topic: Comparing two data points

Tasks to be performed:

1. Review the following stimulus material.

2. Indicate which statistical test you would select for data analysis and why.

Stimulus material: You have been asked to work in an educational teaching laboratory. The topic of your first investigation involves comparing the effectiveness of two different classroom management methods. Two groups of children have been formed by random assignment with 15 participants in each group. Treatment is administered and measurements are then taken. The data are collected rating behavior on a scale of 1 to 7 with 1 representing nondisruptive behavior and 7 representing highly disruptive behavior.

Review briefly what is involved in this study by asking a few specific questions.

1. Is this an independent or a nonindependent comparison?
2. What type of data is being collected, and what does this suggest relative to the selection of parametric versus nonparametric analyses?
3. What is the size of the sample and what does this suggest?

Now, what statistical test would you suggest? Review the relevant chapter pages if you wish.

Write your responses, then turn to page 334 for Simulation Feedback 13.1 and 13.2.

Nonindependent Comparisons

Nonindependent comparisons of two data points represent a considerably different situation from that of independent comparisons just discussed, although they are variations on the same theme. The nonindependent comparison is almost defined by characteristics that are not the case for independent comparisons. In an independent situation, the scores in Condition A are not affected by or do not affect those under Condition B. In practice, this has generally meant that the two groups (Conditions A and B) are constituted from different participants. In a nonindependent situation, on the other hand, there is reason to believe that scores under Condition A have some effect on those under Condition B. This might be the case if repeated measures were taken on the same participants. For example, Fred's performance is measured under Condition A and then again under Condition B. Since Fred's performance is recorded under both conditions, there is reason to believe that the two scores are not independent because his score in one condition may well have some influence on his score in the other. (There is no way that his reading ability in one performance test is not going to have some relationship to his performance on another test.) Similarly, if a participant learns a great deal from taking the pretest, that performance will likely have an influence on the posttest performance. In either of these situations, a different set of statistical procedures is appropriate from those used for independent comparisons. The statistical tests for these conditions are found in the third column of Table 13.2, which is labeled "Nonindependent" to represent the nonindependent comparisons.

Parametric analysis. The most frequently used parametric statistic for this type of comparison is the *t* test for differences between nonindependent means. This analysis is a variation on the *t* test previously discussed for independent comparisons. Since it is a parametric statistic, a minimum of interval data and a sample size of 12 are required. In addition, the assumption of a normally distributed criterion measure should be reasonable. This test could be used in circumstances in which a pretest mean is to be compared with a posttest mean or where two experimental treatments are administered to the same group (in either case, the same group is being tested under both conditions). Remember that for comparing two nonindependent means, the *t* test to be used is different from that used for independent means. Computational procedures may be found in most research texts (e.g., Best & Kahn, 2006; Goodwin, 2005; Urdan, 2005). Several name variations commonly appear for this analysis, including *t* test for nonindependent means, correlated *t* test, and *t* test for related or repeated means. These terms are used interchangeably and all designate the same type of analysis.

Nonparametric analysis. Recall that nonparametric statistics are useful in situations in which parametric analyses are inappropriate. A variety of nonparametric analyses may be used to compare two nonindependent data points. When nominal data have been collected, McNemar's test for significance of changes is a useful analysis and is particularly appropriate for pre-post designs.

If ordinal data have been recorded, two nonparametric analyses are available— the sign test and the Wilcoxon matched-pairs signed-ranks test. Both of these tests are used for situations in which performance is assessed on the same participants at two different times.

The sign test is so named because the signs "+" and "" are used as integral parts of the computation. This test is easy to use and may be applied with rather small samples (e.g., $N = 6$). However, this analysis does require that the variable being assessed and scored in terms of ranks must have a continuous distribution. An example may be one where all the students in a given group are being ranked in terms of height. The continuous distribution requirement simply assumes that there is a continuum of heights possible underlying the ranks of 1 to 15 (if there are 15 in the group). No other assumption is required.

The Wilcoxon matched-pairs signed-ranks test is the second nonparametric statistic mentioned for ordinal data. This analysis is more powerful than the sign test because it takes into account the magnitude of differences between scores rather than merely indicating in what direction change occurred. (Using the sign test, the direction of change is all that is considered. A change in one direction is denoted by a "+," whereas a change in the other direction is designated by a ".") Because the Wilcoxon test makes greater use of the actual ranks, it does require that the experimenter be able to roughly judge the magnitude between ranks. When this can be reasonably done, the Wilcoxon test is preferred over the sign test. Computational procedures may be found in a number of sources (e.g., Urdan, 2005).

It should be kept in mind that both of the above analyses ask the question, "Is there a significant difference between two sets of related performances?" This question may take the form, "Is there a difference in this group's performance on the pretest as compared to the posttest?" These analyses may also be employed in studies where the same group might be given two experimental treatments (e.g., both A and B), which is not the pretest and posttest format.

Comparing More Than Two Data Points

One Experimental Variable

The discussion of statistical analyses thus far has focused on comparing two data points (e.g., comparing performances of two test situations such as two means or medians). This discussion has examined comparisons that were independent as well as those that were nonindependent. In all cases, the comparisons were between two groups or performances with one experimental variable involved. Recall for a moment the many hypothetical examples of Groups A and B in which two treatment techniques are compared. There is one experimental variable and a method of treatment, with two types (Conditions A and B) representing the specific conditions compared. Likewise if a time series study is conducted, baseline performance is compared to performance under treatment. In this case, the experimental variable may be designated as "level of positive reinforcement." The two specific conditions within this experimental variable are the absence versus presence of the treatment (baseline versus treatment). In a similar fashion, a pre-post experiment may be conceived as a comparison of absence versus presence of the treatment with a single experimental variable.

Frequently, a researcher wishes to conduct a study in which one experimental variable is involved, but more than two specific conditions exist within that variable. Expanding the previous example, a study may be conducted that investigates methods of treatment but compares three or more specific types (Groups A, B, C, etc.). Experiments of this type are merely variations on the previous configuration with one experimental variable under study. In Table 13.2, this is labeled "More than two data points" and "One experimental variable" about halfway down in the far left column. The only change is that more than two specific conditions are compared within that experimental variable. Instead of two drug dosages, the researcher may wish to compare performance under five levels of dosage (amount of drug treatment being the experimental variable). This type of situation requires the use of different statistical analyses from those previously discussed.

Independent comparisons. Independent comparisons (second column from the left in Table 13.2) of three or more data points, with one experimental variable, should be viewed in much the same fashion as independent comparisons in general. Independence, once again, means that the scores under Condition C are not influenced by those under Conditions B, A, and so on. As before, this usually takes the form of different groups of participants for each condition. Figure 13.1 illustrates how five conditions might be designed to test the effects of variation in level of drug dosage. For the present purpose, 20 different participants have been assigned to each of the five different experimental groups, making this an independent comparison design.

If the researchers have collected interval or ratio data, they are in a position to consider parametric statistics. Perhaps the most commonly used statistic for this type of comparison is the one-way analysis of variance for comparing independent means (see the second column in Table 13.2). Shortened to one-way analysis of variance, or ANOVA, this test is a powerful technique for comparing three or more means. It is important to emphasize that this discussion is about a one-way ANOVA for independent comparisons. Variations of the basic ANOVA will recur in later discussions with different types of designs. One of the reasons for the popularity of ANOVA is its great flexibility for different designs.

The ANOVA provides a convenient analysis for making a simultaneous test for differences among the five means of performance scores by participants, in Figure 13.1. As noted earlier, the ANOVA is a parametric statistic. Several assumptions must be reasonable before it can be appropriately applied. First, the type of data must be suitable for this type of analysis, interval or ratio. In addition, three major assumptions are usually considered as required: (1) the scores recorded are normally distributed in the population, (2) the variation in scores is approximately the same for all groups in the experiment (i.e., the score variation in Group A is about the same as that in Groups B, C, and so on. This is commonly referred to as the assumption of equal variance, or homogeneous variances.), and (3) the observations or scores are independent. Although these assumptions may appear overwhelming to a beginning researcher,. in practice, some latitude is possible with respect to how rigorous one must be about meeting these assumptions precisely. Considerably more detail regarding these assumptions, as well as computational procedures, may be found in most texts that present inferential analyses (e.g., Frankfort-Nachmias & Leon-Guerrero, 2006; Levin & Fox, 2006; Urdan, 2005).

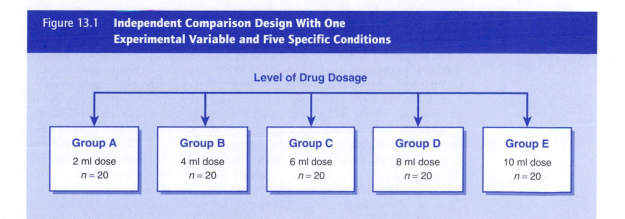

Figure 13.1   Independent Comparison Design With One Experimental Variable and Five Specific Conditions

Level of Drug Dosage

Group A	Group B	Group C	Group D	Group E
2 ml dose	4 ml dose	6 ml dose	8 ml dose	10 ml dose
$n = 20$	$n = 20$	$n = 20$	$n = 20$	$n = 20$

There are occasions when nominal or ordinal data are recorded with the intent to compare more than two data points (still with one experimental variable). Under these conditions, of course, one must turn to nonparametric statistics for analysis purposes. Using the same basic design arrangement that was presented in Figure 13.1, suppose for a moment that you have collected nominal data. This might be the case if there were some sort of dichotomous categories regarding the participants' health status (e.g., "cured" versus "not cured"). The different groups can be statistically compared under this situation by using the chi-square test for k independent samples. You will find this in the "Independent" column of Table 13.2, about two-thirds of the way down; "Nominal data" appears in the far left column. The chi-square test for this comparison is a simple expansion of the analysis that was mentioned previously for comparing two groups. The term k is used to designate the number of groups being compared. For the example in Figure 13.1, k would be equal to 5, since there are five groups. However, as a part of the general title of the analysis, k is used to indicate "several, depending on the exact number of groups in the experiment." The cell size (n) for this analysis needs to be at least 5. Thus, this test would not be appropriate if there were only three or four in any cell. The discussion presented previously for chi-square remains appropriate for its application here and, as before, computational procedures may be found in a variety of statistical textbooks (e.g., Urdan, 2005).

Two statistical analyses are appropriate for comparing more than two independent data points if ordinal data have been collected—the median test and the Kruskal-Wallis one-way analysis of variance by ranks. Look down the left-hand column in Table 13.2 to "More than two data points," under "One experimental variable," to "Nonparametric," and "Ordinal." Then move directly across to the second column where you will see both the "Median test" and the "Kruskal-Wallis test." The median test for this situation is an extension of the median test that was previously mentioned for comparing two data points (in fact, it is frequently designated as the extension of the median test). Computational procedures may be found in many texts covering nonparametric statistics (e.g., Urdan, 2005).

The Kruskal-Wallis one-way analysis of variance by ranks represents a second statistical technique that is useful for comparisons of k independent data points when ordinal data have been collected. The requirements of this analysis are essentially the same as those for the extension of the median test presented above. The Kruskal-Wallis, however, is more efficient because it makes use of more of the available information than does the median test. Consequently, when the situation permits use of either test, the Kruskal-Wallis is preferred.

Nonindependent comparisons. Occasionally, a researcher may wish to compare three or more data points that are not independent. Such a situation might arise if, for example, the same participants were tested three times with some treatment or event occurring between the measurements. Figure 13.2 illustrates how such an investigation might be designed. The same participants are given a pretreatment measure (Measure 1), then the first 20 practice trials of the learning task are administered. This is followed by a mid-experiment assessment (Measure 2); the next 20 practice trials; and, finally, the third test (Measure 3). This type of study can be viewed as an extension of the pre-post design mentioned previously, with the addition of a third test. Expansions may, of course, involve more than three data collection points (e.g., four, five . . . k). On occasion, the treatment that intercedes between measurements may involve only the passage of time rather than application of an active treatment.

If the researcher has collected nominal data and wishes to compare three or more nonindependent data points, a useful analysis is the Cochran Q test. Such a situation might occur if the design involved testing the same participants under three different drug dosages. The data might be recorded as "cured" versus "not cured," thereby falling into the categorical type of measurement. This example is merely used for illustrative purposes, and it is necessary to remain aware of the design problems that

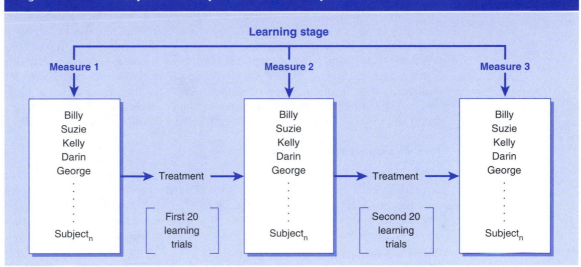

Figure 13.2   Nonindependent Comparison With One Experimental Variable and Three Data Points

would be presented by such an experiment. One obvious difficulty would be a multiple-treatment interference problem, which was noted as affecting both internal and external validity in Chapter 9. Certainly, there would have to be some assurance that the effects of Drug Dosage 1 were not still lingering when the Dosage 2 condition was implemented. Computational procedures for Cochran's Q may be found in many books with nonparametric sections (e.g., McMillan & Schumacher, 2006).

If the recorded data are ordinal, three or more nonindependent data points may be statistically compared using the Friedman two-way analysis of variance by ranks. Although the title includes the term *two-way* (which usually suggests two experimental variables), this analysis is appropriate here because it actually makes a one-way comparison. To illustrate, suppose that the study concerning drug dosage was arranged as in Table 13.4. The Friedman analysis compares the ranks between the dosage conditions, which, since there is one experimental variable (level of drug dosage), is a one-way comparison despite what the analysis title suggests. Because the same participants are tested under all conditions, this situation falls into the nonindependent data point comparison category. The Friedman technique may be used with small samples and is relatively simple to compute (McMillan & Schumacher, 2006).

If a researcher has collected interval or ratio data, parametric statistical techniques may be considered for analysis purposes. With this level of data, and assuming that other factors are present like an adequate sample size and a reasonable

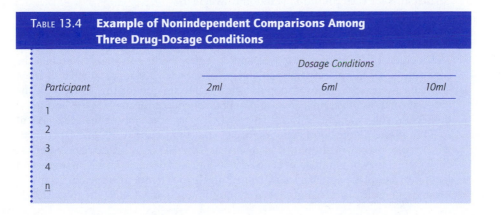

TABLE 13.4   Example of Nonindependent Comparisons Among Three Drug-Dosage Conditions

	Dosage Conditions		
Participant	2ml	6ml	10ml
1			
2			
3			
4			
n			

assurance that assumptions are approximated, the task at hand is essentially one of comparing three or more nonindependent means. Probably the most commonly used statistical test for such a comparison is the analysis of variance for repeated measures (with one experimental variable—thus a one-way ANOVA for repeated measures). The "repeated" distinction is important to highlight. Previously, a one-way ANOVA for comparing independent means was discussed (resulting from different groups' performance). The present discussion refers to a one-way ANOVA for comparing three or more nonindependent means (resulting from repeated measures on the same participants). The computational procedures are somewhat different and may be found in most statistical texts that focus on inferential statistics.

Two Experimental Variables

The discussion of statistical procedures has thus far focused on situations in which one experimental variable is being investigated. (The term *experimental variable* is being used generically here as before; it essentially refers to comparisons that may be made whether the study is an experiment in the true sense or a comparison between data points in a nonexperimental study such as a survey.) Hypothetical studies in which two or more data points are compared (e.g., performance under three different instructional techniques) within the single experimental variable (method of instruction) have been examined. Frequently, studies are conducted in which more than one experimental variable is of interest in the same investigation. This section will discuss statistical data analysis in situations with two experimental variables under study. You may wish to review the design sections on this type of investigation in Chapter 6.

You will note that there will be less emphasis on nonparametric analyses in this discussion than in previous sections, a reflection of a point made earlier in this chapter. Parametric statistics offer greater flexibility in terms of the types of questions asked, particularly where more complex designs are involved with more than one experimental variable. However, do not interpret this as freedom to apply parametric analyses under all conditions where two or more experimental variables are studied. Restrictions concerning the type of data, sample size, and assumptions are still required.

Independent comparisons. An investigation with two experimental variables that involves independent comparisons merely represents a combination of simpler designs. Figure 13.3 illustrates a hypothetical investigation with two experimental variables, material difficulty and amount of practice. Comparison A, which represents the material difficulty variable, has two specific levels, high-difficulty material and low-difficulty material. Comparison B, the amount of practice variable, has three levels of 10 trials, 20 trials, and 30 trials. Thus, there are six different data points to be compared. This is an independent design as there is a separate group of participants for each condition (randomly assigned).

An investigation such as that in Figure 13.3 is usually designed for situations in which parametric analyses can be applied, because nonparametrics are so cumbersome with complex studies. This, of course, means that interval data are collected, cells include 12 or more participants, and the researcher is reasonably sure that the assumptions of normal distribution and equal variance are approximated. If these elements are present, the most popular statistical technique for this situation is the two-way analysis of variance for comparing independent means (see the bottom of the second column in Table 13.2). This analysis is an extension of the independent ANOVA discussed previously under independent comparisons with one experimental variable. By now it should be evident that the ANOVA is an extremely flexible analysis that may be modified to fit a variety of research designs. This is an important factor in its great popularity and contributes to its frequent appearance in the research literature. In addition to its flexibility, however, the ANOVA is an extremely

Figure 13.3   Hypothetical Independent Comparison With Two Experimental Variables

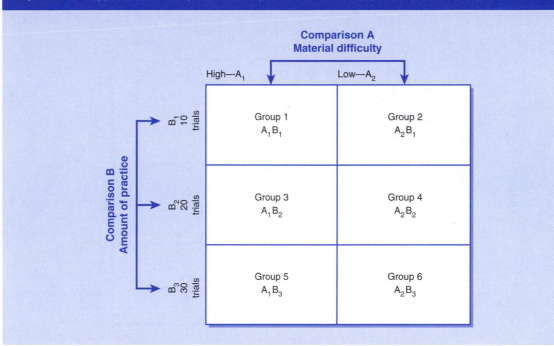

powerful analysis, often viewed as the standard against which other techniques are compared. Computational procedures for this analysis are really rather simple and certainly less formidable than many beginning researchers think. They are found in most statistical texts under titles such as two-way ANOVA or two-factor ANOVA.

If the requirements are not met for parametric statistics, the researcher will have to resort to nonparametric analyses. In an experiment such as the example above, data analysis becomes cumbersome. Common nonparametric techniques previously reviewed are the main choices from which selection may be made. In such a situation, the experimenter has little choice but to analyze one comparison at a time while ignoring the second experimental variable. This would mean, in the example just given, that two independent data points would be compared (high versus low difficulty) by combining the performances of Groups 1, 3, and 5 for high difficulty and Groups 2, 4, and 6 for low difficulty (refer to Figure 13.3). The second variable would then have to be analyzed comparing the three amounts of practice: 10 trials (by combining the performance scores of Groups 1 and 2) versus 20 trials (Groups 3 and 4) versus 30 trials (Groups 5 and 6). Such an approach is obviously more laborious and does not provide as much information. It may, however, be the only option if parametric analysis is not appropriate.

Mixed comparisons. Mixed designs have previously been discussed in Chapter 6. Review of this material will alert the reader to the fact that mixed designs involve studies with at least two experimental variables, in which independent comparisons are made on one variable and repeated measures are used on the second. For the purposes of this section, use the example in Figure 13.3. This independent design would be a mixed design if it were set up with different groups for each level of Variable B (number of learning trials). The different groups for each level result in three different groups of participants—the independent comparison variable. Receiving both high- and low-difficulty material constitutes repeated measures on the difficulty variable. Such a design is illustrated in Figure 13.4.

Figure 13.4   Hypothetical Mixed Comparison With Two Experimental Variables

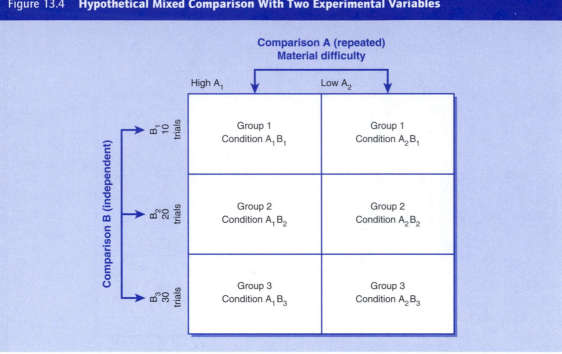

As mentioned earlier, investigations designed in this fashion are usually planned with the intent of using parametric statistical analyses. If the requirements for such computation are met, the two-way mixed analysis of variance would be an appropriate analysis for this type of experiment (see the lower right-hand corner of Table 13.2). This is another variation on the basic ANOVA theme, further illustrating its flexibility. Computational procedures are somewhat different from those presented before and combine the components of independent analysis with those for repeated measures. A "mixed" ANOVA is used in the same sense as the "mixed" design described earlier. Details for computing this analysis may be found in a variety of statistical texts that include discussions of inferential statistics.

Investigations that will not permit the use of parametric analyses (e.g., inappropriate data, small samples, or drastic assumption violation) would again require the application of nonparametric techniques. Basically, the same approach as that described in the previous section would be applied. Data from one variable at a time would be analyzed using the appropriate nonparametric statistic (e.g., either two or k data points, independent or nonindependent, depending on the situation). As with two-factor studies or more complex experiments, nonparametric analyses are considerably more cumbersome.

Logical Extrapolations: More Complex Designs

The phrase "more complex designs" generally refers to studies with more than two experimental variables. The term is not meant to suggest complex in the sense of "difficult." It has been our experience that some of the most difficult experiments are made difficult by virtue of ill-defined problems that have not been distilled to operational form. On the other hand, some of the "easier" pieces of research often involve several experimental variables (that are complex only in the sense of the number of variables) but are made easy because they are clearly and operationally defined in great detail.

Using More Complex Designs

For our purposes here, we are discussing studies asking difference questions with three or more experimental variables. Such designs were introduced in Chapter 6. This type of study is conducted when the researcher wishes to examine three or more experimental variables simultaneously. Diagrams of such studies are somewhat more difficult than with two variables because they have three dimensions. Figure 13.5 illustrates an experiment with three variables. This diagram, although totally hypothetical, involves Variable A (with two levels, A_1 and A_2), Variable B (with three levels, B_1, B_2, and B_3), and Variable C (with two levels, C_1 and C_2). This experiment is often called a 2 x 3 x 2 design, with the numerical designations referring to the specific levels in each variable.

If the experiment illustrated in Figure 13.5 involved different participants for each cell group, it would be considered a totally independent design. This would mean that 12 separate groups of participants would be used. As before, the term *independent* is used to indicate that the scores in any given cell do not have an influence on the scores in any other cell. This, of course, precludes repeated measures on any variable. Using this example, suppose for the moment that the basic requirements for parametric analyses are met. This would mean that interval or ratio data had been collected, that each cell had 12 or more participants, and that the assumptions of normality and equal variance are reasonable. If these elements are present, data could be conveniently analyzed using a three-way analysis of variance for independent comparisons. (A three-way ANOVA is not on Table 13.2.) This analysis will yield a great deal of information and, as before, merely involves computation extensions of the more simple ANOVA procedures discussed earlier. Computation procedures are not difficult but become increasingly tedious as the design becomes more complex if you are calculating by hand.

Figure 13.5   Diagrammatic Representation of a Hypothetical Study With Three Experimental Variables

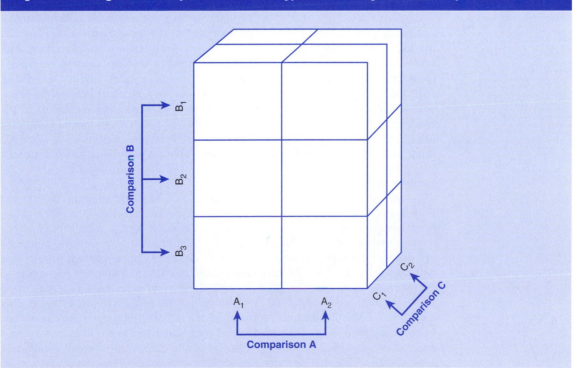

Now consider this same design assuming that it is not possible to use parametric statistics. As noted during the discussion of studies with two experimental variables, such a situation makes data analysis cumbersome because nonparametric statistics are not nearly as flexible when used with more complex designs. Probably the best approach under such conditions would involve analyzing the comparisons separately (e.g., Comparison A, then B, and finally C). The basic nonparametric approaches to performing such analyses have been described earlier in this chapter. It is hoped that the investigator will plan ahead sufficiently and either ensure the appropriateness of the study for parametric analysis or design a simpler investigation.

Reconsider the three-factor experiment illustrated in Figure 13.5. It may be that the researcher will want to obtain repeated measures on one or more of the experimental variables. If this is the case, the design becomes a three-factor mixed design, since it combines independent comparisons on some experimental variables (e.g., different groups for Variables A and B) and repeated measures on others (e.g., Variable C). This type of design was introduced previously in Chapter 6 and is illustrated in Figure 13.6. Note that two examples are shown in Figure 13.6. One indicates Comparisons A and B as being independent, and Comparison C as the variable on which participants receive repeated measures. For this experiment, four different groups of participants would be necessary, and they would all be measured twice (under the two C conditions). The second example in Figure 13.6 indicates only Variable A as independent, and repeated measures are obtained on both Variables B and C. Only two groups of participants would be used in this example, and both groups would be measured under all B and C conditions. Both of these examples are considered mixed designs.

If the studies in Figure 13.6 include the appropriate elements for parametric statistics, the data can be analyzed using the three-way mixed analysis of variance. This technique is an extension of the mixed ANOVA discussed earlier. Slight computational modifications are made depending on whether one or two variables are independent.

Problems With More Complex Designs

The last section described more complex designs that may be used to investigate difference questions and statistical procedures that can be applied for data analysis purposes. Studies were discussed that included three experimental variables. The researcher may wish to conduct an investigation that includes even more experimental variables (e.g., four, five, or more). Such studies may be conducted and data analyzed using logical extrapolations of what has been discussed previously. There are analysis-of-variance procedures that can be computed for such designs, both totally independent as well as mixed (e.g., four-way ANOVA). In fact, as computer use has become increasingly sophisticated, there have been a number of sophisticated analysis procedures that make the computational capability nearly limitless. There are, however, some serious interpretation problems involved in using such complex designs.

As the complexity of an investigation increases, it becomes more difficult to create and maintain a mental image of the various components included in the study. It has been our experience that one of the most effective means of conceptualizing a study is to draw a picture of it, much like the diagrams that have appeared throughout this text. Most people are accustomed to visualizing phenomena primarily in a two-dimensional fashion (particularly as they illustrate on paper). It is possible to draw three-dimensional designs such as those in Figures 13.5 and 13.6, but when presented with additional factors to illustrate, the task becomes difficult. This results in a conceptualization problem, particularly for the beginning researcher. Interpreting results from a complex experiment once the data are analyzed becomes a particular challenge. Remember, analysis of the data is not the end product of research. There is little reason to conduct an investigation unless the results can be

Figure 13.6 **Option Examples for Three-Factor Mixed Design**

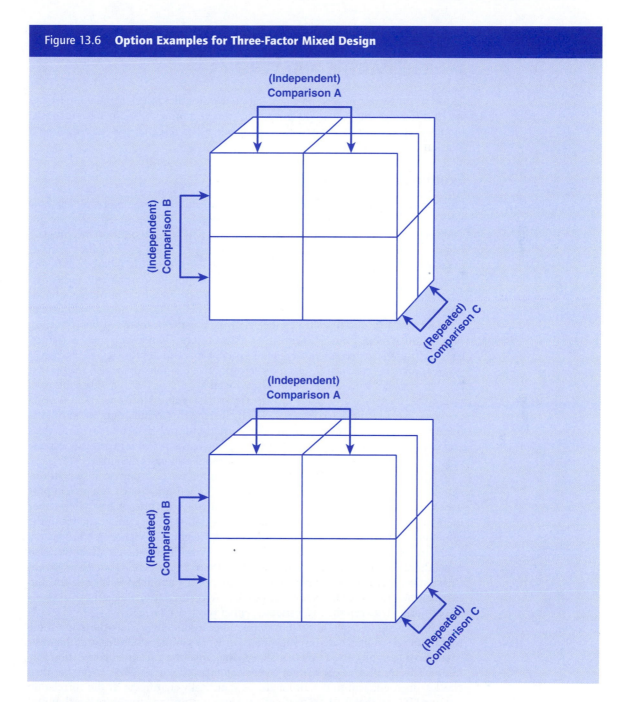

meaningfully interpreted. Such interpretation frequently becomes overwhelming when the design is complex. Thus, although the design and analysis capability exists for highly complex experiments, the interpretation of simpler studies is far easier and more straightforward. More importantly, simpler studies may generate more meaningful outcome for practice and theory.

A variety of statistical procedures have been discussed thus far in this chapter. The questions and conditions under which each might be most appropriately applied have been examined. Obviously, these are general considerations; specifics may alter somewhat the analysis chosen. However, these general guidelines may be very helpful to the beginning researcher and are summarized in Table 13.2.

RELATIONSHIP QUESTIONS: WHICH STATISTIC AND WHEN?

Thus far our focus has been on statistical procedures that may be applied to a variety of difference questions. The purpose of this section is to briefly describe techniques that may be used for data analysis when the researcher is investigating a relationship question.

Examining Correlation Techniques

Once again, relationship questions are involved in studies that explore the *degree to which two or more phenomena relate or vary together*. Such an investigation might examine the relationship between reading scores and writing performance in class (As reading test scores vary, what tends to happen to writing performance in class? Does it tend to improve as reading scores increase?). For this type of study, the researcher records both height and weight on a sample of participants. With two measures on each participant, the data are then analyzed by computing what is known as a *correlation coefficient*. The correlation coefficient provides an estimate of the degree of relationship between the variables. It is the outcome of the computation and may range from +1.00 to −1.00. (Most results fall between these extremes, e.g., +.70, −.50) Correlations that result in coefficients with a plus sign are known as positive correlations. Such results indicate a positive relationship, which means that the two variables tend to vary in the same direction (e.g., as reading scores increase, writing performance also tends to increase, or as reading scores decrease, writing performance also tends to decrease). Coefficients with a minus sign are known as negative correlations. These indicate inverse relationships between the two variables and tend to vary in opposite directions; as one increases the other tends to decrease (e.g., as time on academic tasks increases, classroom outbursts diminish).

A correlation resulting in a +1.00 coefficient indicates a strong positive relationship between the two variables being measured. Sometimes known as a perfect positive correlation, a +1.00 coefficient indicates that each time one variable either increases or decreases, the second variable also exhibits an increment change in the same direction. (i.e., each time height increases, weight also increases.) Similarly, a −1.00 correlation indicates a strong inverse relationship. In such a situation, each time there is an increase in one variable, there is a decrease in the second. Correlation coefficients that are closer to zero indicate a much weaker relationship between the two variables being measured. A zero correlation suggests no systematic variation between the two variables, either positive or negative.

Statistical significance in relationship studies essentially means the same thing that it does in comparative investigations. Once the sample is selected and the measures recorded, the data are then analyzed using one of a variety of correlation formulas. This results in a correlation coefficient as just discussed. The researcher then checks this coefficient to determine if it is statistically significant. If the correlation obtained is such that $P < 0.05$ or $P < 0.01$, it is significant and therefore it is doubtful that the relationship is due to chance. The researcher is then likely to interpret the data as suggesting that a relationship does exist between the two factors measured.

Interpreting Correlational Studies

A word of caution is in order concerning the interpretation of correlational studies: a high correlation coefficient, even if it is statistically significant, should *not* be taken to mean that the variation in one factor (e.g., reading score changes) *caused* the variation in the second factor (e.g., writing performance). Causation should *not* be inferred from correlational data. A high correlation coefficient merely indicates that the two variables tend to vary systematically, either together for positive correlation or inversely in the case of negative correlation. Such a relation permits the prediction of one variable from knowledge about the second, but does not suggest causation. Many factors that vary systematically in this world do not actually act on one another.

A second note is also appropriate at this point in terms of interpreting correlation coefficients. It was noted above that 1.00 correlations (either "+" or "−") rarely occur and that coefficients such as 0.70, 0.50, and so on are more frequent. Perhaps because of the way the correlation coefficient is presented, a 0.70 correlation is occasionally misinterpreted as representing the percentage of variation in common between the two variables being measured. This is an inappropriate interpretation and, in most cases, is inaccurate. A 0.70 correlation does not mean that 70% of the time when one factor varies, the second measure also changes. In fact, if one is interested in the percentage of variation in common, the obtained correlation coefficient should be squared. Using the previous example, a correlation of 0.70 actually indicates less than 50% variation in common between the two measures ($0.70 \times 0.70 = .49$, or 49%). This presents a very different picture from the misinterpretation of a 0.70 coefficient. There are certain formulas that include correction factors in computation (primarily reliability formulas used in test construction). In general, however, a correlation should not be taken as representative of a percentage.

The term *correlation* is a general label for the type of analysis used in relationship investigations. Actually, several specific techniques are used in different situations, much like we encountered with statistics for difference questions. In selecting the appropriate correlation technique for analysis purposes, the researcher must pay close attention to the type of data that have been collected on both variables (i.e., nominal, ordinal, interval, or ratio). The reader may wish to review the discussion concerning different types of data found in Chapter 10.

Perhaps the most commonly known correlation technique is the Pearson product-moment correlation. This analysis may be used when both of the measures recorded are either interval or ratio data (Criterion Measures 1 and 2, reading scores and writing performance in the previous example). The symbol for the product-moment correlation is r, which is occasionally used to refer to correlation in general. This use of the symbol for correlation in general is actually incorrect since it specifically denotes the product-moment analysis. The product-moment r is a highly popular correlation technique, primarily because it provides a stable estimate of relationship. When the data permit its use, this is definitely the preferred analysis. Computational procedures may be found in most standard statistical texts (e.g., Dowdy et al., 2004; Salkind, 2007; Sirkin, 2006). Table 13.5 shows the Pearson at the top of the second column.

Table 13.5 has three columns: the far left labeled "Type of Analysis," the middle column labeled "Parametric Conditions," and the far right column labeled "Nonparametric Conditions." Looking at the left column, we first encounter the label "Same data type on both measures" and immediately under that we find "Interval or ratio." If we have interval or ratio data on both measures, we move to the right under the middle column and find the Pearson product-moment correlation (parametric conditions in this case meaning that we can compute arithmetic on the data—that is, we have interval or ratio data).

Correlation Techniques

Two correlation techniques may be used *if the data collected are ordinal* (i.e., *both Measure 1 and Measure 2 are in the form of ranks*). The more widely known analysis is the Spearman rank-order correlation, also known as rho. The second technique is Kendall's tau, which may also be used when both measures are in the form of ordinal data. Kendall's tau is preferred over the Spearman correlation when only a small sample is available (*N* less than 10). It is, however, somewhat more difficult to compute, and when the sample size permits, the Spearman rho should be employed.

TABLE 13.5 **Summarized Inferential Statistics for Relationship Questions**

Type of Analysis	Parametric Conditions	Nonparametric Conditions
Same data type on both measures		
Interval or ratio	Pearson product-moment correlation	
Ordinal		Spearman rank-order correlation ($N > 10$)
		Kendall's tau ($N < 10$)
Nominal		Phi coefficient (true dichotomy)
		Tetrachoric correlation (artificial dichotomy)
Different data types on the two measures		
Nominal (artificial dichotomy) and ratio or interval		Biserial correlation
Nominal (true dichotomy) and ratio or interval		Point-biserial correlation

Computational procedures for Spearman's analysis may be found in most statistical texts. Computational procedures for Kendall's tau are somewhat less available but may be obtained from Sheskin (2000). Table 13.5 shows both of these analyses in the far right column, which is labeled "Nonparametric Conditions." They appear on the "Ordinal" data line of the left column, indicating that they can be used when ordinal data are collected on both measures.

Type of Dichotomous Data

Data in the form of a dichotomy (e.g., successful-unsuccessful) may also be submitted to correlation analysis. Because a dichotomy represents categories, data of this type fall into the nominal level of measurement (see left-hand column of Table 13.5). Two correlation techniques may be used with this type of data.

If the data on both variables represent an **artificial dichotomy,** the analysis to be applied is the tetrachoric correlation. A note of explanation is in order regarding artificial dichotomy. An artificial dichotomy would exist if the experimenter arbitrarily divided performances into two categories. This might be the case with the "successful-unsuccessful" example above, in which someone has rather arbitrarily defined what is successful and unsuccessful performance. If such data are recorded on both measures, the experimenter can obtain a correlation using the tetrachoric procedure (see right-hand column of Table 13.5).

A second type of dichotomous data may also be correlated. When data on both variables represent true dichotomies, the analysis of choice is the phi coefficient (right-hand column of Table 13.5). A **true dichotomy** exists when the categories are relatively clear-cut and are not determined arbitrarily. An example of this type of situation might be the absence versus presence of a student's response. Assuming that the determination of whether the student responded is clear-cut, such data would be considered a true dichotomy. When such data are recorded on both measures, an estimate of relationship can be obtained with the phi coefficient.

Correlation Procedures

The discussion thus far has examined correlation techniques that may be used with nominal and ordinal data as well as interval and ratio data. In each case, however, the procedure was designed for the same type of data on both of the measures being correlated. That is, if the analysis under discussion was appropriate for rank data (Spearman's rho, Kendall's tau), this type of data was required on both Measure 1 and Measure 2. A limited number of techniques are available that permit correlation when data on one measure are of one type and data on the second measure are of a different type. The remainder of this section will present two such correlation procedures.

The concepts of artificial and true dichotomies. The concepts of artificial and true dichotomies have already been encountered but deserve further discussion. Consider for a moment a situation in which the researcher has data in the form of an artificial dichotomy on one measure and interval or ratio data on the second measure. Recall that the artificial dichotomy data will be the result of two arbitrarily defined categories. If a researcher wishes to correlate artificial dichotomy data with interval or ratio data, a *point-biserial correlation* may be used. This type of situation might be encountered if, for example, the investigator wanted to determine the relationship between success or failure in a physical fitness test and speed in a 100-yard dash. In this example, the time to run the 100-yard dash may be considered interval or ratio data. The other measure, recorded as pass-fail on the physical fitness test, is artificial dichotomous data, since the score represents an arbitrarily determined category.

A precautionary note is in order in terms of use of the biserial correlation. It was previously noted that the extreme limits for any correlation are +1.00 and 1.00. In computation of the biserial correlation, it is mathematically possible to exceed these limits, particularly if the measures are not normally distributed. This is a characteristic of this particular formula of which the researcher should be aware. Otherwise, a correlation of 1.15 might result in wasted searching for a computational error that really is not there. Such a result is generated by the relative lack of precision in the technique, emphasizing the preference of measures other than the artificial dichotomy when possible.

If the data involve a true dichotomy on one measure and interval or ratio data on the second measure, an estimate of relationship may be obtained by using a point-biserial correlation. Recall that a true dichotomy is the result of clear-cut categories such as male and female. This is a different situation from that presented by the artificial dichotomy. The point-biserial correlation is frequently used in investigations that relate gender categories to performance on tasks that generate at least interval data. Modifying the earlier example, the point-biserial procedure might be used to correlate gender categories with performance in a 100-yard dash. This analysis is closely related to the powerful product-moment correlation and does not have the mathematical idiosyncrasy noted for the biserial technique (exceeding the 1.00 range). Computation procedures for the point-biserial correlation may be found in many statistical texts.

Examination of statistical procedures for relationship questions has been limited to situations in which two variables are of interest, such as the well-worn examples of reading and writing as Measures 1 and 2. More complex techniques are available to permit correlation of more than two variables. These analyses, however, generally require a knowledge of and degree of comfort with statistics that are frequently not present in the beginning researcher. Consequently, these procedures have been omitted to focus on an introductory presentation.

A variety of statistical procedures have been discussed here for relationship questions. The conditions under which each might be most appropriately applied have also been examined. Clearly these are general considerations and the particular conditions of a given investigation might alter the analysis used. These general guidelines, however, may prove useful to beginning researchers and are summarized in Table 13.5.

COMMENTS

The discussion of inferential statistics presented in this chapter has by no means been exhaustive. Not all of the many statistical tools have been discussed, nor has any single technique been explored in great depth. The purpose of this chapter was simply to provide an introductory description of selected analyses that might be applied under a variety of research circumstances. The presentation was intended to give the reader an overview of various statistical tools and to provide a guide to when they might be used. More comprehensive knowledge will require consulting a variety of texts that have the sole purpose of presenting statistical analyses. Likewise, information on computational procedures and formulas has intentionally been omitted from this chapter. This was done on the assumption that such inclusions might detract from the student's important understanding of the purposes and uses of various analyses. The result has been frequent references to other sources for computational information. These references have been considered carefully to select those that are elementary and clear yet accurate in their presentation. Hopefully, the student now has a general knowledge (or can refer back to this chapter) of what statistic to use where. Armed with this background, it will be a much simpler task to make sense of and apply the basic statistical tools used in behavioral research. You will find Tables 13.2 and 13.5 very handy as you work through these practice situations, and these are tables you are familiar with by this time. Table 13.6 is also being provided at this point. This is a chart that our students have used for years to remind themselves to check off each point as they proceed down the path of selecting a statistical analysis. Our students have labeled this their "Quick and Dirty Checklist for Statistical Selection." It has been so successful that we use it ourselves to be sure we haven't forgotten something, and we are using their title for the table.

**TABLE 13.6 . Quick and Dirty Checklist for Statistical Selections
(Matters you have to determine in order to select an analysis)**

❑ The Question: What type of question is it, difference, relationship, or descriptive?

❑ The Data: What type of data are collected, nominal, ordinal, interval, ratio?

❑ Distribution of Scores: Is the distribution substantially abnormal? Does it appear to be very different from a bell-shaped distribution?

❑ The N: What is the number of participants? Is there an appropriate n if we are looking at a difference question or an adequate N if it is a relationship question?

❑ Comparison Type: This is only a consideration for difference questions. Is the design an independent comparison, a nonindependent or repeated-measures comparison, or a mixed comparison?

❑ Number of Experimental Variables: This is only a consideration for difference questions. Is there one experimental variable, two experimental variables, or more?

❑ Number of data points: This is only a consideration for difference questions. Data point refers to means, medians, or other representation of a group's performance being compared. How many are to be compared—two, or more than two? These answers will put you in a different part of Table 13.2.

❑ Same or different data types: This is a prominent consideration for relationship questions. If both types of data are the same—say, ordinal—then that puts you in a different part of Table 13.5.

❑ And miscellaneous others: There are some other considerations that occasionally arise, but as a first cut, the eight items above will get you very close to selecting an appropriate analysis.

Chapter Summary

+ Statistical analyses used for inferential research result in a statement of statistical significance that tells a researcher whether the results obtained are different from those that might have resulted by chance. In this manner, statistical significance tells the researcher what the probability is that chance could have generated the results.

+ Three areas are important in selecting parametric versus nonparametric analyses: (1) assumptions about the nature of the population distribution, (2) the type of data that are collected, and (3) the sample size.

+ Selecting the appropriate statistical analysis for a difference question involves determining (1) whether the comparisons involve two data points or more than two data points; (2) the number of experimental variables; 3) whether the comparisons are independent, nonindependent, or mixed; 4) the number of data points (e.g., groups) that are to be compared; 5) the type of data collected, which determines whether parametric or nonparametric analyses are appropriate; and 6) the number of participants.

+ Selecting the appropriate statistical analysis for a relationship question involves determining (1) whether the same or different types of data are collected on both measures, (2) the type of data collected, and (3) the number of participants.

Key Terms

Artificial dichotomy. Artificial dichotomy data are found when data are divided into two arbitrarily defined categories, but these are artificial and the behavior or performance actually does have an underlying continuum between the categories.

Independent comparisons. In an independent comparison, the scores in Condition A are not affected by and do not affect those under Condition B. In practice, this has generally meant that the two groups (Conditions A and B) are constituted from different participants.

Nonindependent comparisons. In a nonindependent situation, there is reason to believe that scores under Condition A have some effect on those under Condition B. In practice, this generally is the case if the same group of participants is measured twice, under Condition A and under Condition B.

Nonparametric statistics. Represent a general category of analysis that includes fewer assumptions about the population of scores, can often be computed with ordinal or nominal data, and may also be used with fewer participants than required by parametric analyses.

Parametric statistics. Statistics representing a general category of analysis that involves selected assumptions about the population of scores, generally uses arithmetic and therefore requires interval or ratio data, and typically needs more participants than do nonparametric analyses.

Statistical significance. Indicates whether the results obtained are different from those that might have resulted by chance.

True dichotomy. A true dichotomy occurs when the data reflect actual categories of behavior and there is no assumed underlying continuum between the categories.

Student Study Site

The companion Web site for *Designing and Conducting Research in Education* www.sagepub.com/drewstudy

Supplement your review of this chapter by going to the companion Web site to take one of the practice quizzes, use the flashcards to study key terms, and check out the many other study aids you'll find there. You'll even find some research articles from the Sage Full-Text Collection and a step-by-step guide that will show you how to read an educational research article.

Simulation Feedback

For additional simulations visit www.sagepub .com/drewstudy

Simulation Feedback 13.1

The general category of nonparametric statistics would be appropriate for use in the study presented. The nonparametric choice is based on the type of data that are collected. The rating scale has been a recurring example of ordinal data throughout the text. Table 13.1 indicates that nonparametric analyses are the only possibility with such data. The sample size was certainly adequate for parametric statistics, but the previously mentioned type of data consideration will not permit parametric statistics use because the property of additivity is not present. Table 13.2 provides more specific selections. For nonparametric analyses, we have two alternatives under independent comparisons with ordinal data: the median test and the Mann-Whitney U test. The Mann-Whitney is used more often and is preferred for group samples (*n*) under 20.

Simulation Feedback 13.2

First run through the questions in the stimulus material.

1. You have information in the stimulus material that indicates two groups of 15 participants each were formed. Consequently, there is little reason to believe that the performances are not independent. It seems you have an independent comparison.

2. As you have noted throughout the text and previous simulations, a rating scale such as this is generally considered to be generating ordinal data. Table 13.1 indicates that nonparametric analyses should be used with ordinal data.

3. The sample size of 15 per group is not terribly relevant, as you must use nonparametrics with ordinal data. It may, however, influence your choice of a specific test within the nonparametric category.

As noted in Table 13.2, two statistical tests are appropriate for ordinal data comparing two independent data points: the median test and the Mann-Whitney U test. Either test will be appropriate, although the Mann-Whitney is more popular with group samples (*n*) under 20.

14

ANALYZING QUALITATIVE DATA

After reading Chapter 14 you should be able to do the following:

✦ Describe the purpose of team meetings.

✦ Describe the purpose of data summaries.

✦ Compare the benefits and drawbacks of different coding and counting techniques.

✦ Describe and differentiate between inductive and deductive analysis approaches.

✦ Describe thick description.

✦ Describe criticism.

✦ Compare grounded theory, ethnography, and narrative construction.

We introduced qualitative principles of research methods and data collection in Chapter 8. The time-consuming nature of qualitative research should by now be very apparent, along with its many advantages. Chapters 12 and 13 presented some commonly employed techniques for analyzing quantitative data. In this chapter, we turn to techniques the qualitative researcher uses for analysis using data recorded as language rather than numbers. Computer software for analyzing qualitative data is becoming increasingly available and effective. As is the case with quantitative analyses, these software packages are primarily designed for use on desktop and notebook computers, which now have ample power to perform the analyses. We do not make specific recommendations here because software titles are upgraded and change so frequently.

Qualitative data are collected over time in the form of systematic field notes, interview notes and transcripts, researcher journals and reflections, and archival records. These data can then be conceptually organized, beginning with preliminary pattern identification while still in the field (Denzin & Lincoln, 2005; Mertens, 2005; Neuman, 2006). Qualitative data require careful analyses that employ much the same logic of finding and matching patterns that dominates quantitative methods in order to reveal patterns and principles that distinguish the social phenomenon under study. In Chapter 8, we emphasized that qualitative methods require rigorous inquiry on which consumers of the research can rely when drawing conclusions. The design and data collection principles we introduced provide the foundation for the inquiry, but, like the raw numbers recorded in a computer data file, they have no inherent knowledge value until they have been carefully analyzed. Many beginning researchers using qualitative methods underestimate the discipline and hard work necessary to turn interesting data into qualitative research through analysis. Collecting data in the field is often fascinating, even fun; analyzing the data systematically once the researcher has left the field is time-consuming and sometimes tedious, particularly if done manually. The rule of thumb that qualitative researchers often use to plan the time they need to complete a qualitative research project is this: "Time in the field equals time in analysis." In this chapter, we introduce the techniques that qualitative researchers use to complete this analysis.

First, we describe a few of the techniques that qualitative researchers use to organize data while still in the field. These techniques help researchers maximize the quality and appropriateness of participants interviewed, observation sampling, and the search for archival data. Later and in greater detail, we discuss the variety of techniques employed to systematically analyze qualitative data once the researchers have left the field. These techniques distinguish the findings of well-designed and executed qualitative research from the insights provided by testimonials and stories. Each has its place and contributions to make. We do not blanch with horror at the audacity of the novelist who takes up a pen (or keyboard) to render insight into the human condition. However, we do advise the committed qualitative researcher to seek patterns and themes in social life and not to commit the error of portraying unique circumstances as though they automatically represent society and human behavior in general. We also remind the beginning researcher that qualitative researchers fall along the entire epistemological continuum from phenomenologist to positivist, and the scholarship they produce in their inquiry may resemble the novelist's or the statistician's.

PRELIMINARY ANALYSIS

Preliminary field analyses can reveal patterns in the data requiring additional data, broader sampling, or new informants. Consequently, unlike the design, data collection, and data analysis steps sequentially followed in quantitative research, qualitative researchers engage in simultaneous and iterative processes of analysis *while still in the field* to point them toward important sources and data not predicted in the design phase of the study. Techniques that assist this are (1) meetings of multiple researchers (data sharing with other researchers), (2) field note summaries, and (3) data summary sheets.

Team Meetings

If a group of researchers is working on a project, meetings to discuss field issues and emerging patterns provide a useful way to enhance the quality of the data-gathering process. By comparing their experiences and preliminary data, researchers can find new data sources and potential interview participants, check information consistency between interviewers or observers, assure consistency and breadth of archival data, and take advantage of insights of other researchers.

If a qualitative researcher is working in the field alone, preliminary data should be shared with other qualitative researchers not engaged in the fieldwork for reactions and suggestions. This is sometimes referred to as an *external audit* or a **data audit.** This step in the research process is not an odious burden on the outside scholar, and it assures the field researcher that the insights and questions of someone removed from the pressures of the field will enhance the quality of the data-gathering process. A critic can point out places in an interview where a follow-up question was warranted, ask about relationships apparent in the data, and query the researcher about procedural decisions being made. An outsider's view on data gathering is invaluable to the solo qualitative researcher.

Data Summaries

Ultimately, the form used for data recording in the field is a personal choice. It depends on the type of study, the focus, and the researcher's preferences. There are numerous techniques for preliminary analysis with multiple researchers while still in the field (Ritchie & Lewis, 2003; Silverman, 2004; Sofaer, 2005). Figures 14.1, 14.2, and 14.3 show data display options researchers can use as data begin to accumulate.

FIGURE 14.1   Contact Summary Form: Illustration With Coded Themes (excerpt)

Contact Summary

Type of: Mtg.   ___Principals___   ___Ken's office___   ___4/2/76___   Site ___Westgate___
Contact: Who, what group   place

Phone   _____   _____   _____   Coder ___MM___
                With whom, by whom   place

Inf. Int. _____   _____   _____   Date
                With whom, by whom   place   Coded ___4/18/76___

1. Pick out the most salient points in the contact. Number in order on this sheet and note page number on which point appears. Number point in text of write-up. Attach theme or aspect to each point in CAPITALS. Invent themes included in double parentheses.

Page	Salient Points	THEMES/ASPECTS
1	1. Staff decisions have to be made by April 30.	STAFF
2	2. Teachers will have to go out of their present grade-level assignment when they transfer.	STAFF RESOURCE MGMT
2	3. Teachers vary in their willingness to integrate special ed kids into their classroom—some teachers are "a pain in the elbow."	*RESISTANCE
2	4. Ken points out that tentativie teacher assignment lists got leaked from the previous meeting (implicitly deplores this).	INTERNAL COMUNIC
2	5. Ken says, "Teachers act as if they had the right to decide who should be transferred." (would make outcry)	POWER DISTRIB
2	6. Tacit/explicit decision: "It's our decision to make." (voiced by Ken, agreed by Ed)	POWER DISTRIB/ CONFLICT MGMT
2	7. Principals and Ken, John, and Walter agree that Ms. Epstein is a "bitch."	*STEREOTYPING
2	8. Ken decides not to tell teachers ahead of time (now) about transfers ("because then we'd have a fait accompli").	PLAN FOR PLANNING\ TIME MGTM

SOURCE: Miles, M. B., & Huberman, A. M., *Qualitative Data Analysis* (2nd ed.) © 1994 by Sage Publications, Thousand Oaks, CA. Reprinted by permission of Sage Publications Inc.

FIGURE 14.2   Document Summary Form: Illustration

Document Form

Name or description of document: Site: Carson
  The Buffalo (weekly sheet)
                                                                                     Document   2

Event or contact, if any, with which
  document is associated: Date received or picked up: Feb.13
  Paul's explanation of the admin. team's functioning

Significance or importance of document:
  Gives schedule for all events in the district for the week.   Date: Feb.13

  Enables coordination, knits two schools together.

Brief summary of contents:
  Schedule of everything from freshman girls' basketball to
    "Secret Pals Week" in the elementary school.
  Also includes "Dis you know" items on the IPA program
    (apparently integrating the IPA News).
  And a description of how admin. team works who is on team,
    what regular meetings deal with, gives working philosophy
    (e.g., "we establish personal goals and monitor progress"
    ... "We coordinate effort, K–12, and all programs" ...
    "We agree on staff selection"). Concluding comment: "It is
    our system of personnel management."
  Also alludes to the 26 OPERATIONAL GUIDELINES
  (Document 16)
  (I'll guess that the admin. explanation does not appear every
  week—need to check this.)

IF DOCUMENT IS CENTRAL OR CRUCIAL TO A PARTICULAR CONTACT (e.g., a meeting agenda, newspaper clipping discussed in an interview) make a copy and include with write-up. Otherwise, put in document file.

SOURCE: From Miles, M. B. & Huberman, A. (1994). *Qualitative Data Analysis* (2nd ed.) p. 55. Reprinted by permission of Sage Publications, Inc.

Beginning qualitative researchers can adopt and adapt tactics specific to their own particular research projects (see Figure 14.4). You should practice using a variety of these summary format techniques so that you are skilled in managing your data *before* you move into the field for an extended qualitative research project. Individual researchers also can use these data display options to query their own data, seek new data sources, and point their data gathering in productive directions. Provisional counts of data points that reveal emerging themes can provide insight into issues around which interviews, instruments, or additional observation plans should be organized. New informants are identified, new document sources are found, and some inferences can begin to be developed based on preliminary data patterns. Qualitative researchers must become expert at maximizing serendipity.

FIGURE 14.3 **Illustration of a Start List of Codes**

INNOVATION PROPERTIES	IP-OBJ	3.1
IP: OBJECTIVES	IP-ORG\DD, LS	3.1.1
IP: IMPLIED CHANGES–ORGANIZATION	IP-CH\CL	3.1.4
IP: IMPLIED SALIENCE	IP-SALIENCE	3.1.5
IP: (INITIAL) USER ASSESSMENT	IP-SIZEUP/PRE., DUR	3.1.3, 3.4, 3.5
IP: PROGRAM DEVELOPMENT (IV-C)	IP-DEV	3.1.1, 3.3.3, 3.3.4
EXTERNAL CONTEXT	EC (PRE) (DUR)	3.2, 3.4, 3.4
EC: DEMOGRAPHICS	EC-DEM	
In country, school personnel	ECCO-DEM	3.2.3, 33, 34
Out country, nonschool personnel	ECEXT-DEM	3.3.3, 33, 34
EC: ENDORSEMENT	EC-END	3.2.3, 3.3, 3.4
In country, school personnel	ECCO-END	3.2.3, 3.3, 3.4
Out country, nonschool personnel	ECEXT-END	3.2.3, 3.3, 3.4
EC: CLIMATE	EC-CLIM	3.2.3, 3.3, 3.4
In country, school personnel	ECCO-CLIM	3.2.3, 3.3, 3.4
Out country, nonschool personnel	ECEXT-CLM	3.2.3, 3.3, 3.4
INTERNAL CONTEXT	IC (PRE) (DUR)	3.2, 3.3, 3.4
IC: CHARACTERISTICS	IC-CHAR	3.2.2, 3.4, 3.5
IC: NORMS AND AUTHORITY	IC-NORM	3.2.2, 3.4.3, 3.5
IC: INNOVATION HISTORY	IC-HIST	3.2.1
IC: ORGANIZATION PROCEDURES	IC-PROC	3.1.1, 3.2.4, 3.3, 3.4
IC: INNOVATION–ORGANIZATION CONGRUENCE	IC-FIT	3.2.2
ADOPTION PROCESS	AP	3.2, 3.3
AP: EVENT CHRONOLOGY–OFFICIAL VERSION	AP-CHRON/PUB	3.2.4, 3.3.1
AP: EVENT CHRONOLOGY–SUBTERRANEAN	AP-CHRON/PRIV	3.2.4, 3.3.1
AP: INSIDE/OUTSIDE	AP-IN/OUT	3.2.5
AP: CENTRALITY	AP-CENT	3.2.2
AP: MOTIVES	AP-MOT	3.2.6
AP: USER FIT	AP-FIT	3.2.7
AP: PLAN	AP-PLAN	3.3.3
AP: READINESS	AP-REDI	3.3.4, 3.2.1
AP: CRITICAL EVENTS	AP-CRIT	3.3.1
TR: SITE DYNAMICS AND TRANSFORMATIONS	TR:	3.4
TR: EVENT CHRONOLOGY–SUBTERRANEAN	TR-CHRON/PUB	3.4.1, 3.4.2, 3.4.3
TR: EVENT CHRONOLOGY–OFFICIAL VERSION	TR-CHRON/PRIV	3.4.1, 3.4.2, 3.4.3
TR: INITIAL USER EXPERIENCE	TR-START	3.4.1, 3.4.2, 3.4.3
TR: CHANGES IN INNOVATION	TR-INMOD	3.4.1
TR: EFFECTS ON ORGANIZATIONAL PRACTICES	TR-ORG\PRAC	3.4.3
TR: EFFECTS ON ORGANIZATIONAL CLIMATE	TR-ORG\CLIM	3.4.3
TR: EFFECTS ON CLASSROOM PRACTICE	TR-CLASS	3.4.2
TR: EFFECTS ON USER CONSTRUCTS	TR-HEAD	3.4.2, 3.4.3
TR: IMPLEMENTATION PROBLEMS	TR-PROBS	3.4.1
TR: CRITICAL EVENTS	TR-CRIT	3.4.1, 3.4.2, 3.4.3
TR: EXTERNAL INTERVENTIONS	TR-EXIT	3.4.3
TR: EXPLANATIONS FOR TRANSFORMATIONS	TR-SIZUP	3.4.1, 3.4.2, 3.4.3
TR: PROGRAM PROBLEM SOLVING	TR-PLAN	3.4.1, 3.4.2, 3.4.3

FIGURE 14.3 (CONTINUED)

NEW CONFIGURATION AND ULTIMATE OUTCOMES	NCO	3.5

NCO: STABILIZATION OF INNOVATION–CLASSROOM	NCO-INNOSTAB/CLASS	3.5.1
NCO: STABILIZATION OF USER BEHAVIOUR	NCO-STAB/USER	3.5.2
NCO: USER FIRST-LEVEL OUTCOMES	NCO-USER IOC	3.5.4
Postive and negative	NCO-USER IOC/+, −	
Anticipated and unanticipated	NCO-USER IOC/A, U	
Combination (when appropriate)	NCO-USER IOC/A+, A−	
	U+, U−	
NCO: USER META OUTCOMES	NCO-USER META	
Positive and negative	NCO-USER META OC/+, −	
Anticipate and unanticpated	NCO-USER META OC/A, U	
Combinations (when appropriate)	NCO-USER META OC/A+, A−	
	U+, U−	
NCO: USER SPINOFFS AND SIDE EFFECTS	NCO-USER SIDE	3.5.5 (3.5.2)
Positive and negative	NCO-USER SIDE OC/+, −	
Anticipated and unanticipated	NCO-USER SIDE OC/A, U	
Combinations (when appropriate)	NCO-USER SIDE OC/A+, A−	
	U+, U−	
NCO: CLASSROOM INSTITUTIONALIZATION	NCO-INST/CLASS	3.5.5
NCO: STABILIZATION OF INOVATION–ORGANIZATION	NCO-INNOSTAB/ORG	3.5.6
NCO: STABILIZATION OF ORGANIZATIONAL BEAVIOUR	NCO-STAB/ORG	3.5.7
NCO: ORGANIZATIONAL INSTITUTIONALIZATION	NCO-INST/ORG	3.5.8
NCO: ORGANIZATIONAL FIRST-LEVEL OUTCOMES	NCO-ORG IOC	3.5.9
Positive and negative	NCO-ORG IOC/+, −	
Anticipated and unanticipated	NCO-ORG IOC/A, U	
Combinations (when appropriate)	NCO-ORG IOC/A+, A−	
	U+, U−	
NCO: ORGANIZATIONAL META OUTCOMES	NCO-ORG META	3.5.9
Positive and negative	NCO-ORG SIDE OC/+, −	
Anticipated and unanticipated	NCO-ORG META OC/A, U	
Combinations (when appropriate)	NCO-ORG META OC/A+, A−	
	U+, U−	
NCO: ORGANIZATIONAL SPINOFFS AND SIDE EFFECTS	NCO-ORG SIDE	3.5.9 (3.5.7)
Positive and negative	NCO-ORG SIDE OC/+, −	
Anticipated and unanticipated	NCO-ORG SIDE OC/A, U	
Combinations (when appropriate)	NCO-ORG META OC/A+, A−	
	U+, U−	
NCO: INSTITUTIONAL EXPANSION	NCO-INNOGRO/ORG	3.5.8
NCO: ORGANIZATIONAL REDUCTION	NCO-INNODWIN/org	3.5.8

EXTERNAL AND INTERNAL ASSISTANCE (SEPARATE CODES FOR EXTERNAL, PEER, ADMINISTRATIVE)		

ASS: LOCATION	AS-LOC	3.6.1
ASS: RULES, NORMS	ASS-RULE	3.6.1
ASS: ORIENTATION	ASS-ORI	3.6.2
ASS: TYPE	ASS-TYPE	3.6.3
ASS: EFFECTS	ASS-EEF	3.6.4
ASS: ASSESSMENT BY RECIPIENTS	ASS-ASS	3.6.5
ASS: LINKAGE	ASS-LINK	3.6.6

(Continued)

FIGURE 14.3   (CONTINUED)

EMERGNG CASUAL LINKS	CL	
CL: NETWORKS	CL-NET	N.A.
CL: RULES	CL-RULE	N.A.
CL: RECURRENT PATTERNS	CL-PATT	N.A.
Within site	CL-PATT/LS	N.A.
Interside	CL-PATT/OS	N.A.
CL: EXPLANATORY CLUSTER (researcher)	CL-EXPL	N.A.
(respondent)	SITECL-EXPL	N.A.
QUERIES	QU	
QU: SURPRISES	QU-I	
QU: PUZZLES	QU-Q	N.A.

SOURCE: From Miles, M. B. & Huberman, A. (1994). *Qualitative Data Analysis* (2nd ed.) p. 59–60. Reprinted by permission of Sage Publications, Inc.

FIGURE 14.4   **Example Protocol Adaptation**

Protocol Question

B. How is the Title I program organized, who is employed by Title I, when are decisions made, and who makes them?

Sources of Data

_____ Title I director

_____ Assistant Superintendent

_____ Organization chart

_____ Job descriptions

Sample Strategies:

_____ Obtain or draw an organizational chart that shows the location of the Title I office

_____ List the type and number of instructional and noninstructional Title I personnel (including Title I specialists, coordinators, managers).

_____ To whom does the Title I director report?

_____ Who reports to the Title I director ?

_____ Whom does the Title I director supervise?

_____ What kinds of decisions does the director have to formally sign off and with whom?

_____ Create an organizational chart of the Title I program (if one doesn't exist) that shows the directors and any intermediaries (either in schools or in the Title I office) and their relations to principals, regular teachers, and Title I teachers.

_____ Fill in the following table by ranking the order in which the following decisions and events occur.

SOURCE: From Yin, R. K. (1989). *Case study research: Designs and methods* (2nd ed.), pp. 76–77. Reprinted by permission of Sage Publications, Inc.

Qualitative researchers also must be sensitive to normative expectations in the setting—what is expected of the members of the group by other members of the group. This is why a researcher's **reflections section** in systematic field notes is so important. It provides a record of the thinking and beliefs of the *field researcher* at each stage of the research. Subjective judgments made by the researcher can unfairly bias attitudes toward normative expectations and lead to premature and inaccurate preliminary conclusions. Eventually, patterns in the data may emerge as trends are identified. However, a prudent qualitative researcher treats all preliminary findings developed in the field cautiously and reflects on his or her thinking at the time the data were recorded or obtained. Preliminary patterns provide insight into promising sources and types of data, but they should not be treated as **findings** until data are reanalyzed from the distance of time and place after the researcher leaves the setting (see Chapter 9 for a discussion of the impact of time away from the setting on the reliability and validity of findings).

Because of the great variability in approaches to analysis in qualitative methods as well as space constraints, a detailed discussion of the analysis stages is not provided here. For a more in-depth guide to how to conduct specific types of qualitative educational research, we suggest you refer to a text specific to that method of research (e.g., Glesne, 2006; Golden-Biddle & Locke, 2006; Silverman, 2006; Strauss & Corbin, 1998; Willis, 2007).

POST–DATA-GATHERING ANALYSIS

At the end of data collection, it is important for a researcher to leave the setting in order to achieve some distance from the people, place, and events studied. Having left the field, a researcher can concentrate on the analytical techniques that will help him or her transition from data gathering to the analytic process that reports the findings for consumers of the research. We will discuss only a few of these techniques in detail and recommend that the beginning researcher take special pains to become acquainted with the many options available. Analytical techniques range from coding and counting, data summary sheets, matrices, charts, graphs, and tables to "thick description" and criticism. Later in the chapter, we will turn to the scholarly writing traditions that flow from these various types of data analysis.

Coding and Counting

Data display and analysis techniques chosen by the researcher reveal very different assumptions about the kind of conclusions that can be drawn from qualitative data. In fact, these processes are also mutually influenced by the demands of rigorous analysis, and the systematic ways in which researchers can explore, explain, describe, and illustrate qualitative data and findings.

Data Display Techniques

Data display techniques such as those illustrated in Figures 14.1 through 14.4 provide systematic processes for distilling data during analysis. These include such things as data coding, analytical matrices, and pattern matching that allow for data audits by other researchers. Such data audits are crucial because they enable the logic of analysis to be retraced and understood by others. They provide a qualitative analog for the statistical techniques discussed in Chapters 12 and 13. They also allow the analysis to reveal frequencies, intervals, intensity, and kinds of behaviors that can also be counted, allowing quantitative analyses of qualitative data. Before data can be recorded in matrices, charts, and tables, however, they must be distilled from language and text into abstract categories. Techniques of presentation and data analysis such as thick description, discourse analysis, criticism, classical, and critical ethnography rely on phenomenological assumptions about the nature of social reality (e.g., Cassell & Symon, 2004; Jupp, 2006; Mertens, 2005).

Distilling words into abstract categories is one of the first tasks faced by a researcher working in positivistic traditions of qualitative methods. These categories or "themes" begin to emerge during preliminary analysis in the field. Through repeated and careful iterations, abstract concepts emerge that can be coded in the text and then displayed in a number of configurations as the researcher gradually comes to understand the social and behavioral implications of the findings (see Figure 14.1).

We need to stress here that this is an iterative process that requires repetition of analysis and re-analysis until a clear picture of the implications emerges. Rarely (if ever) is this process limited to one or two steps. With each iteration of analysis, additional aspects of the data may emerge. As data are found to not fit in one set of categories or themes, additional themes must be added to increase the "fit" of the data. Action research studies also require repeated analysis steps when using qualitative analysis. The Research in Action box illustrates elements of identifying themes in Emily's study.

Increasingly, computer programs are used to organize text by codes and themes. Text that illustrates or represents a concept can be blocked and coded in the text, and then the researcher can use the codes to assemble data for further analysis and writing the research report. For example, the responses from 100 interviews (either transcribed into a text file or recorded as systematic field notes in a text file) can be grouped by date, role of the respondent (e.g., teacher, parent, principal), interviewer, or any other general category. The same interviews also can be quickly reorganized by setting (school), level (elementary, middle, high school), environment (urban, socioeconomic, suburban, rural), or any other category. Once text has been carefully read and coded, it can be reorganized by theme or code. For example, a researcher can prepare a text file of all blocks of text coded as examples of concepts such as competitiveness, frustration, persistence, or any other conceptual category represented in the data, along with identifying information about the source. These processes can be accomplished with hard copies of text and have traditionally been done this way.

Simulation

For additional simulations visit www.sagepub. com/drewstudy

Simulation 14.1

Topic: Writing the research report

Background statement: Like quantitative research, qualitative research reports must not only convey the findings and implications of the systematic inquiry, they must also provide sufficient detail for an informed reader to determine for him- or herself the usefulness and trustworthiness of the findings.

Tasks to be performed:

1. Read a qualitative research report of *your choosing.*

2. Summarize the analytical procedures followed by the author(s).

3. Describe the major qualities and shortcomings of the analyses in the stimulus material below; defend your judgments.

Stimulus material: Choose a qualitative research report you personally find compelling. Be sure to provide complete references (or a copy) to your instructor.

Write your response, then turn to page 353 for Simulation Feedback 14.1.

RESEARCH IN ACTION

KEY POINTS IN THE CHAPTER REFLECTED IN THIS BOX:

- The manner in which this study identified themes in the qualitative data collected
- How the qualitative data may be analyzed to identify themes as a means of discovering staff attitudes toward reading instruction approaches

For more research in action tips visit www.sagepub .com/drewstudy

OBJECTIVES TO LEARN FROM THIS BOX:

- Learn to identify potential themes to help explain study results.
- Notice how the qualitative elements of this study provide information that would not be available otherwise.
- Consider the implications of method selection and determine what effects such a choice might have on the data.

We saw earlier that Emily is planning to use selected qualitative methods as one of the approaches in her study of reading instruction. Viewed in total, her study is one employing mixed methods. Her qualitative data will be recorded as interview commentaries from the teachers involved in her study of reading instruction. Recall that the study involves two approaches to reading instruction. One group intervention involves student engagement through emphasizing concepts of interest to the students (CORI), and the other method uses drill and practice on words and sentences (DAP). The qualitative data will be collected by interviewing the teachers and teachers' aides to determine opinions about the approaches being used for reading instruction.

Interview data indicate that teachers in both the CORI and DAP groups believe very strongly that reading instruction is of central importance to the overall educational success with children. They do not believe that any teacher should be teaching a topic for which he or she does not have a passion. One teacher indicated that, "Some teachers act as if the material they teach is boring and not all that important. How do they think the students react to that because for sure the students can sense it? They shouldn't be allowed in the classroom period!" Emily's initial analysis of these data identified themes of "pride," "conflict," and "concern for students." As indicated in the text, she will have to undertake repeated iterations of theme analysis to feel comfortable that she has identified teachers' perceptions about teaching.

Think about this: For the action research study in this box, what themes do you see that perhaps Emily has not yet identified? Why is repeated analysis needed to fully understand what themes might emerge and what the data mean?

SOURCE: This action research scenario is roughly based on Swan, E. A. (2003). *Concept-oriented reading instruction: Engaging classrooms, lifelong learners.* New York: Guilford Press.

Various tables, charts, figures, and matrices can then be made using these distilled data. Patterns and relationships emerge from this process in vivid and visual ways that provide additional insight in the analysis. There are many different ways in which qualitative data can be displayed to enhance the reliability of the analytical process that can be used by beginning researchers as models (Neuman, 2006; Silverman, 2004; Sofaer, 2005).

These coding processes, whether on paper or using technology, provide an important "audit trail" of the logic employed by the researcher during analysis. You will recall in Chapter 9 that we talked about ways in which the reliability of qualitative research can be enhanced. A *data audit* by another researcher (either part of the team or a colleague not involved in the research) can then test the logic of the analysis. Comparable data displays and presentations can also be used to compare one research setting with another, prepare case studies, or complete any number of analytical tasks. A qualitative researcher must be able to show how conclusions are drawn from the data as part of the analytical process in order for the consumers of the research to have confidence in the findings (e.g., Denzin & Lincoln, 2005; Mertens, 2005).

As analytical codes are developed that represent central concepts emerging from the data, qualitative researchers can count the frequency with which these themes or issues appear to develop a sense of the intensity, relative frequency, or distribution of concepts. Depending on the paradigm from which the researcher approaches the task, these analytical techniques can become increasingly quantitative in nature. When multiple researchers are involved (one way of protecting the reliability of the research), they can conduct parallel analyses on the same raw data, compare their coding judgments, and discuss the emerging conceptual themes until they agree.

Regardless of the perspective applied to the analysis, the record of the analysis should be as systematic as the records kept of raw data. This analytical trail provides a conceptual chain of logic that a peer or colleague can use in an audit of the research. While no two scholars will reach exactly the same conclusions from any single data set, colleagues with similar expertise should be able to follow the data/analysis/conclusion logic backward to understand how the researcher reached his or her conclusions. This process is a critical component of qualitative research and mimics the replicability process in quantitative, statistical analyses in its contribution to research rigor.

Data Summary Sheets

Researchers use a variety of techniques to help organize their data into manageable forms while still in the field. After leaving the field, the need to organize the data becomes even more critical. Like with data analysis in the field, **data summary sheets** are commonly used to summarize such things as findings from observation days, types of events, data related to particular individuals, or emerging themes. These can be arranged by time, setting, type of participant, or individual. Thematic summaries of research on schools might include conversations between key leaders of groups in a school, criticisms shared with the receptionists about a discipline program by the teachers across time and by teacher, information about students referred to the assistant principal for disciplinary action, or previous action taken. Matrices, graphs, and charts also help the qualitative researcher make sense of data (see Chapter 11 for more hints about data tabulation and display).

Matrices

Once coding and counting are completed and summary sheets constructed, comparisons among variables, factors, or emerging themes are facilitated by the use of other data display and analysis techniques. Matrices constructed to promote such comparisons provide one such technique.

A matrix lays out one factor in relation to another, providing for data cells across multiple factors. For example, a researcher investigating the disruptive behavior of children with disabilities in school might collect observation data on a dozen children throughout the school day over a period of several weeks. After summaries of disruptive behavior are collected, a matrix can be constructed that places the 12 participants on one axis, and hours of the school day on another axis. The numbers of disruptive behaviors in the matrix cells provides one look at the children's lives in school. Another might compare children to teachers (if they move to different teachers during the day) and reveal the number of disruptive behaviors occurring under each teacher's supervision. Yet another might be type of behaviors recorded compared with settings in which the children spend the day (classrooms, physical education or recess, lunch, between classes, before and after school). The research focus and types of data will drive the choice of factors along which matrices can be built.

Graphs and Charts

Data points or matrix cell totals can be displayed as graphs and charts that visually represent the findings emerging from analysis. Qualitative researchers interested in developing a sense of time or movement or in comparing cases, settings, groups, or individuals often use graphs and charts to explore differences and similarities. See Chapter 11 for examples of graphs that are commonly used in educational research.

Pattern Matching

All the analytical techniques illustrated above provide ways for a researcher to compare and match patterns among abstract concepts emerging from qualitative data. This step is an important one because it lays a foundation for trustworthy statements about the phenomenon under study. For example, a nonresearcher observing an elementary school when dropping off or picking up a child might say that the children seem to fight a lot. A researcher would observe the elementary school for many days, deliberately sampling observations over all times of the day and making sure to observe the children interacting with all their peers and with their teachers. Fighting patterns would constitute the focus of only one of many factors observed, and the researcher would then approach the analysis by child, by time of day, by teacher, by age of child, and so forth. A statement might then be made that Eric fights more often when he has a substitute teacher than when his regular classroom teacher is present. You can probably think of many matrices, charts, and graphs that a researcher might produce to understand children's behavior.

INDUCTIVE AND DEDUCTIVE ANALYSES

While there are many different approaches to analysis of qualitative data, they can be grouped into two different types of approaches: inductive and deductive analysis. **Inductive analysis** refers to approaches that "follow the data" rather than comparing the data to an a priori construct. **Deductive analysis** refers to approaches that begin with a hypothesis, theoretical framework (to be tested or compared), or strong preconceptions.

Inductive Method

The analytical methods described in the preceding discussion allow for an inductive method of analysis. Concepts, patterns, and themes emerge from the iterative logic employed by the researcher. The more naturalistic the inquiry, the more a researcher seeks to guard against any preconceptions or beliefs on the part of the researcher or any existing social theory to pre-bias the research. What quantitatively grounded researchers call theoretically based research, naturalistic researchers might call pre-conceptions. However, qualitative research also can be designed to test social theories in natural settings characterized by the features we discussed in Chapter 8 (natural settings, small sample size, phenomena that cannot or should not be manipulated). This type of research relies on a more deductive approach in which naturalistic data are analyzed using concepts from a social theory.

Deductive Method

Deductive qualitative research takes several forms. First, systematically collected data using naturalistic methods and very open-ended techniques can be analyzed using codes and variables from existing theory. The coding and counting techniques, data display, and data reduction methods described above can then be employed to "test" hypotheses or theoretical fit. Findings may confirm or disconfirm theory, but the test is in the form of language and text rather than probability data.

Another way in which more deductive methods are used in qualitative research relates to the research design prior to data gathering. A social theory may drive the original impetus for research, and the theory may include a strong conceptual framework proposing relationships and predicting outcomes. When this is the case, the researcher may design a focused interview protocol deliberately designed to elicit responses along a particular vein. Observation and archival research also would be directly related to the theory.

Two dangers face the qualitative researcher employing deductive methods. First, an interview that is too directive or an observation schedule that is too narrow may fail by focusing the research to a degree that guarantees the affirmation of the theory or framework. We warned earlier about "leading the witness" during an interview. In a deductive study, the researcher must take care not to "lead the research," resulting in a self-fulfilling prophecy. This is true whether the data set is collected specifically for the study or whether an existing data set is used that employs a post hoc analysis.

Second, important or even vital information that is more relevant to a particular research setting may be overlooked or misinterpreted. This is why it is so important that qualitative researchers seek out informants known to oppose a prevalent view, check emerging findings with participants to see if they are capturing the emic point of view accurately, and share their analysis and the logic of their data reduction with outside researchers or through a data audit.

Phenomenological Analytical Techniques

The analytical techniques discussed so far tap into traditions within the social sciences rather than more literary traditions. Qualitative scholarship such as discourse analysis, critical theory, and criticism borrow from more philosophical and artistic traditions. While space does not allow for an extensive description of these more phenomenological traditions, they differ enough from analyses described above to warrant some discussion. We urge those interested in these traditions to give rigorous study to the variety of intellectual traditions that inspire high-quality phenomenological inquiry. For our discussion here, we rely on two of the most common in education and social science research—thick description and criticism.

Thick Description

Description that meets criteria for both accuracy and vividness is often called **thick description**. Through the use of prose, it places the consumer of qualitative research personally and explicitly in the setting the researcher observed. Like a gifted novelist describing a scene, the qualitative researcher writes prose that creates clear sensual images of the setting and behaviors being observed. The sights, smells, and feelings of the social setting come alive for a reader. At the same time, the qualitative researcher must be sparse and accurate, avoiding "purple prose" that exaggerates and elaborates in the search for richness. It takes a great deal of talent and practice to be able to create for the reader a sense of being there with the researcher while resisting the temptation to embellish.

Beginning researchers seeking to hone their observation and description skills often spend long hours sitting quietly, observing, and writing. When several students of qualitative inquiry describe the same setting and then critique each others' work, they develop a strong sense of the advantages and drawbacks of qualitative research. The vividness and salience that make thick description and the scholarship based on it compelling reading, also place tremendous responsibility on the researcher. From the outset of conducting the research, the point of view shapes the outcome.

This interdependence between point of view and findings exists in quantitative research as well. We have emphasized that researchers must clearly acknowledge the assumptions on which their inquiry is based. Earlier we discussed the impact of the assumptions on which statistical techniques rely, and the way the outcomes of analysis critically depend on respect for and adherence to these assumptions by the researcher. In both quantitative and qualitative scholarship, the researcher is responsible for stating clearly and directly what his or her assumptions and points of view are. The consumer of the research can then make informed judgments about how best to interpret and use the research.

Criticism

Another commonly used method of data gathering and analysis in qualitative research is **criticism**. Criticism relies on the same kinds of writing skills as thick description but it also adds preferences, likes, and dislikes to the process. Criticism may be used in social and educational research by applying criticism processes to observational research. This perspective relies on the analog of researcher as artistic critic (in the best sense). The observer describes while conveying personal taste and preference, even judgment, to the reader. Such an approach is a way of combining art and science in social inquiry. The accomplished educational critic thus is able to capture the art and craft of teaching along with the science by these methods.

Criticism is firmly established in other traditions of social inquiry as well. Critical theorists take a perspective toward the assumptions and outcomes of traditional social sciences that is often "critical" in the common understanding of the word. The critical perspective they take is designed to peel back the layers of assumed and entrenched practice to examine those attitudes and behaviors that are pushed aside or hidden. This point of view becomes an integral part of their methods and findings. More specifically, 20th-century critical theorists apply the methods of Marx and an anticapitalist perspective to the collection, analysis, and presentation of social science inquiry, arguing that purely positivist traditions carry an equally slanted bias toward Western thought and science. These same criticisms of traditional methodologies are leveled by critical feminist theorists and others, such as critical race theorists, who often use discourse analysis to illustrate how our language biases the outcomes of our research and the implications of our findings.

The critical traditions in qualitative research are varied and complex. Before turning to the ways in which this scholarship is written and presented to consumers, we must emphasize that each new researcher must seek a scholarly tradition that coincides with his or her epistemological view—what is the nature of knowledge, how is it best obtained, how is knowledge conveyed to others? Self-knowledge will help facilitate this search.

REPORTING QUALITATIVE RESEARCH

The final test of qualitative research rests with its ability to convey meaning and expand understanding while contributing to theory development and knowledge. Ultimately, a reader must be convinced when reading the researcher's report that the research conveys reliable and valid information about the situation under study and expands the reader's understanding of social and cultural experiences.

All three major methods for gathering qualitative data—interview, observation, and archival research—are used by qualitative researchers, regardless of the perspective they take during analysis and writing. Once a qualitative researcher leaves the field and switches roles to analyst and writer, different research methods dramatically shape the nature of the study that emerges. One writer may write an extensive ethnography, whereas another scholar may employ the coding and counting methods described earlier that rely on searches for patterns. Many traditional and emerging approaches to analyzing and reporting qualitative research exist. We will describe three formats that are common in qualitative studies in education and social science research—grounded theory, ethnography, and narrative construction.

Grounded Theory

Grounded theory reports present a conceptual framework (i.e., a theory) that explains the process of some substantive topic. The theory is "grounded" in data, meaning that the theory is generated during and after data collection rather than beforehand, which would be done with quantitative methods. As such, the data must be drawn from multiple sources using multiple methods.

With grounded theory approaches, the data analysis will generally take the form of the iterative procedures described above. Because of the desire to generate a conceptual theory, close attention must be paid to the standards of rigor described in Chapter 9. Triangulation, data audits, and member checking are all crucial pieces to assuring that the theory is accurate as well as applicable.

Another key concept in grounded theory is that of **saturation.** Rather than the research process being one of data collection *and then* data analysis, grounded theory often uses an iterative process of data collection, analysis, more collection, more analysis, and so forth. With each iteration, the theory becomes more refined and complete. However, at some point the researcher arrives at a place of diminishing returns such that additional data do not add to the theory. This is the point of saturation. There are no hard and fast rules about identifying when you have reached saturation. It is up to the discretion of the researcher, but can be confirmed by others familiar with the research.

Development of the theory involves development of a core category as well as additional categories that all relate back to the core. These categories and their interrelations form the basis of the theory, which then must be described and applied to not only the situation under study, but also others to which the researcher believes they should be generalized.

Ethnography

Ethnography is the in-depth study of the culture of a particular group of people. The ethnographer seeks to describe this culture and convey the patterns of life, beliefs, and ideologies as well as formal and informal relationships. The ethnographer also describes the way life is represented by technology, architecture, art, literature (or stories), and other traditions that make up the culture. All of this must be done in a way that makes the interpretations credible and assures the reader that the ethnographer approached the study without preconceptions regarding what could be expected (Mertens, 2005). This requires direct, prolonged, on-the-spot observation. While the role of the ethnographer varies from site to site, guidelines regarding what is appropriate and of what will likely succeed can be conveyed by training as well as sensitivity about social interaction, interpersonal relations, and obtrusiveness.

Good ethnography requires extended, meticulous, and perceptive data gathering as well as careful analysis. Many inexperienced researchers choose ethnography or other forms of qualitative research because they are unsure of their statistical skills. These same beginning researchers are often unaware of the major time commitment a good ethnography requires and the intellectual challenge of qualitative data. Before choosing ethnography, care should be given to research design that preserves important criteria for good ethnographic research (Denzin & Lincoln, 2005; Jeffrey & Troman, 2004; Mertens, 2005).

A number of ethnographers take what they call a critical perspective on ethnography. This distinction is important, because the intellectual role the ethnographer plays in the study is that of a critic of the established perspective on knowledge. Critical ethnographers rely on a body of existing theory from critical sociology and philosophy. From this departure, they observe the participants and the environment with an eye toward criticizing that theoretical perspective. A critical ethnographer thus approaches the qualitative research process by focusing on practices that serve to disempower or oppress the group under study. The researcher speaks to the audience (i.e., the readers) on behalf of the group under study with an ultimate purpose of advocacy. Because of this purpose and these procedures, it is very important for the researcher to acknowledge (and sometimes even celebrate) having conscious intentions or "biases" in doing the research.

Ethnographies generally are not undertaken with specific hypotheses determined in advance, coded instruments, or highly defined categories for observation. The danger of carrying preconceptions into a study is too great when these techniques are used for ethnography (unless they become an aspect of the research, as in some critical ethnographies). Questionnaires and interview guides may be used, but they will usually be developed after the investigator has spent time on-site collecting observations.

Narrative Construction

Narrative construction will often look similar to ethnography except that it focuses on an individual. The data that have been collected through interview, observation, or archival searches are organized into specific stories that contribute to that individual's life. These stories must be organized for themes or key elements. These themes should serve to add depth or understanding to a description of the life of that individual. The order in which these stories are collected rarely (if ever) actually aligns with the theme or key elements that would compose the narrative. Once the stories have been identified and organized by theme or element, the researcher must use the technique of **restorying** to put the individual stories into a chronological or logical order that pulls them together into a coherent narrative. This is the process used when writing biographies or autobiographies. It is the same process to conduct a narrative construction for educational research purposes.

A crucial part of pulling individual stories into a coherent whole is to use the thick description technique described above. It is important to provide detailed descriptions of key characters, settings, and elements of each story as well as those of the narrative as a whole. While this is important with other forms of qualitative research reports, it is even more important for narrative construction because it is the basis of the findings. Without a thick description, the findings may be left even more to reader interpretation without the benefit of presentation of the author's interpretation.

Because narrative construction relates the life events of an individual, it is often also important to maintain the interpretation of the subject of the narrative. Narrative construction relies heavily on emic or negotiated data; therefore it is generally a good idea to use the process of member checking to ensure that the researcher has not altered the perspective or interpretations during the process of restorying.

Chapter Summary

+ Many researchers who love statistical analyses find the time in analysis of quantitative data to be more fun than the data collection stage. However, few qualitative researchers describe analysis as more fun than data gathering. This reality is unsurprising, because the deeply human and engaging process of data gathering is often the feature investigators find most appealing about qualitative research in the social sciences.

+ As noted before, the advent of widely available computer analyses has freed quantitative researchers from many of the tedious aspects of analysis; however, qualitative data analysis remains a labor-intensive and time-consuming process, even with the use of computer programs.

+ Nevertheless, for the researcher committed to describing the subtleties and exploring the salient depth and breadth of social life, qualitative research remains the methodology of choice. The rich traditions of qualitative research provide an immediacy of experience and evoke empathy in the reader that is unavailable for most consumers of quantitative research.

+ Assumptions regarding the trustworthiness of analytical techniques require vigilant safeguarding. For those interested in crossing the boundaries, however, qualitative/quantitative mixed-method designs offer an intriguing alternative to traditional research that adheres to the sacred boundaries between research methods.

Key Terms

Criticism. A phenomenological analytic technique that uses the researcher's preferences or opinions to interpret and judge the phenomenon under study. It is often used to expose the biases in common wisdom and how they affect a specific disempowered group.

Data audit. Providing preliminary data to a researcher not participating in the study in order to get feedback.

Data summary sheets. Forms used to summarize field notes or other recorded data. They are often used as an intermediary step in analysis.

Deductive analysis. Approaches to data analysis that begin with a hypothesis, theoretical framework, or strong preconceptions to which the results are compared.

Ethnography. The in-depth study of the culture of a particular group of people that seeks to describe this culture and convey the patterns of life, beliefs, and ideologies as well as formal and informal relationships.

Findings. Results or conclusions in qualitative research.

Grounded theory. A type of qualitative research that presents a conceptual framework (i.e., a theory) that explains the process of some substantive topic.

Inductive analysis. Approaches to data analysis that evolve as analysis is conducted rather than comparing results to an a priori hypothesis.

Narrative construction. Similar to ethnography except that it focuses on an individual. The stories or anecdotes about that person's life are organized for themes and relayed in a fashion that leads to a purpose or lesson.

Reflections section. The section of research field notes that covers the researcher's personal reflections about what is being observed.

Restorying. In narrative construction, the process of taking stories or anecdotes and putting them into a chronological or logical order that conveys a coherent narrative.

Saturation. The point at which collecting additional data will not add to the interpretation of the findings.

Student Study Site

The companion Web site for *Designing and Conducting Research in Education*
www.sagepub.com/drewstudy

Supplement your review of this chapter by going to the companion Web site to take one of the practice quizzes, use the flashcards to study key terms, and check out the many other study aids you'll find there. You'll even find some research articles from the Sage Full-Text Collection and a step-by-step guide that will show you how to read an educational research article.

Simulation Feedback

Simulation Feedback 14.1

Writing the research report poses a daunting challenge to researchers. While many scholars were reared with the injunction, "If you can't write it, you don't know it," writing is the final hurdle many scholars face in their quest to communicate with other scholars. The research report also is the means through which the researcher seeks to communicate with others who could use the findings to improve their lives.

Your analysis should have specifically enumerated the features of a research report drawing on a particular perspective. See **pages 350–351** for more information about the features of the report you should be able to describe and illustrate.

For additional simulations visit www.sagepub .com/drewstudy

15

INTERPRETING RESULTS

CHAPTER OBJECTIVES

After reading Chapter 15, you should be able to do the following:

+ Describe research as an integrated process, from the idea through implementation and interpretation of results.

+ Describe the reasoning process that moves from a theory or idea to a research question.

+ Describe the components found in a method section and how they provide an operational protocol for the study.

+ Describe steps that may be part of interpretation.

It is not uncommon for beginning researchers to labor through the development of a research question, through the design and execution of a study, and even through data analysis, only to find themselves confronted with serious difficulty in terms of interpreting results. The intuitive leaps from data to behavior are difficult at best, but in fact these leaps are representative of a broader problem related to acquiring a unified concept of the research process. Such difficulties should not be surprising because the process of interpreting research results is rarely taught. In fact, a broad conceptualization of the total research process is seldom taught. More often than not, college or university instructors teach limited segments of research methods, such as a statistics course. The segments most often taught lend themselves well to rote memorization but are not placed in the context of research as a thinking activity. Consequently, students may be well equipped with library research information or statistical computation skills, but are unable to even approach the planning and implementation of a study. The absence of an overall concept of the total research process not only impedes conducting research but also often reduces the effective acquisition of even the basic individual research skills because those skills make no sense and have little utility out of context.

This chapter will discuss the relationship between various segments of the research act with the intent of providing a panoramic view of the process, attempting to place these segments in functional perspective. In addition, attention will be given to interpretation of results, which is a factor of vital importance to progress in behavioral science.

RESEARCH AS AN INTEGRATED PROCESS

There are a number of roadblocks that appear to prevent research from being viewed as an integrated process. One significant obstacle is the previously noted fragmentation of the overall research act. This segmenting is generated in a variety of fashions, the most powerful of which may be the approach to teaching. Courses on statistics are often taught with little or no attention to how statistics relate to either the research question or the meaning of results. Similarly, writing is taught primarily from a term paper framework with little attention focused on how to build a logical, reasoned case or how to articulate intuitive leaps from Data Point A to Data Point B to resulting conclusions. Since little effort is exerted to synthesize these disjointed parts, conceptual gaps existing between various segments of the research process handicap beginning researchers. This may result in a limited perspective of research that is incompatible with the total implementation of an investigation, from the beginning of a research question to the interpretation of data collected to answer that question.

As noted before, research actually represents a continuous process beginning with a theory or body of knowledge that generates a research question. The nature of the research question, in turn, dictates to a considerable degree the method to be employed. Finally, all of those relate to the interpretive discussion of results. Certain qualitative researchers would contend that this series or sequence of events is inappropriate, as indicated in Chapter 2. Such researchers allow definitions to emerge as procedures move forward. We acknowledge this viewpoint and have chosen to use the current framework to facilitate discussion. The gaps in conceptual continuity will be addressed in the following sections in an attempt to highlight the relationships among various segments of the research act. Conceptual gaps in the research process represent points where the student has a high probability of encountering difficulties.

One of the first high-risk points encountered in the research process involves the relationship between a theory or piece of theory and the research question. A second high-risk problem arises during translation of the research question into the method (which includes study design, data collection, and analyses). Finally, also of great importance are the conceptual relationships between results and interpretations back to behavioral terms. These problematic areas represent vital and logical relationships that must be well understood if a researcher is to have the functional capacity to work in a variety of settings. Figure 15.1 offers a visualization of how

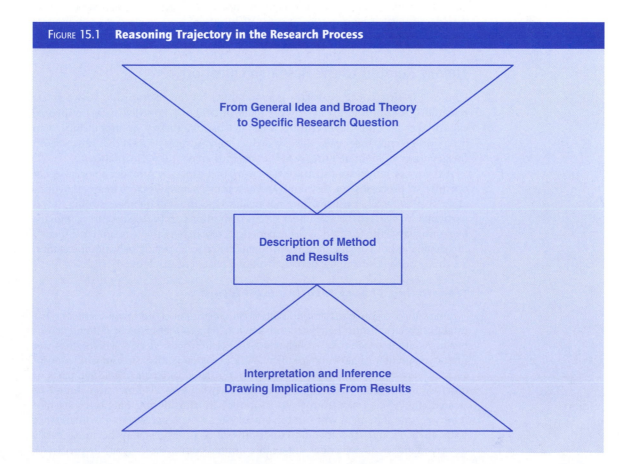

FIGURE 15.1   **Reasoning Trajectory in the Research Process**

From General Idea and Broad Theory to Specific Research Question

Description of Method and Results

Interpretation and Inference Drawing Implications From Results

TABLE 15.1	**Broad Decision Tree of the Research Process**			
Idea Stage	*Research Question*	*Method*	*Analysis*	*Interpretation*
Conduct a study?	Type of Question?	Select Method	Select Analysis	Interpret Results
Check literature,	Descriptive, Difference,	Quantitative,	Based on	Relate to literature,
Lit reviews, Other	Relationship,	Qualitative,	question type,	Relate to theory,
	Combinations	Mixed	data, N, n,	Relate to practice
			distribution,	Suggest new questions

reasoning in the research process progresses: (1) moving from a general idea to a specific research question, (2) describing the methods and design to be used and the results, and (3) reasoning in a way that moves from the specific results back to the broader context of the general world of behavior—this last reasoning is the process of interpreting the results and what it means for the more general context. This visual model also fits the general trajectory of reasoning in a research article as well as in theses and dissertations. Figure 15.1 pictorially represents the flow of reasoning, from the general idea to a focused research question and from that point to selecting the research methods, collecting and analyzing data, and interpreting results. There are a variety of decisions that need to be made through this process. Table 15.1 reflects a broad decision tree of choices that face the researcher (we have seen decision trees before, as in Chapter 10, but those have focused on components of the overall process).

Theory Related to the Research Question

One of the first conceptual gaps is represented by the relationship between the research question and a theoretical model or body of knowledge. Many people experience difficulty determining what an abstract theory or model means in behavioral terms. Essentially this is a deductive reasoning process that moves from the general statement of a theory to the specific behavioral performance.

A theory or model is an abstract framework that generally provides an overview of the inferred processes (e.g., learning) and how they operate. Because theory functions at an abstract level, it usually does not include specific statements regarding how a particular human will behave under specific conditions. In the absence of exemplars, beginning students (and often the experienced researcher) may encounter difficulty in visualizing how the theoretical statements relate to a specific behavioral instance. Yet this process is vital to the development of a related research question.

Translating Theory Into the Big Picture

One source of the translation difficulty is that students tend to view a theory as a total package that must be related to behavior. Yet a model or theory often encompasses a rather broad area of behaviors that, when viewed as a whole, does not intend to predict behavioral specifics. A model is generally a composite concept such as learning, and it should generally be translated in terms of selected parts or dimensions of behavior that are included. Each behavioral dimension should be treated somewhat apart from the total model. By considering only one part of a theory or one statement within a total theory at a time (e.g., learning words, rather than all learning), the specific conditions of a situation may be more easily described and behavior under these more limited circumstances may be predicted.

After the results are obtained, the findings are usually related back to the theory or the part of the theory that explains the behavioral dimension under study. Attempting to consider a total theory from the beginning may seriously impede the development of a researchable question. This process may be compared to eating a pastrami sandwich. If a person tries to swallow the sandwich whole, he or she will likely choke, and certainly not derive pleasure from eating it. On the other hand, one bite at a time from the sandwich is an approach that is easily translatable into operational terms and represents a manageable procedure.

Several steps may be useful in translating this analogy into the context of research. Students initially must hold the totality of a theory in mind while concentrating on one facet or dimension. Then, with this segment of the model under focus, the question seems to be, "What does this theory statement mean in terms of behavior?" The answer to such a question needs to be situation specific if it is to predict behavior. For example, part of a theory under study may suggest, "Under variable reinforcement conditions, a child who is socially immature should perform in a particular way." Because theory represents an abstraction, the empirical test of such a prediction becomes the task of research.

Asking progressively more specific questions, the researcher moves closer to a manageable research question. "If, under *these (hypothetical) conditions, this particular type of child* is expected to perform in a certain way, *then* how might I observe the behavior to either confirm or deny the prediction?" This question leads directly to the initial stages of study design and the specifics involved in the method to be used. It really represents several questions and resulting decisions that need attention. For example, how might the conditions specified by the statement be arranged in the real world (or at least in a laboratory approximation of the real world)? How is the researcher going to know whether these conditions have exerted an influence? What is going to be observed or measured to represent the behavioral performance? (In quantitative studies, what is the researcher going to count? The number of correct responses?)

As suggested by the preceding discussion, the leap in reasoning from a theory to a research question represents a dramatic increase in specificity. Intense application of the deductive process is involved as a researcher moves from a broad theory or model to the particular facet under study and, in turn, to the focused and specific research question. This funnel-like process may be hidden between the two visible end points—the generalized model and the specific, often molecular, research question. The notion of a funnel to visualize conceptually moving from a general idea emerging from theory to a very specific research question is reflected in Figure 15.2. This is the process of distilling an idea we encountered earlier (Chapter 2). Take a moment and review the several steps involved in problem distillation that we have examined before (e.g., determine the type of question as well as operationally define and specify details of the study).

The Question Related to Method and Analysis

One gap to be bridged is between the research question and the experimental method. The method section becomes quite detailed and provides an operational roadmap, permitting measurement aimed at answering the question posed.

Specific Participant Verbiage

The method statement must include detailed descriptions of participants, materials, and procedures. The participants must fit the question. For example, suppose you are studying "socially immature children." This gives us at least two dimensions to consider in our operational definitions. First of all, who are "children"? This term suggests a chronological age range of people who are young enough to be considered

FIGURE 15.2   **Distilling From a Theory to a Specific Research Question**

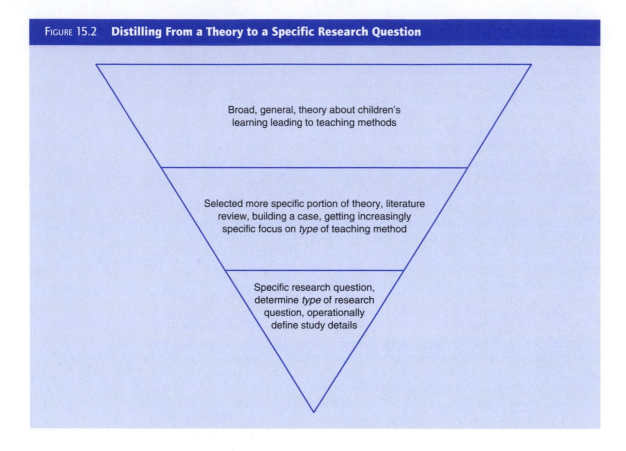

Broad, general, theory about children's
learning leading to teaching methods

Selected more specific portion of theory, literature
review, building a case, getting increasingly
specific focus on *type* of teaching method

Specific research question,
determine *type* of research
question, operationally
define study details

children but not old enough to be thought of as adolescents. For these purposes, just remember that chronological age needs to be specified. The second descriptor suggested by the above phrase is the necessity of determining that the participants are "socially immature." How is this to be accomplished? It may involve some standardized evaluation instrument, or it may mean that children are classified by observations. At any rate, on some logical or empirical basis, if participants are to be selected who are relevant to the research question, they must be sampled from a group who will fall within the framework of "socially immature" children.

Materials in Use

Another area of focus that relates investigation method to the research question is represented by the materials to be used. The materials or apparatus for the example question may include one or two factors depending on how the study will be implemented. For example, suppose we are studying memory and, more specifically, recall. It will be necessary to specify the materials to be used that relate to the phrase "recall performance." What is it that the children are going to recall? Even more specific on this point, how are these materials going to generate the criterion measure? If, for example, geography questions that require written responses are to be used, then is the researcher willing to contend that the number of correct responses represents recall? The point to be made here is simply that the materials chosen must also relate to the research question. In this example, the materials or research task must relate to what is considered to be recall.

Suppose our question has been sorted out and now reads as follows: "What are the effects of a variable reinforcement schedule as compared with continuous reinforcement on the recall performance of socially immature children?" This question now leads us to define a dimension of methods related to reinforcement. If the participants are going to be reinforced with tangible rewards (e.g., candy, tokens), reinforcement probably is best discussed under "materials." On the other hand, if verbal praise is to be used, the reinforcement part of the question receives attention under "procedures." Also, if tangible rewards are to be dispensed by machine or other apparatus, this should be described. These types of details need to be specified and their choice must relate to the research question being explored.

Procedures Put Into Motion

A third area of focus that relates study method to the research question is reflected in the procedures that are put into operation. As with participants and materials, the procedures must be relevant to the research question. This means that the way the experimental conditions are to be implemented must be conceptualized in terms of the research question.

The next intuitive relationship requiring discussion is that which links the research question to the analysis of data. It is not uncommon for beginning students to pose a relationship question when their design and analysis are appropriate for a difference question (or vice versa). The example research question suggests that the effects of variable versus continuous reinforcement are being compared. This is a difference question, which should be reflected by the design and the analysis technique employed. More specific information on the analysis segment was presented earlier, particularly in Chapter 13. The difficulty encountered is how to bridge the conceptual gap between the research question and the selection of *which* analysis technique to use. It simply is *not* appropriate to approach a difference question with a correlation, *or* a relationship question with a *t* test.

This section has emphasized the fact that the research process involves a series of highly interrelated segments. The relationships among these various areas are crucial and require specific focus because they are often overlooked in instruction and frequently not included in the conception of research held by beginning investigators. To review, this section has been a miniature replay of much of what was discussed in greater detail throughout earlier portions of this text.

One important area of the research process remains to be discussed—*interpretation of results*. This area is strongly related to other activities in research and should not be viewed apart from the total research enterprise. It is highly dependent on all that has gone on before.

INTERPRETATION OF RESULTS

Perhaps the most difficult conceptual gap to bridge is the relationship between the results obtained and the inference or interpretation of behavior. This may partially result because many people without research experience extract little meaning from numbers and, in particular, statistical statements such as P < 0.05. Interpretation about the meaning of results in terms of behavior requires that an individual must know what such statements mean. *Inference* is much like interpretation and involves *the researcher explaining what results might suggest or mean.*

Steps to Complete Interpretation

There are several steps involved in the interpretation process. An initial examination of results often includes taking certain steps even before beginning the interpretation. For example, it is often helpful to display the data by constructing a working graph. This assists with visualization and it seems easier to interpret from a graph than from raw numbers. With a graph or set of graphs prepared, it is time to begin interpretation.

Posing Questions

The interpretation of results to make inferences about behavior may begin with a series of questions. If, for example, the study involved a comparison of groups (a difference question), the first query is usually, "Did the groups perform differently?" This question may be answered by reviewing the results of the statistical test. Was there a significant difference? If they were different, which group had the higher (or highest) performance? This latter question can be answered by simply inspecting the group means if mean scores are being used. Simulation 15.1 is an example of a very simple set of study results and is a good place to start. The results in Simulation 15.1 are obvious and easy to interpret. It may not be necessary to construct a graph for these results, but with a little increased complexity, the working graph for interpretation becomes very helpful.

For additional
simulations visit
www.sagepub
.com/drewstudy

Simulation

Simulation 15.1

Topic: Beginning to interpret results from an experiment

Background statement: Below is a diagram from an experiment comparing two teaching methods. There is also a very brief statement about what we know from the analysis. From these, begin drafting an interpretation or discussion section. Even though you do not know the literature, you can begin the process of interpretation. Each time you practice this process, it will become easier and will enhance your interpretation skills when you begin work on your own thesis or dissertation.

What we know from the results: The difference is significant (P < .05), and the experimental variable is teaching method with Group A receiving the cognitive process method and Group B the direct instruction method. The criterion measure is number of correct responses on a test. How do you begin interpreting the results? What are the first words you write in the discussion? What type of an outline might you use for the discussion section?

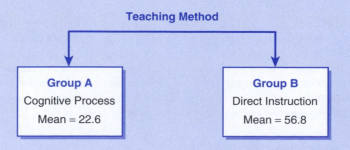

Write your response, then turn to page 369 for Simulation Feedback 15.1.

Process of Inference

The next step really initiates the process of inference. What do the performance differences mean in terms of behavior? The researcher cannot get by with merely answering this question by saying that Group B made more correct responses than Group A. That is evident in the results and adds no interpretive information. Inference requires attention to the performance and deducing not only *what* happened but also relating the results back to the reasons for doing the study. The researcher must make some interpretive leaps or guesses about *why* "Group B made more correct responses than Group A." Would the theoretical model that the researcher discussed when introducing the research question have predicted these differences? If so, in what fashion is the model supported? Would these data suggest that some particular psychological construct is operative in the process of learning? These questions exemplify the process of inference from results to behavior. Research that has an impact on both theory and practice *will attempt to improve our understanding of students and how to teach them by using inference in this way. Implications for theory* are generally included in a discussion of results and are where the researcher interprets what the results might mean for the theory that prompted the research question, or some other theory. The interpretation will probably begin with "Results indicate that direct instruction is more effective than cognitive osmosis in teaching about . . ." The interpretation might continue as follows: "These results are predicted by the teaching model outlined by Smith and Frederick (2006) and suggest that knowledge that is important for students to know may be taught more effectively through direct instruction rather than cognitive osmosis, which is often used in higher education today." This example shows that the interpretation of results relates the data back to the theory as well as the literature that was reviewed initially.

An even greater challenge is represented by results that would not have been predicted by the model or theory being tested. Here again it is not enough to merely say, "These data would not support the theory of Smith and Frederick (2006)." The question must be posed as to *why* the data do not support the theory of these imaginary authors. Do the data instead suggest that an alternative model may be operating in the learning process? If so, this is an important and exciting finding. Perhaps the data suggest a modification of the model. This type of finding exemplifies the process of empiricism as it serves to shape models and theories. Fully interpreted results should include other possible explanations for the data if they do not support the theory under study. Discussion sections of articles and dissertations are full of such statement as, "While the results do not support the teaching model of Smith and Frederick (2006), they do suggest that slight alterations may better predict instructional effectiveness."

Possible Meaning of Results

Another important interpretation element relates to what the results might mean for practice or clinical application. This is particularly important in applied research endeavors. Do the data suggest that teachers might more effectively instruct if they were to use a particular reinforcement or organization technique? Do the data suggest that instructional materials might be more effective for certain children if they were designed in a particular way? Results may suggest that a given counseling strategy might be effective with a particular group of students. The point to be emphasized here is that research results that are interpreted for application require similar intuitive inference processes relating data to the world practice to those that were involved in inference from data to theory.

Interpretation for practice has not always been a respected activity for researchers. There has, however, been a substantial shift in philosophy regarding **interpretation for practice** in recent years. Not only is it given less of a peripheral

Figure 15.3 **Interpretation of Results**

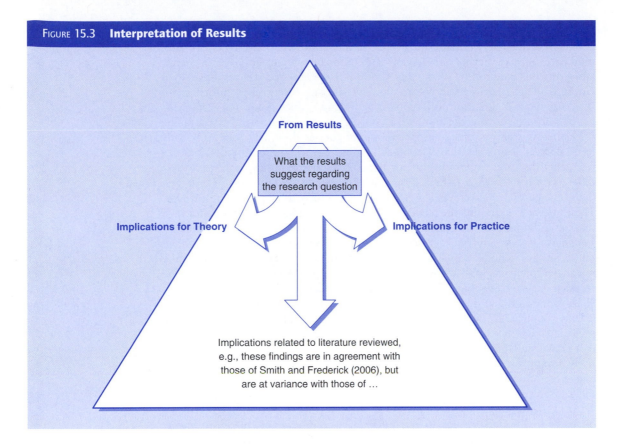

From Results

What the results suggest regarding the research question

Implications for Theory

Implications for Practice

Implications related to literature reviewed, e.g., these findings are in agreement with those of Smith and Frederick (2006), but are at variance with those of …

status than was previously the case, it is also being expected by journal editors under certain conditions. The nature of interpretation for practice depends primarily on the audience for which the report is intended. Figure 15.3 pictorially represents a discussion section and three lines of interpretation that relate the results to the theory, the literature reviewed (which may include the theory), and implications for practice. Notice that Figure 15.3 has a triangle superimposed over the arrows of interpretation lines. This triangle is meant to suggest interpretation in directions from the specific (the data or results) to more general circumstances reflecting implications for the literature reviewed, theory, and practice. *Implications for future research* are also generally included in a discussion of results. Such implications are where the researcher suggests directions for the next study or next series of studies based on the results of the present study.

Drawing implications for practice and inference in terms of alternative theory models are two activities representing a process that may be difficult for experienced researchers as well as the beginning student. One serious roadblock to such interpretation might be called "conceptual rigidity," which can be illustrated by an example. As noted, research often is launched from the framework of a theory, model, or some other conceptual framework. The relevant dimensions of this conceptual model are discussed by the researcher as he or she writes the introduction to the research question, and the review of related literature, both of which give the researcher a mental set to proceed with the study. This set may also work against the researcher when it comes to interpretation of results. If he or she does not conceptually explore beyond the boundaries of the model, the mental set may become too rigid to permit alternative inference. The confinement of oneself *strictly* to the boundaries of the model is what we refer to as conceptual rigidity. The framework of the model is indeed useful

and necessary to launch an investigation. The limits of such a framework, however, may become somewhat like conceptual fences. If researchers never go beyond those conceptual fences once the study is designed, they will find themselves less effective in terms of data interpretation. There are several resulting difficulties.

Initially, difficulty is encountered when the data do not fit between the conceptual fences. A quick examination of nearly any professional journal will indicate that this often occurs, as evidenced by the frequent statements like "results do not support . . ." whatever model is being tested. When data do not fit within the conceptual fences of a model, a statement that "these data do not support . . ." will not alone suffice. It is at this point that the researcher must go beyond the explanations provided by the model and either suggest an alternative theory that the data *will* support or suggest modifications of the model being tested.

Because the theory being tested seldom involves practice, implications in this area also involve conceptual fences. Often implications for practice are made more difficult because researchers are not generally in the field practitioner role on a continuing basis. Thus, in a real sense, the current set of experiences that are temporally and conceptually close to the researcher often do not involve clinical application or practice. Implications for practice therefore may require an even more dramatic assault on conceptual rigidity than model alternatives. However, *implications for practice* are generally included in a discussion of results and are where the researcher interprets what the results might mean for practical application or practice such as teaching.

Researchers who are either unable or unwilling to inferentially explore beyond the boundaries of a model will reduce their impact even if the model predicted the data. It should be emphasized that one must always stay within the legitimate boundaries of the *data*. The researcher should, however, be willing to watch the participants beyond the pure criterion measure level. Such observation often is revealing in a clinical sense and is not infrequently discussed during the interpretation. These observations should always carry a qualifying statement such as, "Subjective experimenter observation suggested . . ."

ACQUIRING INTERPRETATION SKILLS FOR RESEARCH

How does one acquire the skills discussed in this chapter? As mentioned previously, a proven formula for such instruction is not presently known, at least to most professionals involved in research training. What is known is that with some prerequisite level of information acquired, most students progress most rapidly from practice. Once one begins to break down conceptual fences, the divergent thinking necessary seems best nurtured by experience at asking the additional questions: What are other psychological or theoretical explanations for the same results? What are modifications of the theory being tested that would predict the data obtained? To what practical setting might these results be relevant—curriculum planning, student diagnosis, counseling, placement, or treatment development?

Steps for Creating Procedures

It is not necessary for students to wait for their first study to practice the process of inference and data interpretation (although working on your own data is much more fun). In fact, it is desirable to gain some experience before beginning your first study. We have used a simulation technique with our students that has shown considerable success. Simulations have been presented in the previous chapters in this text. You will find your first chances to practice simulated interpretation in the material at the end of this chapter.

In addition to the simulation material provided, you can create your own, which is often quite helpful. If you are interested in such practice, you are encouraged to try the following procedures:

1. Select a journal article that is in an area familiar to you; if possible, let it be one in which you have done considerable reading, have considerable experience, or both.

2. The initial study should have a fairly simple design. As you become more experienced, more complex studies can be used (e.g., select a simple study that compares two groups for the first try).

3. Tape a piece of paper over the author's discussion section.

4. Read the article carefully up to the discussion section.

5. Now, write your own discussion of the results. Interpret the results in terms of the theory or literature reviewed in the introduction and in terms of what the results might mean for practice and future research. Be thoughtful during this process and review the current chapter if needed.

6. Remove the paper from the article and compare your discussion with that of the author. Did you hit the main points? Do not be concerned about the polish of your writing or differences in style. After all, the author may have been working and writing in the area considerably longer than you.

7. Practice, practice, practice.

COMMENTS

This chapter has emphasized some of the lesser-known processes of research, primarily the judicious use of intuition, reasoning, and logic. We do not intend to give the impression that all researchers must do is gather data and then say whatever their imagination suggests. At all times, a researcher must stay in close touch with what the data indicate in terms of logical leaps and inferences. The use of logic and conceptual relationships is, however, one of the most important processes in research. This chapter also highlights research as a dynamic and creative act. Research does not always carry such a connotation for the uninitiated. Beginning researchers must, if they are to achieve the impact that is possible and desirable, learn to incorporate creative thinking into their repertoire of behavior.

It is evident that research is more than statistics. It is, in fact, a series of parts that have specific relationships and that strongly involve the use of mental exploration and intuition as well as logic. We started this process, at the beginning of the book, by moving from broad, general ideas about a phenomenon and distilling that idea to a more specific and focused research question or set of research questions. This is the reasoning process illustrated by Figure 15.2. In that example, we start with a general idea about children's learning and move to how that leads to concepts about teaching methods. After reading the literature and building a logic case, we then funnel down to the specific research question or questions.

Interpretation of results turns the funnel or triangle upside down as suggested in Figure 15.3. In this case, we have conducted the data collection and have the results. Now our logic needs to take those results and conceptualize what they mean. Of course, we want to see what the results suggest in terms of the research question or questions. In most cases we will find partial answers to those questions, but we will also find that a new set of research questions will emerge. (Many researchers spend years or even a career pursuing a set of questions.) The interpretation process examines the results to see how they square with any theory about teaching reading or self-esteem—depending on what launched the study from a theory standpoint. In some cases, the researcher

RESEARCH IN ACTION

KEY POINTS IN THE CHAPTER REFLECTED IN THIS BOX:

- Consider what the results might mean for literature reviewed and the related theory (which is typically outlined in the literature reviewed).
- Consider what the results indicate with respect to the basic research question.
- Consider what the results might mean for practice.

For more research in action tips visit www.sagepub .com/drewstudy

OBJECTIVES TO LEARN FROM THIS BOX:

- A diagram can be very useful in visualizing the research question and the results obtained.
- Interpretation can be accomplished by answering the questions of what happened, what the results suggest regarding the research question, what they mean regarding the literature and the theory, and what they mean for practice.

Emily is continuing the action research study that compares two approaches to reading instruction. One group emphasized student engagement called concept-oriented reading instruction (CORI), and the second focused on drill and practice (DAP). The research was based on earlier work by Professor John Guthrie and Emily (Guthrie & Anderson, 1999), which suggested that engagement of students through concepts would improve reading comprehension. A diagram for Emily's action research study is shown below. She is collected a variety of types of data. One involved reading test scores, and the means are found in the diagram. The data for reading scores involved the number correct on a test. The statistical analysis indicated a significant difference between the CORI group and the DAP group.

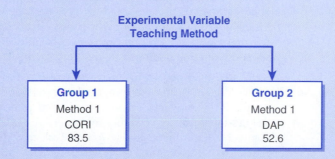

Think about this: Which group performed better? How do these results relate to the literature reviewed? What might the results suggest for teaching reading?

SOURCE: This action research scenario is roughly based on the work of John Guthrie at the University of Maryland and Emily Anderson Swan at the University of Utah (Guthrie & Anderson, 1999; Swan, 2003).

may simply have an idea that leads to reading about a theory. That was certainly the case with Daniel as he pursued his study of self-esteem in Latino and Caucasian students with learning disabilities. Emily's study emerged from earlier research.

The interpretation process moves from answering the research questions, to the literature reviewed (how do the results agree with the literature reviewed—how are the results different from those of earlier researchers). Finally, the interpretative process will draw implications for practice. In this latter part of interpretation, the researcher will ask the question about what the results suggest for practical applications. What do the results indicate in terms of teaching reading with a method that embeds concepts and attempts to engage the students in a very proactive manner? This was the exciting idea that drove Emily's research, which we have seen emerge throughout the book as an action research study. This is the action research example found in the Research in Action box where Emily studied concept-oriented reading instruction (CORI) compared to drill and practice (DAP).

Hopefully, you have begun to see research as the dynamic process that it is and not as sterile and mechanistic. It is exciting, and those that get bit by the research bug are definitely infected in a way that promotes curiosity and creativity. Even as consumers of research, there is always the desire to have some research evidence to answer this question, that notion, or to begin finding a solution to some challenge we face daily.

Chapter Summary

+ Research as an integrated process is one where the reasoning and logic moves from a general idea and broad theory to a focused research question; this then leads to a design, which is followed by conducting the study. The data collected are analyzed and results are interpreted with the reasoning moving back to the question, the theory, and drawing implications for practice and future research.

+ The reasoning leap from a theory to a research question represents a dramatic increase in specificity. Intense application of the deductive process is involved as a researcher moves from a broad theory or model to the particular facet under study and, in turn, to the focused and specific research question.

+ A complete method section becomes quite detailed and provides an operational roadmap or protocol for what is to be done in conducting the study. This includes a description of participants, what is said to them and by them, what materials are used and how, and what measurement is conducted to answer the research question.

+ Several steps may be part of interpreting results, including posing questions, making inferences, and interpreting the possible meaning of the results. For example, if the study involved a comparison of groups (a difference question), one question is usually, "Did the groups perform differently?" As you interpret the possible meaning of results, you may ask something like, "Do the results suggest that instructional materials might be more effective for certain children if they were designed in a particular way?"

Key Terms

Implications for future research. These are generally included in a discussion of results and are where the researcher suggests a direction for the next study or next series of studies, based on the results of the present study.

Implications for practice. Implications for practice are generally included in a discussion of results and are where the researcher interprets what the results might mean for practical application or practice such as teaching.

Implications for theory. Implications for theory are generally included in a discussion of results and are where the researcher interprets what the results might mean for the theory that prompted the research question or some other theory.

Inference. Inference is much like interpretation and occurs when the researcher concludes that something is true, based on what the results suggest.

Interpretation of results. The process of suggesting what results of a study might mean for theory, for practice, and for future research.

Student Study Site

The companion Web site for *Designing and Conducting Research in Education* www.sagepub.com/drewstudy

Supplement your review of this chapter by going to the companion Web site to take one of the practice quizzes, use the flashcards to study key terms, and check out the many other study aids you'll find there. You'll even find some research articles from the Sage Full-Text Collection and a step-by-step guide that will show you how to read an educational research article.

Simulation Feedback

Simulation Feedback 15.1

Giving feedback on how one writes or interprets information is always vulnerable to some error because people express their ideas differently. The words below are fictitious interpretations of fictitious data and yours might look a bit different or use different words. But the process gets you started drawing interpretation inferences and turning results (data) into a story. These are examples.

For additional simulations visit www.sagepub .com/drewstudy

How we might begin: Analysis of the data indicated that subjects receiving direct instruction performed at a superior level compared to those who were taught through cognitive processing. These results are consistent with those found by Smith and Jones (2007), but are at variance with those of Ynowsky (2005).

How we might continue: Results of the current investigation do not support the operation of a higher-level cognitive process organizer, which has been hypothesized by some researchers to enhance subject performance in learning situations (George & Mathias, 2006). They do, however, provide support for the concept that specific instructional objectives and teaching to meet those objectives seem to facilitate learning (Yu, 2004).

How we might continue further: Implications for practice of the current findings are several. Initially, it appears that if there is serious intent that students learn material, the content should probably be taught directly. While this study involved freshman students, such an implication might hold as well for more advanced students. Future research may find it fruitful to . . . (here you might suggest the next study or speculate about future studies).

Appendix

Random Numbers Table

Line/Col.	1	2	3	4	5	6	7
1	07145	45302	74179	45012	77713	56679	09426
2	75560	43006	38575	53850	89107	91968	87837
3	11209	85849	39566	69370	52856	02120	14406
4	02350	15942	54730	25381	59586	91738	60890
5	12696	35654	62129	44835	80712	28068	85326
6	09481	00374	04222	13284	79056	73073	20122
7	10706	58445	85928	58438	46708	58162	16412
8	61569	66413	36171	55676	34235	72620	21208
9	50415	81924	18835	53482	53819	10947	76928
10	87039	43552	65050	39492	52579	19880	36178
11	06538	41043	31483	51946	63099	38493	55908
12	51931	55359	74754	49926	64868	06672	80506
13	35567	95660	66722	13797	02545	45487	91831
14	96455	77953	87583	04965	31341	28268	88237
15	91409	63167	70983	24169	75902	11958	80235
16	93854	64666	99716	68191	28971	78997	39423
17	37251	65269	69085	16888	77504	17680	64594
18	90301	24817	97194	88461	90876	30206	73334
19	15928	49714	94310	02042	31428	59057	60743
20	21576	22124	88803	55328	88750	88487	40404
21	06433	24095	78687	74777	92393	65396	58849
22	11741	06462	05342	82000	45641	84492	55386
23	61159	68816	91661	53037	81463	43484	20767
24	80154	05453	42296	61653	67493	40111	06056
25	35954	39975	34780	30520	24323	61293	84134
26	42066	48118	50339	65754	32522	91394	50313
27	69715	55225	03960	84450	34141	91903	89990
28	66298	82635	21346	60208	27873	86282	84284
29	39477	60043	63775	26247	25969	54786	06134
30	06821	57160	41754	38990	47728	21706	68998
31	73291	84197	24326	84540	71450	42875	51951
32	52186	60096	73327	53278	33528	06065	15122
33	67523	00407	88437	92982	16107	86129	53620
34	98183	16718	93505	08915	24466	01887	82818
35	50950	11086	40425	63708	53664	41084	10462
36	35676	83343	08756	71352	54515	59009	50975
37	84582	69934	43818	13192	95981	60289	93749
38	97472	75592	94323	21657	39944	16877	15118
39	42787	25841	85258	75373	96227	61994	53424
40	83426	26464	54832	97037	75337	17194	97537
41	80927	60722	35251	37874	63545	86637	59490
42	76569	30030	96730	70814	10164	80862	69471
43	27500	99335	35407	11443	63580	54801	39013
44	75153	17436	89974	94444	80977	64627	96928
45	86070	24988	54594	14605	65983	52602	68787
46	20707	75395	06828	38921	69665	83686	81692
47	50207	19937	61048	76262	77197	88036	69459

8	9	10	11	12	13	14
77483	45144	72545	54122	91893	35098	93581
06391	53800	81539	22554	04251	05152	98289
03222	15188	03096	34653	69094	30381	45875
47814	87277	93681	05037	85762	33113	05095
56335	58093	51313	92645	19471	84031	53273
25431	68566	06677	18428	27345	69509	15425
28631	95660	78694	39126	14602	84592	12756
16268	29414	82077	62352	35915	65708	46937
58085	03618	97704	25385	38366	96511	04125
36639	84325	37253	05620	85986	54131	11964
92935	75058	77145	75814	90336	33725	23408
12580	39794	20328	03721	72033	05494	36563
60068	30893	30111	37066	53699	62749	90685
23647	49183	40100	75088	17298	50790	72095
43637	41675	92572	57930	25990	47238	77628
25137	28778	04665	61123	61470	94470	04384
60537	98788	85586	22708	48517	12456	88821
18140	20047	85741	59561	41674	09602	65826
31646	11568	21820	04084	79403	16917	17216
53937	14573	57019	06213	43865	37512	17127
93798	73733	66620	89732	31639	26570	70953
45732	60303	30160	04751	70585	41114	82332
32008	90449	21775	44919	39762	90973	06190
13835	17622	62978	29166	11901	28468	93887
35038	23102	13888	34844	21191	51439	40119
06439	94815	46558	71880	34433	53355	58116
80637	56436	51393	81027	95131	75781	15923
81572	83805	40373	35543	51757	00676	03097
13782	07050	35612	97828	81192	91813	11970
57600	31907	27272	70989	77990	88188	49852
93426	23403	45278	19862	66650	75938	47983
46393	59945	44431	68272	70258	67574	63549
73228	83785	30041	93963	21912	46104	04622
55763	69368	02235	69452	34628	03705	02952
36868	91158	55898	53327	89446	64793	92699
09668	99437	38468	53636	96327	48417	70631
74886	99175	87145	70179	11818	78202	20920
71474	77745	15252	33770	22960	00601	36846
15762	28908	85515	65484	91798	92857	80472
83185	48848	00909	80733	23571	22130	85727
53741	31158	49010	17145	29806	94794	76002
17084	99064	63038	45146	10703	10372	06604
33873	72460	06619	81281	89323	50474	35550
58841	58147	99944	53143	58960	19148	62314
78818	02806	45487	00340	11013	15455	35200
22606	12818	34426	80523	60475	51840	07975
67331	43323	41165	82463	69952	03866	88515

(Continued)

(Continued)

Line/Col.	1	2	3	4	5	6	7
48	17904	75484	61780	91409	31968	57422	47673
49	87970	88899	95520	01325	43030	05273	74712
50	47498	56871	27119	15846	40768	46750	27515
51	58271	33979	90940	45652	81532	72395	51593
52	78416	84785	07610	47422	93799	61248	47909
53	42902	28553	77017	02762	69449	64577	29187
54	98263	68336	43252	95568	73063	17216	31531
55	68173	12748	08425	14154	51846	19379	71104
56	79759	95609	32558	44447	59019	24309	58783
57	85550	51609	96337	72226	04671	84985	29974
58	47624	37131	53008	78928	78803	92932	05370
59	45427	71365	40886	23789	61871	72028	28923
60	25220	29525	53879	60863	92173	04689	14268
61	17222	90226	88556	71149	00926	19828	51515
62	16005	89958	12014	04913	03530	02994	94311
63	32291	61408	45386	51672	56963	15559	03364
64	47929	69613	93957	30556	38295	50183	51705
65	62201	16801	69440	72070	08318	23166	34769
66	77112	21233	15598	96658	53689	69970	31423
67	04482	49362	27178	11533	99930	40915	10671
68	39044	39653	95734	49735	64925	26772	04154
69	38112	43618	81736	27916	46163	48743	29587
70	28620	80204	49860	40806	54150	49764	86990
71	78378	76959	55518	95672	71925	93236	39329
72	80354	18078	45039	73335	55718	08715	81187
73	85783	60874	52086	11240	84501	73946	45270
74	39242	56769	27458	20020	28498	83768	58424
75	24129	77226	62686	49126	19781	89997	29990
76	98934	93004	13565	40930	40458	78767	69061
77	47441	04658	96606	51731	98073	88775	70797
78	98984	78395	74805	88374	83586	05363	72023
79	67873	91512	27376	26813	43913	40035	63102
80	72070	43961	84278	88873	31885	41322	04240
81	69204	27321	87832	68647	17141	45699	75844
82	81876	31666	57244	18007	37320	19010	62857
83	87705	98027	52571	37129	17379	34920	00307
84	39933	33996	87861	40917	44005	24348	16063
85	34672	67287	14042	06919	05411	65884	97047
86	81568	91943	17493	52870	54762	15083	62741
87	23310	21402	50787	21986	16941	18131	03415
88	31558	12606	64321	23872	89621	37761	94858
89	11040	83703	24091	41583	44911	40636	51104
90	00156	83282	60036	81537	52604	97283	58670
91	28137	45500	46018	63496	30942	65192	26238
92	76451	65511	68184	27918	96594	66429	21134
93	07517	33442	56778	14741	01043	54006	97134
94	59264	98164	40338	86001	95711	81884	85273
95	95722	98216	91978	41494	86558	29457	39807
96	59732	01584	58777	22959	42937	05311	89520
97	07935	23847	03335	12660	78134	83373	95358
98	59798	82788	12645	37034	41857	79229	84740
99	88273	17215	90212	93833	10453	23411	10487
100	82965	40281	58849	52969	90078	92269	77907

8	9	10	11	12	13	14
64267	67749	46454	99594	59271	46619	36554
67351	64986	02559	47794	07856	84888	83131
58336	03474	88260	70674	10927	19974	69070
68348	19388	34138	25778	98171	20151	43926
79461	54891	33869	97221	72594	46653	83227
37898	80444	45442	50526	00074	82592	44480
35348	14918	78465	35617	54019	97091	16860
88277	02085	15933	01366	13516	87173	33571
68781	69857	90409	46549	56433	10356	29670
68577	15719	86854	93809	43385	34787	20301
16186	97198	73439	55047	45433	71491	20311
74291	33880	00820	65657	38529	17964	13504
80745	59406	04748	41635	17017	12165	30916
51226	65673	02947	43267	46007	26827	90803
37956	39571	24320	57639	30031	12218	94416
52941	22747	15199	73393	45358	07387	84530
84817	60290	40377	01849	06223	89561	38519
00635	97524	55283	59421	05616	51433	66416
88719	41294	12871	08016	77930	81090	00539
66576	26716	89604	17309	57952	79998	31036
49975	50029	27038	73566	23053	72532	43621
90126	07144	16836	07636	26464	08922	43580
85502	97786	54650	33835	09217	64279	98428
75111	41808	82421	61808	88236	33410	82046
24089	65196	09384	70598	95914	65198	41593
40595	29954	03366	67556	67202	00229	40012
78413	74678	46783	67861	36451	75680	93912
75842	20716	30972	28398	19945	40402	01126
46234	39217	43547	01483	70002	98820	51133
89749	42162	98613	26959	44586	21890	46363
50262	05966	32098	81095	74083	22956	83719
28014	27239	47151	55920	62718	25767	08231
15824	72270	61620	29800	90852	10944	25011
11640	25155	92625	69590	36599	84232	37001
94787	84891	02554	52912	52524	34569	25032
96560	03054	89990	17579	01840	80390	26823
53030	25150	72101	30471	60728	59745	12679
43693	46731	27141	34851	90621	29907	32276
38963	17358	84794	62859	32086	22291	52312
50929	88560	56555	29505	65475	15237	33604
14212	27023	31119	40561	48749	55676	76789
09281	37475	60304	39397	48151	29503	98002
26091	77587	39354	96182	38134	98605	27603
70156	98573	35270	32090	21474	91982	65885
74173	03771	04847	57386	58753	84308	26175
98537	08935	25105	06477	47192	74313	04962
96255	44431	62470	31313	33750	82074	42937
14294	06356	62291	65537	99824	94672	13155
53810	69197	47772	09783	00673	04842	07183
88414	72345	61792	48535	56760	73483	52137
89410	04131	05575	22475	09851	06175	94640
25079	35962	11744	95088	14556	28365	84613
57303	75653	44561	20196	71734	37995	93254

The authors wish to thank Dr. John Kircher, Department of Educational Psychology, University of Utah, for generating this table of random numbers.

Glossary

A-B design. A single-subject design that involves two phases: A, in which the baseline data are collected before treatment is implemented; and B, in which data are recorded while treatment is underway. This design is not widely used because more sophisticated designs have been developed that provide stronger evidence.

A-B-A-B design. A single-subject design that involves four phases. The first A represents the baseline before treatment is implemented. The first B represents initial application of treatment. The second A designates removal of treatment and return to baseline conditions, whereas the second B represents a return to treatment conditions. This is also known as a reversal design.

Action research. Research undertaken to determine results related to a specific action or decision. Action research is often conducted by teachers to determine the effectiveness of a specific teaching intervention in a particular setting.

Additivity. A number property that permits arithmetic on the scores. By adding together two numbers, one can obtain a third number that is different or unique. Numbers with additivity reflect the direction (e.g., greater than or less than) and quantity of the property being measured.

Anonymity. Anonymity refers to keeping the identity of a respondent from being known by the researcher.

Applied research. Research that involves studies that address questions with some clear application rather than testing a theory.

A priori method of knowing. The a priori method of knowing refers to "before the fact" and is primarily based on intuitive knowledge. In subscribing to the a priori method, something is known before information is gathered or even in the absence of experiential data.

Artificial dichotomy. An artificial dichotomy is found when data are divided into two arbitrarily defined categories, but the "dichotomy" is artificial because there actually is an underlying continuum between the categories of behavior or performance. An example would be categories of "well" versus "sick," which is an artificial representation of the underlying continuum of health status.

Artificial research arrangements. A threat to external validity by the fact that participant's behavior or performance is altered because the research setting deviates from the participants' usual routine.

Authority method of knowing. The authority method of knowing or fixing belief cites an eminent person or entity as the source of knowledge. The belief is that, if a well-known authority states that something is the case, then it is so.

Basic research. Basic research involves investigation of questions that are interesting but may have no application at the present time.

Bias in group composition. A threat to internal validity occurring when there are systematic differences between the composition of groups in addition to the treatment under study.

Capacity. An element of consent referring to a person's ability to acquire and retain knowledge.

Captive assignment. The identification and availability of a total sample at the outset of the investigation, as opposed to situations in which all participants are not present at one time.

Ceiling effect. An effect that occurs when the performance range of a task is so restricted or limited on the upper end that the subjects cannot perform to their maximum ability.

Central tendency measures. Statistical computations that describe where the scores tend to bunch together.

Cluster sampling. A sampling procedure involving grouping individuals into clusters (e.g., a third-grade elementary class). The researcher then lists all the clusters and draws samples from the clusters.

Concept of control. The process of holding all possible influences constant except the experimental variable, which is what is being studied. For example, if the researcher is comparing the effectiveness of Reading Programs A and B, the reading programs should be the only factor that is different between the groups. All other influences (e.g., intelligence or age) should be equivalent.

Confidentiality. Confidentiality refers to keeping the identity of a respondent from being known by anyone other than the researcher.

Criterion measure. That which is being measured in a study. If, for example, a study were focusing on the height of a particular group, the criterion measure might be inches. *Criterion measure* is synonymous with the term *dependent variable.*

Criticism. A phenomenological analytic technique that uses the researcher's preferences or opinions to interpret and judge the phenomenon under study. It is often used to expose the biases in common wisdom and how they affect a specific disempowered group.

Data analysis. A step in the research process where the investigator summarizes data collected and prepares it in a format to determine what occurred. For quantitative studies, data analysis means summarizing the numbers, whereas for qualitative studies, data analysis involves reviewing the narrative data to determine trends.

Data audit. Providing preliminary data to a researcher not participating in the study in order to get feedback.

Data collection. The data collection phase of research refers to the actual execution of the investigation and involves recording data in some form. This may include the process of administering a questionnaire, conducting an interview, or presenting a math test to a participant and recording responses.

Data reliability. Data reliability refers to how dependable the information is that the investigator collects. When a researcher repeatedly observes a behavior, data reliability concerns the consistency of his or her recording of what occurred.

Data summary sheets. Forms used to summarize field notes or other recorded data. They are often used as an intermediary step in analysis.

Deception. Research deception involves an intentional misrepresentation of facts related to the purpose, nature, or consequences of an investigation. In this context, deception may involve either an *omission* or a *commission* on the part of the researcher in terms of interactions with participants.

Deductive analysis. Approaches to data analysis that begin with a hypothesis, theoretical framework, or strong preconceptions to which the results are compared.

Dependent variable. That which is being measured in a study. If, for example, a study were focusing on the height of a particular group, the dependent variable might be inches. *Dependent variable* is synonymous with the term *criterion measure.*

Descriptive question. Descriptive questions ask, "What is . . . ?" or "What does . . . ?": What does this culture look like, what does this group look like, or what is the level at which a particular group of participants performs?

Descriptive statistics. Analyses used for descriptive questions such as what is the average age or height of a particular group.

Design flexibility. The ability to add or remove methods of collecting, recording, or analyzing data while the data are being collected (rather than after they have been collected). This provides the researcher the advantage of being sensitive to changing events.

Design validity. The technical soundness of the research study. its rigor and scientific merit. The two primary types of design validity are *internal* and *external.*

Difference question. Difference questions make comparisons and ask, "Is there a difference?" Comparisons may be made either between groups (e.g., between two groups of children receiving different math instruction) or between measurements within a single group (e.g., pre- and posttest performance on the same group).

Directional hypothesis. Hypothesis that predicts a difference and the direction of that difference; for example, "Participants receiving Treatment Method A will make significantly more correct responses than those receiving Treatment Method B."

Dispersion measures. Statistical computations that describe the amount of variability among the scores in the group.

Double sampling. Also known as two-phase sampling. In this procedure, a participant is accessed twice for data collection (e.g., when a situation warrants an intense or more in-depth follow-up of participants).

Duration method. A procedure for recording observations in which the observer records how much time a participant spends engaged in a behavior.

Emic perspective. How the participant(s) views the phenomenon being described or analyzed.

Empathic neutrality. Empathic neutrality is often presented as an alternative to objectivity; however, rather than a researcher expressing no opinion or perspective, the researcher's opinion or perspective is openly acknowledged and described. In doing this, the researcher must also be willing to suspend that view and not make judgments on the views of participants that may differ from his or her own.

Ethics. Ethics in research generally means an investigator has a moral obligation to protect the participants from harm, unnecessary invasion of their privacy, and any other threats to their general well-being.

Ethnography. The in-depth study of the culture of a particular group of people that seeks to describe this culture and convey the patterns of likes, beliefs, and ideologies as well as formal and informal relationships.

Etic perspective. The viewpoint of the researcher as an outsider.

Experimental mortality. A threat to internal validity occurring when there is a differential loss of participants between comparison groups.

Experimental research. In experimental research, an investigator *manipulates* a condition (aka, independent variable or treatment) in order to analyze whether participants who receive the treatment (experimental group) perform differently from those who do not (control group). A researcher using experimental methods would be inclined to impose an intervention, such as a teaching method, on a group of children and measure how well they learned math compared to another group not receiving that intervention.

Experimental variable. That phenomenon that is under study; that factor that the researcher manipulates to see what the effect is. For example, if the researcher were interested in determining which of two teaching methods was more effective, the experimental variable would be the method of teaching. *Experimental variable* is synonymous with the term *independent variable.*

Figures. Any type of graphical display of data included in a report or manuscript, other than the tables.

Findings. Results or conclusions in qualitative research.

Floor effect. An effect that occurs when the performance range of the task is so restricted or limited on the lower end that the subjects' performance is determined by the task rather than by their ability to perform. Under such conditions, the task is so difficult that the researcher is unable to obtain any evidence about how the subjects can perform.

General notes. General notes for a table provide explanations or qualifying statements regarding a whole table rather than a specific portion (see **Specific notes**).

Graphs, charts, plots. Terms for different types of figures.

Grounded theory. A type of qualitative research report that presents a conceptual framework (i.e., a theory) that explains the process of some substantive topic.

Harm. In the context of research ethics, harm may be broadly defined to include extreme physical pain or death, but also involves such factors as psychological stress, personal embarrassment or humiliation, or myriad influences that may adversely affect the participants in a significant way.

Hawthorne effect. A threat to internal validity when there is a change in the sensitivity or performance by the participants that may occur merely as a function of being a part of the research study.

History. A threat to internal validity involving an uncontrolled event during the study that may have an influence on the observed effect other than the variable under study.

Hypothesis. A statement used in research to help clarify the research question. It is presented as a declarative statement of prediction. Two basic formats are used: the *null hypothesis* and the *directional hypothesis.*

Identity. A number property that distinguishes that number as unique and not exactly the same as any other number. Identity merely reflects distinction among numbers and does not indicate greater or lesser amounts of the property being measured.

Implications for future research. These are generally included in a discussion of results and are where the researcher suggests what the next study or next series of studies might be, based on the results of the present study.

Implications for practice. These are generally included in a discussion of results and are where the researcher interprets what the results might mean for practical application or practice such as teaching.

Implications for theory. Implications for theory are generally included in a discussion of results and are where the researcher interprets what the results might mean for the theory that prompted the research question or some other theory.

Independent comparisons. In an independent comparison, the scores in Condition A are not affected by or do not affect those under Condition B. In practice, this has generally meant that the two groups (Conditions A and B) are constituted from different participants.

Independent group comparison. Group research designs in which different subjects are used for each group. A group of subjects receives only one treatment, and therefore, the scores in one condition are presumed independent of scores in another condition. This is distinguished from studies in which subjects may receive two or more assessments or treatments (repeated measures), and the scores in one condition cannot be considered independent of the scores in the other.

Independent variable. That phenomenon that is under study; that factor that the researcher manipulates to see what the effect is. For example, if the researcher were interested in determining which of two teaching methods was more effective, the independent variable would be the method of teaching. *Independent variable* is synonymous with the term *experimental variable*.

Inductive analysis. Approaches to data analysis that evolve as analysis is conducted rather than comparing results to an a priori hypothesis.

Inference. Inference is much like interpretation and occurs when the researcher concludes that something is true, based on what the results suggest.

Inferential statistics. Analyses used for difference and relationship questions. Difference statistics are used for comparisons or difference questions and relationship statistics (also called correlations) are used for relationship questions.

Information. An element of consent requiring that information pertaining to a study be presented in a way that can be completely and fully understood by each participant.

Informed consent. Informed consent ensures that each participant has a complete understanding of the purpose, methods used, the risks involved, and the demands of the study.

Institutional review boards. Institutional review boards (IRBs) are committees of individuals within universities and other organizations to provide assurance that no ethical violations occur in any given study. An IRB is charged with reviewing the purpose of the research and the proposed methodology as it relates to potential risk or benefits to the participants involved.

Instrumentation. A threat to internal validity involving the influences on scores due to calibration changes in any instrument used to measure participant performance, whether those are mechanical changes or changes in the observer.

Integrity. Relates to the honesty of an investigator and how he or she undertakes an investigation. Any breach of integrity during the execution of a research study, whether it be unintentional errors or outright falsification of the data, seriously weakens or even invalidates the investigation.

Interobserver reliability. A procedure to determine the reliability of the observer(s) in collecting data. Interobserver reliability involves determining the percentage of agreement among observers (What percentage of time did the observers agree?). Correlational methods estimate interobserver reliability by determining the degree to which factors relate or vary together.

Interpretation of results. The process of suggesting what results of a study might mean for theory, for practice, and for future research.

Interval data. This type of data has all three number properties of identity, order, and additivity. When interval measurement is possible, the researcher is working with known and equal distances between score units, and arithmetic can be used on the scores. The zero point on interval data is artificial and does not reflect an actual absence of the property being measured.

Interval method. A procedure for recording observations in which the observer records whether or not a behavior occurs during a given interval such as a 10-minute period of time.

Intervals. A process of grouping scores that assigns a common score (the midpoint) to all cases falling within a certain range of performance. Not to be confused with interval-level data.

Interview investigations. These have the same purpose as questionnaires but different data collection procedures, including personal contact and interaction to gather data. Interview studies may include face-to-face interactions, telephone interviews, and/or focus groups.

Literature reviews. Literature reviews are articles (or a portion of an article) where an author interprets the published research studies he or she has read on a given topic such as reading comprehension.

Maturation. A threat to internal validity involving factors that influence a participant's performance because of time passing (e.g., age, fatigue) rather than specific incidents.

Mean. The mean is the arithmetic average of all the scores.

Measure communication value. Refers to how easily understood a term is by a particular audience. A measure that has good communication value is one that is intuitively easily understood and not obscure.

Measure sensitivity. Refers to how sensitive a particular measure is to performance differences; that is, when performance changes, how well does the measure reflect those changes.

Median. The median is a point in the distribution that has exactly the same number of scores above it as below it when all scores are arranged in order.

Midpoint score. The point in the center of an interval or range of scores. It is usually represented by an X.

Mixed-group experimental design. Traditional group investigations in which two or more experimental variables are studied with independent groups on one or some of the variables, and repeated measures are studied on the remaining variable or variables.

Mixed-method research. Mixed-method studies employ elements from more than one approach to research, often capitalizing on the strengths of each procedure. Investigations using mixed-method research may use both quantitative and qualitative methods.

Mode. The mode is the most frequently occurring score.

Multiple-baseline design. A single-subject research design in which data on more than one target behavior are simultaneously recorded. Phase changes from baseline to treatment are then staggered, with each behavior serving as the sequential control for the previously treated behavior as in the diagram in Figure 6.5.

Multiple-treatment interference. A threat to external validity occurring when more than one treatment is administered to the same participants and results in cumulative effects that may not be similar to the outside world and may threaten generalization of the results.

Narrative construction. Similar to ethnography except that it focuses on an individual. The stories or anecdotes about that person's life are organized for themes and relayed in a fashion that leads to a purpose or lesson.

Negotiated perspective. A blend of both the emic and etic perspectives that is discussed and agreed upon by the researcher and participant(s) (*see* **Emic perspective** and **Etic perspective**).

Nominal data. Also called categorical or classification data, nominal data represent the most primitive type of measurement. Such data only have the number property of identity and are useful when all that can be done is the assignment of events to categories.

Nonexperimental research. In nonexperimental research, existing phenomena (e.g., middle school children's *satisfaction* with a math program) are *described* without manipulating (changing) the treatment. Nonexperimental research methods are distinguished from experiments in that they do not impose a treatment or intervention to see how participants respond. Nonexperimental studies are more characterized by gathering data as it occurs or exists in a natural environment.

Nonindependent comparisons. In a nonindependent situation, there is reason to believe that scores under Condition A have some effect on those under Condition B. In practice, this generally is the case if the same group of participants is measured twice, once under Condition A and once under Condition B.

Nonparametric statistics. A general category of analyses that include fewer assumptions about the population of scores, can often be computed with ordinal or nominal data, and may also be used with fewer participants than required by parametric analyses.

Nonparticipant observation. An approach to observation wherein the researcher is not a full, active member of the setting or group being observed.

Null hypothesis. The null hypothesis predicts no difference; for example, "Participants will not differ in mean correct responses as a function of treatment method."

Observation protocol. A description of what behavior is to be observed and how it is to be recorded as data.

Observation studies. Observation studies involve the recording of observations in a given setting that may be structured (e.g., counting specific behaviors using a checklist or rating scale) or unstructured (writing down field notes in a narrative form without a specific protocol).

Order. A number property that indicates one number is less than or greater than another on some continuum. If one number is higher than another number, the higher number reflects a larger amount of the property being measured but the exact *quantity* is not reflected.

Ordinal data. Also known as rank-order data, ordinal data have the properties of identity and order. They move measurement from the discrimination between events to a more quantitative basis of assessment. Ordinal measurement provides the ability to rank order events on the basis of an underlying continuum, and the ranks denote "greater than" or "less than" on the dimension being assessed.

Parametric statistics. A general category of analysis that involve selected assumptions about the population of scores, generally use arithmetic and therefore require interval or ratio data, and typically need more participants than do nonparametric analyses.

Participant. A term that refers to one of the individuals on whom the data are collected in a study.

Participant observation. An approach to observation wherein the researcher is a full, active member of the setting or group being observed. It often involved deception in that the other participants cannot know the observer is actually observing.

Participant reactivity. The degree to which a participant's behavior or performance is altered by the effects of taking the test, completing the instrument, or otherwise participating in the study.

Performance range. Task performance range refers to the variation in responses possible within the limits imposed by highest and lowest possible performance scores on the task.

Population-sample differences. A threat to external validity by the fact that participants in a study are not representative of the population to which generalization is desired.

Pre-post design. A traditional group design in which the researcher administers a pretest, then applies a treatment of some type, followed by a posttest assessment to determine the difference between the two testing sessions. There are also studies where the treatment is a time period intervening between assessments rather than an active treatment.

Pretest influence. A threat to external validity when a pretest activity or warm-up task results in "learning to respond" behaviors that may influence a participant's response during a study.

Privacy. The right of an individual to control distribution of personal information. As a rule of thumb, researchers should invade the privacy of participants as minimally as possible.

Probability levels. An application of inferential statistics that provides levels of decision making based on the probability of finding a result of that magnitude.

Proportional random sampling. A sampling procedure aimed at properly representing characteristics in subgroups, it involves drawing samples from a subgroup only in the proportion that it exists in the larger population.

Qualitative research. Type of research in which data are collected in the form of words or a narrative that describes the topic under study and emphasizes collecting data in natural settings.

Quantitative research. Studies using quantitative methods collect data in the form of numbers. In this approach to research, the occurrence of behaviors is counted, correct answers or errors are counted, and other types of measures are recorded in terms of quantity.

Quasi-experimental design. A group study design in which the groups are formed from subject pools that are different before the experiment is begun, and this difference is the basis for the experimental variable. An example might be the comparing of groups from two levels of intelligence (Group A with an IQ range of 75–90 and Group B with an IQ range of 100–115). In this example, the level of intelligence is the experimental variable under study, and the two groups are pre-experimentally different. Such a design is in contrast to a true experimental design in which both groups are formed from the same subject pool and become different after they are administered the respective treatments.

Questionnaire investigations. Type of investigation that involves mailed or electronic distribution of a written instrument that asks questions of the participants.

Questionnaire legitimacy. Establishment of a study's (and thereby the questionnaire's) degree of respectability, justifiability, or genuine quality through appropriate sponsorship by or affiliation with a respected organization or agency.

Questionnaire sensitivity. The degree to which a questionnaire or other instrument has the potential to be personally or culturally offensive due to "sensitive" or controversial topics.

Range. The range is a measure of dispersion that reflects the difference between the highest and lowest scores in a distribution. The range may be used with ordinal, interval, or ratio data.

Rank order. Describes ordinal-level data that are ranked from first to last on the basis of some characteristic.

Ratio data. Ratio data have all the number properties of identity, order, and additivity. For ratio data, the zero point is not arbitrary and a zero score on a ratio scale signifies total absence of the property being measured.

Reflections section. The section of research field notes that covers the researcher's personal reflections about what is being observed.

Relationship question. Relationship questions explore the degree to which two or more phenomena relate or vary together such as intelligence level and reading skills.

Reliability, of measurement. Reliability refers to the consistency with which a measure reflects a given performance level. A reliable measure should consistently reflect performance change when change occurs.

Repeated-measures comparison. A study design in which the researcher records data on the same subjects under two or more treatment conditions.

Representative sample. A sample in which the group selected for inclusion in a study has similar characteristics to the population that is being studied and therefore accurately reflects that population, so the results can be generalized.

Research idea. Topic identified by researchers that represents an interesting area for investigation. Research ideas often involve rather general topics, which are refined to a more detailed, focused, and specific research question.

Research question. A focused and often detailed statement of the research topic to be studied. The three types of research questions often studied in education are descriptive, difference, and relationship.

Restorying. In narrative construction, the process of taking stories or anecdotes and putting them into a chronological or logical order that conveys a coherent narrative.

Reversal design. *See* A-B-A-B design.

Sample size. The number of participants a researcher selects to be in a study. It is important for a researcher to have an adequate sample of the population under study. The characteristics of a given population will determine how large the sample must be to accurately predict population factors.

Saturation. The point at which collecting additional data will not add to the interpretation of the findings.

Science method of knowing. The method of science as a way of knowing is based on external experience through observation. Data are collected about a topic to determine the existence of a phenomenon.

Semi-interquartile range. Half the range in scores represented by the middle 50% of the scores. The semi-interquartile range is a natural companion for the median, and is useful for ordinal data but can also be used with interval or ratio data.

Sequential assignment. A method used in situations where the researcher does not have the exact sample drawn and is operating from a participant pool. When the participants present themselves to take part in the study, they are assigned to one of the treatment conditions in the sequence that they appear and in a manner that will guard against the formulation of biased or unequal groups.

Simple random sampling. A sampling procedure where each individual has an equal chance of being chosen.

Single-subject design. Single-subject experiments involve investigations where the experimental variable is studied comparing different phases of treatment. These phases compare a participant's performance without treatment (e.g., a baseline phase) and with treatment (generally termed "treatment phase" or labeled by the specific treatment).

Specific notes. Specific notes are used at the bottom of a table to explain or elaborate on the information contained in a table.

Standard deviation. A measure of variability in the scores around the mean. The standard deviation is a companion dispersion measure when the mean is used and requires interval or ratio data because arithmetic is used in computation.

Statistical regression. A threat to internal validity occurring when participants have been assigned to particular group on the basis of atypical or incorrect scores.

Statistical significance. Statistical significance indicates whether the results obtained are different from those that would have occurred by chance.

Statistics. A set of analysis procedures commonly applied to the data in quantitative research. Researchers compute statistics so they can determine what occurred, such as whether one treatment was more effective than another.

Stratified random sampling. A sampling procedure that is useful for obtaining representative samples from different subpopulations.

Survey research. Type of research that involves asking questions of a sample of individuals who are representative of a group or groups under study. Survey research typically uses questionnaires, interviews, or both procedures for data collection.

Systematic sampling. A sampling procedure used in very rare circumstances in which a representative sample can be obtained only if the population frame is arranged appropriately.

Tally method. A procedure for recording observations in which the observer records the number of times that a particular behavior occurs.

Tenacity method of knowing. Thinking that something is true because "it has always been true." This perspective comes from the idea that an individual holds tenaciously to existing beliefs.

Test practice. A threat to internal validity involving the effects of participants taking a test that then influences how they score on a subsequent test.

Thick descriptions. Narrative descriptions that provide a clear and accurate picture of the nature of the phenomenon being described.

Traditional group experimental design. Traditional group experiments are conducted by forming groups of participants for comparisons. These studies are often characterized by the various groups receiving different treatments (e.g., different teaching methods) and then being assessed regarding their performance for comparison purposes.

Triangulation. A process of using a variety of different sources, collection methods, or perspectives to check the consistency or accuracy of research conclusions.

True dichotomy. A true dichotomy occurs when the data reflect actual categories of behavior and there is no assumed underlying continuum between the categories.

Validity, of measurement. Validity means that the criterion measure assesses what it is supposed to be measuring, such as addition skills.

Voluntariness. Voluntariness in consent ensures each participant's ability to exercise the power of free choice without the intervention of force, fraud, deceit, duress, or other forms of coercion.

Working graphs. Displays of data that are used to aid the researcher in interpreting results, but may not necessarily be used in reporting those results to others.

References

Abelson, R. P., Frey, K. P., & Gregg, A. P. (2004). *Experiments with people: Revelations from social psychology.* Mahwah, NJ: Erlbaum.

American Educational Research Association (2002). *Ethical standards of the American Educational Research Association: Cases and commentary.* Washington, DC: Author.

American Psychological Association. (2001). *Publication manual of the American Psychological Association* (5th ed.). Washington, DC: Author.

American Psychological Association. (2002). *Ethical principles of psychologists and code of conduct.* Washington, DC: Author.

American Psychological Association. (2005a). APA Advanced Training Institutes (ATIs). *APA Online.* Available at: http://www.apa.org

American Psychological Association. (2005b). Code of fair testing practices in education. *APA Online.* Available at: http://www.apa.org.

Anderson, N. H. (2002). Methodology and statistics in single-subject experiments. In H. Pashler & J. Wixted (Eds.), *Stevens' handbook of experimental psychology, Vol. 4: Methodology in experimental psychology* (3rd ed., pp. 301–337). New York: Wiley.

Bacon, J., & Olsen, K. (2005). *Doing the right thing* [online]. Retrieved October 2, 2005, from http://www.dwp.gov.uk/asd/asd5/WP11.pdf

Baez, B. (2002). Confidentiality in qualitative research: Reflections on secrets, power and agency. *Qualitative Research, 2,* 35–58.

Behnke, S. (2004). Multiple relationships and APA's new ethics code: Values and applications. *Monitor on Psychology, 35*(1), 66–67.

Belar, C. (2004). Speaking of education: Applying psychological science to education in psychology. *Monitor on Psychology, 35*(7), 56.

Bergin, D. A., & Cooks, H. C. (2002). High school students of color talk about accusations of "acting White." *Urban Review, 34*(2), 113–134.

Berk, L. E. (2006). *Child development* (7th ed.). Boston: Pearson/Allyn & Bacon.

Berthold, H. C., Hakala, C. M., & Goff, D. (2003). An argument for a laboratory in introductory psychology. *Teaching of Psychology, 30,* 55–58.

Best, J. W., & Kahn, J. V. (2006). *Research in education* (10th ed.). Boston: Allyn & Bacon.

Betz, N. E., Hammond, M. S., & Multon, N. E. (2005). Reliability and validity of five-level response continua for the career decision self-efficacy scale. *Journal of Career Assessment, 13,* 131–149.

Black, T. R. (2001). *Understanding social science research.* Thousand Oaks, CA: Sage.

Bradburn, N. M., Sudman, S., & Wansink, B. (2004). *Asking questions: The definitive guide to questionnaire design—for market research, political polls, and social and health questionnaires* (Rev. ed.). New York: Wiley.

Brinkmann, S., & Kvale, S. (2005). Confronting the ethics of qualitative research. *Journal of Constructivist Psychology, 18,* 157–181.

Carradice, A., Beail, N., & Shankland, M. C. (2003). Interventions with family caregivers for people with dementia: Efficacy problems and potential solution. *Journal of Psychiatric and Mental Health Nursing, 10,* 307–315.

Cassell, C., & Symon, G. (2004). *Qualitative methods and intervention in organizational research: A practical guide.* Thousand Oaks, CA: Sage.

Cepeda, A., & Valdez, A. (2003). Risk behaviors among young Mexican American gang-associated females: Sexual relations, partying, substance use, and crime. *Journal of Adolescent Research, 18,* 90–106.

Corrigan, P. W., & Salzer, M. S. (2003). The conflict between random assignment and treatment preference: Implications for internal validity. *Evaluation and Program Planning, 26,* 109–121.

Cote, J., & Ericsson, K. A. (2005). Tracing the development of athletes using retrospective interview methods: A proposed interview and validation procedure for reported information. *Journal of Applied Sport Psychology, 17,* 1–19.

Craighead, W. E., & Nemeroff, C. B. (2004). *The concise Corsini encyclopedia of psychology and behavioral science* (3rd ed.). New York: Wiley.

Creswell, J. W. (2005). *Educational research: Planning, conducting, and evaluating quantitative and qualitative research* (2nd ed.). Upper Saddle River, NJ: Prentice Hall.

Cusick, P. A. (1973). *Inside high school: The student's world.* New York: Holt, Rinehart and Winston.

Dalute, C., & Lightfoot, C. (2004). *Narrative analysis: Studying the development of individuals in society.* Thousand Oaks, CA: Sage.

Davis, S., Darling-Hammond, L., LaPointe, M., & Meyerson, D. (2005). *Developing successful principals: Review of research.* Palo Alto, CA: Stanford Educational Leadership Institute (SELI).

Denzin, N. K., & Lincoln, Y. S. (2005). *The Sage handbook of qualitative research* (3rd ed.). Thousand Oaks, CA: Sage.

Diekema, D. S. (2005). Payments for participation of children in research. In E. Kodish (Ed.), *Ethics and research with children: A case-based approach* (pp. 143–160). New York: Oxford University Press.

Dittman, M. (2004). Expanding geropsychology training. *Monitor on Psychology, 35*(1), 40–41.

Dowdy, S., Wearden, S., & Chilko, D. (2004). *Statistics for research* (3rd ed.). New York: Wiley.

Drew, C. J., & Hardman, M. L. (2007). *Intellectual disabilities across the lifespan* (9th ed.). Upper Saddle River, NJ: Prentice Hall.

Edmonds, M., & Briggs, K. L. (2003). The instructional content emphasis instrument: Observations of reading instruction. In S. Vaughn & K. L. Briggs (Eds.), *Reading in the classroom: Systems for the observation of teaching and learning* (pp. 31–52). Baltimore: Paul H. Brookes.

Evans, J. B. T. (2002). The influence of prior belief on scientific thinking. In P. Carruthers & S. Stich (Eds.), *The cognitive basis of science* (pp. 193–210). New York: Cambridge University Press.

Field, M. J., & Behrman, R. E. (2004). *Ethical conduct of clinical research involving children.* Washington, DC: The National Academies Press.

Fisher, R. A. (1925). *Statistical methods for research workers.* London: Oliver & Boyd.

Fisher, R. A. (1926). The arrangement of field experiments. *Journal of the Ministry of Agriculture, 33,* 503–513.

Fisher, R. A. (1935). *The design of experiments.* London: Oliver & Boyd.

Flick, U., Steinke, I., & Kardoff, E. von (2004). *Qualitative research: Paradigms, theories, methods, practice and contexts.* Thousand Oaks, CA: Sage.

Foorman, B. R., & Schatschneider, C. (2003). Measurement of teaching practices during reading/language arts instruction and its relationship to student achievement. In S. Vaughn & K. L. Briggs (Eds.), *Reading in the classroom: Systems for the observation of teaching and learning* (pp. 1–30). Baltimore: Paul H. Brookes.

Foster, M., Lewis, J., & Onafowora, L. (2003). Anthropology, culture, and research on teaching and learning: Applying what we have learned to improve practice. *Teachers College Record, 105,* 261–277.

Fraenkel, J. R., & Wallen, N. E. (2006). *How to design and evaluate research in education* (6th ed.). New York: McGraw-Hill.

Frankfort-Nachmias, C., & Leon-Guerrero, A. (2006). *Social statistics for a diverse society with SPSS student version* (4th ed.). Thousand Oaks, CA: Sage.

Gay, L. R., Mills, G., & Airasian, P. W. (2006). *Educational research: Competencies for analysis and application* (8th ed.). Upper Saddle River, NJ: Prentice Hall.

Gelfand, D. M., & Drew, C. J. (2003). *Understanding child behavior disorders* (4th ed.). Pacific Grove, CA: Wadsworth.

Gersten, R., Fuchs, L. S., Compton, D., Coyne, M., Greenwood, C., & Innocenti, M. S. (2005). Quality indicators for group experimental and quasi-experimental research in special education, *Exceptional Children, 71,* 149–164.

Giroux, H. H. (1994). *Disturbing pleasures: Learning popular cultures.* New York: Routledge.

Glesne, C. (2006). *Becoming qualitative researchers: An introduction* (3rd ed.). Boston: Allyn & Bacon.

Glotzer, R. (2005). Unequal childhoods: Class, race, and family life. *Journal of Comparative Family Studies, 36,* 152–153.

Goldberg, S., Levitan, R., Leung, E., Masellis, M., Basile, V. S., Nemeroff, C. B., et al. (2003). Cortisol concentrations in 12- to 18-month-old infants: Stability over time, location, and stressor. *Biological Psychiatry, 54,* 719–726.

Golden-Biddle, K., & Locke, K. D. (2006). *Composing qualitative research* (2nd ed.). Thousand Oaks, CA: Sage.

Goodwin, C. J. (2005). *Research in psychology: Methods and design* (4th ed.). Hoboken, NJ: Wiley.

Gross, D. (2005). Editorial: On the merits of attention-control groups. *Research in Nursing & Health, 28,* 93–94.

Guidelines for preparation of applications for review by General Institutional Review Board (1991). *Psychology, 63,* 105–118.

Guthrie, J. T., & Anderson, E. (1999). Engagement in reading: Processes of motivated, strategic, knowledgeable, social readers. In J. T. Guthrie & D. E. Alvermann (Eds.), *Engaged reading: Processes, practices, and policy implications* (pp. 17–45). New York: Teachers College Press.

Guthrie, J. T., & Cox, K. (1998). Portrait of an engaging classroom: Principles of concept-oriented reading instruction for diverse students. In K. Harris (Ed.), *Teaching every child every day: Learning in diverse schools and classrooms* (pp. 77–131). Cambridge, MA: Brookline Books.

Hadden, K. L., & Baeyer, C. L. von (2005). Global and specific behavioral measures of pain in children with cerebral palsy. *Clinical Journal of Pain, 21,* 140–146.

Hagan, F. E. (2006). *Research methods in criminal justice and criminology* (7th ed.). Boston: Pearson/Allyn & Bacon.

Hardman, M. L., Drew, C. J., & Egan, M. W. (2006). *Human exceptionality: School, community, and family* (8th ed.). Boston: Allyn & Bacon.

Hardy, C. L., & Leeuwen, S. A. van (2004). Interviewing young children: Effects of probe structures and focus of rapport-building talk on the qualities of young children's eyewitness statements. *Canadian Journal of Behavioural Science, 36,* 155–165.

Hart, P. (2003). Reflections on reviewing educational research: (Re)searching for value in environmental education. *Environmental Education Research, 9,* 241–256.

Haverkamp, B. E. (2005). Ethical perspectives on qualitative research in applied psychology. *Journal of Counseling Psychology, 52,* 146–155.

Hendricks, C. C. (2006). *Improving schools through action research: A comprehensive guide for educators.* Boston: Pearson/Allyn & Bacon.

Hoover, E. (2005, July 29). The ethics of undercover research. *The Chronicle of Higher Education,* A37.

Horner, R. H., Carr, E. G., Halle, J., McGee, G., Odom, S., & Wolery, M. (2005). The use of single-subject research to identify evidence-based practice in special education. *Exceptional Children, 71,* 165–179.

Hutchinson, S. R. (2004). Survey research. In K. deMarrais & S. D. Lapan (Eds.), *Foundations for research: Methods of inquiry in education and the social sciences* (pp. 283–301). Mahwah, NJ: Erlbaum.

Janesick, V. J. (2004). *"Stretching" exercises for qualitative researchers* (2nd ed.). Thousand Oaks, CA: Sage.

Jeffrey, B., & Troman, G. (2004). Time for ethnography. *British Educational Research Journal, 30,* 535–548.

Jobber, D., Saunders, J., & Mitchell, V. W. (2004). Prepaid monetary incentive effects on mail survey response. *Journal of Business Research, 57,* 21–25.

Johnson, A. P. (2005). *A short guide to action research.* Boston: Pearson/Allyn & Bacon.

Johnson, B., & Christensen, L. (2004). *Educational research: Quantitative, qualitative, and mixed approaches* (2nd ed.). Boston: Allyn & Bacon.

Johnson, R. B., & Onwuegbuzie, A. J. (2004). Mixed method research: A research paradigm whose time has come. *Educational Researcher, 33*(7), 14–26.

Jones, W. P., & Kottler, J. A. (2006). *Understanding research: Becoming a competent and critical consumer.* Upper Saddle River, NJ: Pearson/Prentice Hall.

Joseph, D. (2004). The practice of design-based research: Uncovering the interplay between design, research, and the real-world context. *Educational Psychologist, 39,* 235–242.

Joynson, R. B. (2003). Selective interest and psychological practice: A new interpretation of the Burt affair. *British Journal of Psychology, 94,* 409–426.

Jupp, V. (2006). *Sage dictionary of social and cultural research methods.* Thousand Oaks, CA: Sage.

Katims, D. S. (2000). Literacy instruction for people with mental retardation: Historical highlights and contemporary analysis. *Education and Training in Mental Retardation, 35*(1), 3–15.

Kazdin, A. E., (2003). Methodology: General lessons to guide research. In Kazdin, A. E. (Ed.), *Methodological issues and strategies in clinical research* (3rd ed., pp. 877–887). Washington, DC: American Psychological Association.

Keller, H. E., & Lee, S. (2003). Ethical issues surrounding human participants research using the internet. *Ethics and Behavior, 13,* 211–219.

Kennedy, C. H. (2005). *Single-case designs for educational research.* Boston: Allyn & Bacon.

Kersting, K. (2004). APA initiative connects genetics and psychology. *Monitor on Psychology, 35*(1), 26–27.

Khandelwal, K. A., & Dhillon, P. K. (2004). Study of organizational cultures: A comparison across three multinationals. *Social Science International, 20,* 3–18.

Kleiman, M. (2003). The "brain disease" idea, drug policy and research ethics: Comment. *Addiction, 98,* 871–872.

Knottnerus, P. (2003). *Sample survey theory: Some Pythagorean perspectives.* New York: Springer-Verlag.

Krause, M. S., & Howard, K. I. (2003). What random assignment does and does not do. *Journal of Clinical Psychology, 59,* 751–766.

Lall, V. F., & Levin, J. R. (2004). An empirical investigation of the statistical properties of generalized single-case randomization tests. *Journal of School Psychology, 42,* 61–86.

Lane, J. (2002). Fear of gang crime: A qualitative examination of the four perspectives. *Journal of Research in Crime and Delinquency, 39,* 437–471.

Langhout, R. D., Rappaport, J., & Simmons, D. (2002). Integrating community into the classroom: Community gardens, community involvement, and project-based learning. *Urban Education, 37,* 323–349.

Leece, P., Bhandari, M., Sprague, S., Swiontkowski, M. F., Schemitsch, E. H., Tornetta, P., et al. (2004). Internet versus mailed questionnaires: A randomized comparison (2). *Journal of Medical Internet Research, 6.*

Lei, P. W., & Dunbar, S. B. (2004). Effects of score discreteness and estimating alternative model parameters on power estimation methods in structural equation modeling. *Structural Equation Modeling, 11,* 20–44.

Leithwood, K., Louis, K. S., Anderson, S., & Wahlstrom, K. (2004). *How leadership influences student learning.* Minneapolis, MN: Center for Applied Research and Educational Improvement.

Lepard, D. H., & Foster, A. G. (2003). *Powerful leadership development: Bridging theory and practice using peers and technology.* Thousand Oaks, CA: Corwin Press.

Levin, J., & Fox, J. A. (2006). *Elementary statistics in social research* (10th ed.). Boston: Pearson/Allyn & Bacon.

Levy, P. S., & Lemeshow, S. (2003). *Sampling of populations: Methods and applications, textbook and solutions manual* (3rd ed.). New York: Wiley.

Lichtenberg, P., Heresco-Levy, U., & Nitzan, U. (2004). The ethics of the placebo in clinical practice. *Journal of Medical Ethics, 30,* 551–554.

Light, R. J., & Pillemer, D. B. (1982). Numbers and narrative: Combining their strengths in research reviews. *Harvard Educational Review, 52,* 1–26.

Maris, G., & Maris, E. (2003). Testing the race model inequality: A nonparametric approach. *Journal of Mathematical Psychology, 47,* 507–514.

Matson, J. L., Dixon, D. R., & Matson, M. L. (2005). Assessing and treating aggression in children and adolescents with developmental disabilities: A 20-year overview. *Educational Psychology, 25,* 151–181.

Mauthner, M., Birch, M., Jessop, J. & Miller, T. (2003). *Ethics in qualitative research.* Thousand Oaks, CA: Sage.

Mazzeo, C. (2003). *Improving teaching and learning by improving school leadership.* Washington, DC: National Governors Association Center for Best Practices.

McCall, W. A. (1923). *How to experiment in education.* New York: Macmillan.

McGrath, J. E. (2005). Conversation is a lot more than just talk. *Experimental Psychology, 52,* 80–81.

McMillan, J. H. (2004). *Educational research: Fundamentals for the consumer* (4th ed.). Boston: Pearson/Allyn & Bacon.

McMillan, J., & Schumacher, S. (2006). *Research in education: Evidence-based inquiry* (6th ed.). Boston: Pearson/Allyn & Bacon.

Mead, M. (1928). *Coming of age in Samoa.* New York: Morrow.

Mertens, D. M. (2005). *Research and evaluation in education and psychology: Integrating diversity with quantitative, qualitative, and mixed methods* (2nd ed.). Thousand Oaks, CA: Sage.

Mertler, C. A. (2006). *Action research: Teachers as researchers in the classroom.* Thousand Oaks, CA: Sage.

Middleton, D., & Brown, S. D. (2006). *The social psychology of experience: Studies in remembering and forgetting.* Thousand Oaks, CA: Sage.

Miles, J., & Banyard, P. (2007). *Understanding and using statistics in psychology: A practical introduction.* Thousand Oaks, CA: Sage.

Mishara, B. L., & Weisstub, D. N. (2005). Ethical and legal issues in suicide research. *International Journal of Law & Psychiatry, 28,* 23–41.

Moghaddam, F. M., & Finkel, N. J. (2005). Rights and duties: Psychology's contributions, normative assessments and future research. In N. J. Finkel & F. M. Moghaddam (Eds.), *Psychology of rights and duties: Empirical contributions and normative commentaries* (pp. 271–283). Washington, DC: American Psychological Association.

Moser, D. J., Arndt, S., Kanz, J. E., Benjamin, M. L., Bayless, J. D., Reese, R. L., Paulsen, J. S., & Flaum, M. A. (2004). Coercion and informed consent in research involving prisoners. *Comprehensive Psychiatry, 45,* 1–9.

Murphy, K. R., & Myors, B. (2004). *Statistical power analysis: A simple and general model for traditional and modern hypothesis tests* (2nd ed.). Mahwah, NJ: Erlbaum.

Myers, J. L., & Well, A. D. (2003). *Research design and statistical analysis* (2nd ed.). Mahwah, NJ: Erlbaum.

Nadelman, L. (2004). *Research manual in child development* (2nd ed.). Mahwah, NJ: Erlbaum.

Nadler, G., & Chandon, W. (2004). *Smart questions: Learn to ask the right questions for powerful results.* New York: Wiley.

Nagy, T. F. (2005a). Assessment. In T. F. Nagy (Ed.), *Ethics in plain English: An illustrative casebook for psychologists* (2nd ed., pp. 249–290). Washington, DC: American Psychological Association.

Nagy, T. F. (2005b). Privacy and confidentiality. In T. F. Nagy (Ed.), *Ethics in plain English: An illustrative casebook for psychologist* (2nd ed., pp. 107–130). Washington, DC: American Psychological Association.

Nagy, T. F. (2005c). Research and publication. In T. F. Nagy (Ed.), *Ethics in plain English: An illustrative casebook for psychologist* (2nd ed., pp. 195–248). Washington, DC: American Psychological Association.

Nanna, M. J., & Sawilowsky, S. S. (1998). Analysis of Likert scale data in disability and medical rehabilitation research. *Psychological Methods, 3,* 55–67.

Nardi, P. M. (2006). *Doing survey research* (2nd ed.). Boston: Pearson/Allyn & Bacon.

Natalicio, D., & Pacheco, A. (2005). The future of teacher preparation. *Edutopia: The New World of Learning.* San Rafael, CA: The George Lucas Educational Foundation. Available online at http://www.glef.org

Nathan, R. (2006). *My freshman year: What a professor learned by becoming a student.* Ithaca, NY: Cornell University Press.

Neuman, W. L. (2006). *Social research methods: Quantitative and qualitative approaches* (6th ed.). Boston: Allyn & Bacon.

Nunnally, J. C. (1967). *Psychometric theory.* New York: McGraw-Hill.

Odom, S. L., Brantlinger, E., Gersten, R., Horner, R. H., Thompson, B., & Harris, K. R. (2005). Research in special education: Scientific methods and evidence-based practices. *Exceptional Children, 71,* 137–148.

Odom, S. L., & Strain, P. S. (2002). Evidence-based practice in early intervention/early childhood special education: Single-subject design research. *Journal of Early Intervention, 25,* 151–160.

O'Donnell, A. M. (2004). A commentary on design research. *Educational Psychologist, 39,* 255–260.

Ohghena, P., & Edgington, E. S. (2005). Customizing pain treatments: Single-case design and analysis. *Clinical Journal of Pain, 21,* 56–68.

O'Malley, K. J., Moran, B. J., Haidet, P., Seidel, C. L., Schneider, V., Morgan, R. O., et al. (2003). Validation of an observation instrument for measuring student engagement in health professions settings. *Evaluation and the Health Professions, 26,* 86–103.

Parasuraman, A. (2003). Reflections on contributing to a discipline through research and writing. *Journal of the Academy of Marketing Science, 31,* 314–318.

Pervin, L. A. (2003). *The science of personality* (2nd ed.). London: Oxford University Press.

Pittenger, D. J. (2003). Internet research: An opportunity to revisit classic ethical problems in behavioral research. *Ethics and Behavior, 13*, 45–60.

Post, S. G. (2003). Bodily integrity: A plausible argument. *Journal of Disability Policy Studies, 13*, 261.

Powell, L., & Amsbary, J. H. (2006). *Interviewing: Situations and contexts.* Boston: Allyn & Bacon.

Price, J. H., Yingling, F., Walsh, E., Murnan, J., & Dake, J. A. (2004). Tone of postcards in increasing survey response rates. *Psychological Reports, 94*, 444–448.

Punch, K. F. (2005). *Introduction to social research: Quantitative and qualitative approaches.* Thousand Oaks, CA: Sage.

Quadagno, J. (2005). *Aging and the life course: An introduction to social gerontology* (3rd ed.). New York: McGraw-Hill.

Rae, W. A., & Sullivan, J. R. (2003). Ethical considerations in clinical psychology research. In M. C. Roberts & S. S. Ilardi (Eds.), *Handbook of research methods in clinical psychology. Blackwell handbooks of research methods in psychology* (Vol. 2, pp. 52–70). Malden, MA: Blackwell.

Rasinski, K. A., Viechnicki, P., & O'Muircheartaigh, C. (2005). Methods for studying stigma and mental illness. In P. W. Corrigan (Ed.), *On the stigma of mental illness: Practical strategies for research and social change* (pp. 45–65). Washington, DC: American Psychological Association.

Rausch, J. R., Maxwell, S. E., & Kelley, K. (2003). Analytic methods for questions pertaining to a randomized pretest, posttest, follow-up design. *Journal of Clinical Child and Adolescent Psychology, 32*, 467–486.

Ritchie, J., & Lewis, J. (2003). *Qualitative research practice: A guide for social science students and researchers.* Thousand Oaks, CA: Sage.

Ritter, P., Lorig, K., Laurent, D., & Matthews, K. (2004). Internet versus mailed questionnaires: A randomized comparison. *Journal of Medical Internet Research, 6.*

Roberts, L. W., Geppert, C. M. A., Coverdale, J., Louie, A., & Edenharder, K. (2005). Ethical and regulatory considerations in educational research. *Academic Psychiatry, 29*, 1–5.

Rubin, H. J., & Rubin, I. S. (2004). *Qualitative interviewing: The art of hearing data.* Thousand Oaks, CA. Sage.

Salkind, N. J. (2007). *Statistics for people who (think they) hate statistics* (3rd ed.). Thousand Oaks, CA: Sage.

Salvia, J., Ysseldyke, J. E., & Bolt, S. (2007). *Assessment in special and inclusive education* (10th ed.). Boston: Houghton Mifflin.

Sapsford, R., & Jupp, V. (2004). *Social research methods.* Thousand Oaks, CA: Sage.

Schaffer, H. R. (2004). *Introducing child psychology.* Malden, MA: Blackwell.

Schenk, K., & Williamson, J. (2005). *Ethical approaches to gathering information from children and adults in international settings.* Washington, DC: Population Council.

Schmuck, R. A. (2006). *Practical action research for change* (2nd ed.). Thousand Oaks, CA: Corwin Press.

Sealander, K. A. (2004). Single-subject experimental research: An overview for practitioners. In K. A. Sealander (Ed.), *Foundations for research: Methods of inquiry in education and the social sciences* (pp. 303–327). Mahwah, NJ: Erlbaum.

Silverman, D. (2004). *Qualitative research: Theory, method and practice.* Thousand Oaks, CA: Sage.

Silverman, D. (2006). *Interpreting qualitative data: Methods for analyzing talk, text and interaction* (3rd ed.). London: Sage Ltd.

Sirkin, R. M. (2006). *Statistics for the social sciences* (3rd ed.). Thousand Oaks, CA: Sage.

Smith, D. (2003). Five principles for research ethics: Cover your bases with these ethical strategies. *Monitor on Psychology, 34*(1), 56–57.

Sofaer, B. (2005). *Qualitative methods in health services and policy research.* Hoboken, NJ: Wiley.

Sofuoglu, M., Gonzalez, G., Poling, J., & Kosten, T. R. (2003). Prediction of treatment outcome by baseline urine cocaine results and self-reported cocaine use for cocaine and opioid dependence. *American Journal of Drug and Alcohol Abuse, 29,* 713–727.

Strauss, A., & Corbin, J. (1998). *Basics of qualitative research: Techniques and procedures for developing grounded theory* (2nd ed.). New York: Sage.

Swan, E. A. (2003). *Concept-oriented reading instruction: Engaging classrooms, life-long learners.* New York: Guilford Press.

Tanofsky-Kraff, M., Yanovski, S. Z., & Yanovski, J. A. (2005). Comparison of child interview and parent reports of children's eating disordered behaviors. *Eating Behaviors, 6,* 95–99.

Tashakori, A., & Teddlie, C. (2002). *Handbook of mixed methods in social and behavioral research.* Thousand Oaks, CA: Sage.

Thomas, J. C., & Rosqvist, J. (2003). Introduction: Science in the service of practice. In J. C. Thomas & M. Hersen (Eds.), *Understanding research in clinical and counseling psychology* (pp. 3–26). Mahwah, NJ: Erlbaum.

Thomas, S. J. (2004). *Using web and paper questionnaires for data-based decision making: From design to interpretation of the results.* Thousand Oaks, CA: Sage.

Thompson, S. K. (2002). *Sampling* (2nd ed.). New York: Wiley.

Totten, M. (2003). Girlfriend abuse as a form of masculinity construction among violent, marginal male youth. *Men and Masculinities, 6,* 70–92.

Tourangeau, R. (2004). Survey research and societal change. *Annual review of Psychology, 55,* 775–801.

Trimble, J. E., & Fisher, C. B. (2006). *The handbook of ethical research with ethnocultural populations and communities.* Thousand Oaks, CA: Sage.

Trussell, N., & Lavrakas, P. J. (2004). The influence of incremental increases in token cash incentives on mail survey response: Is there an optimal amount? *Public Opinion Quarterly, 68,* 349–367.

University of Utah. (2005). *University Regulations: Code of Student Rights and Responsibilities, Chapter X, Section V* [online]. Retrieved October 5, 2005, from http://www.admin.utah.edu/ppmanual/8/8-10.html#SECTION%20V

Urdan, T. C. (2005). *Statistics in plain English* (2nd ed.). Mahwah, NJ: Erlbaum.

Vernoy, M. W., & Vernoy, J. (1992). *Behavioral statistics in action.* San Marcos, CA: Wadsworth.

Wacome, D. H. (2003). Ways of knowing in psychological science. In S. W. Vanderstoep (Ed.), *Science and the soul: Christian faith and psychological research* (pp. 25–52). Lanham, MD: University Press of America.

Walzer, S., & Oles, T. P. (2003). Managing conflict after marriages end: A qualitative study of narratives of ex-spouses. *Families in Society, 84,* 192–200.

Weerasekera, P. (2004). Swimming upstream: Reflections of a career educator. *Academic Psychiatry, 28,* 344–346.

Welch, R. F., & Drew, C. J. (1972). Effects of reward anticipation and performance expectancy on the learning rate of EMR adolescents. *American Journal of Mental Deficiency, 77,* 291–295.

Wiersma, W., & Jurs, S. G. (2005). *Research methods in education: An introduction* (8th ed.). Boston: Pearson/Allyn & Bacon.

Williams, R. N. (2005). The language and methods of science: Common assumptions and uncommon conclusions. In B. D. Slife & J. S. Reber (Eds.), *Critical thinking about psychology: Hidden assumptions and plausible alternatives* (pp. 235–249). Washington, DC: American Psychological Association.

Willis, J. (2007). *Foundations of qualitative research: Interpretive and clinical approaches.* New Thousand Oaks, CA: Sage.

Wilson, W. C., Rosenthal, B. S., & Austin, S. (2005). Exposure to community violence and upper respiratory illness in older adolescents. *Journal of Adolescent Health, 36,* 313–319.

Young, D. (2005). Will exercising informed consent stop "unfortunate experiments"? *Birth: Issues in Perinatal Care, 32,* 1–3.

Zoltan, D. (2003). *Questionnaires in second language research: Construction, administration, and processing.* Mahwah, NJ: Erlbaum.

Zwillinger, D. (2000). *CRC standard probability and statistics tables and formulae.* Boca Raton, FL: Chapman & Hall/CRC.

Index

About the Authors

Clifford J. Drew is Associate Dean for Research and Outreach in the College of Education at the University of Utah. He is also a professor in the Special Education and Educational Psychology Departments. Dr. Drew came to the University of Utah in 1971 after serving on the faculties of the University of Texas at Austin and Kent State University. He received his master's degree from the University of Illinois and his Ph.D. from the University of Oregon. He has published numerous articles in education and related areas including intellectual disabilities, research design, statistics, diagnostic assessment, cognition, evaluation related to the law, and information technology. His most recent book, *Human Exceptionality: School, Community, and Family* (Houghton-Mifflin, in press) is Dr. Drew's 29th text. His professional interests include research methods in education and psychology, human development and disabilities, applications of information technology, and outreach in higher education.

Michael L. Hardman is Dean of the College of Education and Professor in the Department of Special Education at the University of Utah. He has also served as Chair of the Department of Special Education and the Department of Teaching and Learning at the University. Dr. Hardman is the University Coordinator for the Eunice Kennedy Shriver National Center for Community of Caring. In 2004–2005, Dr. Hardman was appointed the Matthew J. Guglielmo Endowed Chair at California State University, Los Angeles, and the Governor's Representative to the California Advisory Commission on Special Education. Additionally, Dr. Hardman is Senior Education Advisor to the Joseph P. Kennedy, Jr. Foundation in Washington, D.C., and a member of the Board of Directors for the Council for Exceptional Children.

Dr. Hardman has numerous publications in national journals throughout the field of education and has authored several college textbooks of which two, *Human Exceptionality* and *Lifespan Perspectives on Intellectual Disabilities,* are now both in ninth editions. As a researcher, he has directed international and national demonstration projects in the areas of educational policy and reform, developmental disabilities, professional development, inclusive education, transition from school to adult life, and preparing tomorrow's leaders in special education.

John L. Hosp is on the Research Faculty of the Florida Center for Reading Research. He was an Assistant Professor of special education at the University of Utah during the time this book was prepared. He received his Ph.D. in special education from Vanderbilt University (2002) and M.S. in school psychology from the Rochester Institute of Technology (1995). He is a nationally certified school psychologist who has worked in schools in New York and Nevada. His research focuses on aspects of implementing Response to Intervention (RtI): including disproportionate representation of minority students in special education and aligning assessment and instruction, particularly in the areas of curriculum-based measurement (CBM) and curriculum-based evaluation (CBE). He is one of the founders of the University of Utah's CBM/DIBELS Institute.

Dr. Hosp is one of the external evaluators for the Reading First Program for the State of Utah, which is implementing many of the characteristics of RtI. This work has allowed him the opportunity to work with several other states' Reading First evaluators to examine the process and outcomes of such large-scale reading reform. He has presented at several national and international conferences on reading, Reading First, and RtI. He is also an author of several journal articles and a video on assessment in education. His other books include *The ABCs of CBM: A Practical Guide to Curriculum-Based Measurement* and *Curriculum-Based Evaluation: Linking Assessment and Instruction.*